PELICAN BOOKS

A393

ROMAN READINGS

Michael Grant, C.B.E., Litt.D. (Cambridge), Hon.Litt.D. (Dublin), Hon. LL.D. (Queen's University of Belfast), has written *The World of Rome*, (1960), *Myths of the Greeks and Romans* (1962), *The Civilizations of Europe* (1965), *Ancient History* (new edition 1965), *Cambridge* (1966) *Roman Literature* (Pelican Books, new edition 1967). He is translator for the Penguin Classics of *The Annals of Tacitus* and selected works of Cicero, and is co-author with Don Pottinger of *Greeks* and *Romans*. The writer of several specialist works on coins, he is a former President and Medallist of the Royal Numismatic Society and Huntington Medallist of the American Numismatic Society.

Michael Grant was successively Chancellor's Medallist and Fellow of Trinity College, Cambridge, Professor of Humanity at Edinburgh University, first Vice-Chancellor of Khartoum University, and President and Vice-Chancellor of the Queen's University of Belfast. He has also been Chairman of the National Council for the Supply of Teachers Overseas, Chairman of the Advisory Council for Education (Northern Ireland), and President of the Virgil Society.

ROMAN READINGS

TRANSLATIONS FROM
LATIN PROSE AND POETRY
CHOSEN BY

MICHAEL GRANT

PENGUIN BOOKS

Penguin Books Ltd, Harmondsworth, Middlesex, England
Penguin Books Inc., 3300 Clipper Mill Road, Baltimore, Md 21211, U.S.A.
Penguin Books Australia Ltd, Ringwood, Victoria, Australia

—

First published 1958
Reprinted (with revisions) 1967

—

Copyright © Michael Grant 1958

—

Made and printed in Great Britain
by Richard Clay (The Chaucer Press) Ltd,
Bungay, Suffolk
Set in Monotype Bembo

CONTENTS

SELECTED TRANSLATIONS
(with Introductions to each author)

CONTENTS

GENERAL INTRODUCTION

GOOD translations rank high among the necessities of our times. Peoples and nations need them to escape from the Tower of Babel, and to understand the past. Yet translation has often, and rightly, been called impossible to achieve. For the ideal translation is required to fulfil hopelessly contradictory sets of conditions. It would need (a) to give the words of the original and (b) to give its ideas; (a) to reflect the style of the original and (b) of the translator. There are likewise clashing views about the legitimacy of adding to the original or omitting from it.[1]

The profound conclusion is that two translations are four times as good as one. A translator must start with some sympathy with his author, but he must also do a lot of work to find out what that author says, how he says it, and what he means. Even in modern languages words and phrases do not always have equivalents, – not to speak of proverbs and the like. If you are translating *Mit Wölfen muss man heulen*, are you going to offer a mysterious 'with wolves must one howl', or will you settle for 'when in Rome do as the Romans do'?

The gulfs of time make the task harder still. Scarcely a single ancient Greek word can be matched in English; the emotions and the sounds are an immeasurable distance away. Latin is more deceptive. We recognize words and moods, but they are rarely reliable equivalents. This problem particularly applies to prose translation, an exacting art of which the theory is gravely neglected; there are a thousand words written about verse translation to every one about prose. Yet it is worth considering, for example, how Cicero's rhetoric slides with catastrophic ease into an outdated English which, being unreadable, cannot be called a suitable rendering. The nineteenth century wanted the classical 'best thoughts' in modern languages, but its versions – and indeed even those of a generation or two ago – now seem to have a mouldy semi-Latinized stuffiness. A new version is needed for every generation; *how* and *what* are equally important all the time.

Robert Graves, in attempting to translate the perfumed lateish Latin of Apuleius (p. 429), remarked that 'the effect of oddness is best achieved in convulsed times like the present by writing in as easy and sedate an English as possible.' The word sedate does his own style injustice, but it is true that any attempt to reproduce Apuleius' flamboyant elaborations (or the pregnant point of Tacitus), would be unacceptable nowadays. It worked with the Elizabethans and the readers of Walter Pater and Oscar Wilde, but it will not work with us.

Greek or Latin poetry are equally or even more difficult to translate, because their diction is more elevated than anything produced today.

1. Theodore Savory, *The Art of Translation*, Cape, 1957. See also his lists of books on p. 153.

The Romans had nothing so densely charged or grandiose as Aeschylus, but the bemusing effects which Virgil and Horace create by arranging quite ordinary words set perilous snares for the translator. Matthew Arnold believed that a suitable vehicle was poetic prose, but Walt Whitman, speaking as one poet about another, said this reminded him of hangings, curtains, finger-bowls and chinaware. And indeed poetic prose all too often meant words like eftsoons and forsooth, and other such poisons which give people wrong ideas about the ancient classics.

So the only alternative media for translating poetry are poetry and plain (that is to say non-poetical) prose. Prose *tours de force* such as E. V. Rieu's *Odyssey* have rightly caught people's imagination; yet a prose rendering discards the chief feature and resource of its original. The translation of a poem must have the characteristics of a poem. Certainly, no ancient poem can be made to live *its own* life again. Ancient metre is one obstacle; efforts to reproduce these quantitative metres into modern stress-accent languages, though occasionally successful in sensitive hands, more often became gouty gallops and the setting of railway by-laws to dance music.

Is rhyme a legitimate substitute, to reproduce part of the formality? In any case there really is no choice between poetry and prose for translating a poem; poetry is better. The beauty of the original can awaken phrases in another poet's mind and so make a *modern* poem – not identical with the ancient work or even its formal parallel, but a significant echo and commentary and re-creation in modern terms of the effect the original had exercised on people's minds and feelings. Occasionally some happy sympathy of cultural climates and personalities almost achieves the impossible. Many a modern poet has had a shot – in America even more than in England, and at translating Greek more than Latin – and the last twenty years have been described as the most brilliant period of translation English literature has known since the Elizabethans. In their day, although Arthur Golding was not a poet of the calibre of Ovid, their attitudes of mind and style coincided closely enough to produce something which thousands enjoyed (p. 257). And then again, in Restoration times though no one can pretend that the two men lived under the same linguistic or social or intellectual conditions, Dryden showed an almost uncanny insight into the intricate, lapidary stanzas and quintessential temperament of Horace (p. 186) – adding enough of himself to bring the *Odes* alive for a second time.

Dryden was also the first great theorist of translation, and the first to recognize and describe it clearly as an art. He distinguished between three ways of translating, the literal way, the looser paraphase, and the even looser imitation or adaptation. He himself uses 171 words where Horace used seventy-eight, and so by modern standards he is paraphrasing – though this is perhaps not a final criterion, since English is far more diffuse than Latin; thirteen words of Virgil have been said to need sixty of English, and even then the sonorous, plangent overtones of trumpet-calls like *mortalia* and *lacrimae* are lost. Paraphrases are also needed when the translator is trying to bring out a joke; Edward Marsh brings out Horace's, but only by straying some way from a literal version (p. 201). The classic case is Ezra Pound, whose *Homage to Sextus Propertius* conveys ironic aspects of the poet which no other renderings have caught (p. 247). But its endowment of the original with 'up to date aluminium crutches' includes blatant mistranslations, which Pound brazened out, hinting that they were deliberate and even perhaps better than the original. Fifty years later opinion is still divided, sharply and at length, regarding the legitimacy of these tactics. Cecil Day Lewis' versions of Virgil likewise include a certain number of anachronisms (p. 156). They were originally commissioned by the B.B.C., and he said he introduced these shocking surprises in order to keep the radio audiences awake.

The Roman works and writers represented in this book belong to the central classical tradition. Horace, Ovid, Cicero and the rest were once admired a great deal, perhaps too much. Now, they are admired far too little. They are not widely or voluntarily read, and their names convey to many people a faded, fusty impression. To set right this ludicrous misconception is one of the aims of the present book. Another is to correct the wildly mistaken idea that Latin literature is just a second class reflection of Greek. What struck the Italian Renaissance about these Latin writers was their demonstration that man is significant and has a say in his own destiny. If we can bridge the gulf of time between ourselves and the ancient Romans, a whole civilization is spread out before us, abundant in warnings and guides and forerunners in glorious achievements and tremendous failures, in marvels of literature as well as of art. Although the problems and perils of transmission from Latin to English are great, the attempts to overcome them have added new dimensions to every century in turn, and are exciting, comforting enhancements of life.

The translations I have chosen are those which seem to me, in their own right and in our own day, comprehensible and enjoyable.[1] I want to thank Professor J. H. Bishop, Mr Andreas Mayor and Professor Stuart Piggott for their previously unpublished contributions, and Professor Bishop for checking many references. I also appreciate the help of Professor W. L. Renwick, Dr E. V. Rieu, Mr G. H. W. Rylands, and Mr Ian Scott-Kilvert. At the end of this book there is a list of writers and publishers whose copyright permissions are gratefully acknowledged. My thanks are also due to Penguin Books Ltd for allowing me an advance view of three of their publications and for giving me much help with the preparation of the manuscript.

MICHAEL GRANT

Gattaiola, 1967

1. I apologise to translators for the occasional insertion of small alterations; for example I have anglicized a few Roman technical terms.

NOTE

An asterisk before a footnote indicates that it is not an editorial comment or explanation, but a part of the original text which a modern author would perhaps have relegated to a footnote.

PART I

THE REPUBLICANS

PLAUTUS

TITUS MACCIUS (or MACCUS) PLAUTUS was born at Sarsina (Mercato Saraceno) in Umbria in about 254 B.C., and died in 184 B.C. His life spanned the years in which Rome became an international power and the Romans learnt much more about Greece and its culture. His popular comedies (in verse, like all ancient drama) are almost the first surviving literary productions in Latin. They wore 'Greek dress': they were original adaptations, for not very cultivated Roman audiences, of the Greek New Comedy typified by Menander (342/1–291/0 B.C.). The name of Plautus later came to be attached to a hundred and thirty plays, of which twenty-one are traditionally regarded as his work. With the exception of the *Vidularia* (*Carpet-Bag*), of which part is lost, we have them all. 'Plautus', says J. W. Mackail, 'is the creator for Europe of burlesque, in the *Amphitryo*; of the comedy of plot, in the *Prisoners* (*Captivi*); of farce, in *The Braggart Soldier* (*Miles Gloriosus*); of the comedy of humours, in *The Pot of Gold* (*Aulularia*) and the *Pseudolus*; of the comedy of domestic life in *The Threepenny-Bit* (*Trinummus*); and in *The Rope* (*Rudens*), of the romantic comedy which is one of the chief glories of our own English literature.'

In 1429 twelve of his plays, hitherto lost, were brought to Rome; and the first printed edition appeared at Venice in 1472. A long list of works in modern languages shows how often, thereafter, he was imitated. Ariosto's *Casaria* was a blend of three plays of Plautus and one of Terence (with topical additions). Written in 1498, it was acted in 1508 at the ducal court of Ferrara, which led the Renaissance of ancient drama. The *Miles Gloriosus*, now the fire-eating 'Capitano' of the *Commedia dell' Arte*, was introduced by Italian actors to the France of Henri III. The *Menaechmi*, translated into Italian and performed at Ferrara in 1486 (a German version was written some eleven years earlier), was rendered into English by W. Warner in 1596. Shakespeare's *Comedy of Errors* owes much to it, and is also indebted to the *Amphitryo*, either directly or through W. Courtney's translation (1562/3). This 'tragi-comedy' was adapted by Molière;[1] and the title of a play by Giraudoux, *Amphitryon 38* (1929), implied that this same Plautine theme, of Jupiter's love for a mortal woman, was now being attempted for the thirty-eighth time.

1. So was the *Aulularia*, model of *L'Avare*.

These are extracts from The Haunted House (Mostellaria). *Old Theopropides has returned home from a business trip to find his servant Tranio
outside the house, and the front door shut tight against him. Unknown to
Theopropides, Tranio has led his son astray in his absence, and the boy with
a friend and two girls is inside the house having a lively party. Tranio has
to find a convincing reason for keeping the old man out of the house without
rousing his suspicion.*

THEOPROPIDES: I'm very grateful to you, Neptune, for just manag-
ing to get me home alive. But if you ever hear in the future that I've
taken myself to sea again, then there's no reason why you shouldn't
do to me what you wanted to do to me this time. That's enough of
you for me from this day onward. I've trusted you with everything I'm going to trust you with.

TRANIO (*aside*): Heavens, Neptune, you've been an ass to miss an
opportunity like this.

THEOPROPIDES: After three years away in Egypt, here I am back
home. I expect the people at home are waiting for me.

TRANIO (*aside*): Good heavens, no; we would rather welcome the
man announcing you're dead.

THEOPROPIDES: But what's going on here? The door shut in the
daytime? I'll knock. Hi, there! Is there anyone in to open the door?

TRANIO (*formally*): What man is it that approaches our house?

THEOPROPIDES: Ah look! there's my man, Tranio.

TRANIO: Theopropides, sir, welcome home! I'm delighted to see you
safe and sound. Have you been keeping well?

THEOPROPIDES: So far, as you see.

TRANIO: Good.

THEOPROPIDES: Now, what are you up to? Have you gone mad?

TRANIO: Why?

THEOPROPIDES: Why, because here you are walking about outside.
And there's not a soul in the house on duty to answer the door and
open it. I've almost battered in this pair of doors with knocking.

TRANIO (*shocked*): You didn't actually touch the house, did you?

THEOPROPIDES: Why not? I've told you, I almost battered the door in.

TRANIO: You touched it?

THEOPROPIDES (*irritated*): Yes I touched it. I knocked.
(*Tranio emits a low and ominous moan.*)
  What's the matter?

TRANIO: That was an awful thing you did.

THEOPROPIDES: What's the bother?

TRANIO: It's quite impossible to find words for the sacrilege you've committed.

THEOPROPIDES: Come on, why?

TRANIO: Away, quick, get away from the house. Come over here, (*whispering*) nearer to me. (*Still whispering*) Did you touch the door?

THEOPROPIDES (*more irritated than ever, in a loud voice*): How on earth could I have knocked, if I didn't touch the door?

TRANIO: That's the end of ...

THEOPROPIDES: Who?

TRANIO: Of all your family.

THEOPROPIDES: I hope that heaven for what you've said will really ...

TRANIO (*interrupts*): I'm afraid you won't be able to put things right for yourself and your family.

THEOPROPIDES: And why's that? What news have you got for me?

TRANIO (*pointing to Theopropides' two slaves*): Hi! tell those two to get away from the door.

THEOPROPIDES: Come away, you two.

TRANIO: Don't touch! Did you two touch it, too?

THEOPROPIDES: Look here, for heaven's sake, why shouldn't they touch it?

TRANIO (*mysteriously*): Because it's seven months now since a living soul set foot inside the place, that's why. Once, that is, we had moved out.

THEOPROPIDES: What *are* you talking about?

TRANIO: Look round a minute. There's no one to overhear us, is there?

THEOPROPIDES: No, it's quite safe.

TRANIO: Still, have another look.

THEOPROPIDES: It's all clear. Tell me now.

TRANIO: There's been a murder!

THEOPROPIDES (*yells*): What! I don't get it.

TRANIO: A shocking one, a long, long time ago.

THEOPROPIDES: A long time ago?

TRANIO: But we've only just discovered it was done.

THEOPROPIDES: What sort of a murder? Who did it?

TRANIO: The owner of the house murdered a fellow who was stay-ing with him – after a struggle. (*Casually*) I imagine it was the chap you bought the house from.

THEOPROPIDES: Murdered him?

TRANIO: Yes, and took his money off him and then buried him right there in the house.

THEOPROPIDES: What makes you suspect all this?

TRANIO: Listen, I'll tell you. Your son was out to dinner one night. After he came in, we all went to bed. We were all asleep. It so hap-pened that I'd forgotten to put the light out. And he suddenly let out a yell.

THEOPROPIDES (*loudly*, *in excitement*): Who did? My son?

TRANIO: Ssh! Be quiet and listen. He said he'd seen the dead man's ghost in a dream.

THEOPROPIDES: In a dream?

TRANIO: That's right. But just listen. He said the ghost talked to him like this –

THEOPROPIDES: In his dream?

TRANIO (*sarcastically*): Well, it would be a bit odd if he spoke to him when he was awake, wouldn't it? He'd been dead sixty years, you know. You're an awful ass sometimes, Theopropides.

THEOPROPIDES: All right, I'll be quiet.

TRANIO: This is what the ghost said –

'I am Diapontius, visitor from over the sea. I live here. This is my allotted habitation. The gods below will not welcome me to rest. I died before my time. I was cheated because I was trustful. My host killed me here and put me in a hole secretly in this house, with no last rites, the scoundrel, all for money. You be off. This house is haunted, this dwelling accursed.'

It would take a year to explain what all this meant.

THEOPROPIDES (*alarmed*): Quiet!

TRANIO: In heaven's name, what's up?

THEOPROPIDES (*whispering*): The door creaked.

TRANIO (*to the imagined ghost, pointing to Theopropides*): It was him who knocked.

THEOPROPIDES: There's not a spot of blood on me! The dead are calling me alive to hell!

(*Noises are heard within the house.*)

TRANIO (*aside*): Curse! Those chaps inside will wreck my story now. I'm terrified Theopropides will catch me in the act.

THEOPROPIDES: Why were you talking to yourself?

TRANIO: Get away from the door. Please be off.

THEOPROPIDES: Why should I be off? How about you?

TRANIO (*smugly*): I've no fear: I'm at peace with the dead.

VOICES WITHIN (*very loudly*): Hi! Tranio!

TRANIO (*to the supposed ghost and to the revellers within*): You won't call me, if you've any sense. I don't deserve trouble and (*pointedly to the revellers*) it wasn't me that knocked on the door.

THEOPROPIDES: Why are you standing there muttering? What's the trouble, Tranio? Who are you talking to?

TRANIO (*realizing that, despite his fears, Theopropides has heard nothing from inside*): Oh, it was you that was calling, was it? May the gods bless me, I thought it was the ghost upset because you'd been knocking! But why are you standing there and not doing what I say?

THEOPROPIDES: What am I to do?

TRANIO: Be careful, look round, and run off with your head covered!

THEOPROPIDES: How about you coming too?

TRANIO (*pompously*): I am at peace with the dead.

THEOPROPIDES: You've said that already. But why were you so frightened?

TRANIO: Don't worry about me. I'll look after myself. You run off now, as you were going to, as fast as you can, and say a prayer to Hercules.

THEOPROPIDES: Hercules, on you I call ... (*Exit.*)

TRANIO: And so do I. Give the old boy a packet of trouble today.

J. H. BISHOP (1956)

MONEYLENDER: There's never been a more wretched year for business than this. I spend all day at the exchange from morning till night, and I can't find anyone to lend money to.

TRANIO (*aside*): Now I'm clearly done, for good and all. Here's the moneylender that lent us the cash with which we bought the girl her freedom; and the rest we spent on riotous living. The game's up now, unless I think up something before the old man starts to find out! I'll go up to him. (*Catches sight of Theopropides returning.*) But why's he back home so quickly? I'm afraid he's got wind of all this. I'll go up to him and talk to him instead. Oh dear! there's nothing worse for a man than to have a guilty conscience like mine. Still, things being what they are, I must go on making trouble: that's what the situation demands.

(*To Theopropides*) Where have you come from?

THEOPROPIDES: I met the man who sold me this house.

TRANIO: You didn't tell him what I told you, did you?

THEOPROPIDES: Oh yes I did – the whole story.

TRANIO (*aside*): Oh, good heavens! that's the whole plot ruined for all time.

THEOPROPIDES: What are you mumbling about?

TRANIO: Oh, nothing. Tell me, please, did you mention it to him?

THEOPROPIDES: Yes, the whole story, point by point.

TRANIO: Did he admit to killing his visitor?

THEOPROPIDES: No! he hotly denied it.

TRANIO: The cad denied it?

THEOPROPIDES: Yes, he kept on denying it.

TRANIO: Just think again! You're sure he didn't admit it?

THEOPROPIDES: I'd tell you, if he had. What do you think we ought to do about it now?

TRANIO: Me? What do I think? Go to a good honest judge about it. (*Aside*) But make sure you get one that will believe me: then you'll win your case as easy as falling off a log.

MONEYLENDER (*aloud to himself*): Aha! There's Tranio, Philolaches' man.[1] They haven't repaid my loan or given me any interest yet.

1. Philolaches is the son of Theopropides.

THEOPROPIDES (*to Tranio*): Where are you off to?

TRANIO: I'm not off anywhere. (*Aside*) What bad luck! Damn it all, every one of the gods is against me. He has to come when *he's* here! I really am a most unlucky character: both of them are making trouble for me at once. But I'll forestall him!

MONEYLENDER (*to himself*): He's coming over to me. I'm saved. There's hope for my money.

TRANIO (*to himself*): Look at him grinning. What a hope he's got! (*To the Moneylender*) I bid you good-morning, Mr Macmoneygrub.

MONEYLENDER: Good-morning. What about the money?

TRANIO: Be off, you horror – opening fire on me at once like that.

MONEYLENDER (*to himself*): Dash, there's no cash here.

TRANIO (*to himself*): The man's clearly a prophet.

MONEYLENDER: Don't put me off with evasions.

TRANIO: Then what do you want? Come on.

MONEYLENDER: Where's Philolaches?

TRANIO (*coaxing*): You know, I think you could never have come at a more appropriate moment.

MONEYLENDER: Why?

TRANIO: Come over here.

MONEYLENDER (*shouting*): Am I going to get my money back or not?

TRANIO: All right, I know you're in good voice: don't overdo it.

MONEYLENDER: I'm jolly well going to shout!

TRANIO: Come on, be a good chap and oblige me.

MONEYLENDER: Why should I oblige you?

TRANIO: Go away home.

MONEYLENDER: Me? Go away?

TRANIO: Yes: please come back about midday.

MONEYLENDER: Shall I get the money then?

TRANIO: Yes, you will: go on.

MONEYLENDER: Why should I keep running to and fro, wasting time and trouble? What if I wait here till midday instead?

TRANIO: Look here, be off: listen, for heaven's sake, just clear off home.

MONEYLENDER: No, I won't, not until the interest is –

TRANIO: Go on, I say, just clear off.

MONEYLENDER: No, let's have the interest on that loan. Why are you wasting my time?

TRANIO: Oh, good heavens! if you don't – no, please be off, do as I say.

MONEYLENDER: Right then, I'll shout out his name. That'll do for a summons.

(*Shouts*) PHILOLACHES!

TRANIO: That's a good bellow! You're happy now you're shouting.

MONEYLENDER: I am asking for what's mine. You've already wasted lots of my days like this. If I'm a curse, then pay me the cash and I'll be off. You can stop all my answering back with one word.

TRANIO: Take the lump sum, then.

MONEYLENDER: Oh no! I want the interest first.

TRANIO (*eyeing Theopropides anxiously*): What do you say, most loathsome of all living men? Did you come here to exercise your lungs? Do what you like, he's not giving you anything. He doesn't owe anything.

MONEYLENDER: Doesn't owe anything?

TRANIO: Not a farthing will you take away with you. I suppose you're frightened that he's going to leave town and go into exile all because of the interest he owes you: and that, when you can have your lump sum back!

MONEYLENDER: But it's not what I want. I want the interest.

TRANIO: Oh, damn you! No one's going to pay, do what you will. I suppose you're the only moneylender in town!

MONEYLENDER: Give me the interest: I want the interest. Give me back my interest. Are you going to give me the interest now? Am I going to get my interest?

TRANIO: Interest here, interest there. He can't talk about anything but interest. Get away! Never in my whole life anywhere ever have I seen such a loathsome creature as you.

MONEYLENDER: You don't upset me with words like that.

THEOPROPIDES (*aside*): This is hot stuff: I'm quite a way off, but I can feel the heat. (*To Tranio*) What's this interest, please, that the fellow's after?

TRANIO (*to Moneylender*): His father, look, has just come home from abroad. He'll give you the lump sum and the interest on it – that'll stop you making a nuisance of yourself. Just see if he hesitates.

MONEYLENDER: I'll take anything that's forthcoming.

THEOPROPIDES: What do you say?

TRANIO: I beg your pardon?

THEOPROPIDES: Who is this fellow? What does he want? Why's he calling for Philolaches and kicking up a shindy in front of you here? What's owed to him?

TRANIO: For heaven's sake, order the money to be thrown in the foul fellow's face.

THEOPROPIDES: Me order —?

TRANIO: Order the chap's face to be pelted with silver.

MONEYLENDER: That would be an easy thing to put up with.

THEOPROPIDES: What money is this?

TRANIO: Philolaches owes it to him. It's a tiny sum.

THEOPROPIDES: How tiny?

TRANIO: Well, forty pounds! Now surely that's not much.

MONEYLENDER: There, that's nothing, is it?

TRANIO: Do you hear? Isn't he just the sort of fellow to be a money-lender? They're all outsiders.

THEOPROPIDES: I don't care who he is, what he is, or where he comes from. All I want to know is how much money. But didn't I hear that there was some interest, too?

TRANIO: Yes, forty-four pounds in all. Say you'll give it him – to get rid of him.

THEOPROPIDES: You want me to say that?

TRANIO: Yes.

THEOPROPIDES: Me?

TRANIO: Yes, you. Go on, do as I say. Say you will; come on. That's what I want.

THEOPROPIDES: Tell me – what was done with the money?

TRANIO: Oh, it's quite safe.

THEOPROPIDES: You pay it then, if it's safe.

TRANIO: Your son is buying a house.

THEOPROPIDES (surprised): A house?

TRANIO: Yes, a house.

THEOPROPIDES: Good heavens! He's a chip off the old block. He's turning to business already. You did say a house, didn't you?

TRANIO: I did: but do you know what sort of a house?

THEOPROPIDES: How could I know?

(Tranio makes a loud exclamation of approval.)
What's the matter?

TRANIO: Don't ask me!

THEOPROPIDES: Why?

TRANIO: It's a real beauty, clean as a whistle.

THEOPROPIDES: Jolly good! How much did it cost?

TRANIO: Just as many hundred pounds as you and I come to. But he gave forty pounds as a deposit and borrowed the money from this man here. Do you understand? You see, once the house was – well, as I told you it was – he bought another one straightaway.

THEOPROPIDES: That's fine!

MONEYLENDER: Hi, it's nearly midday.

TRANIO: Come on, pay this fellow off, so that he stops spluttering all over us. Forty-four pounds we owe him, all told.

MONEYLENDER: That's right, I don't ask a penny more.

TRANIO: I wish you would! [1]

THEOPROPIDES (*to the Moneylender*): Young man, you'll deal with me.

MONEYLENDER: Shall I get the cash from you?

THEOPROPIDES: Yes, come tomorrow.

MONEYLENDER: I'm off: that's good enough for me, if I get it tomorrow. (*Exit.*)

TRANIO (*to the departing Moneylender*): May all the gods and goddesses bring down curses on you for ruining my plans through and through! There's no more damnable tribe today than the moneylenders: there's no right on their side.

THEOPROPIDES (*thinking*): And in what district did my son buy his house?

TRANIO (*aside*): That's done it.

THEOPROPIDES: Will you answer me?

TRANIO: Yes, I'll tell you. But I'm trying to get the owner's name.

THEOPROPIDES: Well, come on, think of it.

TRANIO (*aside*): What can I do now? Unless I unload the whole business on to our neighbour here, and say his son bought his house? I've heard it said that the hottest lie's the best to tell. Well, I'm in the lap of the gods; I'll trust them and say that.

THEOPROPIDES: Well, have you remembered?

TRANIO (*pretending to think*): Oh, drat the man – (*aside*) or rather drat

1. This refers to a Roman law: if the plaintiff demanded more than he was entitled to, then he lost his case forthwith.

that man (*pointing to Theopropides*). It's your neighbour's house your son bought.

THEOPROPIDES: Really?

TRANIO: If you pay the money, then really. But not, if you don't. Didn't he buy a house in a good position?

THEOPROPIDES: No, in the very best position. I'd like to have a look round. Knock on the door and get someone out to see you, Tranio.

TRANIO (*aside*): That's the end of me. I can't think of anything to say to that. That's the second time I've foundered on the same rock.

THEOPROPIDES: Now what?

TRANIO (*aside*): I can find no escape. He's got me now, quite obviously.

THEOPROPIDES: Come on, call someone out! Ask him to show us round.

TRANIO: Just a minute! There are ladies inside. First, we must see whether they mind or not.

THEOPROPIDES: Yes, that's fair enough. You investigate and make inquiries, go on! I'll wait here outside until you come out.

TRANIO (*to the departing Theopropides*): A plague upon you, old man. You've wrecked my plan on all counts – ah, good, here's Simo, the owner of the house, coming out. I'll hide for a minute while I call a committee meeting with myself. Then I'll talk to him when I've decided what to do. . . .

J. H. BISHOP (1956)

TERENCE

PUBLIUS TERENTIUS AFER was said to have been born at Carthage of African (Libyan) stock (in about 195 B.C.), and to have come to Rome as a slave. He was freed, and entered the literary circle of the younger Scipio, to whose taste – and even sometimes to whose pen – were attributed the impeccable Latinity and Hellenistic enlightenment of Terence's six comedies. These are: *The Woman of Andros* (*Andria*), *The Mother-in-Law* (*Hecyra*), *The Self-Tormentor* (*Heautontimorumenos*), *The Eunuch* (*Eunuchus*), the *Phormio*, and *The Brothers* (*Adelphi*). Terence died in 159 B.C.

Like the plays of Congreve, his comedies are literary rather than theatrical successes; but it is from them that European dramatists have learnt how to construct and polish a play. A recent census of medieval library catalogues reveals ten copies of Terence in the eleventh century and twenty-five in the twelfth. His plays were printed at Strasbourg in 1470, and the same period produced French (*c.* 1466) and German (1488) translations. Luther often referred to Terence; Erasmus and Melanchthon memorized his works. Several Italian versions appeared between 1533 and 1588; but his appearance on Jesuit reading lists (1551) was shortlived. The *Woman of Andros* was rendered into English by J. Rastell(?) in *c.* 1520 and by T. Kyffin – for schools – in 1588. The French have been particular admirers of Terence. Molière's *École des Maris* and *Fourberies de Scapin* are based on the *Adelphi* and *Phormio*, though Boileau objected that the element of farce which Molière added to his Terentian original displayed undue 'friendship of the people'. The greatest of classical scholars, Richard Bentley, devoted some of his best work to a commentary on Terence (1726). Gibbon's tutor at Magdalen College, Oxford, 'proposed that we should read every morning, from ten to eleven, the comedies of Terence'. But Terence's urbane, lax humanism displeased the nineteenth century. However, it has survived on the stage of Westminster School; and the *Woman of Andros* has been adapted by Thornton Wilder (1934).

Enter Micio calling a slave, who does not answer.

MICIO: Aeschinus has not come back from his dinner appointment yet: nor have any of the slaves sent to fetch him. You know, they are right when they say that if you are out somewhere and stay longer than you're expected to, then it's better to be a husband and have an angry wife suspecting you than be a son and cause anxiety to your kindly parents. If you're out too long, your wife thinks you're making love or else you've become the object of another's affections: or drinking or indulging yourself. You're out enjoying yourself and she's at home suffering for it. But look at me, the things that worry me because my son's still out. What anxieties cross my mind! Perhaps he's caught a chill in the night air or fallen somewhere and hurt himself. O dear! fancy a man taking to his heart something dearer than himself. Yet he's not really my son, he's my brother's.

My brother and I have had quite different tastes ever since we were boys. I have lived a pleasant life in the city here. I have had peace and quiet and I've never married, a thing which people consider fortunate. His life has been quite the opposite. He's lived in the country, and always conducted his affairs with rigorous economy. He got married, and has two sons. Of these two boys, I adopted the elder. I've brought him up from a tiny lad, looked after him and cared for him as though he were my own. In him is my delight, he's my only joy. I do my best to make sure he cares for me, too. I'm generous to him, overlook things, and don't expect him to think as I do about things. And then, the things other boys do without letting their fathers know, the sort of things that young men generally do, I have encouraged him not to hide from me. I feel that anyone who has learned to lie to his father and deceive him will do the same to others all the more readily. I think kindness and a sense of right and wrong are a better curb to children's spirits than fear.

My brother doesn't agree with all this: he disapproves. Often he comes to me and cries 'What are you doing, Micio? Why are you spoiling our boy like this? Why does he go out with girls? And drink? Why do you give him the funds for such luxuries? Why do you let him have so many clothes? You're an awful ass!' But it's he who is too hard-hearted – more than it's right or fair to be. And the fellow who thinks that authority is more securely or firmly based if it rests on force rather than on mutual affection is in my opinion well wide of the truth.

This is how I look at it. I'm sure I'm right. The man who keeps to the path of duty through fear of punishment will be honest just so long as he thinks he'll be found out. If he thinks he can get away with something undetected, then he'll be back to his tricks. But the man who is attached to you by affection is anxious to treat you as you treat him, whether you're there or not. It's a father's job to get his son to do right of his own free will rather than because he's afraid of someone. That's the difference between a father and a tyrant. A man who can't do this should admit that he can't control children!

But isn't this the very man I'm talking about? Yes, it is; and he looks pretty miserable, too. I suppose he'll make some complaint, as usual.

Enter Micio's brother Demea.

I'm delighted to see you well, Demea.

DEMEA: Ah, good! You're the man I've been looking for.

MICIO: Why are you so miserable?

DEMEA: Are you asking me that, when Aeschinus is ours?

MICIO (*aside*): Didn't I say so? (*Aloud*) What's he done?

DEMEA: What's he done? A fellow like him, with no sense of shame or fear, who doesn't think the normal codes of decency apply to him? Leaving aside all he's done in the past, look at his latest misdeed.

MICIO: What is it?

DEMEA: He's broken in someone's front door, broken into his house, beaten the owner and all his household within an inch of their lives, and carried off some girl he's in love with! Everyone's saying what a scandal it is! Everyone I met on the way here told me about it: it's common gossip. If an example is wanted, doesn't he see how his brother gets on with his job at the farm quietly and soberly? *He* never did anything like this. And in blaming Aeschinus, I blame you, too! You've let him go to pieces.

MICIO: There's no one more unjust than a man ignorant of the facts. You don't think anything's right unless you've done it yourself!

DEMEA: What do you mean?

MICIO: You're jumping to conclusions, Demea. Believe me, there's nothing outrageous in a young fellow going out with a girl or having a drink. No! nor breaking into a house for love. If you and I didn't behave like this, it's just because we couldn't afford it. Now you claim credit because you didn't behave like this, when it was poverty that stopped you. It isn't fair. If we'd had the wherewithal, we would have behaved just the same. Now, if you were a man, you'd let that boy of yours carry on like this and make allowance for his youth; otherwise, when he's at last rid of your supervision, he'll act in this way at a more unsuitable time of life.

DEMEA: Jupiter alive, man, you're enough to drive me mad. Not a scandal for a slip of a boy to behave like this?

MICIO: Listen, don't keep on dinning that into me. You gave that boy to me to look after. So he's mine. If he does something wrong, it's my affair and I'll take care of it. He goes out eating and drinking, living a life in high society; I foot the bill. He's in love; I'll keep him in cash while it suits me to: otherwise he'll be shut out in the cold. He breaks into a house; I'll do the repairs. He tears his clothes; they shall be mended. I have the money to do it, thank God, and it doesn't worry me yet. So stop all this grumbling, or call in some adjudicator – I'll show you're more wrong than I am.

DEMEA: Oh dear! You should learn how to be a father from those who really know.

MICIO: You may be his father by blood, but I am because of the good sense I show.

DEMEA: You? common sense?

MICIO: If you're going on like this, I'm off.

DEMEA: Do you persist?

MICIO: Must I hear the same story so often?

DEMEA: But I'm worried.

MICIO: And I'm worried, too. But, Demea, let's each look after our own boy; you after yours, and I after mine. For you to worry about both is almost to ask back the boy you gave me.

DEMEA (aggrieved). Oh, Micio!

MICIO: Well, that's how I see it.

DEMEA: All right! If that's how you want it: let him rot in bottomless perdition, I don't care. But if after this (*raising his voice*) I hear one word –

MICIO: There you go, losing your temper again.

DEMEA: Don't you believe me? Am I asking for him back? It's a hard life. I'm not an outsider. If I take an interest – oh, never mind. You want me to look after one only. Right! And he, thank God, is all I would have him be, and that lad of yours will realize it some day. I'll say nothing harder than that. (*Exit.*)

MICIO (*alone*): He's neither right nor wrong in what he says. I'm rather annoyed about all this, but I didn't want him to know I was put out. He's like that. To mollify him, I am careful to argue against everything he says and upset him that way. Even then, he can hardly bear it. But if I support him, or even join him in anger, then I would go mad like him! Aeschinus, I admit, has behaved rather badly to me over this. There's scarcely a girl he hasn't been out with or given presents to! Still, a little while ago – I suppose he was tired of flirting – he said he wanted to get married. I hoped his youthful passions were passing: I was delighted. And now he's started again: still, whatever it is, I want to find out about it. I'll go and meet him, if he's in town.

J. H. BISHOP (1956)

CICERO

MARCUS TULLIUS CICERO was born in 106 B.C. at Arpinum (Arpino) in central Italy. He was educated at Rome, and – after his début in the courts – at Athens, under the Head of the Academy, Antiochus. Then at Rhodes, his eminent teachers included the rhetorician Molon and the Stoic Posidonius. His reputation as lawyer and politician was made by the speeches *Against Verres*, corrupt governor of Sicily (70 B.C.). As consul in 63 B.C. Cicero took the lead in averting a *coup d'état* by the savage, anarchistic nobleman Catiline, but his dream of a 'harmony of the orders', reconciling the senate and financiers ('knights'), was destroyed by the informal First Triumvirate of Pompey, Caesar, and Crassus. Cicero refused to join the Triumvirate, was exiled in 58–7 and reluctantly went to govern Cilicia (S.E. Asia Minor) in 51–50. After hesitantly joining Pompey against Caesar in the subsequent Civil War, he acquiesced in Caesar's victory but applauded his murder. Then, disgusted by the failure of the Republic to revive, he gradually summoned the determination to attack the new autocrat, Antony, in the *Philippics* (44–3). In the Second Triumvirate the nineteen-year-old Octavian, despite Cicero's tragic trust in his admiring good will, was temporarily reconciled with Antony; the Triumvirs proscribed Cicero and had him murdered on 7 December 43 B.C.

An extraordinary wealth of autobiographical and historical information is available in his more than 800 surviving letters *To His Friends* (whose replies are sometimes available), *To Atticus*, *To His Brother Quintus*, and *To Brutus*. These letters were not written for publication, and were published posthumously. At Verona, in 1345, Petrarch discovered, or brought to the world's notice, the last three of these collections; they shocked him because of their revelations of political inadequacy. The letters were printed in 1470, and A. Fleming's English rendering (of M. Cordier's French version) was published in 1576.

Born outside the magic circle of Roman dynasts – it is unfair of Communists to regard him as a typical, if enlightened, member of a decadent noble caste – Cicero owed his legal and political career to the unique persuasiveness of his oratory. Fifty-eight of his one hundred and six speeches survive. Italian versions of certain of them appeared in *c.* 1290; a landmark in Petrarch's life was his perusal (and transcription) of two speeches at Liège (1333). Cicero's patriotic responsibility became the ideal of the fifteenth-century Italian Renaissance. English translations of the *Pro Marcello* (R. Sherry) and *Pro Archia* (T. Drant) appeared in 1535 and 1571 respectively. Admiration was never long in abeyance. The French and American Revolutions respected his political republicanism; and simultaneously the growth of trial by jury, and free House of Commons debating, stimulated his influence in England.

The style of his speeches had long been as influential as their content.[1] In the Renaissance, when there were endless controversies about the degree of exactitude required by the imitator, it had become the language of governments, papal chanceries, and Universities; bolder spirits reacted towards Seneca. Then Chatham, Pitt, Sheridan, Fox, and especially Burke echoed in some degree his elaborate rhythms, as perhaps, to a lesser extent, has Sir Winston Churchill in our own day – but scarcely any other modern writer or speaker in Britain, where rhetoric is in complete eclipse.[2]

Cicero's views on this art or science of rhetoric, so important a feature of ancient public life and education, are preserved in his treatises *On Invention*, *On the Orator* (*De Oratore*), *On Famous Orators* (the *Brutus*) – containing a survey of the recent history of public speaking – and the *Orator*, mainly autobiographical. Of these the schematic and youthful *On Invention* (together with a treatise *To Herennius*, of unknown authorship) enjoyed special popularity during the Middle Ages. A manuscript containing complete texts of the three other rhetorical works was discovered in 1421, and the *De Oratore* was one of the first books to be printed, at the Monastery of Subiaco in 1465.

Among the most famous of his ethical treatises are the essays *On Duties* (*De Officiis*), *The Boundaries of Good and Evil* (*De Finibus*), *On Old Age*, *On Friendship*, and the political studies *On the Laws* and *On the State*. Though these are for the most part practical and unphilosophical popularizations of Stoic morality presented with the undogmatic modesty Cicero had learnt at the Academy, the doctrines which they described were the most enlightened that the western world had known. Those doctrines can be summed up by Cicero's own word, *humanitas* – the qualities of mind and character of a man who is civilized. A man should treat his fellow-men with kindliness because Man himself is worthy of respect – he has some inherent value. This was a logical deduction from the Stoic Brotherhood of Man, in which by the universal

1. For an ancient appreciation of his style, see below, p.338.
2. Cicero's verse – much of it translation from the Greek – survives in fairly extensive fragments. It had more influence on poetic techniques than the tales to its discredit would suggest.

Law of Nature – under the guidance of Providence – human beings are held to count for something and deserve well of each other regardless of state, race, or caste. Cicero was convinced that no legislation can make right into wrong or wrong into right.

Dante liked the treatise *On Friendship* best of his works. In 1481 Caxton printed an English translation by John Tiptoft, together with a version of *On Old Age* (from the French). *On Duties* had been printed in 1465 both at Subiaco and at Mainz, and R. Whytinton's English rendering was published in 1533. Luther regarded Cicero's treatises as superior to those of Aristotle. Montaigne quotes him 312 times. Humanists, deists, believers in natural religion, rationalists, freethinkers – Lord Herbert, Bolingbroke, Locke – all turned to his 'philosophy'. David Hume had *On Duties* before him in all his thoughts.

Today, the wheel has turned full circle. The reaction against Cicero (of which one of the leaders was Huysmans in *A Rebours*, 1884) is so effective that, absurdly enough, it is almost impossible nowadays to find commentaries on some of his principal works.

With outstanding foresight Romulus saw and understood that cities founded for long life and greatness ought not to be on the sea, chiefly because cities on the sea are liable to many dangers, some of them unpredictable. For the mainland gives many advance warnings about impending invasions, expected and unexpected alike. For example, the noises and din of a marching army travel; and no enemy can swoop on us by land too quickly for us to know that he is coming, and who he is, and where he is from. But an enemy's fleet can arrive by sea before anyone can have any suspicion that he is coming, and when he comes he does not issue any pronouncement concerning his identity or his place of origin or even his intentions; in fact it is not even possible to discover any interpretable clue indicating if he is friend or enemy.

Besides, the morals of coastal cities deteriorate and become corrupt. These towns become adulterated with strange languages and habits, and import not only foreign cargoes but foreign morals, which inevitably pervert their national traditions. Indeed, the inhabitants themselves do not stay attached to their homes but are forcibly transported far away from them by their ambitions and imaginings – even when physically they stay at home, at heart they are wanderers in remote lands. Nothing contributed more greatly to the long decline and final destruction of Carthage and Corinth than the far-flung dispersal of their inhabitants due to their passion for trade and sea-travel: in consequence of this, agriculture and the army were neglected. Moreover, many ruinous incentives to luxurious living – such as the spoils of wars, and commercial imports – are supplied by sea; and even by its pleasant situation a coastal town contributes abundant temptations to the sensuous pleasures – to extravagance or idleness.

Indeed, what I said about Corinth may well be applied very legitimately to the whole of Greece. For practically the whole of the Peloponnese adjoins the sea – Phlius is the only one of its towns which has no territory bounded by a shore; and outside the Peloponnese the Aenianes, Dorians, and Dolopians are the only peoples who are not on the sea. There is no need to mention the Greek islands, which are seagirt and practically drifting – and the same may be said of their institutions and morals. So much for the Greek homeland; and to pass on to the colonies which they have settled in Asia, Thrace, Italy, Sicily, and Africa, is not every single one except Magnesia washed by the waves? Round the countries of the natives there is a Greek coastal fringe; for none of the native peoples themselves were originally sea-farers except the Etruscans and Carthaginians, who went to sea for piracy and trade respectively. Obviously the evils and upheavals from which Greece has suffered have been due to these defects of maritime cities which I have briefly indicated. On the other hand the defects are accompanied by a great advantage: every product in the world can come across the water to your city, and conversely your fellow-citizens can export their own products to whatever country they wish.

How, then, could Romulus more clearly have shown his divine wisdom? He utilized the advantages of the sea and yet avoided its hazards; he founded his city on the bank of an ever and evenly flow-ing river with a broad estuary. That river allows Rome to receive what it needs from the sea and to export its own superfluous products. Moreover, it enables the city to obtain whatever is needful for its sub-sistence and civilization not only from the sea, but from inland too. It looks to me as though he already divined that this city would one day be the heart and capital of a mighty State. For virtually no city in any other part of Italy could possibly have maintained so vast an empire.

As to Rome's natural defences, the least observant person will have a clear outline and perception of them in his mind. The circuit of its walls was cleverly traced by Romulus and the kings who came after him. On every side there were sheer precipices; the single approach – between the Esquiline and Quirinal Hills – was surrounded by a great bastion facing outwards, and a huge ditch. Our citadel was so well protected by the steep, precipitous crags on which it stands that even at the dreadful time of the Gallic invasion it remained impregnable and inviolate.

Moreover, the site which Romulus chose has abundant springs and, unlike the surrounding country, it is healthy. For the hills are open to the breezes, and also bring shade to the valleys which lie between them.

MICHAEL GRANT (1956)

Sometimes expediency and right (as we understand the terms) will appear to clash. In order to avoid mistaken decisions when this happens, we must establish some rule to guide us in making such comparisons and to prevent us from deserting our obligations. That rule will be in accordance with the teaching and system of the Stoics; they are my models in this work – for the New Academy (to which I belong)[1] gives us wide latitude to support any theory which has probability on its side. But to return to my rule.

Well, then, to take something away from someone else – that one man should profit by another's loss – is more unnatural than death, or destitution, or pain, or any other physical or external blow. To begin with, it strikes at the roots of human society and fellowship. For if we each of us propose to rob or injure one another for our personal gain, then we are clearly going to demolish what is more completely natural than anything else in the world: the link that unites every human being with every other. Just imagine if each of our limbs had its own consciousness and decided it would do better if it appropriated the nearest limb's strength! Of course the whole body would inevitably collapse and die. In precisely the same way, if every one of us seizes and appropriates other people's property, the human community, the brotherhood of mankind, collapses. It is natural enough for a man to prefer earning a living for himself rather than for someone else – granted; but what nature forbids is that we should increase our means, property and resources by plundering others.

Indeed this idea – that one must not injure anybody else for one's own advantage – is not only natural law, an internationally valid principle; it is also incorporated in the statutes which individual communities have framed for their national purposes. The whole point and intention of those statutes is that one citizen shall live safely with another: anyone who attempts to undermine that association is punished with fines, imprisonment, exile, or death.

1. This was the ultimate descendant of the Academy founded by Plato. After a phase of scepticism it had become latitudinarian and borrowed much from other schools, and especially from the Stoics, whose moral imperative greatly influenced Cicero.

The same conclusion follows even more forcibly from the *rational principle* in nature, the law that governs gods and men alike. Whoever obeys it – and everyone who wants to live according to nature's laws must obey it – will never be guilty of coveting another man's goods or appropriating for himself what he has taken from someone else. For great-heartedness and loftiness of soul, and courtesy, and justice, and generosity, are far more natural than self-indulgence, or wealth, or even life itself. But to despise this latter category of things, to attach no importance to them in comparison with the common good, really does need a great and lofty heart.

In the same way, it is more truly natural to model oneself on Hercules and undergo the most terrible labours and troubles to help and save all the nations of the earth than (however superior you are in looks or strength) to live a secluded, untroubled life with plenty of money and pleasures. Mankind was grateful to Hercules for his services, and popular belief gave him a place among the gods.

So the finest and noblest characters prefer a life of dedication to a life of self-indulgence: and one may go further, and conclude that such men conform with nature (for that is just what they do) and will therefore do no harm to their fellow-men.

In conclusion: a man who wrongs another for his own benefit either imagines, presumably, that he is not doing anything unnatural, or he does not agree that death, destitution, pain, the loss of children, relations, friends, are less deplorable than doing wrong to another person. But if he sees nothing unnatural in wronging a fellow-being, how can you argue with him? – he is taking away from man all that makes him man. If, however, he concedes that this ought to be avoided, but regards death, destitution, and pain as even more undesirable, he is mistaken in believing that *any* damage, either to his person or to his property, is worse than a moral failure.

So everyone ought to have the same purpose: to make the interest of each the same as the interest of all. For if men grab for themselves, it will mean the complete collapse of human society.

And if Nature prescribes (as she does) that every human being must help every other human being, whoever he is, just precisely because they are all human beings, then – by the same authority – all men have identical interests. Having identical interests means that we are all subject to one and the same Law of Nature: and, that being so, the very least that such a law must enjoin is that we may not wrong one another. The hypothesis of that proposition is true; so the conclusion is true also. People are not talking sense if they claim (as they sometimes do) that they do not intend to rob their parents or brothers for their own gain, but that robbing their other compatriots is a different matter. That is the same as denying any common interest with their fellow-countrymen, or any consequent legal or social obligations. And such a denial shatters the whole fabric of national life.

Another attitude is that one ought to take account of compatriots but not of foreigners. People who argue like this subvert the whole basis of the human community itself – and when that is gone, kind actions, generosity, goodness, and justice are annihilated. And their annihilation is a sin against the immortal gods. For it was they who established the society which such men are undermining. And the tightest bond of that society is the belief that it is more unnatural for one man to rob another for his own benefit than to endure any loss whatsoever, whether to his person or to his property – or even to his very soul, provided that no consideration of justice or injustice is involved: for justice is the queen and sovereign of all the virtues.

Let us consider possible objections.

(1) 'Suppose a man of great wisdom were starving to death: would he not be justified in taking food belonging to someone who was completely useless?' (2) 'Suppose an honest man had the chance to steal the clothes of a cruel and inhuman tyrant like Phalaris,[1] and needed them to avoid freezing to death, should he not do it?'

These questions are very easy to answer. For if you rob even a completely useless man for your own advantage, it is an unnatural, inhuman action. If, however, your qualities were such that, if you stayed alive, you could render great services to your country and to mankind, then it would not be blameworthy to take something from another *for that reason*. But, apart from such cases, every man must bear his own misfortunes rather than damage someone else's interests to remedy them. The exception I have quoted does not mean that stealing and covetousness in general are any less unnatural than illness, want, and the rest: neglect of the common interest is unjust, and therefore unnatural. So Nature's own law, seeing that it promotes and

1. Dictatorial ruler of Acragas (Agrigentum) in Sicily during the fifth century B.C.

coincides with the common interest, will surely ordain that the means of subsistence may, if necessary, be transferred from the feeble, useless person to the wise, honest, brave man, whose death will be a grave loss to society. But in that case the latter must guard against the excessive self-regard and conceit that would make him act wrongly. If he avoids this, he will be doing his duty, working for the interests of his fellow-men and, I say it yet again, of the human community.

It is extremely easy to answer the query about Phalaris. We have nothing in common with autocrats; in fact we and they are totally set apart.[1] There is nothing unnatural about robbing – if you can – a man whom it is morally right to kill, and the whole sinful and pestilential gang of dictatorial rulers ought to be cast out from human society. For limbs, when there is no longer any life-blood and vital energy in them, are sometimes amputated; and in just the same way these ferocious, bestial monsters in human form ought to be severed from the body of mankind.

So let us regard this as settled: that what is morally wrong can never be expedient – not even when it enables you to secure something that you believe to be expedient. For the mere act of thinking something expedient when it is morally wrong is pernicious. But, as I remarked earlier, circumstances often arise in which expediency and right seem to clash. So an investigation is necessary – do they really clash in such cases? or can they be reconciled?

This is the type of problem. Suppose that there is a food-shortage and famine at Rhodes, and the price of corn is extremely high. An honest man has brought Rhodes a large stock of corn from Alexandria. He is aware that a number of other traders are on their way from Alexandria – he has seen their ships making for Rhodes, with substantial cargoes of grain. Ought he to tell the Rhodians? Or is he to say nothing and sell his stock at the best price he can get? I am assuming he is an enlightened, honest person. What I am imagining are the deliberations and self-searchings of a man who would not keep the Rhodians in ignorance if he thought it dishonest to do so, but who is not certain that it would be dishonest.

In cases of this kind that eminent and respected Stoic Diogenes of Babylon habitually takes one side, and his very clever pupil Antipater

1. This was written shortly after the murder of Julius Caesar, when Antony was in power at Rome.

of Tarsus the other.[1] Antipater says that all the facts must be revealed, and the purchaser must be as fully informed as the seller. According to Diogenes, however, the seller must declare the defects of his wares as far as the law of the land requires, but otherwise – provided he tells no untruths – he is entitled, as a seller of goods, to sell them as profitably as he can.

'I have brought my cargo, I have offered it for sale, I offer it as cheap as other dealers – perhaps cheaper, when I am over-stocked. Whom am I cheating?'

Antipater argues on the other side. 'What do you mean? You ought to work for your fellow-men and serve the interests of mankind: those are the conditions under which you were born, those are the principles which it is your duty to follow and obey – you must identify your interests with the interests of the community, and theirs with yours. How, then, can you conceal from your fellow-men that abundant supplies and benefits are due to reach them shortly?'

'Concealing is one thing,' perhaps Diogenes will say, 'but *not revealing* is another. If I do not reveal to you, at this moment, what the gods are like – or the nature of the Supreme Good – I am not *concealing* that information (and it would certainly be more useful to you than the knowledge that wheat prices were down). It is not my duty to tell you everything that it would benefit you to know.'

'Oh yes, it is,' Antipater will reply, 'if you remember that Nature has joined mankind together in one community.'

'I remember that,' the answer will be, 'but surely it is a community in which private property exists? If not, nothing ought to be sold at all – everything ought to be given away.'

In this whole argument, you will observe, neither party is saying 'However morally wrong this action is, I will perform it, because it is expedient.' One side is claiming that it is expedient without being wrong, while the other urges that it should not be performed because it is wrong.

Or suppose that an honest man wants to sell a house because of certain defects which he alone knows. He knows it is insanitary but it is supposed to be quite healthy; or there is vermin in all the bedrooms, it is badly built and falling down, but nobody knows this except the

---

1. These were leaders of Stoicism during its middle period, during the second century B.C., when casuistry was fashionable.

owner. If he does not disclose these facts to purchasers, and sells the house for much more than he expected, has he behaved unfairly and dishonestly?

'Certainly he has,' says Antipater. 'At Athens, not to set a man right when he has lost his way is penalized by general execration: and is it not precisely the same thing to let a purchaser make a mistake and ruin himself with a very heavy loss? That is even worse than not showing a man the way: it is deliberately misleading him.'

'But he did not force you to buy, did he?' objects Diogenes. 'He did not even ask you to. He offered for sale something he did not want; you bought something you wanted. Seeing that men who advertise a bad, ill-constructed house as fine and well-built are not blamed, still less ought people to be blamed if they merely refrain from praising it. For when the purchaser can exercise his own judgement, what fraud can there be on the part of the seller? If you are not obliged to make good everything you say, how can you be responsible for what you do not say? It would surely be exceptionally stupid for a seller to enumerate the defects of what he is selling, and the height of absurdity for the auctioneer to proclaim, at the owner's request, *An Insanitary House for Sale*.'

These, then, are some of the doubtful cases in which one side takes a moral view, and the other pleads expediency by asserting that it is not only right to do what seems to be expedient but wrong not to do it. Such are the conflicts that often arise between right and apparent expediency.

But I must record my opinion about these cases; for I did not write them down merely to raise problems, but to solve them. I believe, then, that the corn-merchant ought not to have concealed the facts from the Rhodians; the man who was selling the house ought not to have concealed them from his purchaser. Holding things back does not always amount to concealment, but it does when you want people, for your advantage, not to know something which *you* know and it would benefit *them* to know. Anyone can see the sort of concealment that this amounts to – and the sort of person who practises it. Certainly he is not an open, straightforward, fair, honest man; no, he is a shifty, deep, artful, treacherous, malevolent, underhand, sly, habitual rogue. Surely it is inexpedient to get oneself called by all those names and a lot more besides!

So, if suppression of the truth deserves censure, what must we think of people who have actually lied? A Roman gentleman called Gaius Canius, quite a witty and cultured man, once went to Syracuse, not on business but (as he himself told the story) on holiday. He often spoke of buying a little property where he could ask his friends and enjoy himself without intrusion. When this became known, a Syracusan banker called Pythius told him that he had such a property; it was not for sale, but Canius could treat it as his own if he wanted to. Pythius forthwith asked him there to dinner on the following day, and Canius accepted. Now Pythius, being a banker, had people of all classes ready to oblige him. So he sent for some fishermen, and requested them to do their next day's fishing in front of his grounds; and he gave them full instructions. Canius arrived to dinner punctually, and Pythius gave him a sumptuous entertainment. Before their gaze there was a fleet of fishing-boats; each fisherman brought in his catch, and deposited it at Pythius' feet. 'Tell me, Pythius,' said Canius, 'what does this mean? – all these fish and all these boats?'

'It is quite natural,' Pythius replied. 'All the fish and water in Syracuse are precisely here; the men couldn't get on without this estate.'

Canius became excited and pressed Pythius to sell it to him. Pythius showed reluctance at first, but finally – to cut the story short – he gave in. Canius was rich and wanted the property, and he paid what Pythius asked for it – and bought all its appointments as well. Pythius clinched the agreement and entered it in his books.

On the following day Canius invited his friends, and arrived early. Of boats he saw not so much as a single thole-pin. He inquired from his next-door neighbour if there was some fisherman's holiday which accounted for their invisibility. 'I don't know of any,' was the answer. 'But nobody does fish here; so yesterday I couldn't think what had happened.'

Canius was furious. But what was he to do? For at that time my friend and colleague Gaius Aquilius had not yet laid down the established forms of pleading in cases of criminal fraud. When he was asked what he meant by criminal fraud in this connexion, Aquilius used to answer: 'pretending one thing and doing another' – a masterly reply, such as one would expect from one so expert at framing definitions. So Pythius and everyone else whose actions belie their words are ill-intentioned, faithless, and dishonest. Nothing that such vice-ridden people do can possibly be expedient.

The sixth book of Hecato's *Moral Obligations*[1] is full of questions like this: 'When food is extremely scarce, is a decent man entitled to let his slaves go hungry?' Hecato gives both sides of the case, but finally bases his decision on expediency – as he understands it – rather than on human feeling.

Here is another of his problems: if there is a storm at sea, and cargo has to be thrown overboard, should a man prefer to lose a valuable horse or a valueless slave? In this case his pocket pulls one way, human feeling the other.

Another question was this: 'If the ship has sunk and a foolish man has grabbed a plank, will a wise man take it away from him if he can?'

'No,' says Hecato, 'that would be wrong.'

'What about the man who owns the ship, then? will *he* take it away?'

'Certainly not – any more than he would want, because the ship belongs to him, to throw a passenger overboard in deep water. For until she reaches the port for which the ship is chartered it does *not* belong to the owner, but to the passengers.'

'Well, then, if there were one plank, and two shipwrecked people – both wise men! – should each of them try to seize it for himself, or should one give way to the other?'

'One should give way; the plank should be left with the man whose life is more valuable to himself or his country.'

'But what if both lives are equally valuable in both respects?'

'Then they will not compete, but one will give way to the other, as though the matter were decided by lot or by the game of odds-and-evens.'[2]

'Again, suppose a man's father were stealing from temples or digging an underground passage to the Treasury – ought his son to report him to the authorities?'

1. Hecato was another leader of the Middle Stoic school. He himself came from Rhodes, which was a philosophical city as well as a great commercial city in which this sort of problem was very real.

2. This is called *morra* in Italy. At a given signal one person quickly opens any number of his fingers. The other throws up his own hand simultaneously in an attempt to open the same number. (An honest man was one with whom you could play this game in the dark.)

'No, that would be a sin. Indeed, if the father were charged, his son ought to defend him.'

'So patriotism does not, then, come before all other obligations?'

'Yes, it certainly does, but it is in our country's interest to have sons who are loyal to their parents.'

'Then if a man's father tries to seize autocratic power or betray his country, will his son say nothing?'

'Of course he will, he will beg his father not to do it. If he fails, he will censure his father and even threaten him, and finally, if the ruin of his country seems imminent, he will put its safety before his father's.'

Hecato also asks: if a wise man inadvertently accepts counterfeit money, when he discovers his mistake will he offer the same coin, and pass it off as good, in payment of a debt? Diogenes says yes, Antipater says no – and I agree with him.

And then, if a man knows that the wine he sells is going bad, ought he to disclose the fact? Diogenes says he need not, Antipater thinks an honest man should. Among the Stoics problems of this kind are like disputed points of law. Again, 'when you are selling a slave ought his defects to be declared? – not only those which it is legally necessary to declare (otherwise the transaction is liable to cancellation), but also the fact that he is a liar or gambler or thievish or that he drinks?' The one says you ought to declare such facts, the other says you need not.

'If a man thinks he is selling brass when he is really selling gold, should an honest man tell him it is gold, or buy it at one-thousandth of its value?'

But it is clear by this time where the two philosophers disagree – and what my own opinion is.

Michael Grant (1956)

RIGHT AND WRONG

True law is Reason, right and natural, commanding people to fulfil their obligations and prohibiting and deterring them from doing wrong. Its validity is universal; it is unchangeable and eternal. Its commands and prohibitions apply effectively to good men and have no effect on bad men. Any attempt to supersede this law, to repeal any part of it, is sinful; to cancel it entirely is impossible. Neither the

Senate nor the Assembly can exempt us from its demands; we need no interpreter or expounder of it but ourselves. There will not be one law at Rome, one at Athens, or one now and one later, but all nations will be subject all the time to this one changeless and everlasting law; and one God will be shared by all of us, our master and our ruler – God, who invented and instituted this law and arbitrates its operation. Whoever does not obey Him, will be trying to escape from himself, will be rejecting his own human nature; and precisely for that reason, even if he avoids what is usually considered punishment, he will suffer the most terrible penalties of all.

The ideal State never begins a war except in defence of itself or of an obligation. Wars begun without provocation are unjust; for no war can be just unless it is a war of revenge or a war of defence. Again, no war can be regarded as just unless it has been declared and announced, and unless satisfaction has first been demanded.

Our people have gained their world-wide empire by protecting their allies. And do we not see that Nature herself has given control to what is superior – to the great benefit of what is inferior? Otherwise why does God dominate Man? And why, in human beings, does mind dominate body, and Reason dominate the evil elements of the mind, such as lust and anger? However, we must distinguish between different sorts of domination and subjection. For when we say that the mind dominates the body and dominates lust, it controls the body as a king rules over his subjects, or a father his children, whereas it dominates the lusts as a master rules his slaves: it keeps them down and crushes them.

MICHAEL GRANT (1956)

GOVERNMENT

This is an imaginary dialogue between two leading political, military, and literary figures of the previous century: Scipio the younger (destroyer of Carthage) and his friend Gaius Laelius.

SCIPIO: When there is a king, everybody except the king has too few rights, and too small a share in what is decided; whereas under an oligarchy, freedom scarcely extends to the populace, since they are not consulted and are excluded from power. When, on the other hand, there is thoroughgoing democracy, however fairly and moderately it is conducted its egalitarianism is automatically unfair since it does not make it possible for one man to rise above another.

Granted, therefore, that the famous King Cyrus of Persia was the justest and wisest of monarchs, nevertheless his people's interests (for that, as I have said, is what 'commonwealth' means) do not seem to me to have been well served by that sort of government; for they were subject to the absolute control of a single man. Or take our own protectorate the city-state of Marseille. Let us admit that it is governed with the greatest integrity by a select group of leading citizens; yet that implies something like slavery for the population as a whole. And then the Athenians: at certain periods after the elimination of their oligarchic council, the Areopagus, they transacted their affairs exclusively by plebiscites and decrees of the National Assembly; yet because they did not allow one man to rise above another their State could not maintain its glorious position.

I am speaking about these three forms of government – monarchy, oligarchy, democracy – when they retain their specific character, not when they are merged and confused with one another. In addition to their liability to the flaws I have just mentioned, each of them suffers from further ruinous defects. For in front of every one of these constitutional forms stands a headlong slippery path to another and more evil one. Thus beneath the endurable or (if you like) lovable Cyrus – to take him as an example – lurks the terribly cruel Phalaris,[1] influencing him towards the arbitrary transformation of his own nature: for any autocracy readily and easily changes into that sort of tyranny. Then the government of Marseille, conducted by a few leading men, is very close to that clique of the Thirty which once tyrannized Athens. And as for the Athenian democracy, its absolute power turned into rule by the masses, that is to say into maniac irresponsibility.

LAELIUS: But which of these three forms of government do you like best, Scipio?

SCIPIO: You may well ask which of them I like best, for I do not approve of any of them when it is by itself and unmodified: my own preference is for a form of government which is a combina-

1. See above, p. 36, n.

tion of all three. But if I were forced to choose one of them in un-mixed form, I would choose kingship. The word 'king' has a paternal ring – the king looks after his people and cherishes them as though they were his children. Yet here are the oligarchs claiming that they do it more efficiently and that several people judge better than one, and are just as fair and scrupulous. And then listen to the people roaring that they want to obey neither one man nor a group of men – that even wild animals regard freedom as the finest of all things, and that no one who obeys a king or an oligarchy can be free.

In other words, kings appeal to us for their benevolence, oli-garchies for their intelligence, democracies for their freedom; so when you compare them it is very hard to make a choice.

LAELIUS: I quite see that; but if you leave this problem unsolved it will hardly be possible to solve the ones which come next.

SCIPIO: Very well; then let us model ourselves on the Greek poet Aratus,[1] who believed a serious poem ought to be prefaced by the words '*Let us begin with Jupiter.*'

LAELIUS: With Jupiter? What has Aratus' poem got to do with our discussion?

SCIPIO: Only this, that we may very properly begin it with the name of Him whom every educated and uneducated person agrees to be the king of all gods and all men.

LAELIUS: Why?

SCIPIO: Why do you think – except for the obvious reason? Very possibly the belief that there is one king in heaven, who moves all Olympus with his nod (as Homer puts it) and is held to be king and father of all, was instituted by the rulers of States for reasons of prac-tical policy. Certainly, there is abundant, or indeed one may say unanimous, authority for this assertion: that the nations of the world have agreed – in other words, their rulers have decided – that there is nothing better than a king, since the gods, too, are be-lieved to have a single king at their head.

Alternatively, we may have been told that these beliefs just come from the mistaken ideas of ignorant people and are to be classed as mere fables: in which case let us listen to the men who rank as the

1. Aratus of Soli in Cilicia, 3rd century B.C.; Stoic poet who was translated by Cicero.

teachers of the educated community – men who have virtually seen
with their own eyes things that we dimly apprehend by hearsay.

LAELIUS: What men do you mean?

SCIPIO: Philosophers; whose investigations of nature have brought
them to the conclusion that the whole universe is controlled by a
single Mind.

MICHAEL GRANT (1956)

AGAINST ANTONY

You grieve, Senators, that three armies of the Roman people have
been slaughtered: Antonius slaughtered them. You mourn the noblest
of your citizens: Antonius robbed us of them too. The authority of
this our Order has been overthrown: Antonius overthrew it. In a
word, all we have seen afterwards – and what evil have we not seen? –
if we reason rightly, we shall credit to Antonius alone. As Helen was
to the Trojans, so that man has been to this State: the cause of war,
the cause of ruin and destruction! The sequel to his tribuneship was
like the beginning. He effected everything that the Senate, while
there was still a constitution, had rendered impossible.

But that, amongst the many exploits of Marcus Antonius, my speech
may not accidentally pass over one act of his – the very fairest of all –
let us come to the Festival of the Lupercalia.[1]

He does not disguise his feelings, Senators; it is clear he is moved, he
sweats, he grows pale! Let him do what he pleases, except being sick,
as he was in the Portico of Minucius. What defence can there be for
such disgraceful conduct? I long to hear.

Your colleague Caesar was seated on the platform, wearing a
purple gown, on a golden chair, with a wreath. You mount up, you
approach the chair – if you were a Lupercus, yet you should have remembered you were consul too – you display a diadem. There is a
groan all over the Forum. Whence came the diadem? For you had not
picked up something cast away, but had brought it from your house,
a crime rehearsed and fully planned. You persisted in putting it on his

---

1. 15 February, 44 B.C. The youths who performed the ritual were known as
Luperci.

head amid the lamentations of the people; he amid their applause persisted in rejecting it. You then, traitor! were discovered to be the one man, who, while establishing a tyranny and willing to have your colleague as your master, were at the same time making trial of what the Roman people could bear and endure.

Nay, you even courted compassion; you threw yourself as a suppliant at his feet. Asking for what? Slavery? You should have asked for it for yourself alone! From us and from the Roman people at least you had not that as a mandate. Oh, how splendid was that eloquence of yours when you harangued naked! What is more disgraceful, more foul than this, what more meriting any punishment? Are you waiting for us to spit you with an ox-goad, like a slave? These words of mine, if you have any particle of feeling, these already tear you, cut you to the heart. I fear I may be lessening the glory of illustrious men; yet I will speak, moved as I am by indignation. What is more shameful than that he should be living who set on the diadem, while all men confess that he was rightly slain who flung it away? But he even ordered this entry under the Lupercalia in the public records: 'To Gaius Caesar, perpetual dictator, Marcus Antonius the consul, by command of the people, offered the kingship: Caesar was unwilling.'

By now I cease wholly to wonder that peace discomposes you; that you hate, not only the city, but even the light; that you live with the most abandoned brigands, not only on what the day brings, but also only for the day. For where in peace will you plant your foot? What place can there be for you, while the laws and the courts survive which, so far as you could, you overthrew by the tyranny of a king? Was it for this Lucius Tarquinius was banished, Spurius Cassius, Spurius Maelius, Marcus Manlius were put to death, that, many generations after, by an act of desecration, there should be set up by Marcus Antonius a king at Rome?

But let us disregard what is past and gone; the doings of this one day, this very present day, I repeat, this point of time in which I am speaking – defend them if you can. Why, Antony, is the Senate hedged in by a cordon of armed men? Why are your henchmen listening to me sword in hand? Why do the doors of Concord not lie open? Why do you bring Ituraeans, of all tribes the most barbarous, down into the Forum with their arrows? It is for his own protection, he says, he does this! Are not, then, a thousand deaths better than not to be able to live in one's own community without a guard of armed men? But that 'protection', believe me, is none; it is by the affection and good will of your fellow-citizens you should be hedged, not by arms. The Roman people will wrest those arms from you, and wrench them out of your grip – may it be while we are still safe! – but in whatever way you deal with us, while you pursue your present policy you cannot, believe me, live long. For that consort of yours who married you after two others – of all wives the least illiberal, whom I portray without irreverence – has been too long a debtor to the Roman people for her third instalment.[1]

The Roman people still has men to whom to commit the helm of State: wherever they are, there is the State's every defence – or rather the State itself, which so far has only avenged itself, and not restored its strength. It has, I say, assuredly young men of the highest birth ready to be its defenders: let them stay apart, regardful of their ease as they choose, yet they will be recalled by the State. And the name of peace is sweet, and the thing itself wholesome; but between peace and servitude the difference is great. Peace is tranquil liberty, servitude the worst of all evils, one to be repelled not only by war but even by death.

But if those our liberators have withdrawn themselves out of our sight, yet they have left the example of what they did. They did what no man had done. Brutus waged war against Tarquin who was a king when to be a king was lawful at Rome; Spurius Cassius, Spurius Maelius, Marcus Manlius, because of the suspicion that they aimed at kingly power, were put to death; the men of today were the first to attack with swords one not aiming at kingly power, but who was already a king. That deed is not only in itself illustrious and godlike, but also set before us for our imitation, all the more because they achieved such a glory as seems scarce to be bounded by heaven itself. For although in the very consciousness of a splendid deed there was sufficient reward, yet by a mortal immortality should not, I think, be despised.

Recall therefore, Marcus Antonius, that day on which you abolished the dictatorship; set before your eyes the joy of the Senate and of the Roman people; compare it with this monstrous marketing con-

1. i.e. the death of her third husband, Antony.

ducted by you and your friends: then will you understand how great the difference between gain and glory. But assuredly, even as some, through a kind of disease and numbness of perception, do not perceive the flavour of food, so the lustful, the avaricious, the criminal, have no estimation of genuine glory. But if glory cannot allure you to right doing, cannot even fear call you away from the foulest deeds? The law-courts you do not fear. If because of your innocence, I praise you; but if because of your violence, do you not understand what he must be afraid of who in such fashion is not afraid of the law-courts? Yet, if you have no fear of brave men and honest citizens because they are kept from your body by an armed guard, your own followers, believe me, will not endure you any longer. And what a life is it, day and night to dread your own followers? Unless indeed you have men bound to you by greater favours than Caesar had bound some of those by whom he was slain, or yourself are in any respect to be compared with him. In him there was genius, calculation, memory, letters, industry, thought, diligence; he had done in war things, however calamitous to the State, yet at least great; having for many years aimed at a throne, he had by great labour, great dangers, achieved his object; by shows, buildings, largesses, banquets he had conciliated the ignorant crowd; his own followers he had bound to him by rewards, his adversaries by a show of clemency: in brief, he had already brought to a free community – partly by fear, partly by endurance – a habit of servitude.

With him I can compare you in lust of domination, but in other things you are in no wise comparable. But out of very many evils which he had inflicted on the Commonwealth, there has emerged this much good: the Roman people has now learned how much to trust each man, on whom to rely, of whom to beware. Think you not of these things? and do you not understand that it is enough for brave men to have learned how beautiful in act, how grateful in benefit, how glorious in report, it is to slay a tyrant? Or will men, when they did not endure him, endure you? In rivalry hereafter, believe me, they will hurry to do this work, and no slow-coming opportunity will be waited for.

Recover your senses, at length, I beseech you! Consider those from whom you are sprung, not those with whom you live! Treat me as you will; be reconciled to the State! But you must look to your own

49

conduct. For myself, I will make my own profession. I defended the State in youth, I will not desert it in old age; I despised the swordsmen of Catiline, I will not dread yours. Aye, and even my body will I gladly offer if the liberty of the State can be realized by my death, so that the anguish of the Roman people may some time bring to birth that with which it has so long travailed. For if nearly twenty years ago, in this very temple, I said that death could not come untimely to a man who had been consul, with how much greater truth shall I say it in old age! By me indeed, Senators, death is even to be wished for, now that the honours I have won and the deeds I have performed are past. These two things only I pray for: one, that in my death I may leave the Roman people free – than this no greater gift can be given me by the immortal Gods – the other, that each man's fortune may be according to his deserts toward the State.

W. C. A. KER (1926)[1]

LETTERS

To his friend Atticus in north-western Greece, from Rome (60 B.C.)

I must say, there is nothing I miss so much at the moment as a man with whom I can share all my worries, who is fond of me and sensible, to whom I can speak without any pretence or reserve or concealment. My brother, so straightforward and affectionate, is away. Metellus suggests not a human being but

> Sands and shores and desert wildernesses.

And as for you, who have so often relieved my anxiety and depression by your talk and advice, who are my constant ally in public affairs, my confidant in private, my partner in every conversation and project, where on earth are you? I am so utterly forlorn that the only peaceful hours I have are those spent with my wife, my little daughter and my darling boy. For my spectacular friendships with the great,

---

1. I have not altered the style but made slight alterations in order to explain technicalities. With respect for the translator's ability, I confess it seems to me almost impossible, today, to reproduce the fiery, persuasive force of Cicero's oratory.

though they are not without glamour in the big world, give me no enjoyment in private. Thus when my house is well filled with callers in the morning, and I go down to the Forum surrounded with troops of friends, I cannot find in all that crowd a single soul with whom I can exchange either an unguarded joke or an intimate grumble. So it is you I'm waiting for, you I'm longing for; in fact you must come. I have many worries and anxieties which I feel could be dissipated in a single walk and talk, if only I could have your ear.

All the pinpricks and sores of my private troubles I will leave undisclosed, and will not commit them to a letter carried by an unknown messenger. True, they are not over-serious – I should not like you to get alarmed; but they are always there, and give me no peace, and I have no sympathetic friend to relieve them with talk and advice. As for the body politic, there is still life in it, but again and again the very remedies applied open fresh wounds. If I were to give you a summary of what has happened since you left, you would exclaim that it is impossible for the State of Rome to stand a day longer. After you left, the first thing that came on the scene was the Clodian drama.[1] There I thought I saw a chance of using the surgeon's knife on immorality and curbing youthful excesses; I blew hot and strong and used all the resources of my mind and powers, not out of hatred for anyone, but in the hope of purging and even curing the body politic. But a great blow has been dealt the State through the corruption and debauching of the jury. Now observe the sequel. We have had a consul thrust upon us whom nobody less philosophic than ourselves can look at without groaning. Was this a serious blow? Yes. Though the Senate passed a motion about bribery and about juries, nothing has been made law; the Senate has been frightened out of it, and the Knights estranged. So a single year has overturned the two bulwarks of the State whose establishment was my particular service: it has thrown away the prestige of the Senate and broken up the harmony of the two Orders. ...

Meanwhile there is not a ghost of a statesman in sight. The man

1. Publius Clodius, a young patrician whom Cicero hated, broke into the rites of the Bona Dea, which were forbidden to men. It was rumoured that his interest was in Caesar's third wife Pompeia; Caesar must have raised a laugh by commenting that 'his family must be above suspicion'. He divorced her, but Clodius was acquitted.

who could be one, my friend Pompey (for such he is, I would have you know), sits silently contemplating the triumphal cloak awarded him. Crassus never utters a word that could make him unpopular. The rest you know well enough: such fools, that they seem to think they can let the country go to rack and ruin and still keep their precious fish-ponds safe. There is one who could help, more I think by his firmness and integrity than by his judgement and ability – Cato: and he has now for nearly three months been worrying the wretched tax-collectors,[1] with whom he used to be so popular, and won't let the Senate give them an answer.

L. P. WILKINSON (1949)

To the historian Lucius Lucceius, from Anzio (56 B.C.)

I have something to say to you which I have often tried to say face to face, only to be deterred by a kind of countrified shyness. Now we are not together I can broach the matter more boldly, since a letter does not blush. I am consumed with an extraordinary and not, I think, discreditable desire that my name should be made illustrious and renowned by a work from your pen. And though you have often assured me that such is your intention, still I trust you will forgive my impatience. The quality of your work always led me to conceive the highest expectations, but it has now surpassed them. I am so impressed, and indeed fired by it, that I wanted my doings to have the benefit of being recorded by you without a moment's delay. For I am inspired not only by the hope of achieving such immortality as posthumous fame can give, but also by a desire to relish in my lifetime the authority of your historical judgement, the token of your esteem, and the charm of your genius.

In asking this I am not unaware of the heavy burden of the works you have undertaken and already begun; but seeing that you had now almost completed your History of the Italian and Civil Wars, and had told me that you were already embarking on the subsequent period, I thought it only fair to myself to suggest that you should consider

1. These were 'Knights', whose interests were always dear to Cicero. Their petition for a rebate on an unprofitable contract (for tax-collection in Asia) was rejected on Cato's initiative.

whether you preferred to weave my exploits into the general texture or (as many Greeks have done, e.g. Callisthenes in his Phocian War, Timaeus in his War of Pyrrhus, Polybius in his Numantine War, all of whom detached the wars I have mentioned from their continuous narrative) to separate the Catilinarian Conspiracy [1] from the wars against foreign enemies. As far as my own credit goes, I do not see that it makes much difference, but it does somewhat concern my impatience that you should not wait till you get to the place, but should immediately tackle that episode and period as a whole. At the same time, if your mind is concentrated on one subject and one personality, I can imagine already how much richer and more artistic the whole thing will be.

I am well aware, of course, how presumptuous I am in first imposing such a burden on you (which you may well refuse on account of pressure of work) and then asking you besides to celebrate my own exploits. What if they should seem to you not so worthy of celebration? However, once one has overstepped the bounds of modesty one ought to be well and truly shameless. So I will blatantly ask you again and again to celebrate them with even more enthusiasm than you perhaps feel, and in this case to disregard the principles of history; and as for that 'personal bias' about which you wrote so charmingly in one of your prefaces, declaring that you could no more be swayed by it than Xenophon's Hercules by pleasure – if it serves to prejudice you in my favour more strongly than it should, do not therefore despise it, but indulge your affection for me a trifle more even than strict truth would allow.

If I can induce you to undertake this, the subject will, I am convinced, be worthy of your talent and eloquence. I think a fair-sized volume could be made out of events from the beginning of the conspiracy down to my return.[2] In it you will be able to use your expert understanding of political unrest, both in explaining the causes of revolution and in suggesting remedies for its evils, criticizing what you think deserves condemnation and giving a reasoned commenda-

---

1. Cicero had taken the lead in unmasking and destroying this during his consulship in 63 B.C. For Catiline see p. 121.

2. Cicero had recently returned from a term of exile imposed (for his execution of Catiline's associates) by the agency of his enemy Clodius. See pp. 61, n. 1, 117.

tion of what you approve; and if you think fit, as your custom is, to be exceptionally outspoken, you will stigmatize the disloyalty, deceit, and treachery that many have displayed towards me. Moreover my fortunes will supply you with plenty of variety, a copious source of pleasure which, you being the writer, could rivet the reader's attention. For there is nothing better suited to please a reader than the changes and chances of Fortune; and however unwelcome these were for me to experience, they will none the less make good reading. For the recollection in tranquillity of troubles past is not without its charm. The rest of the world indeed, which has not experienced any suffering of its own, and can look upon the misfortunes of others without pain, derives a certain pleasure from the emotion of pity itself. Which of us in contemplating the death of Epaminondas at Mantinea is not pleased even as he pities? He did not ask for the javelin to be pulled out of him until he had been assured that his shield was safe, so that in spite of the pain of his wound he died gloriously with his mind at rest. Whose sympathy is not aroused and sustained by the story of the exile and return of Themistocles? The fact is, that a mere chronicle of events does not interest us much, any more than the entries in the official almanac. But the uncertain and varied fortunes of a man who often rises to prominence provoke admiration, suspense, joy, sorrow, hope, and fear; and if they end in a striking *dénouement*, the mind enjoys one of the greatest pleasures that reading can give ...

L. P. WILKINSON (1949)

To Atticus at Rome, from the Appian Way (51 B.C.)

... I come to the marginal postscript to your letter in which you gave me a hint with regard to your sister, my sister-in-law. This is how things stand. When I got home to Arpino and my brother Quintus joined me, we talked first of all about you, and at some length. From that I got on to the conversation you and I had about your sister at my place at Tusculum. I have never seen anyone so sweet or so conciliatory as my brother was on this occasion to your sister; if there was any ill-feeling on the score of expense, it was not apparent. So much for that day.

Next day we left Arpino. In view of the date, Quintus stayed at his place at Arce; I was due at Aquino, but we dined at Arce. You know the farm. When we arrived Quintus said very nicely to his wife, 'Pomponia, you ask the women, and meanwhile I'll invite the men.' To my mind nothing could have been pleasanter – not only his words, but his intention and expression. Yet she said in our hearing, 'I, the mistress, seem to be only a stranger here.' I think the real trouble was that Statius had been sent ahead to get dinner for us. Quintus turned to me and said, 'You see what I have to put up with, day in, day out!' 'Is that all?' you may ask. It was a great deal; and I was quite roused myself. Her words and expression were so rude and uncalled-for. I concealed my distress. We all took our places for dinner except her; even so, Quintus sent her out something, but she refused it. In short, I never saw anything so polite as my brother or so rude as your sister; and I've left out a lot of things that upset me more at the time than they did Quintus himself.

Then I went on to Aquino. Quintus stayed at Arce and joined me next day at Aquino, where he told me that she had refused to sleep with him, and on parting had behaved as I had seen her do. Well? You can tell her this from me: in my opinion she was not at all nice that day.

I have gone on longer perhaps than was necessary to show you that in the matter of giving good advice you too have a part to play . . .

L. P. WILKINSON (1949)

To Atticus at Rome, from Pozzuoli (45 B.C.)

What a blessing to speed so formidable a guest with no unpleasant memories! Caesar proved most affable. When he had arrived at Philippus' house on the evening of 18 December, it was so crowded with soldiers that there was scarcely a room left for himself to dine in; two thousand men there were. I was getting worried about what would happen next day, when Cassius Barba came to the rescue. He lent me a guard. The men camped in the open, and my house was put out of bounds. Caesar stayed at Philippus' until about noon on the 19th, and let no one in; doing accounts with Balbus, I think; then he went for a walk on the shore. After one o'clock he repaired to my bath. Then he heard about Mamurra; [1] it had no visible effect. He made a careful toilet and came to table. He was taking a course of emetics, so he ate and drank fearlessly and with relish, expensively of course and elaborately, and not only that, but

> With food well cooked and seasoned,
> With good talk too, and in a word, with pleasure.

Besides this, his *entourage* were entertained in three rooms on a generous scale. His humbler freedmen and slaves lacked for nothing: the superior ones I entertained in style.

Need I say more? We behaved like human beings together. However, he wasn't a guest to whom you would say, 'Do please come again on your way back.' Once is enough. Our talk kept off serious topics and was largely about literature. In short, he was delighted and enjoyed himself. He said he would be spending a day at Pozzuoli, and another at Baiae.

There you have the story of a visit, or should I say, billeting, which was distasteful to me, as I said, but did not prove embarrassing. I shall stay here for a while, then go to Tusculum.

P.S. When he was passing Dolabella's house, he mounted and paraded the whole of his armed guard to right and left, a thing he did nowhere else. I had this from Nicias.

L. P. WILKINSON (1949)

CICERO'S CORRESPONDENTS

From Servius Sulpicius Rufus – a great lawyer and now governor of Greece – at Athens, to Cicero in Italy (45 B.C.)

When I was told of the death of your daughter Tullia, I was of course as grieved and upset as I was bound to be; I felt that it was my tragedy too, and if I had been there, I should have been at your side, and should have expressed my sympathy to you in person. All condolence is a wretched and painful business, because those who should give it,

1. A senior officer of Caesar's, attacked as a vulgarian by Catullus. We do not know what this news was; perhaps Mamurra was dead. Balbus was Caesar's powerful Spanish chief secretary.

relations and friends, are themselves equally distressed, and can hardly make the attempt for grief, so that they themselves seem to need a comforter instead of being able to serve as comforter to others. For all that, I have decided to write to you briefly a few thoughts for this occasion which have occurred to me, not that I think they will be new to you, but in case your sorrow may have clouded your vision for the moment.

Why should your own private trouble affect you so much? Think how unkindly fate has already treated us, robbing us of things that should be as dear to men as their children – country, reputation, position, our whole career. Could the addition of this one drop add anything to our cup of woe? What mind schooled in such adversity should not be steeled by now to take everything less hardly?

Or can it be for her sake that you are mourning? How often must the idea have occurred to you, as it has to me, that in these times people have not fared badly who have been allowed painlessly to exchange life for death! For what great incentive to living could she have in such an age, what possession or prospect or solace? To have a married life with some distinguished young man? You were welcome no doubt, in virtue of your position, to choose any son-in-law you liked from the youth of today, if you could find one to whom you would confidently entrust any child of yours! So that she might have children, and the joy of seeing their success? Children who would be able to maintain the inheritance their father left them, and to stand in due course for each office, with freedom of action in public life and in promoting the interests of their friends? There is not one of these promises that has not been snatched away before it was fulfilled. To lose one's child, you will say, is a calamity. I agree; but to have to endure all this may well be worse.

There is one thought I should like to put to you which has been a great consolation to me, in case it may also be able to bring you some comfort. On my return journey from Asia Minor, as I was sailing from Aegina towards Megara, I began to look at the lands round about. Behind me was Aegina, before me Megara, to the right the Piraeus, to the left Corinth. There was a time when these were most flourishing cities: now they lie there in dust and ruins. I began to think to myself, 'Why, fancy us insignificant humans taking it hard when one of us dies or is killed, whose life must in any case be short, seeing that in one place "the relics of so many cities lie exposed". Please control yourself, Servius, and remember you were born a mortal.' I assure you, I felt considerably better for that thought. Do try, if you will, to fix your attention on the same idea. Lately, at one fell swoop, many outstanding men perished, the Roman people suffered a crippling loss, and all our overseas possessions were shaken: are you to be so distressed for the loss of the little life of one poor woman? If she had not died now, she would have had to die a few years later, since she was born mortal.

Then take your mind off these things, and turn to thoughts worthy of your position: that she lived while life had anything to give her; that she lived as long as we were still a free people; that she saw her father hold office as praetor, consul, and augur; that she was married to young men of the foremost rank; that she experienced almost every happiness; and that when the Republic fell, she departed this life. What possible quarrel could you or she have with fortune on that score?

Finally, do not forget that you are Cicero, the man who used to give others advice and counsel, and do not be like those bad doctors who, when others are ill, profess to be skilled practitioners, but who cannot cure themselves. Take to heart the advice you always give to others and keep a firm hold on it. There is no sorrow that the passage of time does not diminish and soften. It is unworthy of you to wait for this to happen, and not use your wisdom to anticipate it. If there is any consciousness even after death, you may be sure that she, with her love for you and her devotion to all her family, does not want you to do as you are doing. Think of your lost one; think of your other friends and acquaintances, who are saddened by your sorrow; think of your country, and give it the benefit of your help and counsel wherever it is needed.

And one word more. Since our fortunes have sunk so low that we must stoop even to such considerations as this – do not give anyone the chance to think that you are mourning not so much for your daughter as for the condition of the State and the victory of our opponents. I do not like to say anything more to you on this subject, for fear of seeming to lack confidence in your discretion; so I will end with just this one suggestion. We have often seen you bearing prosperity most finely, and winning great praise for it: let us see this time that you can bear adversity no less well, and that your burden weighs upon you no more heavily than it should, lest people think that of all the virtues there is one that you lack. As for my own affairs, when I hear you are in a calmer frame of mind, I will let you know what is happening here, and all about the state of my province.

L. P. WILKINSON (1949)

From Caesar's Friend Gaius Matius at Rome to Cicero in Italy, after Caesar's Murder (44 B.C.)

I am well aware of the abuse people have heaped upon me since the death of Caesar. They put it down to my discredit that I am sorely grieved at the death of a very intimate friend, and resent the fall of one I loved; for they declare that patriotism must come before friend-ship – speaking as though they have already demonstrated that his death has been of benefit to the State.

But I shall use no ingenious arguments; I frankly confess I have not reached their high level of philosophy. For I was not a follower of Caesar in our civil dissensions, though at the same time I did not abandon a friend, however much I was offended by his action; nor did I ever give my approval to the Civil War, or even to the cause of the quarrel – which I was most anxious to see stifled at its very birth. It follows that in the triumph of my personal friend I was not fascin-ated by the attractions either of promotion or of pecuniary profit – prizes of which the others, though they had less influence with him than I had, availed themselves with unrestrained avidity. I may also add that my own private estate was diminished by that very law of Caesar which enabled the majority of those who now exult over Caesar's death to remain in the State. I strove that mercy should be shown to our defeated fellow-citizens as earnestly as I strove for my own life.

Is it possible then that I, who desired the security of all, should feel no resentment at the fall of the man who achieved that blessing – especially when the very same men were as responsible for his un-popularity as they were for his death? 'You will smart for it,' they say, 'since you dare to condemn what we have done.' What unheard-of insolence, that some men may boast of a crime, which others may not even deplore without being punished for it! Why, even slaves have always had this much freedom, that their fears, their joys, and their sorrows were subject to their own control, and not that of another; and now even those privileges they are trying to wrest from us by intimidation! At any rate, that is what your 'champions of liberty' are perpetually saying.

But they are beating the air, and for this reason – I shall never be so afraid of any danger that I shall desert the cause of duty or humanity; for I have never thought that an honourable death should be shirked, often that it should be even welcomed. But why this indignation against me, if my only wish is that they should regret what they have done? My desire is that all the world should feel the bitterness of Caesar's death. You may object that, as a loyal citizen, it is my duty to desire the safety of the constitution! Well, if my past life, as well as my hopes for the future, does not prove without a word of mine that such is my earnest wish, I make no claim to demonstrate it by speech-making.

For that reason I beg of you with special earnestness to attach more weight to facts than to words, and if you feel that true expediency lies in right conduct, to take my word for it that *to hold any communion with the lawless is impossible*. Am I then, in the evening of my life, to effect a radical change in the principles I maintained in the prime of my youth, when even a serious error might have been excused, and with my own hands unweave the texture of my life? That I will not do. However, I will equally not make the mistake of doing anything to cause offence – except by being pained at the grievous fall of one who was very closely bound to me, and a most illustrious man. But even if I were otherwise minded, I should never disavow my own actions, and thereby get the reputation of being not only a rascal in my actions but a coward and hypocrite in concealing the fact.

Adapted from W. GLYNN WILLIAMS (1928)

From Brutus in Macedonia to Atticus at Rome (43 B.C.)

You say in your letter that Cicero is surprised at my never making any comment on his actions. Since you ask me, I feel obliged to tell you what I think.

I know Cicero has done everything with the best intentions: who should have better cause than I to appreciate his devotion to the Republic? But he sometimes acts – can one say *tactlessly* of a man so eminently prudent, or *selfishly* of a man who for the sake of the Republic did not hesitate to incur the enmity of Antony in all his power? I don't know what to say to you but this: the boy Octavian's ambition and high-handedness have been stimulated rather than curbed by Cicero; and he carries this partiality to such a pitch that he does not refrain from abusive remarks which often, indeed, recoil on him with double force; thus he put more than one person to death himself, so he ought to admit himself to be a murderer before calling Casca the names he does. He is treating Casca as Bestia once treated himself.[1] Just because we are not bragging in season and out of the Ides of March in the way he is always talking about his Nones of December (when he executed the Catilinarians), is Cicero in any better position to malign a most glorious deed than Bestia and Clodius were to be for even criticizing the things he did as consul?

Our friend Cicero boasts to me that he, a civilian, withstood the military power of Antony. What good is that to me if the price demanded for crushing Antony is Antony's place for a successor, and if the chastiser of that evil comes forward as the supporter of another likely, unless we prevent it, to have still firmer foundations and deeper roots. Even supposing his policy is dictated by fear of tyranny, or a tyrant, or Antony, I cannot feel grateful to a man who, in order to avoid being slave to a particular ill-tempered master, refrains from deprecating slavery itself; and worse than that, proposes to give a new master a Triumph and pay for his troops, and by decrees of every kind encourages him not to be ashamed to covet the position once held by the man whose name he has adopted. Is this worthy of an ex-consul, or of Cicero? ...

So although Octavius may call Cicero 'father', consult him in everything, praise him and thank him, yet it will become clear that his acts do not tally with his words.[2] For what can be more repugnant to common sense than to treat a man as a father who is not even to be

1. Cicero had been severely criticized, and finally exiled, for executing those of Catiline's fellow-conspirators who came into his power.

2. Brutus was right. Within the year Octavian (the future Augustus), and his fellow-Triumvirs Antony and Lepidus, had Cicero executed.

reckoned among the free? For my part I set no store by those accomplishments at which I know Cicero is a past master: what good has he been done by all those fulsome writings of his about freedom for the fatherland, and about honour, death, exile, and poverty? How much better versed in these things is Philippus, who refused to concede to his stepson what Cicero concedes to him though he is no relation! So let him cease aggravating our troubles by his boasting: for what does it help us that Antony has been beaten, if the only result is that another steps into his shoes? However, even as it is, there is a note of uncertainty in your letter.

Long live Cicero indeed (and well he may!), to cringe and serve, if he is not ashamed to think of his age and rank and past achievements! I at any rate will be deterred by no conditions of slavery, however favourable, from fighting against the principle, that is, against tyranny and unconstitutional powers and despotism and authority that sets itself up above the laws. Even though Antony may be a good man, as you say, though I have never thought so, yet our ancestors willed that no one, not even a father, should have absolute mastery.

If I were not as devoted to you as Cicero thinks Octavius is to him, I should not have written this to you. It hurts me to think of you getting angry as you read it, you who are so fond of all your friends, and especially of Cicero. But believe me when I say that my personal feelings for Cicero are in no way diminished, though my opinion of him is very much so, since you cannot expect a man to form an opinion save according to his lights.

I wish you had told me what proposals of marriage your dear daughter has had. I could have given you some idea of what I thought. I am not surprised you are anxious about Portia's health. Finally, I will gladly do what you asked, for my sisters ask the same, and I know the man and his requirements.

L. P. WILKINSON (1949)

LUCRETIUS

Titus Lucretius Carus was born in the nineties and died in the fifties B.C. It has been variously suggested that he was a nobleman, an ex-slave, a free but poor Roman, and a small land-owner near Naples. In fact, we know scarcely anything of this man who startlingly converted the mild, pedestrian Greek philosophical prose in which Epicurus had sought to prove his materialist theory of the Universe [1] into the exalted poetry of the *De Rerum Natura* (*On the Nature of the Universe*) – the supreme justification of Wordsworth's belief that 'poetry is the impassioned expression which is in the countenance of all science'.

Apart from its extensive influence on Virgil, this poem made little mark in ancient times; and it was far from fashionable among medieval churchmen. But its essential hopefulness was an inspiration to the humanists. The Florentine Poggio Bracciolini wrote to a friend in 1418 of a manuscript discovered in a 'distant and unfrequented place', and it was printed in 1473 at Brescia. Botticelli's Venus, in his *Primavera*, was suggested to him by Politian, who had in mind Lucretius' Invocation to Venus. The Renaissance rejected Lucretius' philosophy but revered his poetry. Montaigne quotes him 149 times – once more, even, than Horace, and most of all ancient poets. Hobbes broke down some of the prejudice against Lucretius, Pierre Gassendi (d. 1655) tried to reconcile moderate Epicureanism with Christian doctrine, and the Stuart poets enlarged on his theme 'all men are equal in the grave'. Milton, like Lucretius, was a poet with a passionate mission – though their missions were utterly different. Eighteenth-century French rationalists discovered greatness in Lucretius' ethics; Voltaire saw in him a champion of freedom, quoted him frequently and borrowed his biting scorn. But to Byron:

> Lucretius' irreligion is too strong
> For early stomachs to prove wholesome food.

Leopardi was a Lucretius without Lucretius' hope. Shelley partly owed his unbelief to Lucretius; Swinburne placed both of them in an atheist's heaven. Yet Gladstone quoted Lucretius impressively in the House of Commons (and was apparently understood). 'Few minds perhaps', thought Matthew Arnold, 'that were not stiffly cased in foregone

1. Inherited, in large part, from the Atomists Leucippus and Democritus.

conclusions have ever met the storm of his passionate eloquence without bending before the blast.' And he 'carried away and overwhelmed by his poignant force' a group of readers including Lord Tennyson, whose haunted poem *Lucretius* (accepting a tradition that he was mad) dwelt on his Epicurean belief in gods infinitely detached, and, like death itself, deserving no fear:

> The gods, who haunt
> The lucid interspace of world and world,
> Where never creeps a cloud, or moves a wind,
> Nor ever falls the least white star of snow,
> Nor ever lowest roll of thunder moans,
> Nor sound of human sorrow mounts to mar
> Their sacred everlasting calm ...

The didactic poem was an inheritance from Greek philosophers, of whom Empedocles was one of the greatest; Lucretius gave it new life. The twentieth century A.D. is not an age which loves didactic poetry, but modern philosophers and politicians, like Rousseau before them, have greatly admired Lucretius' Epicurean account of the beginnings of ancient civilization.[1]

1. Marxists have seen in this account a foreshadowing of their own beliefs.

What has this bugbear death to frighten man,
If souls can die, as well as bodies can?
For, as before our birth we felt no pain,
When Punic arms infested land and main,[1]
When heaven and earth were in confusion hurled
For the debated empire of the world,
Which awed with dreadful expectation lay,
Sure to be slaves, uncertain who should sway:
So, when our mortal frame shall be disjoined,
The lifeless lump uncoupled from the mind,
From sense of grief and pain we shall be free;
We shall not *feel*, because we shall not *be*.
Though earth in seas, and seas in heaven were lost,
We should not move, we only should be tossed.
Nay, e'en suppose, when we have suffered fate,
The soul could feel in her divided state,
What's that to us? for we are only *we*
While souls and bodies in one frame agree.
Nay, though our atoms should revolve by chance,
And matter leap into the former dance;
Though time our life and motion could restore,
And make our bodies what they were before,
What gain to us would all this bustle bring?
The new-made man would be another thing:
When once an interrupting pause is made,
That individual being is decayed.
We, who are dead and gone, shall bear no part
In all the pleasures, nor shall feel the smart,
Which to that other mortal shall accrue,
Whom of our matter time shall mould anew.

For backward if you look on that long space
Of ages past, and view the changing face

1. During the Carthaginian Wars.

Of matter, tossed and variously combined
In sundry shapes, 'tis easy for the mind
From thence to infer that seeds of things have been
In the same order as they now are seen:
Which yet our dark remembrance cannot trace,
Because a pause of life, a gaping space,
Has come betwixt, where memory lies dead,
And all the wandering motions from the sense are fled.
For whosoe'er shall in misfortunes live,
Must *be*, when those misfortunes shall arrive;
And since the man who *is* not feels not woe
(For death exempts him, and wards off the blow,
Which we, the living, only feel and bear)
What is there left for us in death to fear?
When once that pause of life has come between,
'Tis just the same as we had never been.
And therefore if a man bemoan his lot,
That after death his mouldering limbs shall rot,
Or flames, or jaws of beasts devour his mass,
Know, he's an unsincere, unthinking ass.
A secret sting remains within his mind;
The fool is to his own cast-offals kind.
He boasts no sense can after death remain,
Yet makes himself a part of life again;
As if some other *He* could feel the pain.
If, while we live, this thought molest his head,
What wolf or vulture shall devour me dead?
He wastes his days in idle grief, nor can
Distinguish 'twixt the body and the man:
But thinks himself can still himself survive;
And, what when dead he feels not, feels alive.
Then he repines that he was born to die,
Nor knows in death there is no other He,
No living *He* remains his grief to vent,
And o'er his senseless carcase to lament.

If after death 'tis painful to be torn
By birds, and beasts, then why not so to burn,

Or drenched in floods of honey to be soaked,
Embalmed to be at once preserved and choked?
Or on an airy mountain's top to lie,
Exposed to cold and heaven's inclemency?
Or crowded in a tomb to be oppressed
With monumental marble on thy breast?
But to be snatched from all the household joys,
From thy chaste wife, and thy dear prattling boys,
Whose little arms about thy legs are cast,
And climbing for a kiss prevent their mother's haste,
Inspiring secret pleasure through thy breast –
Ah! these shall be no more: thy friends oppressed
Thy care and courage now no more shall free;
Ah! wretch, thou criest, ah! miserable me!
One woeful day sweeps children, friends, and wife,
And all the brittle blessings of my life!
Add one thing more, and all thou sayest is true;
Thy want and wish of them is vanished too:
Which, well considered, were a quick relief
To all thy vain imaginary grief.
For thou shalt sleep, and never wake again,
And, quitting life, shalt quit thy living pain.

But we, thy friends, shall all those sorrows find,
Which in forgetful death thou leavest behind;
No time shall dry our tears, nor drive thee from our mind.
The worst that can befall thee, measured right,
Is a sound slumber, and a long good night.
Yet thus the fools, that would be thought the wits,
Disturb their mirth with melancholy fits:
When healths go round, and kindly brimmers flow,
Till the fresh garlands on their foreheads glow,
They whine, and cry, 'Let us make haste to live,
Short are the joys that human life can give!'
Eternal preachers, that corrupt the draught,
And pall the god, that never thinks, with thought;
Idiots with all that thought, to whom the worst
Of death is want of drink, and endless thirst,

Or any fond desire as vain as these.
For even in sleep the body, wrapt in ease,
Supinely lies, as in the peaceful grave;
And, wanting nothing, nothing can it crave.
Were that sound sleep eternal, it were death;
Yet the first atoms then, the seeds of breath,
Are moving near to sense; we do but shake
And rouse that sense, and straight we are awake.
Then death to us, and death's anxiety,
Is less than nothing, if a less could be.
For then our atoms, which in order lay,
Are scattered from their heap, and puffed away,
And never can return into their place,
When once the pause of life has left an empty space.

And last, suppose great Nature's voice should call
To thee, or me, or any of us all,
'What dost thou mean, ungrateful wretch, thou vain,
Thou mortal thing, thus idly to complain,
And sigh and sob, that thou shalt be no more?
For if thy life were pleasant heretofore,
If all the bounteous blessings I could give
Thou hast enjoyed, if thou hast known to live,
And pleasure not leaked through thee like a sieve;
Why dost thou not give thanks, as at a plenteous feast,
Crammed to the throat with life, and rise and take thy rest?
But if my blessings thou hast thrown away,
If indigested joys passed through, and would not stay,
Why dost thou wish for more to squander still?
If life be grown a load, a real ill,
And I would all thy cares and labours end,
Lay down thy burden, fool, and know thy friend!'

JOHN DRYDEN (1685)

IN PRAISE OF EPICURUS

When human life lay grovelling on the ground,
A piteous sight, by superstition crushed –
Who lifting high her head from heaven, looked down
With louring look – then first a man of Greece
Dared lift his eyes, and dared to face the foe;
Him not the fables of the gods above,
Nor lightning's flash, nor heaven with threats could stay;
But all the more he set his eager soul
To burst through Nature's portals closely barred,
And his keen soul prevailed, and far beyond
The flaming ramparts of the world did pierce,
With mind and soul surveyed the vast expanse,
Whence crowned with victory he can teach to us
What may or may not be, what power to each
Is given, and its bounds so deeply set:
So superstition dying in its turn,
And trampled underneath the foot of men,
No more alarms; and we are heaven's peers.

SIR ROBERT ALLISON (1919)

EPICURUS AND THE GODS

Thou, who from out such darkness first couldest lift
A torch so bright, illumining thereby
The benefits of life, thee do I follow,
O thou bright glory of the Grecian race,
And in thy deep-set footprints firmly now
I plant my steps, not so much through desire
To rival thee, rather because I love
And therefore long to imitate thee: for how
Should a mere swallow strive with swans? or what
Might kids with staggering limbs, matched in a race,
Achieve against the stalwart strength of a horse?

Thou, father, art the discoverer of truth;
Thou dost enrich us with a father's precepts;
And from thy pages, glorious sage, as bees
In flowery glades sip from all plants, so we
Feed likewise upon all thy golden words,
Golden words, ever worthy of endless life.

For soon as, issuing from thy godlike intellect,
Thy doctrine has begun to voice abroad
The nature of things, straightway the mind's terrors
Take flight; the world's walls open; I behold
Things happening throughout the whole of space.
Revealed is the divinity of the gods,
And their serene abodes, which neither winds
Buffet, nor clouds drench them with showers, nor snow
Congealed by sharp frost, falling in white flakes,
Violates, but an ever-cloudless sky
Invests them, smiling with wide-spreading light.
Moreover all their wants Nature provides,
And there is nothing that at any time
Can minish their tranquillity of soul.

R. C. TREVELYAN (1937)

THE BEGINNINGS OF CIVILIZATION

The *human beings* that peopled these fields were far tougher than the
men of today, as became the offspring of tough earth. They were built
on a framework of bigger and solider bones, fastened through their
flesh to stout sinews. They were relatively insensitive to heat and cold,
to unaccustomed diet and bodily ailments in general. Through many
decades of the sun's cyclic course they lived out their lives in the
fashion of wild beasts roaming at large. No one spent his strength in
guiding the curved plough. No one knew how to cleave the earth
with iron, or to plant young saplings in the soil or lop the old
branches from tall trees with pruning hooks. Their hearts were well
content to accept as a free gift what the sun and showers had given
and the earth had produced unsolicited. Often they stayed their hun-

ger among the acorn-laden oaks. Arbutus berries, whose scarlet tint now betrays their winter ripening, were then produced by the earth in plenty and of a larger size. In addition the lusty childhood of the earth yielded a great variety of tough foods, ample for afflicted mortals. Rivers and springs called to them to slake their thirst, as nowadays a clamorous cataract of water, tumbling out of the high hills, summons from far away the thirsty creatures of the wild. They resorted to those woodland sanctuaries of the nymphs, familiar to them in their wandering, from which they knew that trickling streams of water issued to bathe the dripping rocks in a bountiful shower, sprinkled over green moss, and gushed out here and there over the open plain.

They did not know as yet how to enlist the aid of fire, or to make use of skins, or to clothe their bodies with trophies of the chase. They lived in thickets and hillside caves and forests and stowed their rugged limbs among bushes when driven to seek shelter from the lash of wind and rain.

They could have no thought of the common good, no notion of the mutual restraint of morals and laws. The individual, taught only to live and fend for himself, carried off on his own account such prey as fortune brought him. Venus coupled the bodies of lovers in the greenwood. Mutual desire brought them together, or the male's mastering might and overriding lust, or a payment of acorns or arbutus berries or choice pears. Thanks to their surpassing strength of hand and foot, they hunted the woodland beasts by hurling stones and wielding ponderous clubs. They were more than a match for many of them; from a few they took refuge in hiding-places.

When night overtook them, they flung their jungle-bred limbs naked on the earth like bristly boars, and wrapped themselves round with a coverlet of leaves and branches. It is not true that they wandered panic-stricken over the countryside through the darkness of night, searching with loud lamentations for the daylight and the sun. In fact they waited, sunk in quiet sleep, till the sun with his rose-red torch should bring back radiance to the sky. Accustomed as they were from infancy to seeing the alternate birth of darkness and light, they could never have been struck with amazement or misgiving whether the withdrawal of the sunlight might not plunge the earth in everlasting night. They were more worried by the peril to which unlucky

71

sleepers were often exposed from predatory beasts. Turned out of house and home by the intrusion of a slavering boar or a burly lion, they would abandon their rocky roofs at dead of night and yield up their leaf-strewn beds in terror to the savage visitor.

The proportion of mortal men that relinquished the dear light of life before it was all spent was not appreciably higher then than now. Then it more often happened that an individual victim would furnish living food to a beast of prey: engulfed in its jaws, he would fill thicket and mountainside and forest with his shrieks, at the sight of his living flesh entombed in a living sepulchre. Those who saved their mangled bodies by flight would press trembling palms over ghastly sores, calling upon death in heart-rending voices, till life was wrenched from them by racking spasms.

In their ignorance of the treatment that wounds demand, they could not help themselves. But it never happened then that many thousands of men following the standards were led to death on a single day. Never did the ocean levels, lashed into tumult, hurl ships and men together upon the reefs. Here, time after time, the sea would rise and vainly vent its fruitless ineffectual fury, then lightly lay aside its idle threats. The crafty blandishment of the unruffled deep could not tempt any man to his undoing with its rippling laughter. Then, when the mariner's presumptuous art lay still unguessed, it was lack of food that brought failing limbs at last to death. Now it is superfluity that proves too much for them. The men of old, in their ignorance, often served poison to themselves. Now, with greater skill, they administer it to others.

As time went by, men began to build huts and to use skins and fire. Male and female learnt to live together in stable union and to watch over their joint progeny. Then it was that humanity first began to mellow. Thanks to fire, their chilly bodies could no longer so easily endure the cold under the canopy of heaven. Venus subdued brute strength. Children by their wheedling easily broke down their parents' stubborn temper. Then neighbours began to form *mutual alliances*, wishing neither to do nor to suffer violence among themselves. They appealed on behalf of their children and womenfolk, pointing out with gestures and inarticulate cries that it is right for everyone to pity the weak. It was not possible to achieve perfect unity of purpose. Yet a substantial majority kept faith honestly. Otherwise the entire human race would have been wiped out there and then instead of being propagated, generation after generation, down to the present day.

As for the various sounds of *spoken language*, it was nature that drove men to utter these, and practical convenience that gave a form to the names of objects. We see a similar process at work when babies are led by their speechless plight to employ gestures, such as pointing with a finger at objects in view. For every creature has a sense of the purposes for which he can use his own powers. A bull-calf, before ever his horns have grown and sprouted from his forehead, butts and thrusts with them aggressively when his temper is roused. Panther and lion cubs tussle with paws and jaws when their claws and teeth are scarcely yet in existence. We see every species of winged bird trust in its wings and seek faint-hearted aid from flight. To suppose that someone on some particular occasion allotted names to objects, and that by this means men learnt their first words, is stark madness. Why should we suppose that one man had this power of indicating everything by vocal utterances and emitting the various sounds of speech when others could not do it? Besides, if others had not used such utterances among themselves, from what source was the mental image of its use implanted in him? Whence did this one man derive the power in the first instance of seeing with his mind what he wanted to do? One man could not subdue a greater number and induce them by force to learn his names for things. It is far from easy to convince deaf listeners by any demonstration what needs to be done. They would not endure it or submit for long on any terms to have incomprehensible noises senselessly dinned into their ears.

And what, after all, is so surprising in the notion that the human race, possessed of a vigorous voice and tongue, should indicate objects by various vocal utterances expressive of various feelings? Even dumb cattle and wild beasts utter distinct and various sounds when they are gripped by fear or pain or when joy wells up within them. Indeed we have direct evidence of such distinctions. Molossian hounds, for instance, when first their gaping flabby jowls are drawn back in a grim snarl that bares their hard teeth, give vent to a gruff growl. Very different is the sound when the growl has grown to a loud-mouthed reverberating bay. Different again is the soft crooning with which they fondle their pups when they fall to licking them lovingly with their tongues or toss them with their paws, snapping with open jaws in a playful pretence of gobbling them up with teeth that never close. And different from all these are their howls when left alone in the house, or the whimpering with which they shrink and cringe to avoid the whip. In the same way, when a stallion in the prime of his youth is let loose among the mares, smarting from the prick of winged Cupid's darts, and snorts defiance to his rivals through distended nostrils, his neigh is surely not the same that shakes his limbs on other occasions. So also with the various species of winged birds. The hawks and ospreys and gulls that seek a livelihood among the salt sea-waves all have distinctive cries that show when they are squabbling over their booty or struggling to master a quarry. Some birds even vary their note according to the weather. So the hoarse-throated cawing of long-lived ravens and gregarious rooks varies from time to time according as they are clamouring for showers of rain, as it is said, or summoning wind and storm. If the animals, dumb though they be, are impelled by different feelings to utter different cries, how much the more reason to suppose that men in those days had the power of distinguishing between one thing and another by distinctive utterances!

Here is the answer to another question that you may be putting to yourself. *The agent by which fire was first brought down to earth* and made available to mortal man was lightning. To this source every hearth owes its flames. Think how many things we see ablaze with heaven-sent flame, when a stroke from heaven has endowed them with heat. There is also, however, another possible source. When a branching tree, tossed by the wind, is swaying and surging to and fro and stooping to touch the branches of another tree, the violent friction squeezes out seeds of fire, till sometimes from the rubbing of bough against bough, trunk against trunk, there flashes out a blazing burst of flame. Either of these occurrences may have given fire to mortals. Later it was the sun that taught them to cook food and soften it by heating on the flames, since they noticed in roaming through the fields how many things were subdued and mellowed by the impact of its ardent rays. As time went by, men learnt to change their old way of life by means of fire and other new inventions, instructed by those of outstanding ability and mental energy. *Kings began to found cities* and establish citadels for their own safeguard and refuge. They parcelled out cattle and lands, giving to each according to his looks, his strength and his ability; for good looks were highly prized and strength counted for much. Later came the invention of property and the discovery of gold, which speedily robbed the strong and the handsome of their pre-eminence. The man of greater riches finds no lack of stalwart frames and comely faces to follow in his train. And yet, if a man would guide his life by true philosophy, he will find ample riches in a modest livelihood enjoyed with a tranquil mind. Of that little he need never be beggared. Men craved for fame and power so that their fortune might rest on a firm foundation and they might live out a peaceful life in the enjoyment of plenty. An idle dream. In struggling to gain the pinnacle of power they beset their own road with perils. And then from the very peak, as though by a thunderbolt, they are cast down by envy into a foul abyss of ignominy. For envy, like the thunderbolt, most often strikes the highest and all that stands out above the common level. Far better to lead a quiet life in subjection than to long for sovereign authority and lordship over kingdoms. So leave them to the blood and sweat of their wearisome unprofitable struggle along the narrow pathway of ambition. Since they savour life through another's mouth and choose their target rather by hearsay than by the evidence of their own senses, it avails them now, and will avail them, no more than it has ever done.

So the kings were killed. Down in the dust lay the ancient majesty of thrones, the haughty sceptres. The illustrious emblem of the sovereign head, dabbled in gore and trampled under the feet of the rabble, mourned its high estate. What once was feared too much is now as passionately down-trodden. So the conduct of affairs sank back into the turbid depths of mob-rule, with each man struggling to win dominance and supremacy for himself. Then some men showed how to form a constitution, based on fixed rights and recognized laws. Mankind, worn out by a life of violence and enfeebled by feuds, was the more ready to submit of its own free will to the bondage of laws and institutions. This distaste for a life of violence came naturally to a society in which every individual was ready to gratify his anger by a harsher vengeance than is now tolerated by equitable laws. Ever since then the enjoyment of life's prizes has been tempered by the fear of punishment. A man is enmeshed by his own violence and wrong-doing, which commonly recoil upon their author. It is not easy for one who breaks by his acts the mutual compact of social peace to lead a peaceful and untroubled life. Even if he hides his guilt from gods and men, he must feel a secret misgiving that it will not rest hidden for ever. He cannot forget those oft-told tales of men betraying themselves by words spoken in dreams of delirium that drag out long-buried crimes into the daylight.

Let us now consider why *reverence for the gods is widespread* among the nations. What has crowded their cities with altars and inaugurated those solemn rites that are in vogue today in powerful States and busy resorts? What has implanted in mortal hearts that chill of dread which even now rears new temples of the gods the wide world over and packs them on holy days with pious multitudes? The explanation is not far to seek. Already in those early days men had visions when their minds were awake, and more clearly in sleep, of divine figures, dignified in mien and impressive in stature. To these figures they attributed sentience, because they were seen to move their limbs and give voice to lordly utterances appropriate to their stately features and stalwart frames. They further credited them with eternal life, because the substance of their shapes was perpetually renewed and their appearance unchanging and in general because they thought that beings of such strength could not lightly be subdued by any force. They pictured their lot as far superior to that of mortals, because none of them was tormented by the fear of death, and also because in dreams they saw them perform all sorts of miracles without the slightest effort.

Again, men noticed the orderly succession of celestial phenomena and the round of the seasons and were at a loss to account for them. So they took refuge in handing over everything to the gods and making everything dependent on their whim. They chose the sky to be the home and headquarters of the gods because it is through the sky that the moon is seen to tread its cyclic course with day and night and night's ominous constellations and the night-flying torches and soaring flames of the firmament, clouds and sun and rain, snow and wind, lightning and hail, the sudden thunder-crash and the long-drawn intimidating rumble.

Poor humanity, to saddle the gods with such responsibilities and throw in a vindictive temper! What griefs they hatched then for themselves, what festering sores for us, what tears for our posterity! This is not piety, this oft-repeated show of bowing a veiled head before a graven image; this bustling to every altar; this kow-towing and prostration on the ground with palms outspread before the shrines of the gods; this deluging of altars with the blood of beasts; this heaping of vow on vow. True piety lies rather in the power to contemplate the universe with a quiet mind.

When we gaze up at the supernal regions of this mighty world, at the ether poised above, studded with flashing stars, and there comes into our minds the thought of the sun and moon and their migrations, then in hearts already racked by other woes a new anxiety begins to waken and rear up its head. We fall to wondering whether we may not be subject to some unfathomable divine power, which speeds the shining stars along their various tracks. It comes as a shock to our faltering minds to realize how little they know about the world. Had it a birth and a beginning? Is there some limit in time, beyond which its bastions will be unable to endure the strain of jarring motion? Or are they divinely gifted with everlasting surety, so that in their journey through the termless tract of time they can mock the stubborn strength of illimitable age?

Again, who does not feel his mind quailing and his limbs unnerved with shuddering dread of the gods when the parched earth reels at the dire stroke of the thunderbolt and tumult rolls across the breadth of heaven? Do not multitudes quake and nations tremble? Do not proud monarchs flinch, stricken in every limb by terror of the gods and the thought that the time has come when some foul deed or arrogant word must pay its heavy, heavy, price?

Or picture a storm at sea, the wind scouring the water with hurricane force and some high admiral of the fleet swept before the blast with all his lavish complement of troops and battle elephants. How he importunes the peace of the gods with vows! How fervently he prays in his terror that the winds, too, may be at peace and favouring breezes blow! But, for all his prayers, the tornado does not relax its grip, and all too often he is dashed upon the reefs of death. So irresistibly is human power ground to dust by some unseen force, which seems to mock at the majestic rods and ruthless axes of authority and trample on them for its sport.

Lastly, when the whole earth quakes beneath their feet, when shaken cities fall in ruins or hang hesitantly tottering, what wonder if mortal men despise themselves and find a place in nature for super-human forces and miraculous divine powers with supreme control over the universe?

We come next to *the discovery of copper, gold and iron, weighty silver and serviceable lead*. This occurred when fire among the high hills had consumed huge forests in its blaze. The blaze may have been started by a stroke of lightning, or by men who had employed fire to scare their enemies in some woodland war, or were tempted by the fertility of the country to enlarge their rich ploughlands and turn the wilds into pasturage. Or they may have wished to kill the forest beasts and profit by their spoils; for hunting by means of pitfall and fire developed earlier than fencing round a glade with nets and driving the game with dogs. Let us take it, then, that for one reason or another, no matter what, a fierce conflagration, roaring balefully, has devoured a forest down to the roots and roasted the earth with penetrative fire. Out of the melted veins there would flow into hollows on the earth's surface a convergent stream of silver and gold, copper and lead. After-wards, when men saw these lying solidified on the earth and flashing with resplendent colour, they would be tempted by their attractive lustre and polish to pick them up. They would notice that each lump was moulded into a shape like that of the bed from which it had been lifted. Then it would enter their minds that these substances, when liquefied by heat, could run into any mould or the shape of any object they might desire, and could also be drawn out by hammering into pointed tips of any slenderness and sharpness. Here was a means by which they could equip themselves with weapons, chop down forests, rough-hew timber and plane it into smooth planks and pierce holes in it by boring, punching, or drilling. At the outset they would try to do this with silver and gold no less than with tough and stubborn copper. But this would not work. These metals would give under the strain, lacking strength to stand up to such exacting tasks. So copper was more highly prized, and gold with its quickly blunted edge was despised as useless. Now it is copper that is despised, while gold has succeeded to the highest honours. So the circling years bring round reversals of fortune. What once was prized is afterwards held cheap. In its place, something else emerges from ignominy, is daily more and more coveted and, as its merits are detected, blossoms into glory and is acclaimed by mankind with extravagant praises.

At this point, Memmius,[1] you should find it easy to puzzle out for yourself how men discovered the properties of iron. The earliest weapons were hands, nails, and teeth. Next came stones and branches wrenched from trees, and fire and flame as soon as these were discovered. Then men learnt to use tough iron and copper. Actually the use of copper was discovered before that of iron, because it is more easily handled and in more plentiful supply. With copper they tilled the soil. With copper they whipped up the clashing waves of war, scattered a withering seed of wounds and made a spoil of flocks and fields. Before their armaments all else, naked and unarmed, fell an easy prey. Then by slow degrees the iron sword came to the fore; the bronze sickle fell into disrepute; the ploughman began to cleave the earth with iron, and on the darkling field of battle the odds were made even.

The art of mounting armed on horseback, guiding the steed with reins and keeping the right hand free for action, came earlier than braving the hazards of war in a two-horsed chariot. This again preceded the yoking of two pairs in one harness and the charge of armed warriors in chariots set with scythes. Later the redoubtable snake-handed elephant, its body crowned by a tower, was taught by the men of Carthage to endure the wounds of war and embroil the long-drawn ranks of Mars. So tragic discord gave birth to one invention after another for the intimidation of the nations' fighting men and added daily increments to the horrors of war.

Bulls, too, were enlisted in the service of war, and the experiment was made of launching savage boars against the enemy. Some even tried an advance guard of doughty lions with armed trainers and harsh masters to discipline them and keep them on the lead. But these experiments failed. The savage brutes, inflamed by promiscuous carnage, spread indiscriminate confusion among the cavaliers, as they tossed the terrifying manes upon their heads this way and that. The

1. Lucretius' poem is addressed to Gaius Memmius, a literary dilettante; he was praetor in 58 B.C. and patron of Catullus, who quarrelled with him and complained of his dissolute habits.

79

riders failed to soothe the breasts of their steeds, panic-stricken by the uproar, and direct them with the reins against the enemy. The lionesses hurled their frenzied bodies in a random spring, now leaping full in the face of oncomers, now snatching down unsuspecting victims from behind and dragging them to the ground, mortally wounded in the embrace and gripped fast by tenacious jaws and crooked claws. The bulls tossed their own employers and trampled them underfoot and with their horns gored the flanks and bellies of horses from below and hacked up the very earth with defiant forehead. The infuriated boars with their stout tusks slashed their allies. They reddened with their own blood the weapons broken in their bodies. They mowed down horse and foot pell-mell. The horses would shy away, or rear up and paw the air in a vain attempt to escape the savage onslaught of those tusks. But down you would see them tumble hamstrung, and bury the earth beneath their fallen mass. Even such beasts as their masters had once thought tame enough at home were seen to boil over in the stir of action – wounds, yells, stampedes, panic, and turmoil; and none of them would obey the recall. Brutes of every breed were rushing wildly about. The sight must have been just such as is sometimes seen in our own times when elephants, badly wounded by the steel, run wild after turning savagely upon their own associates. If, indeed, the experiment was ever tried. For my part, I find it hard to believe that men had no mental apprehension and prevision of this mutual disaster and disgrace before it could happen. It would be safer to assert that this has happened somewhere in the universe, somewhere in the multiplicity of diversely formed worlds, than in any one specific globe. In any event it must have been undertaken more to spite the enemy than with any hope of victory, by men mistrustful of their own numbers and armaments but not afraid to die.

As to *costume*, plaited clothes came before woven ones. Woven fabrics came after iron, because iron is needed for making a loom. Apart from it no material can be made smooth enough for treadles and spindles and shuttles and clattering heddles.[1] Nature ordained that this should be men's work before it was women's. For the male sex as a whole is by far the more skilful and gifted in the arts. But eventually it was

1. The small cords through which the warp is passed in a loom after going through the reed.

damned as effeminate by a censorious peasantry, so that they chose rather to leave it to women's hands while they joined in the endurance of hard labour and by the hardness of their toil hardened hands and thews.

For the *sowing and grafting of plants* the first model was provided by creative nature herself. Berries and acorns, lying below the trees from which they had fallen, were seen to put forth a swarm of shoots in due season. From the same source men learnt to engraft slips in branches and to plant young saplings in the soil of their fields. After that they tried one type of cultivation after another in their treasured plot. They saw the wild fruits grow mild in the ground with cosseting and humouring. Day by day they kept forcing the woodland to creep further up the hillside, surrendering the lower reaches to tillage. Over hill and plain they extended meadowland and cornland, reservoirs and water-courses and laughing vineyards, with the distinctive strip of blue-grey olives running between, rippling over hump and hollow and along the level ground. So the countryside assumed its present aspect of variegated beauty, gaily interspersed with luscious orchards and marked out by encircling hedges of luxuriant trees.

Men learnt to mimic with their mouths the trilling notes of birds long before they were able to enchant the ear by joining together in *tuneful song*. It was the whistling of the breeze through hollow reeds that first taught countryfolk to blow through hollow stalks. After that, by slow degrees, they learnt those plaintive melodies that flow from the flute at the touch of the player's fingers, melodies that took shape far from the busy highways, amid groves and glades and thickets in the solitudes where the shepherd spends his sunlit leisure. These are the tunes that soothed and cheered their hearts after a full meal: for at such times everything is enjoyable. So they would often recline in company on the soft grass by a running stream under the branches of a tall tree and refresh their bodies pleasurably at small expense. Better still if the weather smiled upon them and the season of the year emblazoned the green herbage with flowers. Then was the time for joking and talking and merry laughter. Then was the heyday of the rustic Muse. Then lighthearted jollity prompted them to wreath head and shoulders with garlands twisted of flowers and leaves and dance out of step, moving their limbs clumsily and with clumsy foot stamping on mother earth. This was matter enough for mirth and boisterous laughter. For these arts were still in their youth, with all the charm of novelty.

In the same occupation the wakeful found a means to while away their sleepless hours, pitching their voices high or low through the twisted intricacies of song and running over the pipes with curving lips. This remains a recognized tradition among watchmen to this day, and they have now learnt to keep in tune. But this does not mean that they derive any greater enjoyment from it than did the woodland race sprung from the soil. For what we have here and now, unless we have known something more pleasing in the past, gives the greatest satisfaction and is reckoned the best of its kind. Afterwards the discovery of something new and better blunts and vitiates our enjoyment of the old. So it is that we have lost our taste for acorns. So we have abandoned those couches littered with herbage and heaped with leaves. So the wearing of wild beasts' skins has gone out of fashion. And yet I daresay that the invention of this costume provoked such envy that its first wearer met his death in an ambush and the costume itself was so daubed with blood and torn to shreds by rival claimants that it could not be used by anyone. Skins yesterday, purple and gold today – such are the baubles that embitter human life with resentment and waste it with war. In this, I do not doubt, the greater blame rests with us. To the earth-born generation in their naked state the lack of skins meant real discomfort through cold; but we are in no way discommoded by going without robes of purple, brocaded with gold and gorgeously emblazoned, so long as we have some plebeian wrap to throw around us. So mankind is perpetually the victim of a pointless and futile martyrdom, fretting life away in fruitless worries through failure to realize what limit is set to acquisition and to the growth of genuine pleasure. It is this discontent that has driven life steadily onward, out to the high seas, and has stirred up from the depths the surging tumultuous tides of war.

It was the sun and moon, the watchmen of the world, encircling with their light that vast rotating vault, who taught men that the seasons of the year revolve and that there is a constant pattern in things and a constant sequence.

By this time men were living their lives fenced by fortifications and tilling an earth already parcelled out and allotted. The sea was aflutter with flying sails. Societies were bound together by compacts and alliances. Poets were beginning to record history in song. But letters were still a recent invention. Therefore our age cannot look back to see what happened before this stage, except in so far as its traces can be uncovered by reason.

So we find that not only such arts as sea-faring and agriculture, city walls and laws, weapons, roads and clothing, but also without exception the amenities and refinements of life, songs, pictures, and statues, artfully carved and polished, *all were taught gradually by usage* and the active mind's experience as men groped their way forward step by step. So each particular development is brought gradually to the fore by the advance of time, and reason lifts it into the light of day. Men saw one notion after another take shape within their minds until by their arts they scaled the topmost peak.

R. E. LATHAM (1951)

CATULLUS

GAIUS VALERIUS CATULLUS, born in about 84 B.C. at Verona, died in about 54 B.C. Catullus is the supreme writer of Latin love lyrics. In his day he was the most important member of a group of North Italian poets whose impact widened Rome's cultural horizons. His surviving 2,300 lines comprise nine long and 109 short poems, including epigrams, elegies, hymns, personal attacks, and miniature epics. They owe debts – but stimulating, not crippling debts – to various Greek *genres*, and particularly (though here too in his own distinctive vein) to the scholarly but experimental and individualistic Alexandrian movement of later Greece. 'Rome could not have infected Catullus with sophistication as Edinburgh infected Burns', writes E. A. Havelock, 'for he was sophisticated already. ... Yet he is par excellence the poet of intense moods, expressed either singly or in rapid succession. ... In a manner easier to feel than describe, his worship of a woman, his sense of poetry, and his sense of history somehow commingled, without making his love in the least bookish, or on the other hand his poetry sentimental.'

His adoption and refinement of Greek lyric metres and rhythms pointed the way to the Augustans. In the Middle Ages Catullus was neglected [1] – and all 120 manuscripts now known (except one containing a single poem) are believed to go back to a single survivor. This appeared at his native Verona in the fourteenth century and then vanished again – but not until a transcript had reached the Latin Secretary of Florence, Coluccio Salutati (1330–1406). Then Catullus' freshness helped to inspire the Italian humanist poets, and his verses were often on the lips of a great Renaissance teacher, his fellow-townsman Guarino. The poems of Catullus were first printed, together with those of Tibullus, Propertius, and Statius, in 1472. Not long afterwards Skelton (like many after him) imitated his poem to a dead sparrow:

> Whan I remembre agayn
> How mi Philyp was slayn,
> Never halfe the payne
> Was betwene you twayne,

---

1. Though a tenth-century bishop of Ravenna admitted he enjoyed reading him.

Pyramus and Thesbe,
As than befell to me:
I wept and I wayled,
The tearys downe hayled;
But nothynge it avayled
To call Phylyp agayne,
Whom Gib our cat hathe slayne.

This may be contrasted with Alexander Pope's *Rape of the Lock* derived from Catullus' *Lock of Berenice*.[1]

In nineteenth-century Britain the directness of Catullus (though based, as was not always appreciated, on consummate artistry) caused him to seem more spontaneous, and therefore better, than Horace. Among his translators were Ugo Foscolo and Landor, to whom Wordsworth wrote that he, too, possessed an 'intimate acquaintance' with Catullus (as well as with Virgil, Horace, and Lucretius). Tennyson's *Frater Ave atque Vale* was inspired by two poems of Catullus: his eulogy of Sirmio, and a heart-breaking farewell. But when we try to keep up, says Swinburne, with this unflinchingly lucid Latin poet, 'he makes mouths at our speech'. Among his twentieth-century adapters and translators are Arthur Symons, A. C. Benson, Laurence Binyon, and Edna St Vincent Millay. 'A generation,' says R. G. C. Levens, 'which has elevated Donne to the status of a major poet, which has produced and accepted Dylan Thomas, and has come to judge poetry more by the energy it transmits than by the polish of its surface, is naturally drawn to a poet whose sense of form was the servant of his urge to express emotion. The present age is all the more at home with Catullus because the feelings he expressed were those of an individualist clinging, in a disintegrating society, to the one standard which he could feel was secure, that of personal integrity.'

1. This was, in turn, almost a translation from the Greek of Callimachus.

HOW LOVE CHANGES

'Unto nobody,' my woman saith, 'she had rather a wife be
  Than to myself; not though Jove grew a suitor of hers.'
These be her words, but a woman's words to a love that is eager
  In wind or water's stream do require to be writ.

SIR PHILIP SIDNEY (1554–86) [1]

THE SAME

That me alone you loved, you once did say,
Nor should I to the king of gods give way.
Then I loved thee not as a common dear,
But as a father doth his children cheer.
Now thee I know, more bitterly I smart;
Yet thou to me more light and cheaper art.
What power is this? that such a wrong should press
Me to love more, yet wish thee well much less?

I hate and love; wouldst thou the reason know?
I know not; but I burn, and feel it so.

RICHARD LOVELACE (1618–58)

LOVE AND HARSH WORDS

Lesbia for ever on me rails;
To talk of me, she never fails.
Now, hang me, but for all her art
I find that I have gained her heart.
My proof is this: I plainly see
The case is just the same with me;
I curse her every hour sincerely,
Yet, hang me, but I love her dearly.

JONATHAN SWIFT (1667–1745)

1. The second of these elegiac couplets is not from the original.

EVENING WITH LICINIUS

Licinius, yesterday at leisure
We in my tablets took much pleasure,
As either of us then thought fit
To versify, and deal in wit;
Now in this sort of verse, now that,
As mirth and wine indulged the chat.
And thence, Licinius, did I part,
So grieved with thy replies so smart
That even my food denied me ease,
Nor could sleep my eyelids seize:
But tumbling in my bed all night,
I coveted to see the light,
That with Licinius I may be,
And in discourse again be free.
But when my limbs with toil oppressed,
Half dead, half seemed to take their rest,
This I, my merry comrade, sent,
That you might know my discontent.
Take care now, be not proud and high,
Nor slight my prayers with haughty eye,
Lest Nemesis reprisals make,
And of thy pride just vengeance take;
For she's a goddess (oh! take care
How you provoke her) will not spare.

ANONYMOUS (1707)

THE EFFECTS OF LOVE

Equal to Jove that youth must be –
Greater than Jove he seems to me –
Who, free from Jealousy's alarms,
Securely views thy matchless charms.
That cheek, which ever dimpling glows,
That mouth, from whence such music flows,

To him, alike, are always known,
Reserved for him, and him alone.
Ah! Lesbia, though 'tis death to me,
I cannot choose but look on thee;
But, at the sight, my senses fly;
I needs must gaze, but gazing die;
Whilst trembling with a thousand fears,
Parched to the throat my tongue adheres,
My pulse beats quick, my breath heaves short,
My limbs deny their slight support,
Cold dews my pallid face o'erspread,
With deadly languor droops my head,
My ears with tingling echoes ring,
And life itself is on the wing;
My eyes refuse the cheering light,
Their orbs are veiled in starless night;
Such pangs my nature sinks beneath,
And feels a temporary death.

LORD BYRON (1807)

CONSOLATION

If mortal sorrow on the silent dead,
    Calvus! can any touch of joy bestow,
When mourns regret o'er love for ever fled,
    Or weeps for friendship it no more must know,

Oh! then Quintilia's spirit will not grieve
    At early death and fate's unjust decree,
So much as she will gladden to perceive
    How well, how truly, she was loved by thee.

T.L. (before 1809)

THE SAME

Friend, if the mute and shrouded dead
　　Are touched at all by tears,
By love long fled and friendship sped
　　And the unreturning years,
O then, to her that early died,
　　O doubt not, bridegroom, to thy bride
Thy love is sweet and sweeteneth
　　The very bitterness of death.

H. W. GARROD (1912)

AT A BROTHER'S GRAVE

Over the mighty world's highway,
　　City by city, sea by sea,
Brother, thy brother comes to pay
　　Pitiful offerings unto thee.

I only ask to grace thy bier
　　With gifts that only give farewell,
To tell to ears that cannot hear
　　The things that it is vain to tell,

And, idly communing with dust,
　　To know thy presence still denied,
And ever mourn forever lost
　　A soul that never should have died.

Yet think not wholly vain today
　　This fashion that our fathers gave
That hither brings me, here to lay
　　Some gift of sorrow on thy grave.

Take, brother, gifts a brother's tears
　　Bedewed with sorrow as they fell,
And 'Greeting' to the end of years,
　　And to the end of years 'Farewell'.

H. W. GARROD (1912)

A WISH

Colonia,[1] so fain to celebrate
   Games on a bridge of state,
Eager to dance, but fearful lest too frail
   The little bridge should fail,
And in the waters of the marsh should sprawl
   With topsy-turvy fall
(As, propped on ancient posts, done up as new,
   'Tis very like to do),
So may the bridge to which you would aspire
   Fulfil your heart's desire,
A bridge on which the priests of Mars might prance
   And riot in a dance,
If you, Colonia, my eyes delight
   With one most mirthful sight.
I wish a certain townsman, whom I know,
   From yonder bridge to go
Head over heels, and falling unaware
   To plunge, not anywhere,
But in the blackest pool of all the mere
   Wholly to disappear,
Just where the water has the greenest hue,
   And smells most vilely too.
The man's a dolt: a boy of two years old,
   Whom father's arms enfold
And gently rock to sleep, why even he
   More sensitive would be.
For though he has for bride the sweetest flower
   Of girlhood's morning hour
(Was never fawn so exquisite as she,
   Fashioned so tenderly,
Were never purple grapes, however rare,
   More worthy of man's care),
He lets her play and keep or break the law,
   Nor cares a single straw,

1. The modern Cologna, a small town a few miles east of Verona.

Nor stirs to play his part, but sluggishly,
   Like some fallen alder tree
That in the cold Ligurian fen lies low
   Felled by the axe's blow,
As if whether it were not or it were
   The tree was unaware;
Even so that stupid oaf with eyes and ears
   Nor sees at all, nor hears,
And knows not who he is, nay if he be
   Or be not knows not he.
Now from your bridge I long to see him thrown
   Into the water prone,
Just in the hope that he may suddenly
   Awake from lethargy,
And leave his sprawling wits to the end of time
   In that abyss of slime,
As the iron shoe, ill fastened on a mule,
   Sticks in the muddy pool.

               HUGH MACNAGHTEN (1925)

WINE

Bearer of old Falernian wine,
Good boy, a stronger glass be mine.
Mistress of toasts (as drunk as she
Not even the drunken grape can be)
Postumia will have it so.
You, water, wine's destruction, go:
Away with you to folk austere:
The god of wine himself is here.

               HUGH MACNAGHTEN (1925)

HAPPINESS

To sit where I can see your face
And hear your laughter come and go
Is greater bliss than all the gods
    Can ever know.

The bright dream carries me away:
Watching your lips, your hair, your cheek,
I have so many things to say,
  Yet cannot speak.

I look, I listen, and my soul
Flames with a fire unfelt before;
Till sense swims, and I feel and see
  And hear no more.

E. A. HAVELOCK (1939)

TO CICERO

Dear Marcus Cicero, it's true,
No Roman pleads so well as you,
Both past and future you outdo.
To you Catullus gives his thanks,
Worst of all poets though he ranks,
Ranking indeed as much the worst
As you of advocates stand first.

JACK LINDSAY (1948)

LOVE AND HATRED

I hate her – yet I love her too.
  You ask how this can be.
I only know that it is true
  And bitter agony.

JANET MACLEAN TODD (1955)

A PRAYER

If there's some pleasure in remembering
The decent things one did (that one felt true,
And broke no serious oath, and in no compact

Used the Gods' greatness for deceiving men),
Then, in a long life, many joys, Catullus,
Are surely due you for your squandered love!
All gentle things a man can say or do
In love, by you have all been said or done:
All, to a thankless heart entrusted, perished.

Why do you still extend your area of
Self-torture? Why not stiffen up, draw back,
And cease – the Gods dislike it – to be wretched?
It's hard to quench an old love suddenly:
It's hard indeed, but what you've got to do:
You must do this, whether you can or not!
Gods, if there's pity in you, or if ever
To any deathbed you brought any comfort,
Have pity on poor me! Was my life honest?
Then snatch away this plague and ruin from me –
Alas, this slackness in my deepest joints,
Creeping, that drives my heart's delight away!
I ask no longer this: for my love, her love:
Nor wish she'd wish, though vainly, to be chaste.
I want mere health: to lay down this vile sickness.

If I've observed decorum, Gods, grant this!
                              G. S. FRASER (1955)

ATTIS IN EXILE

Are these ungreek landscapes
My new life-home?
Where is Attica?
Where can the pupil open with Attica?
The storm has lifted
And there is no piazza.
Where is the stadium? the wrestling ring? the gymnasium?
A fallen life left to tread sorrow
                              PETER WHIGHAM (1966)

CAESAR

GAIUS JULIUS CAESAR, born in 102 or 101 or 100 B.C., belonged to an ancient but dull aristocratic family, but was nephew to the wife of Marius, the middle-class professional general and stormy politician. Lacking funds, Caesar supported the millionaire Crassus, and by unusually heavy bribery was elected Chief Priest (Pontifex Maximus) in 62 B.C. As consul in 59 he was the ally of Crassus and Pompey in the First Triumvirate. Then followed the eight years of the Gallic War (58–51), and the Wars against Pompey, the Alexandrians, and Pompey's sons (49–45). The dictatorship, designed as an emergency appointment, was assumed by Caesar at first briefly, then for ten years and finally life: this was one of the reasons for his murder by Brutus, Cassius, and their fellow-conspirators.

Caesar's speeches, second only to Cicero's in quality, are lost. But we have his apologia, the *Gallic War* and *Civil War*. These works reveal that Caesar, like very few men (except perhaps Sir Winston Churchill), wrote about his times as ably as he dominated them. His writings provide an outstanding picture of Roman efficiency and discipline. They bear a modest-seeming title, the *Commentaries* – 'Notes' or 'Memoirs', written in the third person. This title is as persuasive and reassuring as the sweetly reasonable evasions of political war-guilt or very occasionally military failure (for instance in Britain), communicated by Caesar's crystalline, ostensibly direct prose.

This calculated absence of rhetoric was too austere for ancient tastes, but has reaped its harvest since. The Commentaries were first published at Rome in 1469, and in 1565 a complete English *Gallic War* [1] was produced by Arthur Golding. In *The Scholemaster* (1570), Ascham asserts that this work should 'be read with all curiosity, wherein specially, without all exception to be made either by friend or foe, is seen the unspotted propriety of the Latin tongue'. A more unqualified admiration is already apparent in Henry Felton (1715): 'he possesseth this almost peculiar to himself that you see the Prince and the Gentleman as well as the Scholar and the Soldier in his memoirs'. Napoleon I said every general ought to read Caesar as part of his education; Napoleon III frankly admired his autocracy and aggression. But 'we cannot', says Trollope, 'take the facts as the Emperor of the French gives

1. It superseded a partial version of 1530.

94

them to us'. W.H.D.Rouse (1898) recommended Caesar as a reading book for school-girls; but he is more suitable for the maturer judgement of University courses, in which, as Sir Frank Adcock regrets, he is seldom included.[1]

1. I have ventured here, as in my Penguin translation of *The Annals* of Tacitus, to modernize 'legions', 'cohorts', 'legates', and 'military tribunes' as 'brigades', 'battalions', 'generals', and 'colonels'. I have not, however, attempted complete consistency throughout the book.

It was now near the end of the summer (55 B.C.), and winter sets in early in those parts, because all that coast of Gaul faces north. Nevertheless, Caesar made active preparations for an expedition to Britain, because he knew that in almost all the Gallic campaigns the Gauls had received reinforcements from the Britons. Even if there was not time for a campaign that season, he thought it would be of great advantage to him merely to visit the island, to see what its inhabitants were like, and to make himself acquainted with the lie of the land, the harbours, and the landing-places. Of all this the Gauls knew next to nothing; for in the ordinary way traders are the only people who visit Britain, and even they know only that part of the coast which faces Gaul. And so, although he interviewed traders from all parts, he could not ascertain anything about the size of the island, the character and strength of the tribes which inhabited it, their manner of fighting and customs, or the harbours capable of accommodating a large fleet of big ships. In order to get this information before risking an expedition, he sent a warship in command of Volusenus, whom he considered a suitable man for the job. His orders were to make a general reconnaissance and return as soon as he could.

Meanwhile, Caesar marched the whole army into the country of the Morini,[1] from which there was the shortest crossing to Britain, and ordered ships to assemble there from all the neighbouring districts, as well as the fleet that had been built the previous summer for the war against the Veneti.[2] His design had become known in the meantime, and when the news was brought by traders to the Britons, envoys were sent by a number of tribes, offering to give hostages and submit to Rome. Caesar gave them audience, made them generous promises, and urged them to abide by their resolve. He then sent them home, accompanied by Commius, whom he had made king of the Atrebates[3] after the conquest of that tribe – a man of whose courage, judgement, and loyalty he had a high opinion, and who was greatly respected in Britain. He instructed Commius to visit as many

1. A tribe living on the coast of Belgium and north-eastern France.
2. Morbihan department, Brittany.
3. A tribe of the Arras district.

tribes as possible, to urge them to entrust themselves to the protection of Rome, and to announce his impending arrival. Volusenus reconnoitred the coast as far as he could without disembarking and putting himself into the power of the natives, which he dared not do, and returned four days later with his report.

While Caesar was waiting in the country of the Morini for his fleet to be assembled, a large section of the tribe sent envoys to apologize for their previous hostile action, pleading that they were foreigners and ignorant of Roman ways, and promising to obey his commands in future. Caesar thought this very fortunate. He did not want to leave an enemy in his rear; yet it would have been too late in the season to start another campaign, and the expedition to Britain was much more important than the conquest of these petty tribes. He therefore demanded a large number of hostages, and on their arrival accepted the submission of the Morini.

In due course about eighty transports, which Caesar considered sufficient to convey two brigades, were obtained and assembled, and also a number of warships, which were assigned to the quaestor, the generals, and the officers of the auxiliary troops. Besides these there were eighteen transports at a point eight miles along the coast, which were prevented by a contrary wind from making the same harbour as the rest; these were allotted to the cavalry. The remainder of the army was entrusted to Sabinus and Cotta, with orders to march against the Menapii [1] and those clans of the Morini which had not sent envoys. Another general, Publius Sulpicius Rufus, was ordered to hold the harbour and was given a force considered adequate for the purpose.

After the completion of these arrangements, Caesar took advantage of favourable weather and set sail about midnight, ordering the cavalry to proceed to the farther port, embark there, and follow him. As these conducted the operation too slowly, their transports were carried back to land by the tide. Caesar himself reached Britain with the first ships about nine o'clock in the morning, and saw the enemy's forces posted on all the hills. The lie of the land at this point was such that javelins could be hurled from the cliffs right on to the narrow beach enclosed between them and the sea. Caesar thought this a quite unsuitable place for landing, and therefore rode at anchor until three

1. Mainly in south Holland.

o'clock, in order to give the rest of the ships time to come up. Meanwhile he assembled the generals and colonels, and, telling them what he had learned from Volusenus, explained his plans. He warned them that the exigencies of warfare, and particularly of naval operations, in which things move rapidly and the situation is constantly changing, required the instant execution of every order. On dismissing the officers he found that both wind and tidal current were in his favour. He therefore gave the signal for weighing anchor, and after proceeding about seven miles ran his ships aground on an evenly sloping beach, free from obstacles.

The natives, on realizing his intention, had sent forward their cavalry and a number of the chariots which they are accustomed to use in warfare; the rest of their troops followed close behind and were ready to oppose the landing. The Romans were faced with very grave difficulties. The size of the ships made it impossible to run them aground except in fairly deep water; and the soldiers, unfamiliar with the ground, with their hands full, and weighed down by the heavy burden of their arms, had at the same time to jump down from the ships, get a footing in the waves, and fight the enemy, who, standing on dry land or advancing only a short way into the water, fought with all their limbs unencumbered and on perfectly familiar ground, boldly hurling javelins and galloping their horses, which were trained to this kind of work. These perils frightened our soldiers, who were quite unaccustomed to battles of this kind, with the result that they did not show the same alacrity and enthusiasm as they usually did in battles on dry land.

Seeing this, Caesar ordered the warships – which were swifter and easier to handle than the transports, and likely to impress the natives more by their unfamiliar appearance – to be removed a short distance from the others, and then to be rowed hard and run ashore on the enemy's right flank, from which position slings, bows, and artillery could be used by men on deck to drive them back. This manœuvre was highly successful. Scared by the strange shape of the warships, the motion of the oars, and the unfamiliar machines, the natives halted and then retreated a little. But as the Romans still hesitated, chiefly on account of the depth of the water, the man who carried the Eagle of the 10th brigade, after praying to the gods that his action might bring good luck to the brigade, cried in a loud voice: 'Jump down, comrades, unless you want to surrender our Eagle to the enemy; I, at any rate, mean to do my duty to my country and my general.' With these words he leapt out of the ship and advanced towards the enemy with the Eagle in his hands. At this the soldiers, exhorting each other not to submit to such a disgrace, jumped with one accord from the ship, and the men from the next ships, when they saw them, followed them and advanced against the enemy.

Both sides fought hard. But as the Romans could not keep their ranks or get a firm foothold or follow their proper standards, and men from different ships fell in under the first standard they came across, great confusion resulted. The enemy knew all the shallows, and when they saw from the beach small parties of soldiers disembarking one by one, they galloped up and attacked them at a disadvantage, surrounding them with superior numbers, while others would throw javelins at the right flank of a whole group. Caesar therefore ordered the warships' boats and the scouting-vessels to be loaded with troops, so that he could send help to any point where he saw the men in difficulties. As soon as the soldiers had got a footing on the beach and had waited for all their comrades to join them, they charged the enemy and put them to flight, but could not pursue very far, because the cavalry had not been able to hold their course and make the island. This was the one thing that prevented Caesar from achieving his usual success.

The defeated enemy, as soon as they rallied after their flight, hastened to send an embassy to ask for peace, promising to give hostages and carry out Caesar's commands. With these envoys came Commius the Atrebatian, whom Caesar had sent on ahead to Britain. When he had disembarked and was delivering Caesar's message to them in the character of an ambassador, the natives had arrested and bound him. Now, after the battle, they sent him back, and in asking for peace threw the blame for this proceeding on the common people, begging Caesar to pardon an error due to ignorance. Caesar reproached them for making war on him without provocation, after sending envoys to the continent of their own accord to sue for peace, but said that he would pardon their ignorance, and demanded hostages. Some of these they handed over at once; the rest they said would have to be fetched from a distance, and should be delivered in a few days' time. Meanwhile they bade their men return to the fields, and the chiefs began to come from all parts to solicit Caesar's favour for themselves and their tribes. Peace was thus concluded.

On the fourth day after Caesar's arrival in Britain, the eighteen transports on which the cavalry had been embarked sailed from the northern port before a gentle breeze. When they were approaching Britain and were visible from the camp, such a violent storm suddenly arose that none of them could hold its course. Some were driven back to their starting-point; others, at great peril, were swept westwards to the south of the island. In spite of the danger they cast anchor, but as they were being filled with water by the waves, they were forced to stand out to sea into the darkness of night and return to the continent.

It happened to be full moon that night, at which time the Atlantic tides are particularly high – a fact unknown to the Romans. The result was that the warships used in the crossing, which had been beached, were waterlogged, and the transports, which were riding at anchor, were knocked about by the storm, without the soldiers' having any chance of interfering to save them. A number of ships were shattered, and the rest, having lost their cables, anchors, and the remainder of their tackle, were unusable, which naturally threw the whole army into great consternation. For they had no other vessels in which they could return, nor any materials for repairing the fleet; and, since it had been generally understood that they were to return to Gaul for the winter, they had not provided themselves with a stock of grain for wintering in Britain.

On learning of this accident, the British chiefs, who had assembled after the battle to execute Caesar's commands, put their heads together. Knowing that Caesar had no cavalry, ships, or corn, and inferring the weakness of his forces from the small size of the camp, which was all the smaller because he had come without most of the heavy luggage, they decided that their best course was to renew hostilities, to hinder the Roman army from obtaining corn and other supplies, and to prolong the war into the winter. If this army was conquered or prevented from returning, they felt confident that no one would come across to invade Britain again. Accordingly, after renewing their promises of mutual loyalty, they slipped away one by one from the camp and secretly called up once more the men who had returned to the fields. Although Caesar had not yet heard of their intention, the disaster which had overtaken his fleet and the fact that they were no longer sending hostages led him to anticipate what was coming. He therefore prepared for anything that might happen. Corn was brought in daily from the fields, timber and bronze from the most severely damaged vessels were used to repair the others, and naval equipment was ordered to be sent from the continent. By the energetic efforts of the soldiers all but twelve ships were saved and rendered tolerably seaworthy.

While this work was proceeding, one brigade, as usual, had been sent out to get corn – in this case the 7th. Nothing had yet occurred to raise any suspicion of a fresh attack, and some of the Britons were still working in the fields, while others were actually going backwards and forwards to the camp. Suddenly the guards on duty at the gates reported to Caesar that an unusually large cloud of dust was visible in the direction in which the brigade had gone. Caesar guessed the truth – that the natives had hatched a new scheme – ordered the battalions on guard duty to set out with him in the direction indicated, two of the others to relieve them, and the rest to arm and follow immediately. After going some way he saw that the brigade was hard pressed by enemy forces and holding its ground with difficulty, packed closely and pelted with missiles from all directions. For as the corn had already been cut everywhere except in one place, the enemy had expected that our men would go there and had hidden by night in the woods. Then, when the soldiers were scattered and busy cutting corn, with their arms laid down, they had made a sudden attack, killing a few and throwing the rest into confusion before they could form up, and also surrounding them with cavalry and chariots.*

The men of the 7th brigade were unnerved by these tactics, and it was just at the right moment that Caesar came to their rescue. At his

* In chariot fighting the Britons begin by driving all over the field hurling javelins, and generally the terror inspired by the horses and the noise of the wheels are sufficient to throw their opponents' ranks into disorder. Then, after making their way between the troops of their own cavalry, they jump down from the chariots and engage on foot. In the meantime their charioteers retire a short distance from the battle and place the chariots in such a position that their masters, if hard pressed by numbers, have an easy means of retreat to their own lines. Thus they combine the mobility of cavalry with the staying-power of infantry; and by daily training and practice they attain such proficiency that even on a steep incline they are able to control the horses at full gallop, and to check and turn them in a moment. They can run along the chariot pole, stand on the yoke, and get back into the chariot as quick as lightning.

approach the enemy halted and the soldiers recovered from their alarm. But as he considered the situation too hazardous for attacking or engaging in battle, he stayed where he was, and after a short interval led the force back to camp. While these events kept all our men occupied, the natives who were still in the fields made off.

There followed several days of continuous bad weather, which kept our men in camp and also prevented the enemy from attacking. During this time the natives sent messengers in all directions, who informed their people of the small numbers of our troops, and pointed out what a good opportunity they had of getting booty and liberating themselves for ever, if they could drive the Romans from their camp. By this means they quickly collected a large force of infantry and cavalry, which advanced towards the camp. Caesar foresaw that what had happened before would happen again: even if the enemy were beaten, their speed would enable them to escape out of harm's way. Nevertheless, having luckily obtained about thirty horsemen whom Commius had brought across, he drew up his brigades in battle-formation in front of the camp. Before the engagement had lasted long the enemy were overpowered and took to flight. The Romans pursued as far as their strength enabled them to run, killing a number of the fugitives, and then set fire to all the buildings over a wide area and returned to camp.

The same day envoys came to Caesar to sue for peace. He demanded twice as many hostages as before, and ordered these to be brought to the continent, as the equinox was close at hand and he thought it better not to expose his damaged ships to the dangers of a voyage in wintry weather. Taking advantage of a favourable wind he set sail shortly after midnight, and the whole fleet reached the continent safely.

Two transports, however, failed to make the same harbours as the rest and were carried a little farther south. When about three hundred soldiers had disembarked from these two ships and were pushing towards the camp, the Morini, whom Caesar had compelled to make peace before setting out for Britain, thought they saw a chance of obtaining booty, and surrounded them, at first with only a small force, bidding them lay down their arms if they did not want to be killed. The Romans formed a ring and defended themselves, but in a short time the shouts of their assailants brought some six thousand natives to the spot. On hearing what was happening Caesar sent all the cavalry to their aid. Meanwhile the soldiers held the enemy's attack, fighting with the utmost bravery for over four hours, and killed a number of them at the cost of only a few men wounded. As soon as the cavalry came in sight the Morini threw down their arms and fled, suffering very heavy casualties.

The next day Caesar sent Labienus against the rebellious Morini with the brigades that had returned from Britain. As the marshes in which they had taken refuge the previous year were now dry, the natives had nowhere to retreat to, and nearly all fell into Labienus' hands. Sabinus and Cotta, however, who had led their forces into the territory of the Menapii, had to content themselves with destroying all the crops, cutting the corn, and burning the buildings, because all the inhabitants had concealed themselves in very dense forests. They then returned to Caesar, who arranged for all formations to winter in Belgic territory.[1] There he received the promised hostages from only two British tribes; the remainder neglected to send them.

On the conclusion of these campaigns and the receipt of Caesar's dispatches, the Senate decreed a public thanksgiving of twenty days.

In the consulship of Lucius Domitius and Appius Claudius (54 B.C.), when Caesar was leaving his winter quarters as usual to go to Italy, he ordered the generals placed in command of the army to have as many ships as possible built during the winter, and the old ones repaired. He specified the dimensions and shape of the new ships. To enable them to be loaded quickly and beached easily he had them made slightly lower than those which we generally use in the Mediterranean – especially as he had found that owing to the frequent ebb and flow of the tides the waves in the Channel were comparatively small. To enable them, however, to carry a heavy cargo, including a large number of animals, they were made somewhat wider than the ships we use in other waters. They were all to be of a type suitable for both sailing and rowing – an arrangement which was greatly facilitated by their freeboard. The materials required for fitting them out were to be imported from Spain.

When Caesar rejoined his army from Italy, he made a tour of all the winter camps, and found that, in spite of a serious shortage of

1. The Belgae inhabited northern France, Belgium, southern Holland, and Germany west of the Rhine.

materials, the men had worked with such enthusiasm that they had built and equipped six hundred vessels of the type described, and twenty-eight warships. These would all be ready for launching in a few days. Caesar congratulated the soldiers and the officers who had superintended the work, gave them further instructions, and ordered all the ships to be assembled at Portus Itius, the starting point for the easiest crossing to Britain – a run of about thirty miles.

When Caesar came to Portus Itius, he found that sixty ships which were built in the country of the Meldi had been driven out of their course by a storm and had returned to their starting-point. All the rest were completely equipped and ready for sea. Four thousand cavalry from all parts of Gaul assembled at the port, and the leaders of all the tribes. Caesar had decided to leave behind only a few of these who had proved their loyalty, and to take all the rest with him as hostages, because he was afraid of a rising in Gaul during his absence.

When Caesar set sail, he left Labienus on the continent with three brigades and two thousand cavalry, with orders to guard the ports, provide for a supply of corn, watch events in Gaul, and act as circumstances from time to time might require. Caesar took with him five brigades and the remaining two thousand cavalry, and putting out about sunset was at first carried on his way by a light south-westerly breeze. But about midnight the wind dropped, with the result that he was driven far out of his course by the tidal current and at daybreak saw Britain left behind on the port side. When the set of the current changed he went with it, and rowed hard to make the part of the island where he had found the best landing-places the year before. The soldiers worked splendidly, and by continuous rowing enabled the heavily laden transports to keep up with the warships. When the whole fleet reached Britain about midday, no enemy was to be seen. Caesar discovered afterwards from prisoners that, although large numbers had assembled at the spot, they were frightened by the sight of so many ships * and had quitted the shore to conceal themselves on higher ground.

Caesar disembarked his army and chose a suitable spot for a camp. On learning from prisoners where the enemy were posted, he left ten

* Including those retained from the previous year and the privately owned vessels built by individuals for their own use, over eight hundred were visible simultaneously.

battalions and three hundred cavalry on the coast to guard the fleet and marched against the Britons shortly after midnight, feeling little anxiety about the ships because he was leaving them anchored on an open shore of soft sand. The fleet and its guard were put under the command of Quintus Atrius. A night march of about twelve miles brought Caesar in sight of the enemy, who advanced to a river with their cavalry and chariots and tried to bar his way by attacking from a position on higher ground. Repulsed by his cavalry they hid in the woods, where they occupied a well-fortified post of great natural strength, previously prepared, no doubt, for some war among themselves, since all the entrances were blocked by felled trees laid close together. Scattered parties made skirmishing attacks out of the woods, trying to prevent the Romans from penetrating the defences. But the soldiers of the 7th brigade, locking their shields together over their heads and piling up earth against the fortifications, captured the place and drove them out of the woods at the cost of only a few men wounded. Caesar forbade them to pursue far, however, because he did not know the ground, and because he wanted to devote the few remaining hours of the day to the fortification of his camp.

The next morning he sent out a force of infantry and cavalry in three columns to pursue the fleeing enemy. They had advanced some way and were in sight of the nearest fugitives, when dispatch-riders brought news from Atrius of a great storm in the night, by which nearly all the ships had been damaged or cast ashore; the anchors and cables had not held, and the sailors and their captains could not cope with such a violent gale, so that many vessels were disabled by running foul of one another. Caesar at once ordered the brigades and cavalry to be halted and recalled. He himself went back to the beach, where with his own eyes he saw pretty much what the messengers and the dispatch described. About forty ships were a total loss; the rest looked as if they could be repaired at the cost of much trouble. Accordingly he called out all the skilled workmen from the infantry, sent to the continent for more, and wrote to tell Labienus to build as many ships as possible with the troops under his command. Further, although it was a task involving enormous labour, he decided that it would be best to have all the ships beached and enclosed together with the camp by one fortification. This work, although it was continued day and night, took some ten days to complete. As soon as the ships were hauled up and the camp strongly fortified, Caesar left the same units as before to guard them, and returned to the place from which he had come. On arriving there he found that larger British forces had now been assembled from all sides by Cassivellaunus, to whom the chief command and direction of the campaign had been entrusted by common consent. Cassivellaunus' territory is separated from the maritime tribes by a river called the Thames, and lies about seventy-five miles from the sea.* Previously he had been continually at war with

* The interior of Britain is inhabited by people who claim, on the strength of an oral tradition, to be aboriginal; the coast, by Belgic immigrants who came to plunder and make war – nearly all of them retaining the names of the tribes from which they originated – and later settled down to till the soil. The population is exceedingly large, the ground thickly studded with homesteads, closely resembling those of the Gauls, and the cattle very numerous. For money they used either bronze, or gold coins, or iron ingots of fixed weights. Tin is found inland, and small quantities of iron near the coast; the copper that they use is imported. There is timber of every kind, as in Gaul, except beech and fir. Hares, fowl, and geese they think it unlawful to eat, but rear them for pleasure and amusement. The climate is more temperate than in Gaul, the cold being less severe.

The island is triangular, with one side facing Gaul. One corner of this side, on the coast of Kent, is the landing-place for nearly all the ships from Gaul, and points east; the lower corner points south. The length of this side is about 475 miles. Another side faces west, towards Spain. In this direction is Ireland, which is supposed to be half the size of Britain, and lies at the same distance from it as Gaul. Midway across is the Isle of Man, and it is believed that there are also a number of smaller islands, in which, according to some writers, there is a month of perpetual darkness at the winter solstice. Our inquiries on this subject were always fruitless, but we found by accurate measurements with a water-clock that the nights are shorter than on the continent. The third side faces north; no land lies opposite it, but its eastern corner points roughly in the direction of Germany. Its length is estimated at 760 miles. Thus the whole island is 1,900 miles in circumference.

By far the most civilized inhabitants are those living in Kent (a purely maritime district), whose way of life differs little from that of the Gauls. Most of the tribes in the interior do not grow corn but live on milk and meat, and wear skins. All the Britons dye their bodies with woad, which produces a blue colour, and this gives them a more terrifying appearance in battle. They wear their hair long, and shave the whole of their bodies except the head and the upper lip. Wives are shared between groups of ten or twelve men, especially between brothers and between fathers and sons; but the offspring of these unions are counted as the children of the man with whom a particular woman cohabited first.

the other tribes, but the arrival of our army frightened them into appointing him their supreme commander.

The British cavalry and charioteers had a fierce encounter with our cavalry on the march, but our men had the best of it everywhere and drove them into the woods and hills, killing a good many, but also incurring some casualties themselves by a too eager pursuit. The enemy waited for a time, and then, while our soldiers were off their guard and busy fortifying the camp, suddenly dashed out of the woods, swooped upon the outpost on duty in front of the camp, and started a violent battle. Caesar sent two battalions – the first of their respective brigades – to the rescue, and these took up a position close together; but the men were unnerved by the unfamiliar tactics, and the enemy very daringly broke through between them and got away unhurt. That day Quintus Laberius Durus, a colonel, was killed. The attack was eventually repulsed by throwing in some more battalions. Throughout this peculiar combat, which was fought in front of the camp in full view of everyone, it was seen that our troops were too heavily weighted by their armour to deal with such an enemy: they could not pursue them when they retreated, and dared not get separated from their standards. The cavalry, too, found it very dangerous work fighting the charioteers; for the Britons would generally give ground on purpose, and after drawing them some distance from the infantry would jump down from their chariots and fight on foot, with the odds in their favour. In engaging their cavalry our men were not much better off: their tactics were such that the danger was exactly the same for both pursuers and pursued. A further difficulty was that they never fought in close order, but in very open formation, and had reserves posted here and there; in this way the various groups covered one another's retreat, and fresh troops replaced those who were tired.

Next day the enemy took up a position on the hills at a distance from the camp. They showed themselves now only in small parties and harassed our cavalry with less vigour than the day before. But at midday, when Caesar had sent three brigades and all the cavalry on a foraging expedition under his general Gaius Trebonius, they suddenly swooped down on them from all sides, pressing their attack right up to the standards of the brigades. The Roman infantry drove them off by a strong counter-attack, and continued to pursue until the cavalry, emboldened by the support of the brigades which they saw close behind them, made a charge that sent the natives flying headlong. A great many were killed, and the rest were given no chance of rallying or making a stand or jumping from their chariots. This rout caused the immediate dispersal of the forces that had assembled from various tribes to Cassivellaunus' aid, and the Britons never again joined battle with their whole strength.

On learning the enemy's plan of campaign, Caesar led his army to the Thames in order to enter Cassivellaunus' territory. The river is fordable at one point only, and even there with difficulty. At this place he found large enemy forces drawn up on the opposite bank. The bank was also fenced by sharp stakes fixed along the edge, and he was told by prisoners and deserters that similar ones were concealed in the river-bed. He sent the cavalry across first, and then at once ordered the infantry to follow. But the infantry went with such speed and impetuosity, although they had only their heads above water, that they attacked at the same moment as the cavalry. The enemy was overpowered and fled from the river-bank.

Cassivellaunus had now given up all hope of fighting a pitched battle. Disbanding the greater part of his troops, he retained only some four thousand charioteers, with whom he watched our line of march. He would retire a short way from the route and hide in dense thickets, driving the inhabitants and cattle from the open country into the woods wherever he knew we intended to pass. If ever our cavalry incautiously ventured too far away in plundering and devastating the country, he would send all his charioteers out of the woods by well-known lanes and pathways and deliver very formidable attacks, hoping by this means to make them afraid to go far afield. Caesar was thus compelled to keep the cavalry in touch with the column of infantry, and to let the enemy off with such devastation and burning as could be done under the protection of the Roman infantry – tired as they often were with marching.

During this march envoys arrived from the Trinovantes,[1] about the strongest tribe in south-eastern Britain. Mandubracius, a young prince of this tribe, had gone over to the continent to put himself under Caesar's protection, having fled for his life when his father, the king of the Trinovantes, was killed by Cassivellaunus. The envoys promised to

1. In Essex.

surrender and obey Caesar's commands, and asked him to protect Mandubracius from Cassivellaunus and send him home to rule his people as king. Caesar demanded forty hostages and grain for his troops, and then allowed Mandubracius to go. The Trinovantes promptly sent the required number of hostages and the grain.

When they saw that the Trinovantes had been protected against Cassivellaunus and spared any injury on the part of the Roman troops, several other tribes * sent embassies and surrendered. From them Caesar learnt that he was not far from Cassivellaunus' stronghold,† which was protected by forests and marshes, and had been filled with a large number of men and cattle. He marched to the place with his infantry, and found that it was of great natural strength and excellently fortified. Nevertheless, he proceeded to assault it on two sides. After a short time the enemy proved unable to resist the violent attack of the brigades, and rushed out of the fortress on another side. A quantity of cattle was found there, and many of the fugitives were captured or killed.

While these operations were proceeding in his territory, Cassivellaunus sent envoys to Kent ordering the four kings of that region ‡ to collect all their troops and make a surprise attack on the naval camp. When these forces appeared the Romans made a sortie, in which without suffering any loss they killed a great many of them and captured Lugotorix, a leader of noble birth. On receiving news of this action, Cassivellaunus, alarmed by so many reverses, by the devastation of his country, and above all by the defection of his allies, sent envoys to Caesar to obtain terms of surrender, employing Commius as an intermediary. Caesar had decided to return to the continent for the winter, for fear any sudden rising should break out in Gaul. The summer, too, was nearly over, and he knew that the Britons could easily hold out for the short time that remained. Accordingly he granted Cassivellaunus' request for terms, demanding hostages, fixing an annual tribute to be paid by the Britons to the Roman government, and strictly forbidding Cassivellaunus to molest Mandubracius or the Trinovantes.

* The Cenimagni, Segontiaci, Ancalites, Bibroci, and Cassi.

† The Britons apply the term 'strongholds' to densely wooded spots fortified with a rampart and trench, to which they retire in order to escape the attacks of invaders.

‡ Cingetorix, Carvilius, Taximagulus, and Segovax.

As soon as the hostages were delivered he led the army back to the coast, where he found the ships repaired. He had them launched, and as he had a large number of prisoners, and some of the ships had been destroyed by the storm, decided to make the return voyage in two trips. It happened that of all these large fleets, which made so many voyages in this and the preceding year, not a single ship with troops on board was lost, while very few of the vessels coming over empty from the continent * reached their destination, nearly all the rest being forced back to land. After waiting a long time for them in vain, Caesar was afraid of being prevented from sailing by the approaching season of the equinox, and so had to pack the men more tightly than usual on the ships he had. The sea becoming very calm, he set sail late in the evening and brought all the fleet safely to land at dawn.

S. A. HANDFORD (1951)

CAESAR DEFEATS POMPEY AT THE BATTLE OF DYRRHACHIUM [1]

Pompey's camp was on the hill. He kept his forces lined up on its lowest slopes, evidently waiting to see if Caesar would risk the unfavourable ground. Caesar concluded that there was no way of enticing Pompey to fight; so his most suitable plan of campaign, he judged, was to strike camp and keep on the move. His intentions were, by moving camp and transferring his army from place to place, to facilitate the receipt of supplies, to secure occasion to fight as he proceeded, and also to give Pompey's army – which was unaccustomed to hard work – the fatigue of daily marching. When these plans were completed, the signal was given for departure, and the tents unstretched. But then it was observed that Pompey's line had, a short time previously, been advanced somewhat further beyond his stockade than was the daily custom. So it seemed possible to fight a battle on quite favourable ground. Caesar's column was already at the gates when he addressed the men. 'For the time being,' he said, 'we must postpone our march and think of battle – which is what we have al-

---

* i.e. those which had returned to Gaul after landing troops in Britain, and sixty that Labienus had built after the start of the expedition.

1. Durazzo in Albania (48 B.C.).

ways wanted! Let us nerve ourselves for a fight. The opportunity will not easily return.' Then he rapidly led out his force, light-armed.

Pompey too (it was later discovered) had decided, with universal encouragement from his troops, to fight a pitched battle. Indeed he had actually claimed at his council of war, on previous days, that Caesar's army would be routed even before the engagement began. When this assertion caused considerable surprise, Pompey continued: 'I know that what I am promising sounds almost incredible; but listen to the reasoning behind my plan, and then you will be heartened for the battle. I have induced my cavalry (and they have assured me of their determination) to wait until the armies are in reach, and then to attack Caesar's right wing, where the flank is open. For, by surrounding his line from the rear, they will throw the whole enemy force into panic and rout before we have launched a single missile against them. So we shall end the war without risking the infantry brigades – almost without a wound. It is not difficult; we are so strong in cavalry.' Then Pompey told them to be in good spirit the next day. They had often demanded the opportunity to fight, he said, and now that they had it they must not disappoint his and everyone else's hopes.

Next Labienus spoke, depreciating Caesar's army and warmly praising Pompey's strategy. 'Pompey,' he said, 'do not imagine that Caesar's army is the one which conquered Gaul and Germany. I took part in all those battles, so I am not talking at random about a matter of which I know nothing. Only a tiny part of that army survives! A large part of it has perished – as was inevitable in all that fighting. Many more died in the autumn's epidemic in Italy; many went home; many were left across the Adriatic. You have heard, have you not, how battalions were formed at Brindisi out of the men who had been left behind there as invalids? The units in front of you have been reconstituted by levies in north Italy during the past few years – most of the men come from settlements north of the Po. Besides, the best of them were killed in the two previous engagements in this Durazzo area.'

After this speech, Labienus swore he would never return to the camp except as conqueror, and he incited the others to say the same. Pompey approved, and took the same oath himself; and every member of the council unhesitatingly did likewise. After these proceedings the meeting broke up amid high hopes and unanimous rejoicing.

They fully anticipated that they would win: it seemed unlikely that optimism in so important a matter and from so experienced a general could be unfounded.

On approaching Pompey's camp Caesar noted that his order of battle was as follows. On the left wing were the two brigades – known as the First and the Third – which Caesar had handed over to him at the beginning of the civil war in accordance with a senatorial decree. Pompey was with them; Scipio was in the centre, with the brigades from Syria. On the right wing was the brigade from Cilicia and the battalions which, as was said above, were transported from Spain by Afranius. Pompey regarded these as his most reliable formations. His remaining troops were stationed between the centre and the wings. Altogether he had one hundred and ten battalions, amounting to forty-five thousand men. In addition there were about two thousand reserves who had come to him from the personal staffs of his former armies; these he distributed throughout the whole force. Seven other battalions were stationed to defend the camp and adjacent forts. A stream with difficult banks covered his right wing; so all the cavalry, archers, and slingers were placed in support of the left wing.

Caesar kept to his previous habit and posted the Tenth Brigade on his right wing, and the Ninth on his left, although it had been seriously weakened in the engagements round Durazzo. He supplemented the Ninth by the Eighth brigade, ordering them to operate in support of one another almost as if they formed a single unit. He had eighty battalions stationed in the line, amounting to twenty-two thousand men; seven battalions were left to protect his camp. He put Antony, Publius Sulla, and Cnaeus Domitius Calvinus in command of the left wing, right wing, and centre respectively, and took up his own station opposite Pompey. At the same time, he took precautions against a massive cavalry envelopment of his right wing, which his study of the above-mentioned order of battle caused him to feel was a danger. Rapidly withdrawing certain battalions from his third line, he made them into a fourth line, which he posted opposite Pompey's cavalry. As he indicated what he wanted done, he added that it was on their courage that the issue of the day's engagement depended. He then ordered the third line, and the rest of the army, not to start fighting until he gave the word – when he wanted them to, he said, he would signal them with a standard.

Next, as generals usually do, he addressed his troops. Recalling the unfailing good treatment they had received from him, he particularly emphasized certain points: his earnest endeavours for peace, of which they were the witnesses – the conferences to which he had sent Vatinius, his dispatch of Aulus Clodius to negotiate with Scipio, his efforts with Libo at Oricum [1] for an exchange of envoys. He had never wanted to waste his men's blood, he said, or to deprive the nation of either of its armies. His speech moved the soldiers, and as they passionately clamoured to meet the enemy his trumpet sounded for the battle to begin.

In Caesar's army there was an outstandingly brave reservist called Gaius Crastinus, who in the previous year had served under him as senior company commander in the Tenth Brigade. When the signal was given, he cried out: 'Follow me! You who have served with me, support your commanding officer as you always have! This is the last of the battles; when it is over Caesar's honour will be his again – and our freedom ours!' Then he looked at Caesar and called out: 'General, today I shall give you occasion to thank me – alive or dead!' With these words he charged ahead of the entire right wing, followed by some hundred and twenty picked volunteers from his own battalion.

Between the two lines there was only just enough space to allow the armies to charge. Pompey, however, had previously instructed his men to wait for Caesar's attack without moving from where they were, thus allowing the attackers' formation to become ragged. The object of these tactics – proposed to him, it was said, by Gaius Triarius – was that the initial onslaught and impetus of the charging men should be broken and their line spread out and scattered: at which moment the Pompeians, all in their proper places, would fall upon them. Pompey also hoped that the enemy's javelins would be less effective if his men stayed where they were posted, instead of discharging their own missiles and moving forwards; and that Caesar's men, the length of their charge doubled, would become breathless and exhausted. In our opinion this was a miscalculation by Pompey, since every man possesses by nature a capacity for keenness and enthusiasm: and this capacity is increased by excitement for battle. There is good reason for the ancient customs of a great blare of trumpets and loud

1. South of Durazzo, on the strait of Otranto.

shouting by the whole army; the belief has always been that this in-timidates the enemy and spurs on one's own side.

When the signal was given, our men rushed forward with levelled javelins. But when they saw that the Pompeians were not coming out to meet them, they acted on their experience gained in previous battles, slowed down of their own accord, and finally halted about half-way – in order not to be exhausted when they reached the enemy. Then, after a brief pause, they continued their advance at full speed, launched their javelins, and, as Caesar had ordered, rapidly drew their swords. The Pompeians reacted effectively, parrying the missiles. They bore the shock of the charge without falling out of formation, and then discharged their own javelins and took to their swords. Meanwhile the cavalry on Pompey's left wing, acting on orders, charged in a body, and simultaneously the whole mass of his archers pressed forward. This onslaught was too much for our cavalry, which gradually lost ground and fell back. Whereupon Pompey's cavalry intensified its pressure and, wheeling troop by troop, began to envelop our lines on their exposed flank. When Caesar became aware of this he gave the signal to the six battalions which formed his fourth line. These pressed rapidly forwards, facing the enemy, and charged his cavalry with such ferocity that the entire Pompeian force gave ground, turned about and not merely evacuated their positions but immediately fled at top speed towards the heights. Once they were dislodged, all the archers and slingers, left unprotected and de-fenceless, were slaughtered. Caesar's battalions, continuing their charge, surrounded the enemy left wing, where the Pompeians fought back without leaving their lines; but they were soon taken in the rear.

At this stage Caesar ordered into action his third line, which had so far had nothing to do and had not budged from its position. As these fresh and vigorous troops replaced tired units, the Pompeian in-fantry – which were simultaneously being attacked in the rear – gave way and fled, one and all. Caesar had been right in forecasting that victory would be initiated by the battalions posted in his fourth line opposite the enemy cavalry; indeed he had published this view in his speech of encouragement to his army. For it was they, first of all, who routed Pompey's cavalry, they who massacred his archers and slingers, they who enveloped the enemy's left wing and started the rout.

When Pompey saw his cavalry in flight and realized that the troops on whom he had placed most reliance were demoralized, he lost all confidence in his army, left the field, and rode straight to his camp. There he gave the company commanders, whom he had stationed at the gate nearest the enemy, the following order – loudly, so that the soldiers should hear him: 'Guard the camp – if things go wrong do everything to protect it! I am going round the other gates to encourage the camp garrison.' But after this pronouncement he retired to his tent – waiting pessimistically for the outcome.

When the fleeing Pompeians had been driven inside their rampart, Caesar decided that, panic-stricken as they were, they must be allowed no respite. So he proposed to his men that they should profit by fortune's favours and storm the enemy camp. And they, though weary from the great heat – the battle had lasted until midday – obeyed his orders with an inexhaustible spirit. Pompey's camp was vigorously defended by the battalions left for its protection; and the determination of their Thracian and native auxiliaries considerably exceeded theirs. But the men who had fled from the battlefield were intimidated and tired out. In many cases they had thrown away their weapons and their standards, and their minds were occupied with continuing their flight rather than with defending the camp. Moreover, those stationed along the rampart could no longer stand up to the rain of missiles. After suffering severe wounds, they evacuated their posts, and in no time the entire garrison, under the leadership of its colonels and company commanders, took refuge on some very high hills close to the camp.

There were things to see in Pompey's camp: specially constructed summer-houses, tables laid with massive silver plate, soldiers' tents lined with freshly cut turf; the tents of Lucius Lentulus and others covered with ivy – and many other signs of excessive luxury, and confidence that they were going to win: the elaborate profusion of unnecessary self-indulgences showed that they had felt no fears for the day's outcome. Yet these were the men who sneered at the alleged extravagances of Caesar's wretchedly frugal and long-suffering army, which had unceasingly lacked even the necessities of life.

When our men were already inside the rampart, Pompey took a horse and, removing his general's badges, left his camp by the gate farthest from the enemy, and galloped straight to Larisa. He did not stop there, however, but joining up with a few fugitives from his army proceeded at the same rapid rate – without pausing at night – until, accompanied by thirty cavalrymen, he reached the coast. There he embarked on a corn-ship. He complained incessantly, it was said, that the complete failure of his forecasts almost made him suspect betrayal: for the rout had begun in precisely that part of his army on which he had relied for victory.

MICHAEL GRANT (1956)

SALLUST

GAIUS SALLUSTIUS CRISPUS, born at Amiternum (San Vittorno) in central Italy in 86 B.C., served under Caesar, was made governor of Numidia (north Africa), survived accusations of large-scale embezzlement there, and purchased a magnificent estate in Rome, where he laid out the famous 'Gardens of Sallust'. He died in about 34 B.C. His *Histories*, now almost wholly lost, greatly influenced the rhetorical academies of Silver and later Latin. His two surviving works are the first important Roman historical monographs. One of them, the *Catiline* (or more accurately, *War Against Catiline*), is the story of that impoverished aristocrat's conspiracy in 63 B.C.[1] The other, the *War Against Jugurtha*, is named after the king of Numidia who fought a long war against the Romans (111–106 B.C.). Jugurtha's conqueror was Marius, uncle by marriage to Caesar – and Sallust wrote as Caesar's political partisan.

Despite the real affinities (stressed by Cicero) between Roman historiography and oratory, there was – even in ancient times – an impression that Sallust was closer to the latter than to the former. Yet in the scintillating, calculated ruggedness of his prose, so effective when read aloud, it was widely felt that history in Latin was, for the first time, written in the distinguished style that it deserved. To Martial he seemed 'the first of historians', to the eleventh and twelfth centuries a major source of history and also of ethics. German and French translations date from the fourteenth century, the first printed edition was published at Venice in 1470, and English versions of the *Jugurtha* by A. Barclay and the *Catiline* by T. Paynell appeared in 1520–3 and 1541 respectively. In the same period Erasmus recommended Sallust, rather than Livy or Tacitus, for school reading. Milton took Sallust at his own word as a high moralist; and, anti-Republican though Sallust was, the French Revolutionaries praised his invective against that other kind of anti-Republican, Catiline.

Recent research has sought to determine whether he was more than a mere propagandist. 'A senator's experience endowed him with a keen and unfriendly insight into human behaviour, a flair for hypocrisy and fraudulence'.[2] Marxist schools in Poland are instructed to pay closer attention to him than to any other Roman historian, since he 'throws an interesting light on the morals of a decadent aristocratic class'.

1. For Cicero's version of this, see above p. 53.   2. R. Syme.

Beyond question Fortune holds sway everywhere. It is she that makes all events famous or obscure according to her caprice rather than in accordance with the truth. The acts of the Athenians, in my judgement, were indeed great and glorious enough, but nevertheless somewhat less important than fame represents them. But because Athens produced writers of exceptional talent, the exploits of the men of Athens are heralded throughout the world as unsurpassed. Thus the merit of those who did the deeds is rated as high as brilliant minds have been able to exalt the deeds themselves by words of praise.

But the Roman people never had that advantage, since their ablest men were always most engaged with affairs. Their minds were never employed apart from their bodies. The best citizen preferred action to words, and thought that his own brave deeds should be lauded by others rather than that theirs should be recounted by him.

Accordingly, good morals were cultivated at home and in the field. There was the greatest harmony and little or no avarice. Justice and probity prevailed among them, thanks not so much to laws as to nature. Quarrels, discord, and strife were reserved for their enemies. Citizen vied with citizen only for the prize of merit. They were lavish in their offerings to the gods, frugal in the home, loyal to their friends. By practising these two qualities, boldness in warfare and justice when peace came, they watched over themselves and their country. In proof of these statements I present this convincing evidence: first, in time of war punishment was more often inflicted for attacking the enemy contrary to orders, or for withdrawing too tardily when recalled from the field, than for venturing to abandon the standards or to give ground under stress; and secondly, in time of peace they ruled by kindness rather than fear, and when wronged preferred forgiveness to vengeance.

But when our country had grown great through toil and the practice of justice, when great kings had been vanquished in war, savage tribes and mighty peoples subdued by force of arms, when Carthage, the rival of Rome's sway, had perished utterly, and all seas and lands were open, then Fortune began to grow cruel and to bring confusion into all our affairs. Those who had found it easy to bear hardship and dangers, anxiety and adversity, found leisure and wealth – so desirable under the circumstances – a burden and a curse. Hence the lust for power first, then for money, grew upon them. These were, I may say, the root of all evils. For avarice destroyed honour, integrity, and all other noble qualities; taught in their place insolence, cruelty, to neglect the gods, to set a price on everything. Ambition drove many men to become false; to have one thought locked in the breast, another ready on the tongue; to value friendships and enmities not on their merits but by the standard of self-interest, and to show a good front rather than a good heart. At first these vices grew slowly, from time to time they were punished. Finally, when the disease had spread like a deadly plague, the State was changed and a government second to none in equity and excellence became cruel and intolerable.

But at first men's souls were actuated less by avarice than by ambition – a fault, it is true, but not so far removed from virtue; for the noble and the base alike long for glory, honour, and power, but the former mount by the true path, whereas the latter, being destitute of noble qualities, rely upon craft and deception. Avarice implies a desire for money, which no wise man covets: as though steeped with noxious poisons, it renders the most manly body and soul effeminate. It is ever unbounded and insatiable, nor can either plenty or want make it less. But after Sulla,[1] having gained control of the State by arms, brought everything to a bad end from a good beginning, all men began to rob and pillage. One coveted a house, another lands. The victors showed neither moderation nor restraint, but shamefully and cruelly wronged their fellow citizens. Besides all this, Sulla, in order to secure the loyalty of the army which he led into Asia,[2] had allowed it a luxury and licence foreign to the habits of our forefathers; and in the intervals of leisure those charming and voluptuous lands had easily demoralized the warlike spirit of his soldiers. There it was that an army of the Roman people first learned to indulge in women and drink; to admire statues, paintings, and chased vases, to steal them from private houses and public places, to pillage shrines, and to desecrate everything, both sacred and profane. These soldiers, therefore, after they had won the victory, left nothing to the vanquished. In truth, prosperity tries the souls even of the wise. How then

1. Dictator 81–79 B.C.
2. For the war against King Mithridates of Pontus.

should men of depraved character like these make a moderate use of victory?

As soon as riches came to be held in honour, when glory, political control, and economic power followed in their train, virtue began to lose its lustre, poverty to be considered a disgrace, blamelessness to be termed malevolence. There – as the result of riches – luxury and greed, united with insolence, took possession of our young manhood.

The institution of parties and factions, with all their attendant evils, originated at Rome as the result of peace and of an abundance of everything that mortals prize most highly. For before the destruction of Carthage the people and Senate of Rome together governed the State peacefully and with moderation. There was no strife among the citizens either for glory or for power; fear of the enemy preserved the good morals of the nation. But when the minds of the people were relieved of that dread, wantonness and arrogance naturally arose – vices which are fostered by prosperity. Thus the peace, for which they had longed in time of adversity, after they had gained it proved to be more cruel and bitter than adversity itself. For the nobles began to abuse their position and the people their liberty, and every man for himself robbed, pillaged, and plundered. Thus the community was split into two parties, and between these the State was torn to pieces.

But the nobles had the more powerful organization, while the strength of the commons was less effective because it was uncompact and divided among many. Affairs at home and in the field were managed according to the will of a few men, in whose hands were the treasury, the provinces, public offices, glory and triumphs. The people were burdened with military service and poverty. The generals divided the spoils of war with a few friends. Meanwhile the parents or little children of the soldiers, if they had a powerful neighbour, were driven from their homes. Thus, by the side of power, greed arose – unlimited and unrestrained – violated and devastated everything, respected nothing, and held nothing sacred, until it finally brought about its own downfall. For as soon as nobles were found who preferred true glory to unjust power, the State began to be disturbed and civil dissension to arise like an upheaval of the earth.

For example, when Tiberius and Gaius Gracchus, whose forefathers had added greatly to the power of Rome in the Punic and other wars, began to assert the freedom of the commons and expose the crime of the oligarchs, the nobility, who were guilty, were therefore panic-stricken. They accordingly opposed the acts of the Gracchi, now through the allies and the Latin cities and again through the Knights, whom the hope of an alliance with the Senate had estranged from the commons. And first Tiberius, then a few years later Gaius, who had followed in his brother's footsteps, were slain with the sword,[1] although one was a tribune and the other a commissioner for founding colonies; and with them fell Marcus Fulvius Flaccus. It must be admitted that the Gracchi were so eager for victory that they had not shown a sufficiently moderate spirit; but a good man would prefer to be defeated rather than to triumph over injustice by establishing a bad precedent.

The nobles then abused their victory to gratify their passions; they put many men out of the way by the sword or by banishment, and thus rendered themselves for the future rather dreaded than powerful. It is this spirit which has commonly ruined great nations, when one party desires to triumph over another by any and every means and to avenge itself on the vanquished with excessive cruelty. But if I should attempt to speak of the strife of parties and of the general character of the State in detail or according to the importance of the theme, time would fail me sooner than material.

J. C. ROLFE (1921)[2]

CATILINE

Lucius Catilina, member of a noble family, had great vigour both of mind and of body, but an evil and depraved nature. From youth up he revelled in civil wars, murder, pillage, and political dissension, and amid these he spent his early manhood. His body could endure hunger, cold, and want of sleep to an incredible degree; his mind was reckless, cunning, treacherous, capable of any form of pretence or concealment. Covetous of others' possessions, he was prodigal of his

---

1. In 133 and 122 B.C. respectively. For the Knights, see above, pp. 29, 52.
2. These versions have been very slightly altered, and one or two technicalities removed.

own. He was violent in his passions. He possessed a certain amount of eloquence, but little discretion. His disordered mind ever craved the monstrous, incredible, gigantic.

After the domination of Sulla the man had been seized with a mighty desire of getting control of the government, caring little by what manner he should achieve it, provided he made himself supreme. His haughty spirit was goaded more and more every day by poverty and a sense of guilt, both of which he had augmented by the practices of which I have already spoken. He was spurred on, also, by the corruption of the public morals, which were being ruined by two great evils of an opposite character, extravagance and avarice.

At no other time has the condition of imperial Rome, as it seems to me, been more pitiable. The whole world, from the rising of the sun to its setting, subdued by her arms, rendered obedience to her; at home there was peace and an abundance of wealth, which mortal men deem the greatest of blessings. Yet there were citizens who from sheer perversity were bent upon their own ruin and that of their country. For in spite of the two decrees of the Senate, not one man of all that great number was led by the promised reward to betray the conspiracy, and not a single one deserted Catiline's camp. Such was the potency of the malady which like a plague had infected the minds of many of our countrymen.

This insanity was not confined to those who were implicated in the plot, but the whole body of the commons through desire for change favoured the designs of Catiline. In this very particular they seemed to act as the populace usually does. For in every community those who have no means envy the good, exalt the base, hate what is old and established, long for something new, and from disgust with their own lot desire a general upheaval. Amid turmoil and rebellion they maintain themselves without difficulty, since poverty is easily provided for and can suffer no loss. But the city populace in particular acted with desperation for many reasons. To begin with, all who were especially conspicuous for their shamelessness and impudence, those too who had squandered their patrimony in riotous living, finally all whom disgrace or crime had forced to leave home, had all flowed into Rome as into a cesspool. Many, too, recalled Sulla's victory. They had seen common soldiers risen to the rank of senator, and others become so rich that they feasted and lived like kings, and now every man hoped that his fruits of victory would be the same, if he took the field. Besides this the young men who had maintained a wretched existence by manual labour in the country, tempted by governmental and private aid had come to prefer idleness in the city to their hateful toil; these, like all the others, profited while the nation suffered. Therefore it is not surprising that men who were beggars and without character, with illimitable hopes, should respect their country as little as they respected themselves. Moreover, those to whom Sulla's victory had meant the proscription of their parents, loss of property, and curtailment of their rights, looked forward in a similar spirit to the issue of a war. Finally, all who belonged to another party than that of the Senate preferred to see the government overthrown rather than be out of power themselves.

Such, then, was the evil which after many years had returned upon the State.

J. C. ROLFE (1921)

CATO AND CAESAR

When I read and heard of the many illustrious deeds of the Roman people at home and abroad, on land and sea, I was seized by a strong desire of finding out what quality in particular had been the foundation of so great exploits. I knew that often with a handful of men they had encountered great armies of the enemy. I was aware that with small resources they had waged wars with mighty kings; also that they had often experienced the cruelty of Fortune; that the Romans had been surpassed by the Greeks in eloquence and by the Gauls in warlike glory. After long reflection I became convinced that it had all been accomplished by the eminent merit of a few citizens; that it was due to them that poverty had triumphed over riches, and a few over a multitude. But after the State had become demoralized by extravagance and sloth, it was the commonwealth in its turn that was enabled by its greatness to sustain the shortcomings of its generals and magistrates, and for a long time, as when a mother is exhausted by child-bearing, no one at all was produced at Rome who was great in merit. But within my own memory there have appeared two men of towering merit, though of diverse character, Marcus Cato and Gaius Caesar. Since the occasion has presented itself, it is not my intention to pass these men by in silence, or fail to give, to the best of my ability, an account of their disposition and character.

In birth then, in years and in eloquence, they were about equal; in greatness of soul they were evenly matched, and likewise in renown, although the renown of each was different. Caesar was held great because of his benefactions and lavish generosity, Cato for the uprightness of his life. The former became famous for his gentleness and compassion, the austerity of the latter had brought him prestige. Caesar gained glory by giving, helping, and forgiving; Cato by never stooping to bribery. One was a refuge for the unfortunate, the other a scourge for the wicked. The good nature of the one was applauded, the steadfastness of the other. Finally, Caesar had schooled himself to work hard and sleep little, to devote himself to the welfare of his friends and neglect his own, to refuse nothing which was worth the giving. He longed for great power, an army, a new war to give scope for his brilliant merit. Cato, on the contrary, cultivated self-control, propriety, but above all austerity. He did not vie with the rich in riches nor in intrigue with the intriguer, but with the active in good works, with the self-restrained in moderation, with the blameless in integrity. He preferred to be, rather than to seem, virtuous; the less, therefore, that he sought fame, the more it pursued him.

J. C. Rolfe (1921)

PART II

THE AUGUSTANS

VIRGIL

PUBLIUS VERGILIUS MARO, born on a farm at Andes near Mantua in 70 B.C.; educated at Cremona, Milan, and Rome. His townsmen, and perhaps his own family, lost their land in the Civil Wars. Subsequently Virgil lived at Naples. He died at Brundusium (Brindisi) in 19 B.C.[1]

The ten pastoral *Eclogues*, written 42–37 B.C., are set in a golden Arcadia and inspired by the more realistic Greek bucolic poetry of Theocritus, whose Romanizer Virgil claimed to be. The impact of the *Eclogues* on Roman culture was great and immediate. In late antiquity and the Middle Ages the Fourth Eclogue, foretelling the birth of a (variously identified) child, created the widespread Messianic belief – shared by Constantine the Great – that Virgil was prophesying the birth of Christ: he was celebrated in churches as the Prophet of the Gentiles. The twelfth-century *trouvères* had their *pastourelle*. After Virgil's works had been printed at Rome in about 1469, Italian translations of the *Eclogues* began to appear (from 1481), and within the next century this and other classical traditions were blended with new forms and feelings to produce the first of many *Arcadias* by Jacopo Sannazaro (1504–14) and the Italian pastoral drama. Sir Philip Sidney adapted Sannazaro, and George Turberville (soon followed by others) translated the *Eclogues* into English in 1567. Spenser's *Shepheard's Calendar* (1579) is divided into twelve 'Eclogues', one for each month. The pastoral tradition is strong in Milton's *L'Allegro*, *Il Penseroso*, and *Comus*, and Virgil's farewell to the *genre* is echoed in *Lycidas*. In the two centuries that followed, Arcadia had countless manifestations in many media; Alexander Pope's early pastoral poems are especially sensitive to the Virgilian tradition.

In *The Princess*, Tennyson means to reveal his debt to the Virgilian pastoral:

> So waste not thou: but come: for all the vales
> Await thee: azure pillars of the hearth
> Arise to thee: the children call, and I
> Thy shepherd pipe, and sweet is every sound,

1. He died after a visit to Greece as a prelude to philosophical work – in which he had also, reputedly, been engaged in early life. A collection of poems known as the *Appendix Vergiliana* may include short specimens of his youthful writings.

> Sweeter thy voice, but every sound is sweet;
> Myriads of rivulets hurrying through the lawn,
> The moan of doves in immemorial elms,
> And murmuring of innumerable bees.

Even today, echoes of the pastoral tradition have been detected in Mallarmé's *Après-midi d'un Faune* (1865–76), Debussy's *Prélude*, Nijinsky's ballet on the same theme, and Picasso's *Joy of Life*. Louis MacNeice chose to entitle his longer poems of the 1930s the *Eclogues*.

The four Georgics (*c.* 36–29 B.C.) were written in praise of the Italian countryside – at the request, Virgil tells us, of his patron and friend Maecenas, who had introduced him to Octavian, soon to be called Augustus. The *Georgics* are cast in a familiar didactic form owing debts to Hesiod, the Alexandrians, and Lucretius. But this is no true didactic, no sequel to Varro's recent text-book for farmers; it is a new sort of descriptive poetry, glorifying the land of Italy.

> Virgil – a tall man, dark and countrified
> In looks, they say: retiring: no rhetorician:
> Of humble birth: a Celt, whose first ambition
> Was to be a philosopher: Dante's guide.
> But chiefly dear for his gift to understand
> Earth's intricate, ordered heart, and for a vision
> That saw beyond an imperial day the hand
> Of man no longer armed against his fellow
> But all for vine and cattle, fruit and fallow,
> Subduing with love's positive force the land.[1]

Numerous translations of the *Georgics* appeared during the sixteenth century – including, finally, the first English version (1589, by A. Fleming). The *Georgics* were Montaigne's favourite reading, and Dryden called them 'the best poem of the best poet'. The innumerable eighteenth-century adaptations included James Thomson's *Seasons*; and Cowper too, in his way, expresses part of the spirit of the *Georgics*. The Pyrenees moved Francis Jammes to *Les Géorgiques Chrétiennes* (1911), and in America Robert Frost has inspired Virgilian comparisons.

The *Aeneid* (published in twelve books, not wholly complete, after Virgil's death) has, for all its overwhelming reputation, often suffered from

---

1. One of the *Dedicatory Stanzas* of Cecil Day Lewis's translation. Virgil *may* have been partly Celtic; but his racial ingredients, like those of most other Latin writers, are wholly uncertain, and were almost certainly mixed.

inevitable but misleading comparisons with the *Odyssey* and the *Iliad*, of which it combines the themes. But it is the product of a society utterly remote from Homer's and even remoter from the societies Homer is describing; and the *Aeneid* is intended not for singing, but for reading aloud and reading silently. It owes much to the Hellenistic romantic epic of Apollonius Rhodius (librarian at Alexandria), much also to earlier Roman national epics of Naevius and Ennius, and to innumerable other sources – but far more to the astounding talent of Virgil. Already in ancient times he had become, to an extent almost beyond description, linguistic and metrical model, spiritual leader and oracle – and a great crop of learned commentators had sprung up around his poems.

'When I should have been weeping for my own sins,' said St Augustine, 'I wept for Dido.' Virgil's fabulous and unceasing fame was a dominant factor in medieval culture. Educated people venerated him incessantly and unreservedly; and the legends and folk-lore of thousands of superstitious men and women – who knew no Latin or any other letters – made him a superhuman sage, an astrologer and a magician. To Dante, whom he guides to the underworld as the Sibyl had guided Aeneas, he is supreme *maestro* and creator of *lo bello stile*.

The *Aeneid* was foremost in the great Tudor output of translations.[1] Gawain Douglas' Scottish version was finished in 1513 and published in 1553; within a further decade the Earl of Surrey had translated Books II and IV, and Thomas Phaer the whole poem. Scaliger (1561) much preferred Virgil to Homer. Ronsard did not complete *La Franciade* (1572); no French Virgilian epic has ever come to fruition. But Milton owed an immeasurable debt to the beautiful, sonorous, complex rhythmical patterns of the *Aeneid*.

In Wordsworth's

> sense sublime
> Of something far more deeply interfused

is mirrored the philosophical vision of Anchises at the centre of the *Aeneid*. Tennyson, too, invokes the same vision:

> Thou that seest Universal
> Nature moved by Universal Mind;
> Thou majestic in thy sadness
> At the doubtful doom of human kind;

1. There had already been Spanish and Italian translations (1428, 1476) and a French paraphrase (before 1483).

Light among the vanished ages;
　　Star that gildest yet this phantom shore;
Golden branch among the shadows,
　　Kings and realms that pass to rise no more.

In the twentieth century it is often asked: can State patronage be good for poetry? But a great gulf seems to be fixed between modern performances, under such auspices, and Virgil's awe-inspiring *Aeneid*. Yet, State-encouraged though it undoubtedly was, 'the things he really understands', as E. M. Forster says, 'are not heroic – the dancing reflection of water on a ceiling, the whizz of tops in a courtyard, the departure of Colours at nightfall, sea that trembles under the moon, the poor woman who must rise early, the sufferings of animals and flowers. ...'

THE ECLOGUES

THE SONG OF SILENUS

Proceed, my Muse!

           Two satyrs, on the ground,
Stretched at his ease their sire Silenus found.
Dosed with his fumes, and heavy with his load,
They found him snoring in his dark abode,
And seized with youthful arms the drunken god.
His rosy wreath was dropped not long before,
Borne by the tide of wine, and floating on the floor.
His empty can, with ears half worn away,
Was hung on high, to boast the triumph of the day.
Invaded thus, for want of better bands,
His garland they unstring, and bind his hands:
For, by the fraudful god deluded long,
They now resolve to have their promised song.
Aegle came in, to make their party good,
The fairest Naïs of the neighbouring flood,
And, while he stares around with stupid eyes,
His brows with berries, and his temples, dyes.
He finds the fraud, and, with a smile, demands
On what design the boys had bound his hands.
'Loose me!' he cried: ' 'twas impudence to find
A sleeping god; 'tis sacrilege to bind.
To you the promised poem I will pay;
The nymph shall be rewarded in her way.'
He raised his voice; and soon a numerous throng
Of tripping satyrs crowded to the song;
And sylvan fauns, and savage beasts, advanced;
And nodding forests to the numbers danced.
Not by Haemonian hills the Thracian bard,
Nor awful Phoebus, was on Pindus heard
With deeper silence or with more regard.
  He sung the secret seeds of nature's frame;

How seas, and earth, and air, and active flame,
Fell through the mighty void, and, in their fall,
Were blindly gathered in this goodly ball.
The tender soil then, stiffening by degrees,
Shut from the bounded earth the bounding seas.
Then earth and ocean various forms disclose,
And a new sun to the new world arose;
And mists, condensed to clouds, obscure the sky;
And clouds, dissolved, the thirsty ground supply.
The rising trees the lofty mountains grace:
The lofty mountains feed the savage race,
Yet few, and strangers, in the unpeopled place.
From thence the birth of man the song pursued,
And how the world was lost, and how renewed:
The reign of Saturn, and the Golden Age;
Prometheus' theft, and Jove's avenging rage:
The cries of Argonauts for Hylas drowned,
With whose repeated name the shores resound . . . .

He sung the lover's fraud; the longing maid,
With golden fruit, like all the sex, betrayed;
The sisters mourning for their brother's loss;
Their bodies hid in bark, and furred with moss:
How each a rising alder now appears,
And o'er the Po distils her gummy tears:[1]
Then sung how Gallus,[2] by a Muse's hand,
Was led and welcomed to the sacred strand,
The Senate rising to salute their guest;
And Linus thus their gratitude expressed:
'Receive this present, by the Muses made,
The pipe on which the Ascraean pastor [3] played;
With which of old he charmed the savage train,
And called the mountain ashes to the plain.

1. The 'longing maid' is Atalanta, who lost the race (and so her freedom) to Milanion because she stopped to pick up the golden apples he dropped. The sisters wept for their brother Phaethon (see below, p. 261) until they were turned into alders (or poplars).
2. A friend of Virgil, and the reputed founder of Latin elegiac poetry.
3. Hesiod.

Sing thou, on this, thy Phoebus; and the wood
Where once his fane of Parian marble stood:
On this his ancient oracles rehearse;
And with new numbers grace the god of verse.'
Why should I sing the double Scylla's fate? [1]
The first by love transformed, the last by hate –
A beauteous maid above; but magic arts
With barking dogs deformed her nether parts:
What vengeance on the passing fleet she poured,
The master frighted and the mates devoured,
Then ravished Philomel the song expressed: [2]
The crime revealed; the sisters' cruel feast;
And how in fields the lapwing Tereus reigns,
The warbling nightingale in woods complains;
While Procne makes on chimney-tops her moan,
And hovers o'er the palace once her own.
Whatever songs besides the Delphian god
Had taught the laurels, and the Spartan flood,
Silenus sung: the vales his voice rebound,
And carry to the skies the sacred sound.

And now the setting sun had warned the swain
To call his counted cattle from the plain;
Yet still the unwearied sire pursues the tuneful strain,
Till, unperceived, the heavens with stars were hung,
And sudden night surprised the yet unfinished song.

JOHN DRYDEN (1697)

1. The monster opposite Charybdis in the Straits of Messina, and Scylla daughter of Nisus king of Megara who killed her father and was changed into a bird.

2. Philomela, to revenge herself on her husband Tereus for having also married her sister Procne, served up to him her own son Itys at a feast. Tereus was then transformed into a hoopoe, Philomela into a nightingale, and Procne into a swallow (in earlier accounts their fates were reversed).

THE BIRTH OF THE SAVIOUR [1]

Muses of Sicily, let us attempt a rather more exalted theme. Hedge-row and humble tamarisk do not appeal to all. If we must sing of woodlands, let them be such as may do a Consul honour.

We have reached the last Era in Sibylline song. Time has conceived and the great Sequence of the Ages starts afresh. Justice, the Virgin, comes back to dwell with us, and the rule of Saturn is restored. The Firstborn of the New Age is already on his way from high heaven down to earth.

With him, the Iron Race shall end and Golden Man inherit all the world. Smile on the Baby's birth, immaculate Lucina; your own Apollo is enthroned at last.

And it is in your consulship, yours, Pollio,[2] that this glorious Age will dawn and the Procession of the great Months begin. Under your leadership all traces that remain of our iniquity will be effaced and, as they vanish, free the world from its long night of horror.

He will foregather with the gods; he will see the great men of the past consorting with them, and be himself observed by these, guiding a world to which his father's virtues have brought peace.

Free-roaming ivy, foxgloves in every dell, and smiling acanthus mingled with Egyptian lilies – these, little one, are the first modest gifts that earth, unprompted by the hoe, will lavish on you. The goats, unshepherded, will make for home with udders full of milk, and the ox will not be frightened of the lion, for all his might. Your very cradle will adorn itself with blossoms to caress you. The snake will come to grief, and poison lurk no more in the weed. Perfumes of Assyria will breathe from every hedge.

Later, when you have learnt to read the praises of the great and what your father achieved, and come to understand what manhood

1. This is the poem which, as mentioned in the Introduction to Virgil, caused many early and medieval Christians to believe that the poet was prophesying the birth of Christ. But, at the time when he was writing, the wives both of Antony and Octavian were pregnant (though neither child proved to be a boy).

2. Gaius Asinius Pollio, historian, statesman, and patron of letters (and perhaps of Virgil) was consul in 40 B.C. and negotiated the Treaty of Brundisium between Antony and Octavian, which greatly raised hopes of world peace and a new Golden Age.

is, the waving corn will slowly flood the plains with gold, grapes hang in ruby clusters on the neglected thorn, and honeydew exude from the hard trunk of the oak.

Even so, faint traces of our former wickedness will linger on, to make us venture on the sea in ships, build walls around our cities, and plough the soil. With a new Tiphys at the helm, a second Argo will set out, manned by a picked heroic crew. Wars even will repeat themselves and the great Achilles be dispatched to Troy once more.

Later again, when the strengthening years have made a man of you, even the trader will forsake the sea, and pine-wood ships will cease to carry merchandise for barter, each land producing all its needs. No mattock will molest the soil, no pruning-knife the vine; and then at last the sturdy ploughman will free his oxen from the yoke. Wool will be taught no more to cheat the eye with this tint or with that, but the ram himself in his own meadows will change the colour of his fleece, now to the soft glow of a purple dye, now to a saffron yellow. Lambs at their pastures will find themselves in scarlet coats.

The Fates have spoken, in concord with the unalterable decree of destiny. 'Run, spindles,' they have said. 'This is the pattern of the age to come.'

Enter – for the hour is close at hand – on your illustrious career, dear child of the gods, great increment of Jove. Look at the world, rocked by the weight of its overhanging dome; look at the lands, the far-flung seas and the unfathomable sky. See how the whole creation rejoices in the age that is to be!

Ah, if the last days of my life could only be prolonged, and breath enough remain for me to chronicle your acts, then neither Thracian Orpheus nor Linus could out-sing me, not though the one had his mother and the other had his father at his side, Orpheus, his Calliope, and Linus, Apollo in all his beauty. If Pan himself, with Arcady for judge, were to contend with me, the great god Pan, with Arcady for judge, would own defeat.

Begin, then, little boy, to greet your mother with a smile: the ten long months have left her sick at heart. Begin, little boy: no one who has not given his mother a smile has ever been thought worthy of his table by a god, or by a goddess of her bed.

E. V. RIEU (1949)

THE GEORGICS

RUSTIC HAPPINESS

Ye sacred Muses! with whose beauty fired,
My soul is ravished, and my brain inspired –
Whose priest I am, whose holy fillets wear –
Would you your poet's first petition hear;
Give me the ways of wandering stars to know,
The depths of heaven above, and earth below:
Teach me the various labours of the moon,
And whence proceed the eclipses of the sun;
Why flowing tides prevail upon the main,
And in what dark recess they shrink again;
What shakes the solid earth; what cause delays
The summer nights, and shortens winter days.
But, if my heavy blood restrain the flight
Of my free soul, aspiring to the height
Of Nature, and unclouded fields of light –
My next desire is, void of care and strife,
To lead a soft, secure, inglorious life –
A country cottage near a crystal flood,
A winding valley, and a lofty wood.
Some god conduct me to the sacred shades,
Where Bacchanals are sung by Spartan maids,
Or lift me high to Haemus' hilly crown,
Or in the plains of Tempè lay me down,
Or lead me to some solitary place,
And cover my retreat from human race.
Happy the man [1] who, studying Nature's laws,
Through known effects can trace the secret cause –
His mind possessing in a quiet state,
Fearless of Fortune, and resigned to Fate!
And happy too is he, who decks the bowers
    Of sylvans, and adores the rural powers –
Whose mind unmoved the bribes of courts can see,

1. Virgil is thought by some to mean Lucretius.

Their glittering baits, and purple slavery –
Nor hopes the people's praise, nor fears their frown,
Nor, when contending kindred tear the crown,
Will set up one, or pull another down.
 Without concern he hears, but hears from far,
Of tumults, and descents, and distant war;
Nor with a superstitious fear is awed
For what befalls at home, or what abroad;
Nor his own peace disturbs with pity for the poor:
Nor envies he the rich their happy store.
He feeds on fruits which, of their own accord,
The willing ground and laden trees afford.
From his loved home no lucre him can draw;
The Senate's mad decrees he never saw;
Nor heard, at bawling bars, corrupted law.
Some to the seas, and some to camps, resort,
And some with impudence invade the court:
In foreign countries others seek renown;
With wars and taxes, others waste their own,
And houses burn, and household gods deface,
To drink in bowls which glittering gems enchase,
To loll on couches, rich with citron steads,
And lay their guilty limbs in Tyrian beds.
This wretch in earth entombs his golden ore,
Hovering and brooding on his buried store.
Some patriot fools to popular praise aspire
Of public speeches, which worse fools admire,
While, from both benches, with redoubled sounds,
The applause of lords and commoners abounds.
Some, through ambition, or through thirst of gold,
Have slain their brothers, or their country sold,
And, leaving their sweet homes, in exile run
To lands that lie beneath another sun.
 The peasant, innocent of all these ills,
With crooked plough the fertile fallows tills,
And the round year with daily labour fills.
And hence the country markets are supplied:
Enough remains for household charge beside,

His wife and tender children to sustain,
And gratefully to feed his dumb deserving train.
Nor cease his labours till the yellow field
A full return of bearded harvest yield –
A crop so plenteous as the land to load,
O'ercome the crowded barns, and lodge on ricks abroad.

   Thus every several season is employed,
Some spent in toil, and some in ease enjoyed.
The yeaning ewes prevent the springing year;
The laden boughs their fruits in autumn bear:
'Tis then the vine her liquid harvest yields,
Baked in the sunshine of ascending fields.
The winter comes; and then the falling mast
For greedy swine provides a full repast:
Then olives, ground in mills, their fatness boast,
And winter fruits are mellowed by the frost.
His cares are eased with intervals of bliss;
His little children, climbing for a kiss,
Welcome their father's late return at night;
His faithful bed is crowned with chaste delight.
His kine with swelling udders ready stand,
And, lowing for the pail, invite the milker's hand.
His wanton kids, with budding horns prepared,
Fight harmless battles in his homely yard:
Himself, in rustic pomp, on holidays,
To rural powers a just oblation pays,
And on the green his careless limbs displays.
The hearth is in the midst; the herdsmen, round
The cheerful fire, provoke his health in goblets crowned.
He calls on Bacchus, and propounds the prize;
The groom his fellow-groom at butts defies,
And bends his bow, and levels with his eyes;
Or, stript for wrestling, smears his limbs with oil,
And watches, with a trip his foe to foil.

   Such was the life the frugal Sabines led;
So Remus and his brother-god were bred,
From whom the austere Etrurian virtue rose;
And this rude life our homely fathers chose.

Old Rome from such a race derived her birth,
(The seat of empire and the conquered earth,)
Which now on seven high hills triumphant reigns,
And in that compass all the world contains.
Ere Saturn's rebel son usurped the skies,
When beasts were only slain for sacrifice,
While peaceful Crete enjoyed her ancient lord,
Ere sounding hammers forged the inhuman sword,
Ere hollow drums were beat, before the breath
Of brazen trumpets rung the peals of death,
The good old god his hunger did assuage
With roots and herbs, and gave the Golden Age.

JOHN DRYDEN (1697)

THE BEES

Next I come to the manna, the heavenly gift of honey.
Look kindly on this part too, my friend. I'll tell of a tiny
Republic that makes a show well worth your admiration –
Great-hearted leaders, a whole nation whose work is planned,
Their morals, groups, defences – I'll tell you in due order.
A featherweight theme: but one that can load me with fame, if only
No wicked fairy cross me, and the Song-god come to my call.
    For a start you must find your bees a suitable home, a position
Sheltered from wind (for wind will stop them carrying home
Their forage), a close where sheep nor goats come butting in
To jump on the flowers, nor blundering heifer stray to flick
The dew from the meadow and stamp its springing grasses down.
Discourage the lizard, too, with his lapis-lazuli back,
From their rich folds, the bee-eater and other birds,
And the swallow whose breast was blooded once by a killer's hand:
For these wreak wholesale havoc, snap up your bees on the wing
And bear them off as a tit-bit for their ungentle nestlings.
But mind there's a bubbling spring nearby, a pool moss-bordered,
And a rill ghosting through the grass:
See, too, that a palm or tall oleaster shadow the entrance,

For thus, when the new queens lead out the earliest swarms –
The spring all theirs – and the young bees play, from hive un-
  prisoned,
The bank may be handy to welcome them in out of the heat
And the tree meet them half-way and make them at home in its
  foliage.
Whether the water flows or is stagnant, fling in the middle
Willow boughs criss-cross and big stones,
That the bees may have plenty of bridges to stand on and dry their
  wings
At the summer sun, in case a shower has caught them loitering
Or a gust of east wind ducked them suddenly in the water.
Green spurge-laurel should grow round about, wild thyme that
  perfumes
The air, masses of savory rich-breathing, and violet beds
Sucking the channelled stream.
   Now for the hive itself. Remember, whether you make it
By stitching concave bark or weaving tough withies together,
To give it a narrow doorway: for winter grips and freezes
The honey, and summer's melting heat runs it off to waste.
Either extreme is feared by the bees. It is not for fun
That they're so keen on caulking with wax the draughty chinks
In their roof, and stuff the rim of their hive with flowery pollen,
Storing up for this very job a glue they have gathered
Stickier than bird-lime or pitch from Anatolia.
Often too, if reports are true, they dig deep shelters
Underground and keep house there, or out of the way are found
In a sandstone hollow or the heart of a rotten tree.
None the less, you should smear with smooth mud their chinky
  chambers
Solicitously for warmth, and lay a thin dressing of leaves.
Don't have a yew too close to their house, or burn in a brazier
Reddening crab-shells: never risk them near a bog,
Or where there's a stink of mud, or a rock formation echoes
Hollow when struck and returns your voice like a ghostly reflection.
   For the rest, when the golden sun has driven winter to ground
And opened up all the leagues of the sky in summer light,
Over the glades and woodlands at once they love to wander

And suck the shining flowers and delicate sip the streams.
Sweet then is their strange delight
As they cherish their children, their nestlings: then with craftsmanship they
Hammer out the fresh wax and mould the tacky honey.
Then, as you watch the swarm bursting from hive and heavenward
Soaring, and floating there on the limpid air of summer –
A vague and wind-warped column of cloud to your wondering eyes: –
Notice them, how they always make for fresh water and leafy
Shelter. Here you shall sprinkle fragrances to their taste –
Crushed balm, honeywort humble –
Make a tinkling noise round about and clash the Mother-god's cymbals.
They will settle down of their own accord in the place you have perfumed,
And crawl to the innermost room for rest, as their custom is.
   But now, suppose they have sallied to battle: for between
Two queens there often arises trouble that comes to war.
At once, from afar, forewarned you will be of the mob's anger,
Their hearts spoiling for a fight:
Martial, a brazen harshness, a roar rebuking the laggard
You hear, and a cry that is like the abrupt blasts of a trumpet.
Then, all agog, their wings quivering, they come together,
Stings are sharpened on beaks, sinews braced for action,
And around the queen in their hordes, right up to the queen's head-quarters
They demonstrate, they challenge the foe with fearsome shouts.
So, on a dry spring day, when the sky's prairies are open,
They deploy from their gates, they charge together, in heaven's height
There's a din; they meet and scrimmage, forming a monster ball, and
Headlong they tumble down, thicker than hail in the air
Or a shower of acorns raining down from a shaken oak.
Illustrious of wing, through the battle-line the monarchs
Move, vast passions agitating their little breasts,
Obstinate not to give in till superior weight of numbers
Has forced one side or the other to turn their backs in flight.

And all these epic battles and turbulent hearts you can silence
By flinging a handful of dust.

    But, when you have recalled both the leaders from combat,
The one that appears worsted you must kill, lest she prove a waste
And a nuisance, and let the winner be absolute in the kingdom.
The one will be all aglow in golden-patined mail –
Two kinds there are – this one is the better, taking the eye
With her form and the flash of her shining scales; that other is shaggy
From laziness, a low and pot-bellied crawler, a bad lot.
As the two queens differ in aspect, so in physique their subjects.
For some are unkempt and squalid, like a traveller when he comes
Athirst off a dusty road and spits the grit from his dry mouth;
While others gleam and glitter,
Their bodies perfectly marked in a pattern of shining gold.
These are the better breed: from these at the right season
Sweet honey you'll get – not sweet so much as pure, and fit
To soften your wine's harsh flavour.
But when the swarms fly aimlessly and sport in the sky,
Looking down on their combs, leaving the hives to cool,
You must put a stop to this empty and irresponsible play.
It is not hard to stop.
Tear off the wings of their queens: while these wait on the ground,
No bee will dare to leave his base or take off for a flight.
Let gardens breathing a scent of yellow flowers allure them:
Let the god of gardens, who watches for birds and robbers, keep them
Safe with his hook of willow.
The bee-keeper for his part should fetch down thyme and pine
From the hills above, and plant them broadly around the bees' home:
His hands should grow work-hardened, bedding the soil with fertile
Shoots, watering them well.

    Indeed, were it not that already my work has made its landfall
And I shorten sail and eagerly steer for the harbour mouth,
I'd sing perhaps of rich gardens, their planning and cultivation,
The rose beds of Paestum that blossom twice in a year,
The way endive rejoices to drink from a rivulet,
The bank all green with celery, the cucumber snaking
Amid the grass and swelling to greatness: I'd not forget
Late-flowering narcissus or gum-arabic's ringlet shoots,

Pale ivy, shore-loving myrtle.
I remember once beneath the battlements of Oebalia,
Where dark Galaesus waters the golden fields of corn,
I saw an old man, a Corycian, who owned a few poor acres
Of land once derelict, useless for arable,
No good for grazing, unfit for the cultivation of vines.
But he laid out a kitchen garden in rows amid the brushwood,
Bordering it with white lilies, verbena, small-seeded poppy.
He was happy there as a king. He could go indoors at night
To a table heaped with dainties he never had to buy.
His the first rose of spring, the earliest apples in autumn:
And when grim winter still was splitting the rocks with cold
And holding the watercourses with curb of ice, already
That man would be cutting his soft-haired hyacinths, complaining
Of summer's backwardness and the west winds slow to come.
His bees were the first to breed,
Enriching him with huge swarms: he squeezed the frothy honey
Before anyone else from the combs: he had limes and a wealth of pine
     trees:
And all the early blossom, that clothed his trees with promise
Of an apple crop, by autumn had come to maturity.
He had a gift, too, for transplanting in rows the far-grown elm,
The hardwood pear, the blackthorn bearing its weight of sloes,
And the plane that already offered a pleasant shade for drinking.
But these are matters the strict scope of my theme forbids me:
I must pass them by, and leave them for later men to enlarge on.

   Well then, let me speak of the natural gifts that God himself
Bestowed on the bees, their reward
For obeying the charms – the chorus and clashing brass of the priests –
And feeding the king of heaven when he hid in that Cretan cave.
They alone have their children in common, a city united
Beneath one roof and a life under established laws:
They know a native country, are sure of hearth and home.
Aware that winter is coming, they use the summer days
For work, and put their winnings into a common pool.
Some are employed in getting food, and by fixed agreement
Work on the fields: some stay within their fenced abode,
With tear of daffodil and gummy resin of tree-bark

Laying the first foundation of the honeycomb, then hanging
The stickfast wax: others bring up the young bees, the hope
Of their people: others press
The pure honey and cram the cells with that crystal nectar.
Some, allotted the duty of sentry-go at the gates,
Keep an eye out for showers and a sign of clouds in heaven,
Relieve incoming bees of their burden, or closing ranks
Shoo the drones – that work-shy gang – away from the bee-folds.
The work goes on like wildfire, the honey smells of thyme.
Thus when the Blacksmith Giants work double shifts to forge
Thunderbolts out of the stubborn ore, some ply the bellows
Of bull-skin, and others plunge the hissing metal in troughs:
And while Mount Aetna moans beneath their anvils' stress
They raise their arms with the powerful alternate rhythm of cranks,
They keep the iron turning in the close grip of their tongs.
So, to compare small things
With great, an inborn love of possession impels the bees
Each to his own office. The old are the town's wardens,
Who wall the honeycombs and frame the intricate houses.
Tired, as the night deepens, the young return from labour,
Their legs laden with thyme: they feed afar on the arbute,
The silvery willow, the spurge-laurel, the fire-blush saffron,
The lime blossom so rich, the rust-red martagon lily.
For one and all one work-time, and a like rest from work.
At morning they hurry from the hives, all helter-skelter: again,
When the Evening Star has told them to leave their meadow pasture,
They make for home, they refresh themselves. What a murmuring
You hear as they drone around their policies and doorsteps!
Later, they settle down in their cells for the night, a silence
Falls, a drowsy fatigue falls.
If rain threatens, be sure they'll not roam too far afield
From their hives: they mistrust the sky, should an east wind be due:
At such times safely beneath the walls of their town they forage
Around, making brief excursions, and often carry some ballast,
As dinghies do to stiffen them in a high sea – they lift
Wee stones, and with these they weather the cloud-tossed solitudes.
    Most you shall marvel at this habit peculiar to bees –
That they have no sexual union: their bodies never dissolve

Lax into love, nor bear with pangs of birth their young.
But all by themselves from leaves and sweet herbs they will gather
Their children in their mouths, keep up the queenly succession
And the birth-rate, restore the halls and the realm of wax.
Often, too, as they wander they bruise their wings on hard
Rocks, happy to die in harness beneath their burdens –
Such is their love for flowers, their pride in producing honey.
Though short their course of life, and death may catch them early,
(Seven summers they have at most,)
The race remains immortal, for many years survive
The family fortunes, their fathers are known to the fourth generation.
Besides, they esteem royalty more than Egypt does or enormous
Lydia even, or the peoples of Parthia, or the Mede by Hydaspes.
Let the queen be safe – they are bound by a single faith and purpose:
Lose her – then unity's gone, and they loot the honey cells
They built themselves, and break down the honeycomb's withy wall.
Guardian of all their works she is. They hold her in awe.
Thick is their humming murmur as they crowd around her and mob
      her.
Often they chair her shoulder high: and in war they shelter
Her body with theirs, desiring the wounds of a noble death.
    Influenced by these signs and images, some have said
That bees partake of an Essence Divine and drink Heaven's well-
      springs.
For God (they hold) pervades
All lands, the widespread seas, the abysms of unplumbed sky:
From Whom flocks, herds, men, every wild creature in its kind
Derive at birth the slight, precarious breath of life:
To Him, therefore, all things return at last and in Him
Are re-absorbed – no room for death – and they soar to join
The stars' immortal muster, and reach the heights of heaven.
    If ever you wish to unseal the treasure-vaults of their palace
Where the honey's hoarded, first sprinkle yourself with water,
Rinse your mouth, and release a smoke to chivvy them out.
Twice a year men gather their harvest and heavy produce: –
As soon as Taygete the Pleiad has turned her handsome
Face to the earth and spurned with her foot the repulsed ocean;
Or again when, fleeing the star of the rainy Fish, she goes

Gloomily down the sky and is drowned in a winter sea.
Unbounded then is the rage of the bees, provoked they breathe
Venom into their stabs, they cling to your veins and bury
Their stings – oh yes, they put their whole souls into the wound.
But if you fear a hard winter for them and wish to provide for
The future, pitying their bruised spirits and bankrupt estate,
Even then you should trouble to fumigate with thyme
And cut back the empty cells. For often the newt unnoticed
Nibbles the combs, their cubicles are black with light-shunning
    beetles,
And the drone gate-crashes their dinner:
There's the assassin hornet who, heavier armed than they,
Mixes it: there's the sinister tribe of moths: and Minerva's
Bugbear, the spider, draping his slack nets over the doorway.
But the more exhausted the bees, the keener they'll be to mend
The wreck of their ruined state,
Re-stock the store-rooms and fashion the flowery granaries.

CECIL DAY LEWIS (1940)

ORPHEUS AND EURYDICE

         She never saw,
Poor girl, her death there, deep in the grass before her feet –
The watcher on the river-bank, the savage watersnake.
The band of wood-nymphs, her companions, filled with their crying
The hilltops: wailed the peaks of Rhodope: high Pangaea,
The unwarlike land of Rhesus,
The Getae lamented, and Hebrus, and Attic Orithyia.
Orpheus, sick to the heart, sought comfort of his hollow lyre:
You, sweet wife, he sang alone on the lonely shore,
You at the dawn of day he sang, at day's decline you.
The gorge of Taenarus even, deep gate of the Underworld,
He entered, and that grove where fear hangs like a black fog:
Approached the ghostly people, approached the King of Terrors
And the hearts that know not how to be touched by human prayer.
But, by his song aroused from Hell's nethermost basements,
Flocked out the flimsy shades, the phantoms lost to light,

In number like to the millions of birds that hide in the leaves
When evening or winter rain from the hills had driven them –
Mothers and men, the dead
Bodies of great-heart heroes, boys and unmarried maidens,
Young men laid on the pyre before their parents' eyes –
And about them lay the black ooze, the crooked reeds of Cocytus,
Bleak the marsh that barred them in with its stagnant water,
And the Styx coiling nine times around corralled them there.
Why, Death's very home and holy of holies was shaken
To hear that song, and the Furies with steel-blue snakes entwined
In their tresses; the watch-dog Cerberus gaped open his triple mouth;
Ixion's wheel stopped dead from whirling in the wind.
And now he's avoided every pitfall of the homeward path,
And Eurydice, regained, is nearing the upper air
Close behind him (for this condition has Proserpine made),
When a moment's madness catches her lover off his guard –
Pardonable, you'd say, but Death can never pardon.
He halts. Eurydice, his own, is now on the lip of
Daylight. Alas! he forgot. His purpose broke. He looked back.
His labour was lost, the pact he had made with the merciless king
Annulled. Three times did thunder peal over the pools of Avernus.
'Who,' she cried, 'has doomed me to misery, who has doomed us?
What madness beyond measure? Once more a cruel fate
Drags me away, and my swimming eyes are drowned in darkness.
Good-bye. I am borne away. A limitless night is about me
And over the strengthless hands I stretch to you, yours no longer.'
Thus she spoke: and at once from his sight, like a wisp of smoke,
Thinned into air, was gone.
Wildly he grasped at shadows, wanting to say much more,
But she did not see him; nor would the ferryman of the Inferno
Let him again cross the fen that lay between them.
      What could he do, where go, his wife twice taken from him?
What lament would move Death now? What deities hear his song?
Cold she was voyaging now over the Stygian stream.
Month after month, they say, for seven months alone
He wept beneath a crag high up by the lonely waters
Of Strymon, and under the ice-cold stars poured out his dirge
That charmed the tigers and made the oak trees follow him.

As a nightingale he sang that sorrowing under a poplar's
Shade laments the young she has lost, whom a heartless ploughman
Has noticed and dragged from the nest unfledged; and the nightin-
gale
Weeps all night, on a branch repeating the piteous song,
Loading the acres around with the burden of her lament.
No love, no marriage could turn his mind away from grief:
Alone through Arctic ice, through the snows of Tanais, over
Frost-bound Riphaean plateaux
He ranged, bewailing his lost Eurydice and the wasted
Bounty of Death. In the end Thracian Bacchantes, flouted
By his neglect, one night in the midst of their Master's revels
Tore him limb from limb and scattered him over the land.
But even then that head, plucked from the marble-pale
Neck, and rolling down mid-stream on the river Hebrus –
That voice, that cold, cold tongue cried out 'Eurydice!'
Cried 'Poor Eurydice!' as the soul of the singer fled,
And the banks of the river echoed, echoed 'Eurydice!'

CECIL DAY LEWIS (1940)

A FARMER'S CALENDAR

Above all, many things are better done
In chill of night, or when the Morning-star
Bedews the earth. Light stubble and dry meads
Are better cut at night, when moisture clings.
I know of one whom winter firelight keeps
Wakeful, whittling his torches with sharp steel.
His wife, her shuttle singing, sings herself
To cheer long hours aweave, or at the fire
Boils down the liquor of sweet must, and skims
With leaves the bubbling froth. In midsummer
You'll cut your reddening crops: in midsummer
You'll thresh the grain you've dried with parching heat.
Plough when you have to strip for it, strip to sow!
For winter is the farmer's holiday.
In this chill time farmers enjoy their gains,

And merrily feast together: winter cheer
Invites, dispelling care; as when, at last,
The laden keels have anchored, and the crews
Joyously wreathed the poops. Yet now's the time
To gather acorns, olives, bay-berries,
And blood-red myrtle, set your snares for cranes
And nets for stags, and chase the lop-eared hare,
Now slay the doe, whirling the hempen thong
Of a Balearic sling, while snow lies deep,
While rivers pack their ice.

                      Why should I sing
Of autumn's weather and autumnal stars,
Or, when days shorten and the heat grows mild,
What signs must closely be observed of men?
Or too, when spring comes down in torrent rain,
Or bearded crops have bristled on the land,
Or when the green corn swells with milky sap?
Oft as the farmer led his harvesters
On to the golden fields, and even now
Was stripping barley from its brittle stalks,
I've seen the embattled winds hurtle together,
Uprooting, tossing high and scattering
The lush-eared crop; then the onrushing gale
With black tornado carry off light stalk
And flying stubble. Oft advances huge
A host of waters in the sky, and clouds,
Gathering from the sea, marshal the storm,
Foul, dark with rain. Down pour the heavens sheer,
In mighty flood sweeping away glad crops
And labours of the ox. The ditches fill:
Deep rivers rise in thundering spate: the seas
Breathe and boom in the narrows. Jove himself,
In blackest darkness of the storm-cloud, wields
With flickering hand his bolt, at whose dread shock
Earth trembles, wild things scurry, and stark fear
Lays prostrate, nation-wide, the hearts of men.
With shaft of blinding light Athos he fells,

Or Rhodopë, or high Ceraunia:
The South-West blows a gale: rain crashes down:
Loud wails the tempest over weald and shore.

L. A. S. JERMYN (1947)

PESTILENCE

Once to this land of Italy there came
A season pitiable in tainted air,
Glowing with full autumnal heat, and brought
Death to all kinds of cattle and wild beasts,
Poisoned the lakes, infecting with disease
Even the hay. Nor was the manner of death
Uniform; but where fevered thirst had driven
Through every vein, and cramped the limbs, once more
Water welled up and drew into itself
The putrid bones that crumbled to decay.
Oft at the very service of the gods
The victim, standing at the altar while
The ministrant about its temples hung
The fillet with its snow-white garland, fell
Dead, as the priests around were slow to strike.
Or, if a priest struck home and in good time,
No flame rose from the altar at the gift
Of omened entrails, and the questioned seer
Had naught in answer for the questioner.
Scarce was the knife laid to the throat before
Blood spattered it, and with its flow, though scant,
Darkened the sanded ground. Then everywhere
Among the luscious grasses calves lay dying,
Or near the well-filled byre gave back a life
That once was sweet. Upon the fawning hound
Came madness: swine fell dead, or shook with coughs
And panting; and a swelling of the throat
Choked them. No longer joyous to his toil
Stepped forth the lordly steed, but, food untouched,
Forbode even to water at the stream,

And stamped and pawed the ground, his ears adroop
And fitful sweat about them – cold if death
Were imminent – the hide rough, hard, and dry
To the caressing hand. Such were the signs
They gave in early days of the fell plague.
But as its progress grew to violence,
Then was there burning of the eyes, the breath
Was deep-drawn, oft-times labouring up with groans:
Their flanks were stretched to bursting with their sobs:
Black blood poured from the nostrils: the rough tongue
Clove to the palate and besieged the throat.
It gave relief then to insert a horn
And pour in draughts of wine; and this appeared
The one hope for the dying. Remedy
Soon proved a bane! for so their fevered rage
Returned; and on the verge of weary death
(O may the gods vouchsafe a happier fate
To virtue, but like madness to our foes!),
They wrenched and tore their own limbs with bared teeth.
And lo! the bull, blood frothing at his lips,
Fell as he laboured at the plough, and groaned
His last. And sadly fared the ploughman then,
Freeing the ox that mourned his yoke-fellow,
Leaving the plough mid-field, his work half-done.
No shade of lofty woodlands, not the mead
Soft with deep grasses, could avail to raise
The spirit of his beasts, no burn that flowed
Clearer than amber, rippling to the plain.
Their flanks fell loose and sagging, while a film
Crept over eyes now lifeless, and the neck
Drooped to the ground, too weak for its own weight.
What boot was it to toil and tend? what use
To churn up with the share the heavy clods?
No draughts of Massic wine, no twice-laid feasts
Had turned their stomachs: for their food was leaves
And purest grass; their drink, the limpid rill
Fussily flowing; nor did cares disturb
Their healthful slumbers. At no other time

Were heifers lacking for the sacrifice
To Juno, nor were bison roughly paired
To pull the festal chariots to her fane.
Men therefore laboured to scratch up the earth
With mattocks, and with their own finger-nails
Dug in the corn-seed, over lofty hills
Dragging with straining necks the creaking wains.
No wolf sought out an ambush for the flock,
Or nightly prowled against it. Heavier care
O'ercame him. Timid deer and fleeing stags
Now roamed the farmstead, all among the hounds.
And now the wave rolled shoreward denizens
Of the unmeasured sea, all things that swim,
And flung them up like shipwrecked mariners.
Seals, breaking custom, fled to estuaries:
His winding lair served no more to defend
The viper, but he perished: perished, too,
The water-snake, his scales erect with fear.
Even birds knew the pestilential air,
Died in the clouds, and headlong plunged to earth.
No remedy was found in change of food:
New arts availed not: physic was all vain,
Though learned of Chiron, son of Phillyra,
Or of Melampus, Amythaon's child.
Bursting from Stygian gloom to light of suns,
Raged the pale Fury, and before her drove
Disease and Dread, and ever day by day
Surged loftier, raising her insatiate head.
Streams and dry banks and hills that seem to drowse
Echoed the bleat of sheep, the frequent groans
Of oxen; and within the very stalls
The plague brought death to multitudes, and heaped
The bodies rotting in corruption foul,
Until men learned to cover them with earth,
Burying them deep. For no use was the hide,
Nor could the stench be washed out of the flesh
Or overcome by roasting, nor the fleece
Be shorn, all eaten through with putrid filth.

And if't were tried, the web set up would break
In pieces at a touch; and, worse than this,
Should any seek to don such tainted cloth,
The burning pustules and foul sweat ran o'er
His fetid limbs, and, biding for no time,
The accursèd fire consumed his stricken joints.

L. A. S. JERMYN (1947)

THE AENEID

THE UNDERWORLD

They went obscure in lowering lone night
Through lodges of King Dis, untenanted –
Featureless lands. Thus goes a forest pathway
Beneath the curst light of the wavering moon,
When Jove has gloomed the sky, and pitchy dark
Uncoloured all the world. In Hell's first reach
Fronting the very vestibule of Orcus
Griefs and the Cares have set their couches down –
The vengeful Cares. There pale Diseases dwell,
Sad Eld and Fear and loathsome Poverty
And Hunger, that bad counsellor – dire shapes –
And Death and Toil, and Sleep brother of Death
And soul-corrupting joys. Opposed he viewed
War the great murderer, and those steel bowers
The Furies deck for bridal, and Discord
Daft, with blood-ribbons on her serpent hair.

But straight in front a huge black knotted elm
Stood branching: here, they say, the Vain Dreams roost –
There's not a leaf without one stuck behind.
Next he saw twisted beasts of the old tales:
Centaurs were stabled at the gates: Scyllas
Spread their twin shapes, Briareus his hundred arms.
And Lerna's beast behold hissing out fear,

Chimaera too, who fights with fire, and Gorgons,
And Harpies, and a shade with a triple form.
Such was the horror seized Aeneas then
He made to meet their onset with cold steel,
And had the instructed Sibyl not advised
That these were gossamer vitalities
Flitting in stuffless mockery of form,
He'd have leapt on and lashed the empty air.

Hence leads a road to Acheron, vast flood
Of thick and restless slime: all that foul ooze
It belches in Cocytus. Here keeps watch
That wild and filthy pilot of the marsh
Charon, from whose rugged old chin trails down
The hoary beard of centuries: his eyes
Are fixed, but flame. His grimy cloak hangs loose
Rough-knotted at the shoulder: his own hands
Pole on the boat, or tend the sail that wafts
His dismal skiff and its fell freight along.
Ah, he is old, but with that toughening eld
That speaks his godhead! To the bank and him
All a great multitude came pouring down,
Brothers and husbands, and the proud-souled heroes,
Life's labour done: and boys and unwed maidens
And the young men by whose flame-funeral
Parents had wept. Many as leaves that fall
Gently in autumn when the sharp cold comes
Or all the birds that flock at the turn o' the year
Over the ocean to the lands of light.[1]
They stood and prayed each one to be first taken:
They stretched their hands for love of the other side.
But the grim sailor takes now these, now those:
And some he drives a distance from the shore.
Aeneas, moved and marvelling at this stir,
Cried – 'O chaste Sibyl, tell me why this throng
That rushes to the river? What desire
Have all these phantoms? and what rule's award

---

1. For Virgil's earlier version of this passage, rendered by a different translator, see above, pp. 146 f.

Drives these back from the marge, let those go over
Sweeping the livid shallows with the oar?'
The old priestess replied in a few words:
'Son of Anchises of true blood divine,
Behold the deep Cocytus and dim Styx
By whom the high gods fear to swear in vain.
This shiftless crowd all is unsepulchred:
The boatman there is Charon: those who embark
The buried. None may leave this beach of horror
To cross the growling stream before that hour
That hides their white bones in a quiet tomb.
A hundred years they flutter round these shores:
Then they may cross the waters long desired.'

JAMES ELROY FLECKER (1914)

THE FURY ALLECTO AROUSES WAR

From some high rock the hateful goddess spies
Her chance for mischief: to the roof she flies
Of the tall stable, from whose summit sheer
She gives the danger-call that shepherds fear.
Through the curved horn her hellish music rang;
Trembled the woodland, and the forest sang;
Diana's lake and Veline springs afar
Heard, and the milky streams of sulphurous Nar,
And trembling mothers to their children clung.
And swiftly as the rallying horn gave tongue,
From far and near the stalwart yeoman ran;
What nearest lay of weapons, armed each man.
Now, to their prince's aid, the hosts of Troy,
Crowding the sally-ports, their ranks deploy:
No more, alas, with rustic arms they brawl –
Stout clubs, charred stakes, to fend themselves withal –
But steel its stern arbitrament affords,
And the field darkens with a shock of swords:
Flashing of brass gives back the sun's hard rays,
And on the clouds its shimmering lightning plays.

So, when the wave first whitens with the breeze,
By little and by little swell the seas,
Higher the water leaps, and still more high,
Churned from its depths, and challenges the sky.
Amid the foremost ranks an arrow flew,
And Almo, first of Tyrrhus' sons, o'erthrew:
Deep in his throat it struck, and stopped in death
His voice's passage and his vital breath.

RONALD KNOX (1924)

DIDO AND AENEAS

But now for some while the queen had been growing more griev-
    ously love-sick,
Feeding the wound with her life-blood, the fire biting within her.
Much did she muse on the hero's nobility, and much
On his family's fame. His look, his words had gone to her heart
And lodged there: she could get no peace from love's disquiet.
    The morrow's morn had chased from heaven the dewy darkness,
Was carrying the sun's torch far and wide over earth,
When, almost beside herself, she spoke to her sister, her confidante:
    Anna, sister, why do these nerve-racking dreams haunt me?
This man, this stranger I've welcomed into my house – what of him?
How gallantly he looks, how powerful in chest and shoulders!
I really do think, and have reason to think, that he is heaven-born.
Mean souls convict themselves by cowardice. Oh, imagine
The fates that have harried him, the fight to a finish he told of!
Were it not that my purpose is fixed irrevocably
Never to tie myself in wedlock again to anyone,
Since that first love of mine proved false and let death cheat me;
Had I not taken a loathing for the idea of marriage,
For him, for this one man, I could perhaps have weakened.
Anna, I will confess it, since poor Sychaeus, my husband,
Was killed and our home broken up by my brother's murderous act,
This man is the only one who has stirred my senses and sapped
My will. I feel once more the scars of the old flame.
But no, I would rather the earth should open and swallow me
Or the Father of heaven strike me with lightning down to the shades –

The pale shades and deep night of the Underworld – before
I violate or deny pure widowhood's claim upon me.
He who first wedded me took with him, when he died,
My right to love: let him keep it, there, in the tomb, for ever.
  So Dido spoke, and the rising tears flooded her bosom.
Anna replied:
               You are dearer to me than the light of day.
Must you go on wasting your youth in mourning and solitude,
Never to know the blessings of love, the delight of children?
Do you think that ashes, or ghosts underground, can mind about such
     things?
I know that in Libya, yes, and in Tyre before it, no wooers
Could touch your atrophied heart: Iarbas was rejected
And other lords of Africa, the breeding-ground of the great.
Very well: but when love comes, and pleases, why fight against it?
Besides, you should think of the nations whose land you have settled
     in –
Threatening encirclement are the Gaetuli, indomitable
In war, the Numidians (no bridle for them), the unfriendly Syrtes;
On your other frontier, a waterless desert and the far-raging
Barcaei: I need not mention the prospect of Tyrian aggression,
Your brother's menacing attitude.
I hold it was providential indeed, and Juno willed it,
That hither the Trojan fleet should have made their way. Oh, sister,
Married to such a man, what a city you'll see, what a kingdom
Established here! With the Trojans as our comrades in arms,
What heights of glory will not we Carthaginians soar to!
Only solicit the gods' favour, perform the due rites,
And plying our guest with attentions, spin a web to delay him,
While out at sea the winter runs wild and Orion is stormy,
While his ships are in bad repair, while the weather is unacquiescent.
  These words blew to a blaze the spark of love in the queen's heart,
Set hope to her wavering will and melted her modesty's rigour.
So first they went to the shrines, beseeching at every altar
For grace: as religion requires, they sacrificed chosen sheep to
Ceres, giver of increase, to Phoebus, and to the Wine-god;
To Juno, chief of all, for the marriage-bond is her business.
Dido herself, most beautiful, chalice in hand, would pour

Libations between the horns of a milk-white heifer, and slowly
Would pace by the dripping altars, with the gods looking on,
And daily renew her sacrifice, poring over the victims'
Opened bodies to see what their pulsing entrails signified.
Ah, little the soothsayers know! What value have vows or shrines
For a woman wild with passion, the while love's flame eats into
Her gentle flesh and love's wound works silently in her breast?
So burns the ill-starred Dido, wandering at large through the town
In a rage of desire, like a doe pierced by an arrow – a doe which
Some hunting shepherd has hit with a long shot while unwary
She stepped through the Cretan woods, and all unknowing has left his
Winged weapon within her: the doe runs fleetly around the Dictaean
Woods and clearings, the deathly shaft stuck deep in her flank.
Now she conducts Aeneas on a tour of her city, and shows him
The vast resources of Carthage, the home there ready and waiting;
Begins to speak, then breaks off, leaving a sentence unfinished.
Now, as the day draws out, she wants to renew that first feast,
In fond distraction begs to hear once again the Trojan
Story, and hangs on his words as once again he tells it.
Then, when the company's broken up, when the moon is dimming
Her beams in turn and the dipping stars invite to sleep,
Alone she frets in the lonely house, lies down on her bed,
Then leaves it again: he's not there, not there, but she hears him and
    sees him.
Or charmed by his likeness to his father, she keeps Ascanius
Long in her lap to assuage the passion she must not utter.
Work on the half-built towers is closed down meanwhile; the men
Of Carthage have laid off drilling, or building the wharves and vital
Defences of their town; the unfinished works are idle –
Great frowning walls, head-in-air cranes, all at a standstill.

    Now as soon as Jupiter's consort perceived that Dido was mad
With love and quite beyond caring about her reputation,
She, Juno, approached Venus, making these overtures: –
    A praiseworthy feat, I must say, a fine achievement you've brought
    off,
You and your boy; it should make a great, a lasting name for you –
One woman mastered by the arts of two immortals.
It has not entirely escaped me that you were afraid of my city

And keenly suspicious of towering Carthage's hospitality.
But how will it all end? Where is our rivalry taking us?
Would it not be far better, by arranging a marriage, to seal
A lasting peace? You have got the thing you had set your heart on:
Dido's afire with love, wholly infatuated.
Well then, let us unite these nations and rule them with equal
Authority. Let Dido slave for a Trojan husband,
And let the Tyrians pass into your hand as her dowry.

   Venus, aware that this was double-talk by which
Juno aimed at basing the future Italian empire
On Africa, countered with these words:

                              Senseless indeed to reject
Such terms and prefer to settle the matter with you by hostilities,
Provided fortune favour the plan which you propose.
But I'm in two minds about destiny, I am not sure if Jupiter
Wishes one city formed of Tyrians and Trojan exiles,
Or would approve a pact or miscegenation between them.
You are his wife: you may ask him to make his policy clearer.
Proceed, I will support you.

                       Queen Juno replied thus:
   That shall be my task. Now, to solve our immediate problem,
I will briefly put forward a scheme – pray give me your attention.
Aeneas and his unfortunate Dido plan to go
A-hunting in the woods tomorrow, as soon as the sun
Has risen and unshrouded the world below with his rays.
On these two, while the beaters are scurrying about and stopping
The coverts with cordon of nets, I shall pour down a darkling rain-
    storm
And hail as well, and send thunder hallooing all over the sky.
Dispersing for shelter, the rest of the hunt will be cloaked in the mirk:
But Dido and lord Aeneas, finding their way to the same cave,
Shall meet. I'll be there: and if I may rely on your goodwill,
There I shall join them in lasting marriage, and seal her his,
With Hymen present in person.

                     Venus made no opposition
To Juno's request, though she smiled at the ingenuity of it.
So now, as Aurora was rising out of her ocean bed
And the day-beam lofted, there sallied forth the *élite* of Carthage:

With fine-meshed nets and snares and the broad hunting lances
Massylian riders galloped behind a keen-nosed pack.
The queen dallies: the foremost Carthaginians await her
By the palace door, where stands her horse, caparisoned
In purple and gold, high-spirited, champing the foam-flecked bit.
At last she comes, with many courtiers in attendance:
She wears a Phoenician habit, piped with bright-coloured braid:
Her quiver is gold, her hair bound up with a golden clasp,
A brooch of gold fastens the waist of her brilliant dress.
Her Trojan friends were there too, and young Ascanius
In high glee. But by far the handsomest of them all
Was Aeneas, who came to her side now and joined forces with hers.
It was like when Apollo leaves Lycia, his winter palace,
And Xanthus river to visit Delos, his mother's home,
And renew the dances, while round his altar Cretans and Dryopes
And the tattooed Agathyrsi are raising a polyglot din:
The god himself steps out on the Cynthian range, a circlet
Of gold and a wreath of pliant bay on his flowing hair,
The jangling weapons slung from his shoulder. Nimble as he,
Aeneas moved, with the same fine glow on his handsome face.
When they had reached the mountains, the trackless haunt of game,
Wild goats – picture the scene! started from crags up above there,
Ran down the slopes: from another direction stags were galloping
Over the open ground of a glen, deserting the heights –
A whole herd jostling together in flight, with a dust-cloud above it.
But young Ascanius, proud of his mettlesome horse, was riding
Along the vale, outstripping group after group of hunters,
And praying hard that, instead of such tame quarry, a frothing
Boar might come his way or a sand-coloured mountain lion.

    At this stage a murmur, a growling began to be heard
In the sky: soon followed a deluge of rain and hail together.
The Trojan sportsmen, their Carthaginian friends and the grandson
Of Venus, in some alarm, scattered over the terrain
Looking for shelter. Torrents roared down from the mountain-tops.
Now Dido and the prince Aeneas found themselves
In the same cave. Primordial Earth and presiding Juno
Gave the signal. The firmament flickered with fire, a witness
Of wedding. Somewhere above, the Nymphs cried out in pleasure.

That day was doom's first birthday and that first day was the cause of
Evils: Dido recked nothing for appearance or reputation:
The love she brooded on now was a secret love no longer;
Marriage, she called it, drawing the word to veil her sin.

  Straightaway went Rumour through the great cities of Libya –
Rumour, the swiftest traveller of all the ills on earth,
Thriving on movement, gathering strength as it goes; at the start
A small and cowardly thing, it soon puffs itself up,
And walking upon the ground, buries its head in the cloud-base.
The legend is that, enraged with the gods, Mother Earth produced
This creature, her last child, as a sister to Enceladus
And Coeus – a swift-footed creature, a winged angel of ruin,
A terrible, grotesque monster, each feather upon whose body –
Incredible though it sounds – has a sleepless eye beneath it.
And for every eye she has also a tongue, a voice, and a pricked ear.
At night she flits midway between earth and sky, through the gloom
Screeching, and never closes her eyelids in sweet slumber:
By day she is perched like a look-out either upon a roof-top
Or some high turret; so she terrorizes whole cities
Loud-speaker of truth, hoarder of mischievous falsehood, equally.
This creature was now regaling the people with various scandal
In great glee, announcing fact and fiction indiscriminately:
Item, Aeneas has come here, a prince of Trojan blood,
And the beauteous Dido deigns to have her name linked with his;
The couple are spending the winter in debauchery, the whole long
Winter, forgetting their kingdoms, rapt in a trance of lust.
Such gossip did vile Rumour pepper on every mouth.
Not long before she came to the ears of king Iarbas,
Whispering inflammatory words and heaping up his resentment.

  He, the son of Ammon by a ravished African nymph,
Had established a hundred shrines to Jove in his ample realm,
A hundred altars, and consecrated their quenchless flames
And vigils unceasing there; the ground was richly steeped in
Victims' blood, and bouquets of flowers adorned the portals.
He now, driven out of his mind by that bitter blast of rumour,
There at the altar, among the presences of the gods,
Prayed, it is said, to Jove, with importunate, humble entreaty:
  Almighty Jove, whom now for the first time the Moorish people

Pledge with wine as they banquet on ornamental couches,
Do you observe these things? Or are we foolish to shudder
When you shoot fire, O Father, foolish to be dismayed
By lightning which is quite aimless and thunder which growls with-
out meaning?
That woman who, wandering within our frontiers, paid to establish
Her insignificant township, permitted by us to plough up
A piece of the coast and be queen of it – that woman, rejecting my
offer
Of marriage, has taken Aeneas as lord and master there.
And now that philanderer, with his effeminate following –
His chin and oil-sleeked hair set off by a Phrygian bonnet –
That fellow is in possession; while we bring gifts to your shrine,
If indeed you are there and we do not worship a vain myth.

    Thus did Iarbas pray, with his hands on the altar; and Jove
Omnipotent, hearing him, bent down his gaze upon Dido's
City and on those lovers lost to their higher fame.
Then he addressed Mercury, entrusting to him this errand: –
    Go quick, my son, whistle up the Zephyrs and wing your way
Down to the Trojan leader, who is dallying now in Carthage
Without one thought for the city which fate has assigned to be his.
Carry my dictate along the hastening winds and tell him,
Not for such ways did his matchless mother guarantee him
To us, nor for such ends rescue him twice from the Greeks;
Rather, that he should rule an Italy fertile in leadership
And loud with war, should hand on a line which sprang from the
noble
Teucer and bring the whole world under a system of law.
If the glory of such great exploits no longer fires his heart
And for his own renown he will make no effort at all,
Does he grudge his son, Ascanius, the glory of Rome to be?
What aim, what hope does he cherish, delaying there in a hostile
Land, with no thought for posterity or his Italian kingdom?
Let him sail. That is the gist. Give him that message from me.
    Jove spake. Mercury now got ready to obey
His father's command. So first he bound on his feet the sandals,
The golden sandals whose wings waft him aloft over sea
And land alike with the hurrying breath of the breezes. Then

He took up his magic wand (with this he summons wan ghosts
From Orcus and consigns others to dreary Tartarus,
Gives sleep or takes it away, seals up the eyes of dead men).
Now, with that trusty wand, he drove the winds and threshed
    through
The cloud-wrack; descried as he flew the peak and precipitous flanks
    of
Atlas, that dour mountain which props the sky with his summit –
Atlas, his pine-bristled head for ever enwrapped in a bandeau
Of glooming cloud, for ever beaten by wind and rain;
Snow lies deep on his shoulders, and watercourses plunge down
That ancient's chin, while his shaggy beard is stiff with ice.
Here first did Mercury pause, hovering on beautifully-balanced
Wings; then stooped, dived bodily down to the sea below,
Like a bird which along the shore and around the promontories
Goes fishing, flying low, wave-hopping over the water.
Even so did Mercury skim between earth and sky
Towards the Libyan coast, cutting his path through the winds,
On his way from that mountain giant, Atlas, his mother's sire.
As soon as his winged feet had carried him to the shacks there,
He noticed Aeneas superintending the work on towers
And new buildings: he wore a sword studded with yellow
Jaspers, and a fine cloak of glowing Tyrian purple
Hung from his shoulders – the wealthy Dido had fashioned it,
Interweaving the fabric with threads of gold, as a present for him.
Mercury went for him at once:

                        So now you are laying
Foundations for lofty Carthage, building a beautiful city
To please a woman, lost to the interests of your own realm?
The king of the gods, who directs heaven and earth with his deity,
Sends me to you from bright Olympus: the king of the gods
Gave me this message to carry express through the air: What do you
Aim at or hope for, idling and fiddling here in Libya?
If you're indifferent to your own high destiny
And for your own renown you will make no effort at all,
Think of your young hopeful, Ascanius, growing to manhood,
The inheritance which you owe him – an Italian kingdom, the soil of
    Rome.

Such were the words which Mercury delivered;
And breaking off abruptly, was manifest no more,
But vanished into thin air, far beyond human ken.

Dazed indeed by that vision was Aeneas, and dumbfounded:
His hair stood on end with terror, the voice stuck in his throat.
Awed by this admonition from the great throne above,
He desired to fly the country, dear though it was to him.
But oh, what was he to do? What words could he find to get round
The temperamental queen? How broach the matter to her?
His mind was in feverish conflict, tossed from one side to the other,
Twisting and turning all ways to find a way past his dilemma.
So vacillating, at last he felt this the better decision:
Sending for Mnestheus, Sergestus, and brave Serestus, he bade them
Secretly get the ships ready, muster their friends on the beach,
Be prepared to fight: the cause of so drastic a change of plan
They must keep dark: in the meanwhile, assuming that generous
    Dido
Knew nothing and could not imagine the end of so great a love,
Aeneas would try for a way to approach her, the kindest moment
For speaking, the best way to deal with this delicate matter. His
    comrades
Obeyed the command and did as he told them with cheerful alacrity.

But who can ever hoodwink a woman in love? The queen,
Apprehensive even when things went well, now sensed his deception,
Got wind of what was going to happen. That mischievous Rumour,
Whispering the fleet was preparing to sail, put her in a frenzy.
Distraught, she witlessly wandered about the city, raving
Like some Bacchante driven wild, when the emblems of sanctity
Stir, by the shouts of 'Hail, Bacchus!' and drawn to Cithaeron
At night by the din of revellers, at the triennial orgies.
Finding Aeneas at last, she cried, before he could speak:

Unfaithful man, did you think you could do such a dreadful thing
And keep it dark? yes, skulk from my land without one word?
Our love, the vows you made me – do these not give you pause,
Nor even the thought of Dido meeting a painful death?
Now, in the dead of winter, to be getting your ships ready
And hurrying to set sail when northerly gales are blowing,
You heartless one! Suppose the fields were not foreign, the home was

Not strange that you are bound for, suppose Troy stood as of old,
Would you be sailing for Troy, now, in this stormy weather?
Am I your reason for going? By these tears, by the hand you gave
    me –
They are all I have left, today, in my misery – I implore you,
And by our union of hearts, by our marriage hardly begun,
If I have ever helped you at all, if anything
About me pleased you, be sad for our broken home, forgo
Your purpose, I beg you, unless it's too late for prayers of mine!
Because of you, the Libyan tribes and the Nomad chieftains
Hate me, the Tyrians are hostile: because of you I have lost
My old reputation for faithfulness – the one thing that could have
    made me
Immortal. Oh, I am dying! To what, my guest, are you leaving me?
'Guest' – that is all I may call you now, who have called you husband.
Why do I linger here? Shall I wait till my brother, Pygmalion,
Destroys this place, or Iarbas leads me away captive?
If even I might have conceived a child by you before
You went away, a little Aeneas to play in the palace
And, in spite of all this, to remind me of you by his looks, oh then
I should not feel so utterly finished and desolate.

    She had spoken. Aeneas, mindful of Jove's words, kept his eyes
Unyielding, and with a great effort repressed his feeling for her.
In the end he managed to answer:

                          Dido, I'll never pretend
You have not been good to me, deserving of everything
You can claim. I shall not regret my memories of Elissa
As long as I breathe, as long as I remember my own self.
For my conduct – this, briefly: I did not look to make off from here
In secret – do not suppose it; nor did I offer you marriage
At any time or consent to be bound by a marriage contract.
If fate allowed me to be my own master, and gave me
Free will to choose my way of life, to solve my problems,
Old Troy would be my first choice: I would restore it, and honour
My people's relics – the high halls of Priam perpetuated,
Troy given back to its conquered sons, a renaissant city,
Had been my task. But now Apollo and the Lycian
Oracle have told me that Italy is our bourne.

There lies my heart, my homeland. You, a Phoenician, are held by
These Carthaginian towers, by the charm of your Libyan city:
So can you grudge us Trojans our vision of settling down
In Italy? We too may seek a kingdom abroad.
Often as night envelops the earth in dewy darkness,
Often at star-rise, the troubled ghost of my father, Anchises,
Comes to me in my dreams, warns me and frightens me.
I am disturbed no less by the wrong I am doing Ascanius,
Defrauding him of his destined realm in Hesperia.
What's more, just now the courier of heaven, sent by Jupiter –
I swear it on your life and mine – conveyed to me, swiftly flying,
His orders: I saw the god, as clear as day, with my own eyes,
Entering the city, and these ears drank in the words he uttered.
No more reproaches, then – they only torture us both.
God's will, not mine, says 'Italy'.
     All the while he was speaking she gazed at him askance,
Her glances flickering over him, eyes exploring the whole man
In deadly silence. Now, furiously, she burst out: –
     Faithless and false! No goddess mothered you, no Dardanus
Your ancestor! I believe harsh Caucasus begat you
On a flint-hearted rock and Hyrcanian tigers suckled you.
Why should I hide my feelings? What worse can there be to keep
          them for?
Not one sigh from him when I wept! Not a softer glance!
Did he yield an inch, or a tear, in pity for her who loves him?
I don't know what to say first. It has come to this – not Juno,
Not Jove himself can view my plight with the eye of justice.
Nowhere is it safe to be trustful. I took him, a castaway,
A pauper, and shared my kingdom with him – I must have been
          mad –
Rescued his lost fleet, rescued his friends from death.
Oh, I'm on fire and drifting! And now Apollo's prophecies,
Lycian oracles, couriers of heaven sent by Jupiter
With stern commands – all these order you to betray me.
Oh, of course this is just the sort of transaction that troubles the
          calm of
The gods. I'll not keep you, nor probe the dishonesty of your words.
Chase your Italy, then! Go, sail to your realm overseas!

I only hope that, if the just spirits have any power,
Marooned on some mid-sea rock you may drink the full cup of
agony
And often cry out for Dido. I'll dog you, from far, with the death-
fires;
And when cold death has parted my soul from my body, my spectre
Will be wherever you are. You shall pay for the evil you've done me.
The tale of your punishment will come to me down in the shades.
    With these words Dido suddenly ended, and sick at heart
Turned from him, tore herself away from his eyes, ran indoors,
While he hung back in dread of a still worse scene, although
He had much to say. Her maids bore up the fainting queen
Into her marble chamber and laid her down on the bed.
    But the god-fearing Aeneas, much as he longed to soothe
Her anguish with consolation, with words that would end her
troubles,
Heavily sighing, his heart melting from love of her,
Nevertheless obeyed the gods and went off to his fleet.
Whereupon the Trojans redoubled their efforts, all along
The beach dragging down the tall ships, launching the well-tarred
bottoms,
Fetching green wood to make oars and baulks of unfashioned timber
From the forest, so eager they were to be gone.
You could see them on the move, hurrying out of the city.
It looked like an army of ants when, provident for winter,
They're looting a great big corn-heap and storing it up in their own
house;
Over a field the black file goes, as they carry the loot
On a narrow track through the grass; some are strenuously pushing
The enormous grains of corn with their shoulders, while others
marshal
The traffic and keep it moving: their whole road seethes with activity.
Ah, Dido, what did you feel when you saw these things going
forward?
What moans you gave when, looking forth from your high roof-top,
You beheld the whole length of the beach aswarm with men, and the
sea's face
Alive with the sound and fury of preparations for sailing!

Excess of love, to what lengths you drive our human hearts!
Once again she was driven to try what tears and entreaties
Could do, and let love beggar her pride – she would leave no appeal
Untried, lest, for want of it, she should all needlessly die.

    Anna, you see the bustle down there on the beach: from all sides
They have assembled; their canvas is stretched to the winds already,
And the elated mariners have garlanded their ships.
If I was able to anticipate this deep anguish,
I shall be able to bear it. But do this one thing, Anna,
For your poor sister. You were the only confidante
Of that faithless man: he told you even his secret thoughts:
You alone know the most tactful way, the best time to approach him.
Go, sister, and make this appeal to my disdainful enemy:
Say that *I* never conspired with the Greeks at Aulis to ruin
The Trojan people, nor sent squadrons of ships against Troy;
I never desecrated the ashes of dead Anchises,
So why must Aeneas be deaf and obdurate to my pleading?
Why off so fast? Will he grant a last wish to her who unhappily
Loves him, and wait for a favouring wind, an easier voyage?
Not for our marriage that was do I plead now – he has forsworn it,
Nor that he go without his dear Latium and give up his kingdom.
I ask a mere nothing – just time to give rein to despair and thus calm it,
To learn from ill luck how to grieve for what I have lost, and to bear it.
This last favour I beg – oh, pity your sister! – and if he
Grants it, I will repay him; my death shall be his interest.

    Such were her prayers, and such the tearful entreaties her agonized
Sister conveyed to Aeneas again and again. But unmoved by
Tearful entreaties he was, adamant against all pleadings:
Fate blocked them, heaven stopped his ears lest he turn complaisant.
As when some stalwart oak-tree, some veteran of the Alps,
Is assailed by a wintry wind whose veering gusts tear at it,
Trying to root it up; wildly whistle the branches,
The leaves come flocking down from aloft as the bole is battered;
But the tree stands firm on its crag, for high as its head is carried
Into the sky, so deep do its roots go down towards Hades:
Even thus was the hero belaboured for long with every kind of
Pleading, and his great heart thrilled through and through with the
    pain of it;

Resolute, though, was his mind; unavailing rolled her tears.[1]

But the hapless Dido, frightened out of her wits by her destiny,
Prayed for death: she would gaze no more on the dome of daylight.
And now, strengthening her resolve to act and to leave this world,
She saw, as she laid gifts on the incense-burning altars –
Horrible to relate – the holy water turn black
And the wine she poured changing uncannily to blood.
She told no one, not even her sister, of this phenomenon.
Again, she had dedicated a chantry of marble within
The palace to her first husband; held it in highest reverence;
Hung it with snow-white fleeces and with festoons of greenery:
Well, from this shrine, when night covered the earth, she seemed
To be hearing words – the voice of that husband calling upon her.
There was something dirge-like, too, in the tones of the owl on the
        roof-top
Whose lonely, repeated cries were drawn out to a long keening.
Besides, she recalled with horror presages, dread forewarnings
Of the prophets of old. Aeneas himself pursued her remorselessly
In dreams, driving her mad; or else she dreamed of unending
Solitude and desertion, of walking alone and eternally
Down a long road, through an empty land, in search of her Tyrians.
Just so does the raving Pentheus see covens of Furies and has the
Delusion of seeing two suns in the sky and a double Thebes:
Just so on the stage does Orestes, the son of Agamemnon,
Move wildly about while his mother pursues him with torches and
        black snakes,
And at the door the avenging Furies cut off his retreat.

So when, overmastered by grief, she conceived a criminal madness
And doomed herself to death, she worked out the time and method
In secret; then, putting on an expression of calm hopefulness
To hide her resolve, she approached her sorrowing sister with these
        words: –

I have found out a way, Anna – oh, wish me joy of it –
To get him back or else get free of my love for him.
Near Ocean's furthest bound and the sunset is Aethiopia,
The very last place on earth, where giant Atlas pivots

1. Virgil does not say whose are the tears; and according to another interpretation it is Aeneas who weeps.

The wheeling sky, embossed with fiery stars, on his shoulders.
I have been in touch with a priestess from there, a Massylian, who
    once,
As warden of the Hesperides' sacred close, was used to
Feed the dragon which guarded their orchard of golden apples,
Sprinkling its food with moist honey and sedative poppy-seeds.
Now this enchantress claims that her spells can liberate
One's heart, or can inject love-pangs, just as she wishes;
Can stop the flow of rivers, send the stars flying backwards,
Conjure ghosts in the night: she can make the earth cry out
Under one's feet, and elm trees come trooping down from the
    mountains.
Dear sister, I solemnly call to witness the gods and you whom
I love, that I do not willingly resort to her magic arts.
You must build up a funeral pyre high in the inner courtyard,
And keep it dark: lay on it the arms which that godless man
Has left on the pegs in our bedroom, all relics of him, and the
    marriage-bed
That was the ruin of me. To blot out all that reminds me
Of that vile man is my pleasure and what the enchantress directs.
    So Dido spoke, and fell silent, her face going deadly white.
Yet Anna never suspected that Dido was planning her own death
Through these queer rites, nor imagined how frantic a madness
    possessed her,
Nor feared any worse would happen than when Sychaeus had died.
So she made the arrangements required of her.
    When in the innermost court of the palace the pyre had been built
    up
To a great height with pinewood and logs of ilex, the queen
Festooned the place with garlands and wreathed it with funereal
Foliage: then she laid on it the clothes, the sword which Aeneas
Had left, and an effigy of him; she well knew what was to happen.
Altars are set up all round. Her hair unloosed, the enchantress
Loudly invokes three hundred deities – Erebus, Chaos,
Hecate, three in one, and three-faced Diana, the virgin.
She had sprinkled water which came, she pretended, from Lake
    Avernus;
Herbs she had gathered, cut by moonlight with a bronze knife –

Poisonous herbs all rank with juices of black venom;
She has found a love charm, a gland torn from the forehead of a new-
    born
Foal before its mother could get it.
Dido, the sacramental grain in her purified hands,
One foot unsandalled, her dress uncinctured, stood by the altars
Calling upon the gods and the stars that know fate's secrets,
Death at her heart, and prayed to whatever power it is
Holds unrequited lovers in its fair, faithful keeping.

    Was night. All over the earth, creatures were plucking the flower
Of soothing sleep, the woods and the wild seas fallen quiet –
A time when constellations have reached their mid-career,
When the countryside is all still, the beasts and the brilliant birds
That haunt the lakes' wide waters or the tangled undergrowth
Of the champain, stilled in sleep under the quiet night –
Cares are lulled and hearts can forget for a while their travails.
Not so the Phoenician queen: death at her heart, she could not
Ever relax in sleep, let the night in to her eyes
Or mind: her agonies mounted, her love reared up again
And savaged her, till she writhed in a boiling sea of passion.
So thus she began, her thoughts whirling round in a vicious circle:

    What shall I do? Shall I, who've been jilted, return to my former
Suitors? Go down on my knees for marriage to one of the Nomads
Although, time and again, I once rejected their offers?
Well then, am I to follow the Trojan's fleet and bow to
Their lightest word? I helped them once. Will that help me now?
Dare I think they remember with gratitude my old kindness?
But even if I wished it, who would suffer me, welcome me
Aboard those arrogant ships? They hate me. Ah, duped and ruined! –
Surely by now I should know the ill faith of Laomedon's people?
So then? Shall I sail, by myself, with those exulting mariners,
Or sail against them with all my Tyrian folk about me –
My people, whom once I could hardly persuade to depart from
    Sidon –
Bidding them man their ships and driving them out to sea again?
Better die – I deserve it – end my pain with the sword.
Sister, you started it all: overborne by my tears, you laid up
These evils to drive me mad, put me at the mercy of a foe.

Oh, that I could have been some child of nature and lived
An innocent life, untouched by marriage and all its troubles!
I have broken the faith I vowed to the memory of Sychaeus.

Such were the reproaches she could not refrain from uttering.
High on the poop of his ship, resolute now for departure,
Aeneas slept; preparations for sailing were fully completed.
To him in a dream there appeared the shape of the god, returning
Just as he'd looked before, as if giving the same admonitions
Mercury's very image, the voice, the complexion, the yellow
Hair and the handsome youthful body identical:

Goddess-born, can you go on sleeping at such a crisis?
Are you out of your mind, not to see what dangers are brewing up
Around you, and not to hear the favouring breath of the West wind?
Being set upon death, her heart is aswirl with conflicting passions,
Aye, she is brooding now some trick, some desperate deed.
Why are you not going, all speed, while the going is good?
If dawn finds you still here, delaying by these shores,
You'll have the whole sea swarming with hostile ships, there will be
Firebrands coming against you, you'll see this beach ablaze.
Up and away, then! No more lingering! Woman was ever
A veering weathercock creature.

                         He spoke, and vanished in the darkness.
Then, startled by the shock of the apparition, Aeneas
Snatched himself out of sleep and urgently stirred up his comrades:

Jump to it, men! To your watch! Get to the rowing benches!
Smartly! Hoist the sails! A god from heaven above
Spurs me to cut the cables, make off and lose not a moment:
This was his second warning. O blessed god, we follow you,
God indeed, and once more we obey the command joyfully!
Be with us! Look kindly upon us! Grant us good sailing weather!

Thus did Aeneas cry, and flashing his sword from its scabbard,
With the drawn blade he severed the moorings. The same sense of
Urgency fired his comrades all; they cut and ran for it.
The shore lay empty. The ships covered the open sea.
The oarsmen swept the blue and sent the foam flying with hard
    strokes.

And now was Aurora, leaving the saffron bed of Tithonus,
Beginning to shower upon earth the light of another day.

The queen, looking forth from her roof-top, as soon as she saw the sky
Grow pale and the Trojan fleet running before the wind,
Aware that the beach and the roadstead were empty, the sailors gone,
Struck herself three times, four times, upon her lovely breast,
Tore at her yellow hair, and exclaimed:
                                        In god's name! shall that foreigner
Scuttle away and make a laughing-stock of my country?
Will not my people stand to arms for a mass pursuit?
Will some not rush the warships out of the docks? Move, then!
Bring firebrands apace, issue the weapons, pull on the oars!
What am I saying? Where am I? What madness veers my mind?
Poor Dido, the wrong you have done – is it only now coming home
    to you?
You should have thought of that when you gave him your sceptre.
                                        So this is
The word of honour of one who, men say, totes round his home-gods
Everywhere, and bore on his back a doddering father!
Why could I not have seized him, torn up his body and littered
The sea with it? finished his friends with the sword, finished his own
Ascanius and served him up for his father to banquet on?
The outcome of battle had been uncertain? – Let it have been so:
Since I was to die, whom had I to fear? I should have stormed
Their bulwarks with fire, set alight their gangways, gutted the whole
    lot –
Folk, father and child – then flung myself on the conflagration.
O sun, with your beams surveying all that is done on earth!
Juno, the mediator and witness of my tragedy!
Hecate, whose name is howled by night at the city crossroads!
Avenging Furies, and you, the patrons of dying Elissa! –
Hear me! Incline your godheads to note this wickedness
So worthy of your wrath! And hear my prayer! If he,
That damned soul, must make port and get to land, if thus
Jove destines it, if that bourne is fixed for him irrevocably,
May he be harried in war by adventurous tribes, and exiled
From his own land; may Ascanius be torn from his arms; may he
    have to
Sue for aid, and see his own friends squalidly dying.
Yes, and when he's accepted the terms of a harsh peace,

Let him never enjoy his realm or the allotted span,
But fall before his time and lie on the sands, unburied.
That is my last prayer. I pour it out, with my lifeblood.
Let you, my Tyrians, sharpen your hatred upon his children
And all their seed for ever: send this as a present to
My ghost. Between my people and his, no love, no alliance!
Rise up from my dead bones, avenger! Rise up, one
To hound the Trojan settlers with fire and steel remorselessly,
Now, some day, whenever the strength for it shall be granted!
Shore to shore, sea to sea, weapon to weapon opposed –
I call down a feud between them and us to the last generation!
    These things she said; then tried to think of every expedient,
Seeking the quickest way out of the life she hated.
Briefly now she addressed Barce, the nurse of Sychaeus,
Her own being dust and ashes, interred in her native land:
    Dear nurse, please will you get my sister, Anna. She must
Hasten to purify herself with living water, and fetch
The cattle, tell her – the atonement offerings, as directed;
Then let her come. And do you go and put on the holy head-band.
These rites to Jove of the Underworld, duly made ready and started,
I mean to go through with now, and put an end to my troubles,
Committing to the flames the funeral pyre of that Trojan.
    She spoke. The nurse hurried off with senile officiousness.
But Dido, trembling, distraught by the terrible thing she was doing,
Her bloodshot eyes all restless, with hectic blotches upon
Her quivering cheeks, yet pale with the shade of advancing death,
Ran to the innermost court of the palace, climbed the lofty
Pyre, frantic at heart, and drew Aeneas' sword –
Her present to him, procured once for a far different purpose.
Then, after eyeing the clothes he had left behind, and the memoried
Bed, pausing to weep and brood on him for a little,
She lay down on the bed and spoke her very last words:
O relics of him, things dear to me while fate, while heaven allowed it,
Receive this life of mine, release me from my troubles!
I have lived, I have run to the finish the course which fortune gave
    me:
And now, a queenly shade, I shall pass to the world below.
I built a famous city, saw my own place established,

Avenged a husband, exacted a price for a brother's enmity.
Happy I would have been, ah, beyond words happy,
If only the Trojan ships had never come to my shore!
   These words; then, burying her face in the bed:
                                 Shall I die unavenged?
At least, let me die. Thus, thus! I go to the dark, go gladly.
May he look long, from out there on the deep, at my flaming pyre,
The heartless! And may my death-fires signal bad luck for his voyage!
  She had spoken; and with these words, her attendants saw her
    falling
Upon the sword, they could see the blood spouting up over
The blade, and her hands spattered. Their screams rang to the roofs of
The palace; the rumour ran amok through the shocked city.
All was weeping and wailing, the streets were filled with a keening
Of women, the air resounded with terrible lamentations.
It was as if Carthage or ancient Tyre should be falling,
With enemy troops breaking into the town and a conflagration
Furiously sweeping over the abodes of men and of gods.
Anna heard it: half dead from extreme fear, she ran through
The crowd, tearing her cheeks with her nails, beating her breast
With her fists, and called aloud by name on the dying woman:
  So this was your purpose, Dido? You were making a dupe of me?
That pyre, those lighted altars – for me, they were leading to this?
How shall I chide you for leaving me? Were you too proud to let
    your
Sister die with you? You should have called me to share your end:
One hour, one pang of the sword could have carried us both away.
Did I build this pyre with my own hands, invoking our family gods,
So that you might lie on it, and I, the cause of your troubles, not be
    there?
You have destroyed more than yourself – me, and the lords
And commons and city of Sidon. Quick! Water for her wounds!
Let me bathe them, and if any last breath is fluttering from her mouth,
Catch it in mine!
              So saying, she had scaled the towering pyre,
Taken the dying woman into her lap, was caressing her,
Sobbing, trying to staunch the dark blood with her own dress.
Dido made an effort to raise her heavy eyes,

Then gave it up: the sword-blade grated against her breast bone.
Three times she struggled to rise, to lift herself on an elbow,
Three times rolled back on the bed. Her wandering gaze went up
To the sky, looking for light: she gave a moan when she saw it.
   Then did almighty Juno take pity on her long-drawn-out
Sufferings and hard going, sent Iris down from Olympus
To part the agonized soul from the body that still clung to it.
Since she was dying neither a natural death nor from others'
Violence, but desperate and untimely, driven to it
By a crazed impulse, not yet had Proserpine clipped from her head
The golden tress, or consigned her soul to the Underworld.
So now, all dewy, her pinions the colour of yellow crocus,
Her wake a thousand rainbow hues refracting the sunlight,
Iris flew down, and over Dido hovering, said: –
   As I was bidden, I take this sacred thing, the Death-god's
Due: and you I release from your body.

                                   She snipped the tress.
Then all warmth went at once, the life was lost in air.

                                   CECIL DAY LEWIS (1952)

HERCULES AND CACUS

                              When hunger
Was satisfied, and the wine went round, Evander
Told them a story [1]:
                        'No vain superstition,
No ignorance of the gods, enjoins upon us
These solemn rites, this feast, this deep devotion
To a mighty power's altar. O Trojan guest,
We are grateful men, saved from a cruel danger;
We pay these rites each year, each year renewing

---

1. Aeneas and his followers have arrived at the site of the future Rome, and
hear this tale from the king who ruled on the Palatine Hill, beneath which was
the Ara Maxima, the great altar of Hercules.

A worship justly due. Look up at the cliff
Hung on the high rocks yonder, see the scattered
Rubble of rock, the ruin of a dwelling,
The jumble of toppled crags. There was a cave there
Once on a time; no man had ever measured
Its awful depth, no sunlight ever cheered it.
The half-man, Cacus, terrible to look at,
Lived in that cave, and the ground was always reeking
With the smell of blood, and, nailed to the doors, the faces
Of men hung pale and wasted. Vulcan fathered
This monster; you would know it if you saw him
With the black fire pouring from mouth and nostrils,
A bulk of moving evil. But time at last
Brought us the help we prayed for; a great avenger,
A god, came to our rescue, Hercules,
Proud in the death and spoil of triple Geryon,
Drove his huge bulls this way, the great herd filling
Valley and river. And the crazy Cacus,
Who never would lose a chance for crime or cunning,
Made off with four of the bulls and four sleek heifers,
Dragging them by their tails; the tracks would never
Prove he had driven them to his rocky cavern.
He hid them in the darkness; whoever looked
Would think they had gone not to, but from, the cave.
Meanwhile, as Hercules drove the well-fed herd
Out of the stables to the road again,
Some of them lowed in protest; hill and grove
Gave back the sound, and from the cave one heifer
Lowed in return. That was the doom of Cacus.
Black bile burned hot in Hercules; he grabbed
His weapons, his great knotted club, went rushing
Up to the mountain-top. Never before
Had men seen terror in the eyes of Cacus.
Swifter than wind, he dove into his cavern,
Shut himself in, shattered the links of iron
That held aloft the giant boulder, dropped it
To block the doorway, and Hercules came flinging
His angry strength against it, to no purpose.

This way he faced, and that, and gnashed his teeth
In sheer frustration; he went around the mountain
Three times, in burning rage; three times he battered
The bulkhead of the door; three times he rested,
Breathless and weary, on the floor of the valley.
Above the cavern ridge, a pointed rock,
All flint, cut sharp, with a sheer drop all around it,
Rose steep, a nesting place for kites and buzzards.
It leaned a little leftward toward the river.
This Hercules grabbed and shook, straining against it;
His right hand pushed and wrenched it loose; he shoved it,
With a sudden heave, downhill, and the heaven thundered,
The river ran backward and the banks jumped sideways,
And Cacus' den stood open, that great palace
Under the rock, the chambered vault of shadows.
An earthquake, so, might bring to light the kingdoms
Of the world below the world, the pallid regions
Loathed by the gods, the gulf of gloom, where phantoms
Shiver and quake as light descends upon them.
So there was Cacus, desperate in the light,
Caught in the hollow rock, howling and roaring
As Hercules rained weapons down upon him,
Everything he could use, from boughs to millstones.
But Cacus still had one way out of the danger:
A cloud of smoke rolled out of his jaws; the cave
Darkened to utter blackness, thick night rolling
With fitful glints of fire. This was too much
For Hercules in his fury; he jumped down through it,
Through fire, where the smoke came rolling forth the thickest,
Where the black billows seethed around the cavern.
And Cacus, in the darkness, to no purpose
Poured forth his fire and smoke. Hercules grabbed him,
Twisted him into a knot, hung on, and choked him
Till the eyes bulged out and the throat was dry of blood.
He tore the doors loose, and the house was open;
People could see the lost and stolen plunder,
And Hercules dragged the shapeless ugly carcass
Out by the feet, a fascinating object

For the gaze of men, the terrible eyes, the muzzle,
The hairy chest, and the fire dead in the gullet.
Ever since then we keep this day, rejoicing
In honour of our deliverance.

ROLFE HUMPHRIES (1951)

HORACE

QUINTUS HORATIUS FLACCUS, born at Venusia in south-east Italy in 65 B.C., fought on the losing (Republican) side at Philippi (42) but was amnestied; joined the literary circle of Maecenas (37); after Virgil's death became Augustus' poet laureate, being commissioned to write the *Secular Hymn*; died 8 B.C., a few months after Maecenas.

His early works included the harsh *Epodes* (published *c.* 30–29 B.C.), in the iambic verse traditionally dedicated to invective themes (as later in the *Iambes* of Chénier and Barbier). The four books of *Odes*, works of his maturity (published 23–13 B.C.), are not the spontaneous lyric of Alcaeus and Sappho – whose 'Romanizer' Horace, despite his singularly different talent, claims to be. Besides, Horace's poems are nearly all written for recitation, not singing. He mixes *le vers donné* and *le vers calculé* in different proportions from Catullus, whose passionate love was alien to his temperament. As Sir Maurice Bowra remarks of Horace, 'the first wild onslaught', as in Donne and Baudelaire, 'yields to something more meditated and more complex.' Horace was too good to have Roman lyrical successors – until the Christian Latinists, Prudentius and Paulinus of Nola.

The *Odes* came into their own with Petrarch, who purchased a manuscript in 1347 and quoted Horace more than any other poet except Virgil. In the next century his fellow-Florentine Landino and Landino's pupil Politian founded Horace's modern fame; his poems were printed in about 1470. Torquato Tasso's father, Bernardo, published Italian imitations (1531), and there were translations into Italian, French, German, and Spanish within the next sixty years. The French Pléiade, like Horace, combined lyrical and national themes. In England, Ben Jonson has been called the first true Horatian, since he admired the *Odes* as well as the *Satires* and *Epistles*. There is also a fine imitation by Thomas Campion (*The man of life upright ....*). Herrick liked Horace's nature poems; and the *Odes* on life and death, and on patriotic themes, also began to have their vogue. Andrew Marvell's *Horatian Ode upon Cromwell's Return from Ireland* sounds some authentic echoes:

> 'Tis madness to resist or blame
> The force of angry heaven's flame;
> And if we would speak true,
> Much to the man is due

> Who from his private gardens, where
> He lived reservèd and austere,
>   As if his highest plot
>   To plant the bergamot,
> Could by industrious valour climb
> To ruin the great work of Time,
>   And cast the kingdoms old
>   Into another mould.

Horace's Golden Mean, interpreted by Frederick the Great and Louis XIV as encouraging quietism under autocratic rule, naturally proved less attractive to the French Revolution. But he was Wordsworth's favourite poet, and was well-known to Browning and much quoted by him. 'Overdosed with Horace' as a boy, Tennyson came to regard Horace and Keats as his two masters, and always took a Horace with him on his travels: stanzas of *In Memoriam* resemble the compact stanzas of a Horatian Ode, in which the lines are

> jewels five words long
> That on the stretched fore-finger of all time
> Sparkle for ever.

The *Satires* and maturer *Epistles* and *Art of Poetry* [1] have, for all their strong individuality, a complicated pedigree of Greek *genres*, and many special debts to Latin forerunners of whose work we can only imperfectly judge, including Ennius and particularly Lucilius. In the Middle Ages Horace's *Satires* and *Epistles* exercised much more influence than his *Odes*, because many of them are moralistic. Their survival was due to Benedictine copyists – and to Charlemagne; a commentary on *The Art of Poetry* has sometimes been attributed to his educational adviser Alcuin of York. It was as *satiro* that Dante admired Horace. Ariosto's seven *Satires* on social corruption are Horatian poems with some of Juvenal's acid. L. Evans published English versions of two *Satires* in 1564, and T. Drant a complete translation of the *Satires*, *Epistles*, and *Art of Poetry* in 1567.

Ben Jonson imitated the *Satires* and *Epistles*, and translated – and noted well – *The Art of Poetry*, once thought of as a final Epistle. Through Boileau's *L'Art Poétique* (1674),[2] this treatise on Poetry and Poet's Manual became, in France, canonical – and misunderstood as a

1. The *Satires* were published in *c.* 35 and *c.* 29 B.C., and the *Epistles* between 20 and Horace's death; the *Ars Poetica* belongs to his last years.

2. Verlaine revived the title – but to strike against contemporary Parnassians. Claudel too had his *Art Poétique*.

systematic treatise; and it was adapted in Byron's *Hints from Horace* (1811) – though Byron had hated Horace at school. Boileau and Byron come roughly at the beginning and the end of an age when much of the finest poetic talent was devoted to the adaptation of classical writers, and especially of Horace. 'I resolved', said Oldham in presenting his own version of the *Ars Poetica* (1681), 'to alter the Scene from Rome to London, and to make use of English names of Men, Places, and Customs, where the Parallel would decently permit, which I conceived would give a kind of new Air to the Poem, and render it more agreeable to the relish of the present Age.' In the same spirit, when the English Augustan Age had dawned, Alexander Pope composed his *Imitations of Horace* [1] – justifying his satire, in accordance with custom, by the public interest. Though Pope is by no means Horace, his *Essay on Criticism* makes explicit acknowledgement:

> Horace still charms with graceful negligence,
> And without method talks us into sense;
> Will like a friend familiarly convey
> The truest notion in the easiest way.

In a later and more solemn epoch, Keble observed: 'I reluctantly confess myself hitherto unable to discover any peculiar and dominating spring of Horace's poetry.' Yet if no single theme dominates, that is because of his astonishing variety and classic balance. Keble went on to censure his light touch. But that is one of the few features of Horace which has won some appreciation from our own unprecedentedly un-Horatian age.

1. Pope started work on these in 1733. He was influenced by the fifteenth-century *Ars Poetica* of Marco Girolamo Vida, edited in England in 1702.

ODES AND EPODES

THE GOLDEN MEAN [1]

You better, sure, shall live, not evermore
Trying high seas; nor, while sea's rage you flee,
Pressing too much upon ill-harboured shore.
The golden Mean who loves, lives safely free
From filth of foreworn house, and quiet lives,
Released from Court, where envy needs must be.
The wind most oft the hugest pine-tree grieves;
The stately towers come down with greater fall;
The highest hills the bolt of thunder cleaves;
Evil haps do fill with hope, good haps appal
With fear of change the courage well prepared:
Foul winters, as they come, away they shall.
Though present times and past with evils be snared,
They shall not last: with cithern silent Muse
Apollo wakes, and bow hath sometime spared.
In hard estate, with stout show valour use,
The same man still, in whom wisdom prevails;
In too full wind draw in thy swelling sails.

SIR PHILIP SIDNEY (1554–86)

GATHER YE ROSEBUDS

Strive not, Leuconoë, to know what end
The gods above to me or thee will send;
Nor with astrologers consult at all,
That thou mayst better know what can befall:
Whether thou livest more winters, or thy last
Be this, which Tyrrhene waves 'gainst rocks do cast.

1. The Licinius to whom this Ode is addressed may be Varro Murena (brother-in-law of Maecenas), an insolent man who was soon afterwards executed by Augustus for alleged conspiracy.

Be wise! Drink free, and in so short a space
Do not protracted hopes of life embrace:
Whilst we are talking, envious time doth slide;
This day's thine own; the next may be denied.

SIR THOMAS HAWKINS (d. 1640)

A NARROW ESCAPE

What slender youth bedewed with liquid odours
Courts thee on roses in some pleasant cave,
 Pyrrha, for whom bindest thou
 In wreaths thy golden hair,

Plain in thy neatness? O how oft shall he
On faith and changèd gods complain: and seas
 Rough with black winds and storms
 Unwonted shall admire,

Who now enjoys thee credulous, all gold,
Who always vacant, always amiable
 Hopes thee; of flattering gales
 Unmindful. Hapless they

To whom thou untried seemest fair. Me in my vowed
Picture the sacred wall declares to have hung
 My dank and dropping weeds
 To the stern god of sea.

JOHN MILTON (1608–74)

ENJOY THE PRESENT HOUR

Behold yon mountain's hoary height,
 Made higher with new mounts of snow;
Again, behold the winter weight
 Oppress the labouring woods below;
And streams with icy fetters bound
Benumbed and cramped to solid ground.

With well-heaped logs dissolve the cold,
   And feed the genial hearth with fires:
Produce the wine that makes us bold,
   And love of sprightly wit inspires.
For what hereafter shall betide,
God, if 'tis worth his care, provide.

Let Him alone, with what He made,
   To toss and turn the world below;
At His command the storms invade,
   The winds by His commission blow,
Till, with a nod, He bids them cease,
And calm returns, and all is peace.

Tomorrow and her works defy;
   Lay hold upon the present hour,
And snatch the pleasures passing by,
   To put them out of Fortune's power.
Nor Love nor Love's delights disdain;
Whate'er thou gettest today is gain.

Secure those golden, early joys,
   That youth unsoured by sorrow bears,
Ere withering Time the taste destroys
   With sickness and unwieldy years.
For active sports, for pleasing rest,
This is the time to be possessed:
The best is but in season best.

The appointed hour of promised bliss,
   The pleasing whisper in the dark,
The half-unwilling, willing kiss,
   The laugh that guides thee to the mark,
When the kind nymph would coyness feign,
And hides but to be loved again;
These, these are joys, the gods for youth ordain.

JOHN DRYDEN (1685)

Descended of an ancient line,
   That long the Tuscan sceptre swayed,
Make haste to meet the generous wine
   Whose piercing is for thee delayed.
The rosy wreath is ready made
   And artful hands prepare
The fragrant Syrian oil that shall perfume thy hair.

When the wine sparkles from afar
   And the well-natured friend cries 'Come away',
Make haste, and leave thy business and thy care:
   No mortal interest can be worth thy stay.

Leave for awhile thy costly country seat,
   And – to be great indeed – forget
The nauseous pleasures of the great:
   Make haste and come,
Come, and forsake thy cloying store,
   Thy turret that surveys from high
The smoke and wealth and noise of Rome,
   And all the busy pageantry
That wise men scorn and fools adore:
Come, give thy soul a loose, and taste the pleasures of the poor.

Sometimes 'tis grateful to the rich to try
A short vicissitude and fit of poverty;
   A savoury dish, a homely treat,
   Where all is plain, where all is neat,
   Without the stately spacious room,
The Persian carpet or the Tyrian loom,
Clear up the clouded foreheads of the great.

The Sun is in the Lion mounted high,
   The Syrian star
   Barks from afar,

And with his sultry breath infects the sky;
The ground below is parched, the heavens above us fry;
 The shepherd drives his fainting flock
  Beneath the covert of a rock
  And seeks refreshing rivulets nigh.
 The Sylvans to their shade retire,
Those very shades and streams new streams require,
And want a cooling breeze of wind to fan the raging fire.

 Thou, what befits the new Lord Mayor,
  And what the city faction dare,
  And what the Gallic arms will do,
  And what the quiver-bearing foe,
  Art anxiously inquisitive to know.
 But God has wisely hid from human sight
  The dark decrees of future fate,
 And sown their seeds in depth of night:
He laughs at all the giddy turns of state
When mortals search too soon and learn too late.

 Enjoy the present smiling hour,
  And put it out of Fortune's power.
The tide of business, like the running stream,
 Is sometimes high and sometimes low,
 A quiet ebb or a tempestuous flow,
  And always in extreme.
 Now with a noiseless gentle course
 It keeps within the middle bed,
  Anon it lifts aloft its head
And bears down all before it with tempestuous force;

 And trunks of trees come rolling down,
  Sheep and their folds together drown,
 Both house and homestead into seas are borne,
 And rocks are from their old foundations torn,
And woods, made thin with winds, their scattered honours mourn.

Happy the man – and happy he alone –
   He who can call today his own,
   He who, secure within, can say
'Tomorrow, do thy worst, for I have lived today:
   Be fair or foul or rain or shine,
The joys I have possessed in spite of Fate are mine:
   Not Heaven itself upon the Past has power,
But what has been has been, and I have had my hour.'

Fortune, that with malicious joy
   Does Man, her slave, oppress,
Proud of her office to destroy,
   Is seldom pleased to bless;
Still various and unconstant still,
   But with an inclination to be ill,
Promotes, degrades, delights in strife
   And makes a lottery of life.

I can enjoy her while she's kind,
But when she dances in the wind,
   And shakes the wings and will not stay,
     I puff the prostitute away.
The little or the much she gave is quietly resigned:
   Content with poverty my soul I arm,
  And Virtue, though in rags, will keep me warm.

     What is't to me,
Who never sail in her unfaithful sea,
   If storms arise and clouds grow black,
    If the mast split and threaten wrack?
Then let the greedy merchant fear
    For his ill-gotten gain,
And pray to gods that will not hear,
While the debating winds and billows bear
    His wealth into the main.

For me, secure from Fortune's blows,
Secure of what I cannot lose,

In my small pinnace I can sail,
Contemning all the blustering roar:
   And running with a merry gale
With friendly stars my safety seek
Within some little winding creek,
   And see the storm ashore.

JOHN DRYDEN (1685)

FAITHLESS

Did any punishment attend
   Thy former perjuries,
I should believe, a second time,
   Thy charming flatteries:
Did but one wrinkle mark thy face,
Or hadst thou lost one single grace.

No sooner hast thou, with false vows,
   Provoked the powers above;
But thou art fairer than before,
   And we are more in love.
Thus heaven and earth seem to declare
They pardon falsehood in the fair.

SIR CHARLES SEDLEY (1639–1701)

A QUIET LIFE

In storms when clouds the moon do hide,
And no kind stars the pilot guide,
Show me at sea the boldest there
Who does not wish for quiet here.

For quiet, friend, the soldier fights,
Bears weary marches, sleepless nights,
For this feeds hard and lodges cold,
Which can't be bought with hills of gold.

Since wealth and power too weak we find
To quell the tumults of the mind,
Or from the monarch's roofs of state
Drive thence the cares that round him wait,

Happy the man with little blest
Of what his father left possessed;
No base desires corrupt his head,
No fears disturb him in his bed.

What then in life which soon must end
Can all our vain designs intend?
From shore to shore why should we run,
When none his tiresome self can shun?

For baneful care will still prevail,
And overtake us under sail,
'Twill dodge the great man's train behind,
Outrun the roe, outfly the wind.

If then thy soul rejoice today,
Drive far tomorrow's cares away.
In laughter let them all be drowned;
No perfect good is to be found.

One mortal feels fate's sudden blow,
Another's lingering death comes slow;
And what of life they take from thee
The gods may give to punish me.

Thy portion is a wealthy stock,
A fertile glebe, a fruitful flock,
Horses and chariots for thine ease,
Rich robes to deck and make thee please.

For me, a little cell I choose,
Fit for my mind, fit for my Muse,
Which soft content does best adorn,
Shunning the knaves and fools I scorn.

THOMAS OTWAY (1652–85)

THE POET'S EXALTED TASK

He on whose natal hour the queen
   Of verse hath smiled, shall never grace
The Isthmian gauntlet, or be seen
   First in the famed Olympic race;

He shall not, after toils of war,
   And taming haughty monarchs' pride,
With laurelled brows conspicuous far
   To Jove's Tarpeian temple ride:

But him the streams which warbling flow
   Rich Tibur's fertile vales along,
And shady groves, his haunts, shall know
   The master of the Aeolian song.[1]

The sons of Rome, majestic Rome,
   Have placed me in the poet's choir,
And envy now, or dead or dumb,
   Forbears to blame what they admire.
             FRANCIS ATTERBURY (1662–1732)

TRUE GREATNESS

Virtue concealed within our breast
Is inactivity at best;
But never shall the Muse endure
To let your virtues lie obscure,
Or suffer Envy to conceal
Your labours for the public weal.
   Within your breast all wisdom lies,
Either to govern or advise;

1. The Greek lyric poets of Aeolis (Lesbos and the coast of Asia Minor), of whom Horace claimed to be the follower and Romanizer, were Alcaeus and Sappho.

Your steady soul preserves her frame
In good and evil times the same.
Pale Avarice and lurking Fraud
Stand in your sacred presence awed;
Your hand alone from gold abstains,[1]
Which drags the slavish world in chains.
Him for a happy man I own
Whose fortune is not overgrown;
And happy he who wisely knows
To use the gifts that heaven bestows;
Or if it please the powers divine,
Can suffer want and not repine.
The man who, infamy to shun,
Into the arms of death would run,
That man is ready to defend
With life his country or his friend.

JONATHAN SWIFT (1667–1745)

JUNO'S DECREE TO ROME [2]

The thin remains of Troy's afflicted host,
In distant realms may seats unenvied find,
And flourish on a foreign coast;
But far be Rome from Troy disjoined,
Removed by seas from the disastrous shore;
May endless billows rise between, and storms unnumbered
roar.
Still let the cursed, detested place,
Where Priam lies, and Priam's faithless race,
Be covered o'er with weeds, and hid in grass.
There let the wanton flocks unguarded stray;

1. The poem is addressed to Marcus Lollius, who later met his end ostensibly for accepting Parthian bribes, but really perhaps because of his enmity to Tiberius. His memory was subsequently attacked for an alleged military defeat in Germany.

2. Though Troy is Rome's ancestor (the legend had been gradually built up, and perpetuated by the *Aeneid*), Juno warns Rome not to emulate its fatal oriental luxury – the luxury of a Cleopatra as opposed to the western, old Roman austerity. Addison's version is an expanded paraphrase.

Or, while the lonely shepherd sings,
Amidst the mighty ruins play,
And frisk upon the tombs of kings.

May tigers there, and all the savage kind,
Sad, solitary haunts and silent deserts find;
In gloomy vaults, and nooks of palaces,
May the unmolested lioness
Her brindled whelps securely lay,
Or, couched, in dreadful slumbers waste the day.

While Troy in heaps of ruins lies,
Rome and the Roman Capitol shall rise;
The illustrious exiles unconfined
Shall triumph far and near, and rule mankind.

In vain the sea's intruding tide
Europe from Afric shall divide,
And part the severed world in two:
Through Afric's sands their triumphs they shall spread,
And the long train of victories pursue
To Nile's yet undiscovered head.
Riches the hardy soldier shall despise,
And look on gold with undesiring eyes,
Nor the disbowelled earth explore
In search of the forbidden ore;
Those glittering ills concealed within the mine,
Shall lie untouched, and innocently shine.
To the last bounds that nature sets,
The piercing colds and sultry heats,
The godlike race shall spread their arms:
Now fill the polar circle with alarms,
Till storms and tempests their pursuits confine;
Now sweat for conquest underneath the line.

This only law the victor shall restrain,
On these conditions shall he reign:
If none his guilty hand employ
To build again a second Troy,
If none the rash design pursue,
Nor tempt the vengeance of the gods anew.

JOSEPH ADDISON (1672–1719)

Lest you should think that verse shall die,
    Which sounds the silver Thames along,
Taught on the wings of truth, to fly
    Above the reach of vulgar song;

Though daring Milton sits sublime,
    In Spencer native Muses play;
Nor yet shall Waller yield to time,
    Nor pensive Cowley's moral lay.

Sages and chiefs long since had birth
    Ere Caesar was, or Newton named:
These raised new empires o'er the earth,
    And those new Heavens and systems framed;

Vain was the chief's and sage's pride;
    They had no poet, and they died.
In vain they schemed, in vain they bled:
    They had no poet, and are dead.
           ALEXANDER POPE (1688–1744)[1]

WE ALL MUST DIE

Alas, dear friend, the fleeting years
    In everlasting circles run,
In vain you spend your vows and prayers,
    They roll, and ever will roll on.

Should hecatombs each rising morn
    On cruel Pluto's altar dye,
Should costly loads of incense burn,
    Their fumes ascending to the sky;

1. This poem should not perhaps, strictly speaking, have been included, since it replaces old names by new, and is therefore an adaptation rather than even the looser sort of translation. See also below, p. 203.

You could not gain a moment's breath,
  Or move the haughty king below,
Nor would inexorable death
  Defer an hour the fatal blow.

In vain we shun the din of war,
  And terrors of the stormy main,
In vain with anxious breasts we fear
  Unwholesome Sirius' sultry reign;

We all must view the Stygian flood
  That silent cuts the dreary plains,
And cruel Danaus' bloody brood
  Condemned to everduring pains.

Your shady groves, your pleasing wife,
  And fruitful fields, my dearest friend,
You'll leave together with your life:
  Alone the cypress shall attend.[1]

After your death, the lavish heir
  Will quickly drive away his woe;
The wine you kept with so much care
  Along the marble floor shall flow.

                    SAMUEL JOHNSON (1709–84)

STEADFAST OF PURPOSE AND LOVE

The man, my friend, whose conscious heart
  With virtue's sacred ardour glows,
Nor taints with death the envenomed dart,
  Nor needs the guard of Moorish bows.

O'er icy Caucasus he treads,
  Or torrid Afric's faithless sands,
Or where the famed Hydaspes spreads
  His liquid wealth through barbarous lands.

  1. The cypress was sacred to Pluto.

For while in Sabine forests, charmed
    By Lalage, too far I strayed,
Me singing, careless and unarmed,
    A furious wolf approached, and fled.

No beast more dreadful ever stained
    Apulia's spacious wilds with gore;
No beast more fierce Numidia's land,
    The lion's thirsty parent, bore.

Place me where no soft summer gale
    Among the quivering branches sighs,
Where clouds, condensed, for ever veil
    With horrid gloom the frowning skies:

Place me beneath the burning zone,
    A clime denied to human race;
My flame for Lalage I'll own;
    Her voice and smiles my song shall grace.

SAMUEL JOHNSON (1757) [1]

RUSTIC JOYS

Blest as the immortal Gods is he
Who lives from toilsome business free,
Like the first race in Saturn's reign
When floods of nectar stained the main;
Manuring with laborious hand
His own hereditary land;
Whom no contracted debts molest,
No griping creditors infest.
No trumpet's sound, no soldier's cries,
Drive the soft slumbers from his eyes,
He sees no boisterous tempests sweep
The surface of the boiling deep,
Him no contentious suits in law
From his beloved retirement draw,

1. The revised version of a poem written in 1743.

He ne'er with forced submission waits,
Obsequious, at his patron's gates;
But round the lofty poplar twines
With artful hand the teeming vines,
Or prunes the barren boughs away;
Or sees from far his bullocks play
Or drains the labour of the bees,
Or sheers the lambkins' snowy fleece.
Or when with golden apples crowned
Autumn o'erlooks the smiling ground
When ripening fruits perfume the year,
Plucking the blushing grape and pear,
Grateful, rewards the deities
That, favouring, listen to his cries.
Beneath some spreading ilex shade
On some green bank supinely laid,
Where rivulets gently purl along
And, murmuring, balmy sleep prolong,
Whilst each musician of the grove
Lamenting warbles out his love,
In pleasing dreams he cheats the day
Unhurt by Phoebus' fiery ray.
But when increased by winter showers
Down cliffs the roaring torrent pours,
The grizzly foaming boar surrounds
With twisted toils, and ravening hounds;
Betimes the greedy thrush to kill
He sets his nets, employs his skill,
With secret springes oft ensnares
The screaming cranes and fearful hares.

    Would not these pleasures soon remove
The bitter pangs of slighted love?
If to complete this heavenly life
A frugal, chaste, industrious wife,
Such as the sun-burnt Sabines were,
Divide the burden of his care,
And heap the fire, and milk the kine,
And crown the bowl with new-pressed wine,

And waiting for her weary lord
With unbought dainties load the board,
I should behold with scornful eye
The studied arts of luxury:
No fish from the Carpathian coast
By Eastern tempests hither tossed,
Nor Libyan fowls, nor snipes of Greece,
So much my appetite would please
As herbs of which the forests nigh
Wholesome variety supply.
Then to the gods, on solemn days,
The farmer annual honours pays,
Or feasts on kids the wolves had killed
And, frighted, left upon the field.
How pleased he sees his cattle come,
Their dugs with milk distended, home!
How pleased beholds his oxen bow
And faintly draw the inverted plough.
His cheerful slaves, a numerous band,
Around in beauteous order stand.

Thus did the usurer Alfius praise,
With transports kindled, rural ease.
His money he collected straight,
Resolved to purchase a retreat.
But still desires of sordid gain
Fixed in his cankered breast remain:
Next month he sets it out again.

SAMUEL JOHNSON (1709–1784)

CEASE TO MOURN

Not always, Valgius, from the bursting cloud
On ruffled plains descends the rain;
Not always fitful gales and darkness shroud
The Caspian main;

Not always on the bleak Armenian shore
Inert and rigid stands the winter snow.
Sunshine returns; the torpid waters flow;
  The storm-tossed oak-tree rests its branches hoar;
And the pale ash bewails its shattered leaves no more.

Thou, friend, in endless anguish day by day
  Mournest thy Mystes snatched away;
  Weeping, when Hesper rises on the night;
Weeping, when Phosphor flies the sun's returning light.
  Not thus on Ilion's fatal plain
  Grey Nestor mourned Antilochus:
  Not thus for ever and in vain
His Phrygian sisters wept their youthful Troilus.

  Cease, Valgius, cease thy wailing,
Those sad soft sighs, that sorrow unavailing;
And sing with me great Caesar's trophies won
From conquered realms beneath the orient sun,
  Frozen Niphates, and the flood
Of broad Euphrates dyed with Median blood.
More slow today it whirls its humbled tide
And now in narrowed bounds the Phrygian horsemen ride.

SIR STEPHEN DE VERE (1812–1904)

THE GOOD MAN NEED FEAR NOTHING

Not the rage of the million commanding things evil,
Not the doom frowning near in the brows of the tyrant,
  Shakes the upright and resolute man
    In his solid completeness of soul;

No, not Auster, the Storm-King of Hadria's wild waters,
No, not Jove's mighty hand when it launches the thunder;
  If in fragments were shattered the world,
    Him its ruins would strike undismayed.

LORD LYTTON (1831–92)

ENJOY YOUR POSSESSIONS WHILE THEY ARE YOURS

Where the high pine and the white poplar mix,
With twining boughs, their hospitable shade,
And bright streams flee between the crooked banks,
Bid them bring wines, and unguent rich, and flowers;
While age, and wealth, and the black fateful threads
Of the three Sisters join to suffer you.
For soon you leave your purchased groves, and home,
Your villa, which the yellow Tiber laves;
And heirs will seize upon the hoarded gold.

ROBERT LOUIS STEVENSON (1850–94)

ODE TO SPRING

The snows are fled away, leaves on the shaws
   And grasses in the mead renew their birth,
The river to the river-bed withdraws,
   And altered is the fashion of the earth.
The Nymphs and Graces three put off their fear
   And unapparelled in the woodland play.
The swift hour and the brief prime of the year
   Say to the soul, *Thou wast not born for aye.*
Thaw follows frost; hard on the heel of spring
   Treads summer sure to die, for hard on hers
Comes autumn, with his apples scattering;
   Then back to wintertide, when nothing stirs.
But oh, whate'er the sky-led seasons mar,
   Moon upon moon rebuilds it with her beams;
Come we where Tullus and where Ancus are
   And good Aeneas, we are dust and dreams.
Torquatus, if the gods in heaven shall add
   The morrow to the day, what tongue hath told?
Feast then thy heart, for what thy heart has had
   The fingers of no heir will ever hold.

When thou descendest once the shades among,
　　The stern assize and equal judgement o'er,
Not thy long lineage nor thy golden tongue,
　　No, nor thy righteousness, shall friend thee more.
Night holds Hippolytus the pure of stain,
　　Diana steads him nothing, he must stay;
And Theseus leaves Pirithous in the chain
　　The love of comrades cannot take away.

　　　　　　　　　A. E. HOUSMAN (1859–1936)

CELEBRATION

No history, please! Work out some other time
The pedigree of Aeacus,
Settle the dates of Inachus
And Codrus, in his death sublime.
Even your outline of the Trojan War,
Just now, would be a bore.
Far sooner would we have you say
What price a cask of Chian is today,
Or where, and what o'clock, we dine,
Who warms the water for the wine,
And shields us from this Arctic winter's nip.

Now, boy, the toasts! Murena's augurship! [1]
New Moon! and Midnight! shall the bumpers be
Nine ladlefuls, or three?
Our frenzied bard, the Muses' votary,
Will plump, of course, for nine;
While they who, like the Graces, hate a riot,
Choose three, to keep the table quiet.
　　Now we'll go berserk – let the binge begin!
Pipe up, thou Berecynthian flute!
Down from your pegs, ye lyre and lute!
I hate a stingy host like sin.

1. For Murena, see above, p. 183 n. 'Chian' is wine from Chios.

More roses! wake the neighbours with the din –
Crusty old Lycus and his Pretty Poll,
Who has no use for him at all.
Here Love be lord! flushed Rhoda find her heaven
In Bassus, shining like the star of even
With his bright curly hair; while I,
Burning for Chloe, lingeringly die.

SIR EDWARD MARSH (1941)

CONVERSION

Little and seldom to the gods I gave
   Due worship once, a wanderer in the ways
Of crazy science. Now my sails I have
   Turned round to sail the course of earlier days;

For Jupiter, who splits the clouds asunder
   With flashing fire, drives often in clear air
The horses and the chariots of thunder,
   By which dull earth and rivers wandering there,

And Styx and the dark place of dreadful nights,
   And Atlas mountain to the furthest end,
Are shaken. Yet the lowly to the heights
   He lifts, and brings the mighty low, the friend

Of poor and humble. Ravening fortune takes,
   With roar of pinions, here from one man's head
His diadem, and her delight she makes
   To place it on another man's instead.

LORD DUNSANY (1947)

THE SATIRES AND EPISTLES

WISDOM

'Tis the first virtue, vices to abhor;
And the first wisdom, to be fool no more.
But to the world, no bugbear is so great
As want of figure, and a small estate.
To either India see the merchant fly,
Scared at the spectre of pale poverty!
See him, with pains of body, pangs of soul,
Burn through the tropic, freeze beneath the pole!
Wilt thou do nothing for a nobler end,
Nothing, to make philosophy thy friend?
To stop thy foolish views, thy long desires,
And ease thy heart of all that it admires?
   Here, wisdom calls: 'Seek virtue first! be bold!
As gold to silver, virtue is to gold.'
There, London's voice: 'Get money, money still!
And then let virtue follow, if she will.'

                ALEXANDER POPE (1738)[1]

ANCIENTS AND MODERNS

If time improve our wit as well as wine,
Say at what age a poet grows divine?
Shall we, or shall we not, account him so,
Who died, perhaps, an hundred years ago?
End all dispute; and fix the year precise
When British bards begin to immortalize?
'Who lasts a century can have no flaw;
I hold that wit a classic, good in law.'

1. Alexander Pope's Horatian poems are, as he called them, *Imitations*, but
they contain passages that correspond fairly closely with the originals.

Suppose he wants a year, will you compound?
And shall we deem him ancient, right and sound,
Or damn to all eternity at once,
At ninety-nine, a modern, and a dunce?'

I lose my patience, and I own it too,
When works are censured, not as bad, but new;
While if our elders break all reason's laws,
These fools demand not pardon, but applause.

ALEXANDER POPE (1737)

THE ORIGIN OF SATIRE

Our rural ancestors, with little blest,
Patient of labour when the end was rest,
Indulged the day that housed their annual grain
With feasts, and offerings, and a thankful strain:
The joy their wives, their sons, and servants share,
Ease of their toil, and partners of their care:
The laugh, the jest, attendants on the bowl,
Smoothed every brow, and opened every soul:
With growing years the pleasing licence grew,
And taunts alternate innocently flew.
But times corrupt, and nature ill-inclined,
Produced the point that left a sting behind;
Till, friend with friend and families at strife,
Triumphant malice raged through private life.
Who felt the wrong, or feared it, took the alarm,
Appealed to law, and justice lent her arm.
At length, by wholesome dread of statutes bound,
The poets learned to please, and not to wound:
Most warped to flattery's side; but some, more nice,
Preserved the freedom, and forbore the vice.
Hence satire rose, that just the medium hit,
And heals with morals what it hurts with wit.

ALEXANDER POPE (1737)

'Twas a long journey lay before us
When I and honest Heliodorus,
Who far in point of rhetoric
Surpasses every living Greek,
Each leaving our respective home,
Together sallied forth from Rome.
    First at Aricia we alight,
And there refresh and pass the night,
Our entertainment rather coarse
Than sumptuous, but I've met with worse.
Thence o'er the causeway soft and fair
To Appii Forum we repair.
But as this road is well supplied
(Temptation strong!) on either side
With inns commodious, snug, and warm,
We split the journey, and perform
In two days' time what's often done
By brisker travellers in one.
Here rather choosing not to sup
Than with bad water mix my cup,
After a warm debate in spite
Of a provoking appetite,
I sturdily resolve at last
To balk it, and pronounce a fast,
And in a moody humour wait,
While my less dainty comrades bait.
    Now o'er the spangled hemisphere
Diffused the starry train appear,
When there arose a desperate brawl;
The slaves and bargemen, one and all,
Rending their throats (have mercy on us!)
As if they were resolved to stun us:
'Steer the barge this way to the shore!
I tell you we'll admit no more!

Plague! will you never be content?'
Thus a whole hour at least is spent,
While they receive the several fares,
And kick the mule into his gears.
Happy, these difficulties past,
Could we have fallen asleep at last!
But, what with humming, croaking, biting,
Gnats, frogs, and all their plagues uniting,
These tuneful natives of the lake
Conspired to keep us broad awake.
Besides, to make the concert full,
Two maudlin wights, exceeding dull,
The bargeman and a passenger
Each in his turn, essayed an air
In honour of his absent fair.
At length the passenger, oppressed
With wine, left off, and snored the rest.
The weary bargeman too gave o'er,
And hearing his companion snore,
Seized the occasion, fixed the barge,
Turned out his mule to graze at large,
And slept forgetful of his charge.

　　And now the sun o'er eastern hill
Discovered that our barge stood still;
When one whose anger vexed him sore,
With malice fraught, leaps quick on shore,
Plucks up a stake, with many a thwack
Assails the mule and driver's back.

　　Then slowly moving on with pain,
At ten Feronia's stream we gain,
And in her pure and glassy wave
Our hands and faces gladly lave.
Climbing three miles, fair Anxur's height
We reach, with stony quarries white.

　　While here, as was agreed, we wait,
Till, charged with business of the State,
Maecenas and Cocceius come
(The messengers of peace) from Rome.

My eyes, by watery humours blear
And sore, I with black balsam smear.

    With smiles the rising morn we greet,
At Sinuessa pleased to meet
With Plotius, Varius,[1] and the bard
Whom Mantua first with wonder heard.
The world no purer spirits knows,
For none my heart more warmly glows.
Oh! what embraces we bestowed,
And with what joy our breasts o'erflowed!
Sure while my sense is sound and clear,
Long as I live, I shall prefer
A gay, good-natured, easy friend
To every blessing Heaven can send.
    At a small village, the next night,
Near the Vulturnus, we alight;
Where, as employed on State affairs,
We were supplied by the purveyors
Frankly at once, and without hire,
With food for man and horse, and fire.
Capua next day betimes we reach,
Where Virgil and myself, who each
Laboured with different maladies,
His such a stomach, mine such eyes,
As would not bear strong exercise,
In drowsy mood to sleep resort;
Maecenas to the tennis-court.
Next at Cocceius' farm we're treated,
Above the Caudian tavern seated;
His kind and hospitable board
With choice of wholesome food was stored.

    To Beneventum next we steer;
Where our good host by over-care

---

1. Plotius Tucca and Varius Rufus (a distinguished elegiac, epic, and tragic poet, whose works are lost) became Virgil's literary executors, and edited the *Aeneid*.

In roasting thrushes lean as mice
Had almost fallen a sacrifice.
The kitchen soon was all on fire,
And to the roof the flames aspire.
There might you see each man and master
Striving, amidst this sad disaster,
To save the supper. Then they came
With speed enough to quench the flame.
From hence we first at distance see
The Apulian hills, well known to me,
Parched by the sultry western blast;
And which we never should have past,
Had not Trivicus by the way
Received us at the close of day.
But each was forced at entering here
To pay the tribute of a tear,
For more of smoke than fire was seen,
The hearth was piled with logs so green.

    From hence in chaises we were carried
Miles twenty-four, and gladly tarrïed
At a small town, whose name my verse
(So barbarous is it) can't rehearse.
Know it you may by many a sign –
Water is dearer far than wine;
There bread is deemed such dainty fare
That every prudent traveller
His wallet loads with many a crust;
For at Canusium you might just
As well attempt to gnaw a stone
As think to get a morsel down.

              WILLIAM COWPER (1731–1800)

HORACE ON LUCILIUS [1]

Yes, I did say that, view him as a bard,
Lucilius is unrhythmic, rugged, hard.

1. The founder of Roman satire (*c.* 180–120 B.C.). Less than 1,300 of his lines
survive.

Lives there a partisan so weak of brain
As to join issue on a fact so plain?
But that he had a gift of biting wit,
In the same page I hastened to admit.
Now understand me: that's a point confessed;
But he who grants it grants not all the rest:
For, were a bard a bard because he's smart,
Laberius' mimes were products of high art.
'Tis not enough to make your reader's face
Wear a broad grin, though that too has its place:
Terseness there wants, to make the thought ring clear,
Nor with a crowd of words confuse the ear:
There wants a plastic style, now grave, now light,
Now such as bard or orator would write,
And now the language of a well-bred man,
Who masks his strength, and says not all he can:
And pleasantry will often cut clean through
Hard knots that gravity would scarce undo.
On this the old comedians rested: hence
They're still the models of all men of sense.

Well, but I called him muddy, said you'd find
More sand than gold in what he leaves behind.
And you, sir Critic, does your finer sense
In Homer mark no matter for offence?
Or e'en Lucilius, our good-natured friend,
Sees he in Accius [1] nought he fain would mend?
Does he not laugh at Ennius' [2] halting verse,
Yet own himself no better, if not worse?
And what should hinder me, as I peruse
Lucilius' works, from asking, if I choose,
If fate or chance forbade him to attain
A smoother measure, a more finished strain,
Than he (you'll let me fancy such a man)
Who, anxious only to make sense and scan,

1. Roman tragic poet (170–c. 85 B.C.). All (except fragments) of Republican
tragedy is lost.
2. 'The father of Roman poetry' and ancestor of Virgil's epic (239–169 B.C.).

Pours forth two hundred verses ere he sups,
Two hundred more, on rising from his cups;
Like to Etruscan Cassius'[1] stream of song,
Which flowed, men say, so copious and so strong
That, when he died, his kinsfolk simply laid
His works in order, and his pyre was made.
No; grant Lucilius arch, engaging, gay;
Grant him the smoothest writer of his day;
Lay stress upon the fact that he'd to seek
In his own mind what others find in Greek;
Grant all you please; in turn you must allow,
Had fate postponed his life from then to now,
He'd prune redundancies, apply the file
To each excrescence that deforms his style;
Oft in the pangs of labour scratch his head,
And bite his nails, and bite them, till they bled.
Oh yes! believe me, you must draw your pen
Not once nor twice but o'er and o'er again
Through what you've written, if you would entice
The man that reads you once to read you twice,
Not making popular applause your cue,
But looking to fit audience, although few.

JOHN CONINGTON (1904)

THE TOWN MOUSE AND THE COUNTRY MOUSE

There lived
Once on a time a country mouse, who welcomed a town mouse,
So the tale tells, in his poor hole, host and guest old friends both.
Though strict and frugal of his store, yet in hospitalities
He could unbend his thrifty soul. He, in short, was not the mouse
To grudge his hoarded chickpeas or long oats, but in his mouth
Bringing dried berries and nibbled scraps of bacon, served them up,
Eager by varied fare to coax the daintiness of his friend,
Who with fastidious tooth would barely touch each bit in turn;
While himself, couched on this year's chaff, the father of the house,

1. Cassius Etruscus, a poet.

Chewed spelt and darnel, leaving the choice morsels to his guest.
At length the town mouse says to him, 'Friend, what pleasure can you
    find
In living a life of hardship on a steep wooded ridge?
Why not set men and cities above these savage forests?
There lies the road: let's take it, comrade; since with mortal souls
All creatures upon earth were born; and no escape from death
Shall ever be for either great or small. Therefore, good sir,
While yet you may, live happily among glad and pleasant things;
Live mindful of how brief your day must be.' These words went home
To the rustic's soul: forth from his house lightly he leaps: then both
Set out upon the journey they have planned, eager to creep
After dark through the city walls. Already now the night
Was tenanting the middle space of heaven, when the two
Set foot within a wealthy palace, where bright coverlets,
Dyed by the scarlet berry, upon ivory couches gleamed;
And there in baskets, that lay piled hard by, was many a course,
Remnants left over from some grand banquet of the day before.
So when the host had couched upon a cloth of crimson grain
His rustic friend, like a brisk waiter he scurries to and fro,
Presenting courses without end, nay even acts the part
Of a home-bred slave, tasting beforehand every dish he serves.
The other, reclined at ease, rejoices in his altered lot,
And plays the jovial guest amid good cheer – when on a sudden
A huge banging of doors tumbled them out of their couches both.
In panic the whole length of the hall they race; and yet more scared
They tremble half dead, when with the barking of Molossian dogs
The lofty roofs resound. Then says the country mouse, 'No use
For such a life have I: and so farewell. My wood and hole,
Safe from alarms and terrors, with plain vetch will solace me.'

R. C. TREVELYAN (1940)

PRESENTATION COPY FOR AUGUSTUS

As I explained to you often and at length
When you set out, Vinius, you will deliver
These rolls to Augustus, under seal, but only

If he is well, if he's in cheerful mood,
If finally he asks for them. I fear
Lest in your blundering eagerness to serve me
You cause my poor works to be frowned upon
Through officious diligence and excess of zeal.
If my book's burden gall you with its weight,
Fling it away at once, rather than dash
Your pack down wildly where you had been bidden
To carry it, and turn your father's name
Of Asina to a jest, and so become
The talk of the whole town. Push stoutly on
Over hills, streams, and bogs. When you've achieved
Your task and reached your journey's end, take care
To guard your burden in the way you should.
A parcel of my books should not be carried
Under your armpit, as a countryman
Carries a lamb, as typsy Pyrria a ball
Of stolen wool, as a poor tribesman, asked
To a rich man's dinner, his felt cap and slippers.
And mind, you are not to boast to everyone
How you have sweated under the weight of poems
Destined to charm the eyes and ears of Caesar.
Though questioners crowd round and seek to stay you,
Press onward. – Go now: farewell. But take care
You do not stumble and break your precious charge.

R. C. TREVELYAN (1940)

THE ART OF POETRY

If in a picture, Pisos,[1] you should see
A handsome woman with a fish's tail,
Or a man's head upon a horse's neck,
Or limbs of beasts of the most different kinds,
Covered with feathers of all sorts of birds,
Would you not laugh, and think the painter mad?

1. The poem is addressed to the sons of a nobleman named Calpurnius Piso (probably Lucius, consul 15 B.C. and later Prefect of the City).

Trust me, that book is as ridiculous,
Whose incoherent style (like sick men's dreams)
Varies all shapes, and mixes all extremes.
Painters and poets have been still allowed
Their pencils, and their fancies, unconfined.
This privilege we freely give and take;
But nature, and the common laws of sense,
Forbid to reconcile antipathies,
Or make a snake engender with a dove,
And hungry tigers court the tender lambs.

  Some that at first have promised mighty things
Applaud themselves, when a few florid lines
Shine through the insipid dullness of the rest;
Here they describe a temple, or a wood,
Or streams that through delightful meadows run,
And there the rainbow, or the rapid Rhine:
But they misplace them all, and crowd them in,
And are as much to seek in other things
As he, that only can design a tree,
Would be to draw a shipwreck or a storm.
When you begin with so much pomp and show,
Why is the end so little and so mean?
Be what you will, so you be still the same.

  Most poets fall into the grossest faults,
Deluded by a seeming excellence:
In striving to be short, they grow obscure;
And when they would write smoothly, they want strength,
Their spirits sink; while others that affect
A lofty style, swell to a tympany.
Some timorous wretches start at every blast,
And, fearing tempests, dare not leave the shore;
Others, in love with wild variety,
Draw boars in waves, and dolphins in a wood;
Thus fear of erring, joined with want of skill,
Is a most certain way of erring still.

The meanest workman in the Aemilian square,[1]
May grave the nails, or imitate the hair,
But cannot finish what he hath begun;
What is there more ridiculous than he?
For one or two good features in a face,
Where all the rest are scandalously ill,
Make it but more remarkably deformed.

Let poets match their subjects to their strength,
And often try what weight they can support,
And what their shoulders are too weak to bear.
After a serious and judicious choice,
Method and eloquence will never fail.

As well the force as ornament of verse
Consists in choosing a fit time for things,
And knowing when a Muse should be indulged
In her full flight, and when she should be curbed.

Words must be chosen, and be placed with skill:
You gain your point, if your industrious art
Can make unusual words easy and plain;
But if you write of things abstruse or new,
Some of your own inventing may be used,
So it be seldom and discreetly done:
But he that hopes to have new words allowed,
Must so derive them from the Grecian spring
As they may seem to flow without constraint.

If your bold Muse dare tread unbeaten paths,
And bring new characters upon the stage,
Be sure you keep them up to their first height.
New subjects are not easily explained,
And you had better choose a well-known theme
Than trust to an invention of your own;
For what originally others write

1. Horace is said to have been referring to the Aemilian gladiatorial school near the Forum.

May be so well disguised, and so improved,
That with some justice it may pass for yours;
But then you must not copy trivial things,
Nor word for word too faithfully translate,
Nor (as some servile imitators do)
Prescribe at first such strict uneasy rules,
As they must ever slavishly observe,
Or all the laws of decency renounce.

Now hear what every auditor expects;
If you intend that he should stay to hear
The epilogue, and see the curtain fall,
Mind how our tempers alter with our years,
And by those rules form all your characters.
One that hath newly learned to speak and go
Loves childish plays, is soon provoked and pleased,
And changes every hour his wavering mind.
A youth that first casts off his tutor's yoke
Loves horses, hounds, and sports and exercise,
Prone to all vice, impatient of reproof,
Proud, careless, fond, inconstant, and profuse.
Gain and ambition rule our riper years,
And make us slaves to interest and power.
Old men are only walking hospitals,
Where all defects, and all diseases, crowd
With restless pain, and more tormenting fear,
Lazy, morose, full of delays and hopes,
Oppressed with riches, which they dare not use;
Ill-natured censors of the present age,
And fond of all the follies of the past.
Thus all the treasure of our flowing years
Our ebb of life for ever takes away.
Boys must not have the ambitious care of men,
Nor men the weak anxieties of age.

Unpolished verses pass with many men,
And Rome is too indulgent in that point;
But then, to write at a loose rambling rate,

In hope the world will wink at all our faults,
Is such a rash, ill-grounded confidence
As men may pardon, but will never praise.
Consider well the Greek originals,
Read them by day, and think of them by night.
But Plautus was admired in former time
With too much patience (not to call it worse);
His harsh, unequal verse was music then,
And rudeness had the privilege of wit.
But you (brave youth), wise Numa's worthy heir,
Remember of what weight your judgement is,
And never venture to commend a book
That has not passed all judges and all tests.

  Greece had a genius, Greece had eloquence,
For her ambition and her end was fame.
Our Roman youth is bred another way,
And taught no arts but those of usury;
And the glad father glories in his child,
When he can subdivide a fraction:
Can souls, who by their parents from their birth
Have been devoted thus to rust and gain,
Be capable of high and generous thoughts?
Can verses writ by such an author live?

  A poet should instruct, or please, or both;
Let all your precepts be succinct and clear,
That ready wits may comprehend them soon,
And faithful memories retain them long;
For superfluities are soon forgot.
Never be so conceited of your parts,
To think you may persuade us what you please,
Or venture to bring in a child alive,
That cannibals have murdered and devoured.
Old age explodes all but morality;
Austerity offends aspiring youths;
But he that joins instructions with delight,
Profit with pleasure, carries all the votes:

These are the volumes that enrich the shops,
These pass with admiration through the world,
And bring their author an eternal fame.

    Be not too rigidly censorious:
A string may jar in the best master's hand,
And the most skilful archer miss his aim;
But in a poem elegantly writ,
I will not quarrel with a slight mistake,
Such as our nature's frailty may excuse;
But he that hath been often told his fault,
And still persists, is as impertinent
As a musician that will always play,
And yet is always out at the same note;
When such a positive abandoned fop
(Among his numerous absurdities)
Stumbles upon some tolerable line,
I fret to see them in such company,
And wonder by what magic they came there.
But in long works sleep will sometimes surprise:
Homer himself hath been observed to nod.

    Poems, like pictures, are of different sorts,
Some better at a distance, others near;
Some love the dark, some choose the clearest light,
And boldly challenge the most piercing eye;
Some please for once, some will for ever please.

    Some think that poets may be formed by art,
Others maintain that nature makes them so;
I neither see what art without a vein,
Nor wit without the help of art can do,
But mutually they need each other's aid.
He that intends to gain the Olympic prize
Must use himself to hunger, heat, and cold,
Take leave of wine, and the soft joys of love;
And no musician dares pretend to skill,
Without a great expense of time and pains;

But every little busy scribbler now
Swells with the praises which he gives himself;
And taking sanctuary in the crowd,
Brags of his impudence, and scorns to mend.

   The prudent care of an impartial friend
Will give you notice of each idle line,
Shew what sounds harsh, and what wants ornament,
Or where it is too lavishly bestowed;
Make you explain all that he finds obscure,
And with a strict inquiry mark your faults;
Nor for these trifles fear to lose your love;
Those things which now seem frivolous and slight,
Will be of serious consequence to you,
When they have made you once ridiculous.

EARL OF ROSCOMMON (1680)

THE ART OF POETRY AGAIN [1]

Poets and painters, as all artists know,
May shoot a little with a lengthened bow;
We claim this mutual mercy for our task,
And grant in turn the pardon which we ask;
But make not monsters spring from gentle dams –
Birds breed not vipers, tigers nurse not lambs.

   In fine, to whatsoever you aspire,
Let it at least be simple and entire.

   The greater portion of the rhyming tribe
(Give ear, my friends, for thou hast been a scribe)
Are led astray by some peculiar lure.
I labour to be brief – become obscure;
One falls while following elegance too fast;
Another soars, inflated with bombast;

1. Byron's *Hints from Horace* range widely over the contemporary field, but include passages of loose translation – though it is hardly fair to the poem to offer these excerpts from them.

Too low a third crawls on, afraid to fly:
He spins his subject to satiety;
Absurdly varying, he at last engraves
Fish in the woods, and boars beneath the waves!

Unless your care's exact, your judgement nice,
The flight from folly leads but into vice.

Dear authors! suit your topics to your strength,
And ponder well your subject and its length;
Nor lift your load before you're quite aware
What weight your shoulders will, or will not, bear.
But lucid Order, and Wit's siren voice,
Await the poet, skilful in his choice;
With native eloquence he soars along,
Grace in his thoughts, and music in his song.

Let judgement teach them wisely to combine
With future parts the now omitted line:
This shall the author choose, or that reject,
Precise in style, and cautious to select;
Nor slight applause will candid pens afford
To him who furnishes a wanting word.
Then fear not, if 'tis needful, to produce
Some term unknown, or obsolete in use.

As forests shed their foliage by degrees,
So fade expressions which in season please;
And we and ours, alas! are due to fate,
And works and words but dwindle to a date.
Though as a monarch nods, and commerce calls,
Impetuous rivers stagnate in canals;
Though swamps subdued and marshes drained sustain
The heavy ploughshare and the yellow grain,
And rising ports along the busy shore
Protect the vessel from old Ocean's roar,
All, all, must perish; but, surviving last,
The love of letters half preserves the past.

True, some decay, yet not a few revive;
Though those shall sink which now appear to thrive,
As custom arbitrates, whose shifting sway
Our life and language must alike obey.

'Tis hard to venture where our betters fail,
Or lend fresh interest to a twice-told tale;
And yet, perchance, 'tis wiser to prefer
A hackneyed plot, than choose a new, and err;
Yet copy not too closely, but record,
More justly, thought for thought than word for word;
Nor trace your prototype through narrow ways,
But only follow where he merits praise.

But many a skilful judge abhors to see
What few admire – irregularity.
This some vouchsafe to pardon; but 'tis hard
When such a word contents a British bard.
And must the bard his glowing thoughts confine,
Lest censure hover o'er some faulty line?
Remove whate'er a critic may suspect,
To gain the paltry suffrage of '*correct*'?
Or prune the spirit of each daring phrase,
To fly from error, not to merit praise?

Ye, who seek finished models, never cease,
By day and night, to read the works of Greece.

Sometimes a sprightly wit, and tale well told,
Without much grace, or weight, or art, will hold
A longer empire o'er the public mind
Than sounding trifles, empty, though refined.

Two objects always should the poet move,
Or one or both – to please or to improve.
Whate'er you teach, be brief, if you design
For our remembrance your didactic line;
Redundance places memory on the rack,
For brains may be o'erloaded, like the back.

Young men with aught but elegance dispense;
Maturer years require a little sense.
To end at once: – that bard for all is fit
Who mingles well instruction with his wit.

But everything has faults, nor is't unknown
That harps and fiddles often lose their tone,
And wayward voices, at their owner's call,
With all his best endeavours, only squall.
Where frequent beauties strike the reader's view,
We must not quarrel for a blot or two;
But pardon equally to books or men,
The slips of human nature, and the pen.

Yet if an author, spite of foe or friend,
Despises all advice too much to mend,
But ever twangs the same discordant string,
Give him no quarter, howsoe'er he sing.

As pictures, so shall poems be; some stand
The critic eye, and please when near at hand;
But others at a distance strike the sight;
This seeks the shade, but that demands the light,
Nor dreads the connoisseur's fastidious view,
But, ten times scrutinized, is ten times new.

LORD BYRON (1811)[1]

1. Published in part 1824, in full 1831.

LIVY

Titus Livius was born at Patavium (Padua) in 59 b.c. and died in a.d. 17. His History of Rome from the earliest times (*Ab Urbe Condita*) would probably have filled twenty or thirty modern volumes; it included 142 books, of which 107 are lost – owing to the bulkiness of the work, and its replacement by epitomes. Yet his history enjoyed great immediate success. His most permanent claim to fame, besides the aesthetic achievement of a richly fluent style, is his splendid glorification of the story of Rome. Rather as Michelet was to ennoble the idea of France, Livy conferred glamour and grandeur on *Romanità*. He was a humanist too, deeply interested in great men and how they behave on great occasions. The ancients were accustomed to compare history with poetry, and Livy's earlier books are poetical evocations of Rome's legendary origins. The first four books were all that Dante knew, and yet he wrote of Livy as infallible.

Petrarch knew twenty-nine books, searched unceasingly for the rest, and based on Livy's account of the Punic Wars his own Latin epic *Africa*, of which he was especially proud. His friend Bersuire made a French version (1352). The humanists of the Renaissance, because they sought for heroes, preferred Livy to Tacitus. Partial Italian renderings date back to the mid-fifteenth century, shortly before the first printing (at Rome, 1469). Montaigne knew Livy well, but Erasmus (1511) omitted him from his reading list for schools – perhaps because the cult of heroes had begun to be frowned upon. Soon afterwards (1516–19) came Machiavelli's *Discourses on the First Decade of Livy* – but in the following century, a committee of Venetian senators exonerated Livy (blaming Tacitus instead) for Machiavelli's undesirable views. Shakespeare's *Rape of Lucrece* is taken from Livy, Book I, as well as from Ovid's *Fasti*. Philemon Holland published an English translation in 1600 (a version of the Hannibal and Scipio passages by A. Cope had appeared in 1544). The first complete edition of all the books now extant appeared at Rome in 1616.

Livy's account of the youthful Republic was a favourite source-book of the French Revolution; Alfieri's *Virginia*, too, comes from him. Niebuhr, though recognizing in Livy the same richness and warmth of colouring which had reappeared in Venetian painting, rejected his early books as history, while Macaulay's *Lays of Ancient Rome* revived them as the poetry which they almost are. Today many have been obliged to read at school his account of the Second Punic War, but an adult taste for Livy has become rare – perhaps partly because it is unfashionable to idealize history's Great Men so unreservedly. Yet Soviet-inspired ministries recommend his account of the struggle between patricians and plebeians for its 'ideological material'.

If I succeed in writing the history of the Romans – going right back
to the foundation of the city – I am by no means sure that the achievement will be worth the trouble; and if I were sure, I should not venture to say so. For I know how stale and platitudinous such boasts are.
Every new writer who appears thinks he is going to provide some
original research about the facts, or write cleverly enough to supersede old-fashioned styles. However, whether I am successful or not,
it will give me satisfaction to have done my part, to the best of my
ability, in contributing to the record of the greatest people in the
world. And if I fail to make my mark among historical writers – who
are very numerous – it will be some comfort to think of the importance and distinction of the men by whom my reputation is
eclipsed.

Besides, my subject is of formidable dimensions. It goes back more
than seven hundred years; from small beginnings it has grown to a
vastness which threatens to be its ruin. Now I am well aware that
many readers will not be so very interested in Rome's origins and
initial stages. They will be impatient to get on to contemporary history, which displays our nation suicidally eating up its own mighty
resources. I, on the other hand, will feel rewarded for my labours by
the chance to rest my eyes from the miseries which for years have beset this generation of ours – to rest my eyes just for so long as I con-
centrate on reconstructing the remote past. This is a task that I can
approach without any of the nervousness felt by the historian who
deals with contemporary events. And that nervousness, even if it does
not cause lapses from truthfulness, can be a worrying thing.

Traditions relating to the period before the foundation of the city
was carried out or contemplated, I propose neither to establish nor to
refute: they belong to poetic fiction rather than to the authentic records of historical fact. Prehistory is allowed the indulgence of blend-
ing the doings of men and gods in order to make the origins of cities
more impressive; and if any country is entitled to sanctify its beginnings by attributing them to divine action, that is true of the Romans.
So tremendous is their military glory that, when they claim their
Father, their Founder's Father, to be none other than Mars, the

nations of the earth must needs endure it patiently – as they endure Roman rule.

Nevertheless, whatever judgements and opinions there may be about such stories, I do not intend to attach much weight to them. The matters in which, instead, I want every reader to be absorbed are these: how did people live? how did they behave? what were the men and the methods, in peace and in war, that won and expanded the empire? Then let it be noted how the moral rot started, how standards were gradually sapped, then crumbled more and more ominously, and finally began to collapse into utter ruin. That is the stage we have now reached; our defects are unendurable to us – and so are their cures.

History possesses the outstandingly beneficial merit of setting all its varied lessons luminously on record for our attention. From these, one may select models for oneself and one's country; and causes that turned out as evilly as they began may be avoided. Now, unless my passion for the task I have undertaken is blinding me, no State has ever possessed more abundant greatness, higher principles, and nobler examples, than Rome. No State was invaded by meanness and extravagance so late in its development. No State honoured simplicity and frugality so signally and so long, during that epoch when men were as lacking in greed as they were lacking in wealth. In recent years, riches have imported avarice; and from unlimited self-indulgence has come a longing to pursue vicious extravagance to the point of personal and universal annihilation.

But protests, however necessary they may be, are unlikely to be acceptable: so from the beginning, at least, of this huge enterprise let them be absent. I should much prefer to inaugurate it with good omens and – if historians had the same customs as poets – with vows and prayers to the gods and goddesses; entreating them to bring my great project to a successful conclusion.

MICHAEL GRANT (1956)

THE SABINE WOMEN

Meanwhile, the city was expanding and reaching out its walls to include one place after another; for the Romans built their defences with an eye rather to the population which they hoped one day to have than to the numbers they had then. Next, lest his big city should be empty, Romulus resorted to a plan for increasing the inhabitants which had long been employed by the founders of cities, who gather about them an obscure and lowly multitude and pretend that the earth has raised up sons to them. In the place which is now enclosed between the two groves as you go up the Capitoline hill, he opened a sanctuary. Thither fled, from the surrounding peoples, a miscellaneous rabble, without distinction of bond or free, eager for new conditions; and these constituted the first advance in power towards that greatness at which Romulus aimed. He had now no reason to be dissatisfied with his strength, and proceeded to add policy to strength. He appointed a hundred senators, whether because this number seemed to him sufficient, or because there were no more than a hundred who, as heads of clans, could be designated Fathers. At all events, they received the designation of Fathers from their rank, and their descendants were called patricians.

Rome was now strong enough to hold her own in war with any of the adjacent States; but owing to the want of women a single generation was likely to see the end of her greatness, since she had neither prospect of posterity at home nor the right of intermarriage with her neighbours. So, on the advice of the Senate, Romulus sent envoys round among all the neighbouring nations to solicit for the new people an alliance and the privilege of intermarrying. Cities, they argued, as well as all other things, take their rise from the lowliest beginnings. As time goes on, those which are aided by their own worth and by the favour of Heaven achieve great power and renown. They said they were well assured that Rome's origin had been blessed with the favour of Heaven, and that worth would not be lacking; their neighbours should not be reluctant to mingle their stock and their blood with the Romans, who were as truly men as they were.

Nowhere did the embassy obtain a friendly hearing. In fact men spurned, at the same time that they feared, both for themselves and their descendants, that great power which was then growing up in their midst; and the envoys were frequently asked, on being dismissed, if they had opened a sanctuary for women as well as for men, for in that way only would they obtain suitable wives.

This was a bitter insult to the young Romans, and the matter seemed certain to end in violence. Expressly to afford a fitting time and place for this, Romulus, concealing his resentment, made ready solemn games in honour of the Equestrian Neptune,[1] which he called Consualia. He then bade proclaim the spectacle to the surrounding peoples, and his subjects prepared to celebrate it with all the resources within their knowledge and power, that they might cause the occasion to be noised abroad and eagerly expected. Many people – for they were also eager to see the new city – gathered for the festival, especially those who lived nearest, the inhabitants of Caenina, Crustumeria, and Antemnae. The Sabines, too, came with all their people, including their children and wives.

They were hospitably entertained in every house, and when they had looked at the site of the city, its walls, and its numerous buildings, they marvelled that Rome had so rapidly grown great. When the time came for the show, and people's thoughts and eyes were busy with it, the preconcerted attack began. At a given signal the young Romans darted this way and that, to seize and carry off the maidens. In most cases these were taken by the men in whose path they chanced to be. Some, of exceptional beauty, had been marked out for the chief senators, and were carried off to their houses by plebeians to whom the office had been entrusted. The sports broke up in a panic, and the parents of the maidens fled sorrowing. They charged the Romans with the crime of violating hospitality, and invoked the gods to whose solemn games they had come, deceived in violation of religion and honour. The stolen maidens were no more hopeful of their plight, nor less indignant. But Romulus himself went amongst them and explained that the pride of their parents had caused this deed, when they had refused their neighbours the right to intermarry; nevertheless the daughters should be wedded and become co-partners in all the possessions of the Romans, in their citizenship and, dearest privilege of all to the human race, in their children; only let them moderate their anger, and give their hearts to those to whom fortune had given their persons. A sense of injury had often given place to affection, and they would find their husbands the kinder for this reason, that every man would earnestly endeavour not only to be a good husband, but also to console his wife for the home and parents she had

1. A Romanized form of the cult of Poseidon of the Horses, which was especially active in horse-breeding Thessaly. At Rome this deity was identified with the native Consus.

lost. His arguments were seconded by the wooing of the men, who excused their act on the score of passion and love, the most moving of all pleas to a woman's heart.

The resentment of the brides was already much diminished at the very moment when their parents, in mourning garb and with tears and lamentations, were attempting to arouse their States to action . . . .

B. O. FOSTER (1919)

HORATIUS ON THE BRIDGE

By this time the Tarquins had sought refuge with Lars Porsenna, king of Clusium.[1] There they mingled advice and entreaty, now imploring him not to permit them, Etruscans by birth and of the same blood and the same name as himself, to suffer the privations of exile, and again even warning him not to allow the growing custom of expelling kings to go unpunished. Liberty was sweet enough in itself. Unless the energy with which nations sought to obtain it were matched by the efforts which kings put forth to defend their power, the highest would be reduced to the level of the lowest; there would be nothing lofty, nothing that stood out above the rest of the State: there was the end of monarchy, the noblest institution known to gods or men.

Porsenna, believing that it was not only a safe thing for the Etruscans that there should be a king at Rome, but an honour to have that king of Etruscan stock, invaded Roman territory with a hostile army. Never before had such fear seized the Senate, so powerful was Clusium in those days, and so great Porsenna's fame. And they feared not only the enemy but their own citizens – they feared that the general body of the citizens, terror-stricken, should admit the princes into the city and even submit to enslavement, for the sake of peace. Hence the Senate at this time granted many favours to the general body of the citizens. The question of subsistence received special attention, and some were sent to the Volsci and others to Cumae [2] to buy up corn. Again, the monopoly of salt, the price of which was very high, was taken out of the hands of individuals and wholly assumed by the

1. In Etruria, to which the exiled Tarquins also belonged.
2. The Volsci were a tribe living south-east of Rome. Cumae (north-west of Naples) was the most ancient Greek settlement in Italy, from which the Romans derived many of their ideas of Greek culture.

government. Imposts and taxes were transferred from the ordinary citizens to the well-to-do, who were equal to the burden: the poor paid dues enough if they reared children. Thanks to this liberality on the part of the Fathers, the distress which attended the subsequent blockade and famine was powerless to destroy the harmony of the State, which was such that the name of king was not more abhorrent to the highest than to the lowest; nor was there ever a man in after years whose demagogic arts made him so popular as its wise governing at that time made the whole Senate.

When the enemy appeared, the Romans all with one accord withdrew from their fields into the city, which they surrounded with guards. Some parts appeared to be rendered safe by their walls, others by the barrier formed by the river Tiber. The bridge of piles almost afforded an entrance to the enemy, had it not been for one man, Horatius Cocles; he was the bulwark of defence on which that day depended the fortune of the city of Rome. He chanced to be on guard at the bridge when the Janiculum Hill [1] was captured by a sudden attack of the enemy. He saw them as they charged down on the run from Janiculum, while his own people behaved like a frightened mob, throwing away their arms and quitting their ranks. Catching hold first of one and then of another, blocking their way and conjuring them to listen, he called on gods and men to witness that if they forsook their post it was vain to flee: once they had left a passage in their rear by the bridge, there would soon be more of the enemy on the Palatine and the Capitol than on Janiculum. He therefore warned and commanded them to break down the bridge with steel, with fire, with any instrument at their disposal; and promised that he would himself receive the onset of the enemy, so far as it could be withstood by a single body.

Then, striding to the head of the bridge, conspicuous amongst the fugitives who were clearly seen to be shirking the fight, he covered himself with his sword and buckler and made ready to do battle at close quarters, confounding the Etruscans with amazement at his audacity. Yet were there two who were prevented by shame from leaving him. These were Spurius Larcius and Titus Herminius, both famous for their birth and their deeds. With these he endured the peril of the first rush and the stormiest moment of the battle. But after

1. On the right bank of the Tiber.

a while he forced even these two to leave him and save themselves, for there was scarcely anything left of the bridge, and those who were cutting it down called to them to come back. Then, darting glances of defiance around at the Etruscan nobles, he now challenged them in turn to fight, now railed at them collectively as slaves of haughty kings, who, heedless of their own liberty, were come to overthrow the liberty of others. They hesitated for a moment, each looking to his neighbour to begin the fight. Then shame made them attack, and with a shout they cast their javelins from every side against their solitary foe. But he caught them all upon his shield, and, resolute as ever, bestrode the bridge and held his ground; and now they were trying to dislodge him by a charge, when the crash of the falling bridge and the cheer which burst from the throats of the Romans, exulting in the completion of their task, checked them in mid-career with a sudden dismay. Then Cocles cried, 'O Father Tiber, I solemnly invoke thee; receive graciously into your waters these arms and this soldier!' So praying, all armed as he was, he leaped down into the river, and under a shower of missiles swam across unhurt to his fellows, having given a proof of valour which was destined to obtain more fame than credence with posterity.

B. O. FOSTER (1919) [1]

CLASS WARFARE

The senators became alarmed, for they feared that if the army should be disbanded there would again be secret gatherings and conspiracies. And so, although the levy had been held by order of the dictator, yet because the men had been sworn in by the consuls they regarded the troops as bound by their oath, and, under the pretext that the Aequi [2] had recommended hostilities, gave orders to lead the army out of the city. This brought the revolt to a head. At first, it is said, there was talk of killing the consuls, that men might thus be freed from their oath; but when it was explained to them that no sacred obligation could be dissolved by a crime, they took the advice of one Sicinius, and without orders from the consuls withdrew to the Sacred Mount,

1. These passages are slightly adapted at one or two points.
2. Mountaineers north and north-east of Rome.

which is situated across the river Anio, three miles from the city. (This version of the story is more general than that given by Piso, namely that the Aventine was the place of their secession.)[1]

There, without any leader, they fortified their camp with stockade and trench, and continued quietly, taking nothing but what they required for their subsistence, for several days – neither receiving provocation nor giving any. There was a great panic in the city, and mutual apprehension caused the suspension of all activities. The ordinary citizens, abandoned by their friends, feared violence at the hands of the senators; the senators feared the ordinary citizens who were left behind in Rome, being uncertain whether they had rather they stayed or went. Besides, how long would the seceding multitude continue peaceable? What would happen next if some foreign war should break out in the interim? Assuredly no hope was left save in harmony amongst the citizens, and this they concluded they must restore to the State by fair means or foul. They therefore decided to send as an ambassador to the commons Menenius Agrippa, an eloquent man and dear to the ordinary citizens as being one of themselves by birth. On being admitted to the camp he is said merely to have related the following story, in the quaint and uncouth style of that age.

In the days when man's members did not all agree amongst themselves, as is now the case, but had each its own ideas and a voice of its own, the other parts thought it unfair that they should have the worry and the trouble and the labour of providing everything for the belly, while the belly remained quietly in their midst with nothing to do but to enjoy the good things which they bestowed upon it. They therefore conspired together that the hands should carry no food to the mouth, nor the mouth accept anything that was given it, nor the teeth grind up what they received. While they sought in this angry spirit to starve the belly into submission, the members themselves and the whole body were reduced to the utmost weakness. Hence it had become clear that even the belly had no idle task to perform, and was no more nourished than it nourished the rest, by giving out to all parts of the body that by which we live and thrive, when it has been divided equally amongst the veins and is enriched with digested food – that is, the blood. Drawing a parallel from this to show how like

1. This secession was traditionally ascribed to 494 B.C.; four others were believed to have occurred, the last (indisputably historical) in 287.

was the internal dissension of the bodily members to the anger of the plebs against the Fathers, he prevailed upon the minds of his hearers.

Steps were then taken towards harmony, and a compromise was effected on these terms: the general body of citizens were to have magistrates of their own, who should be inviolable, and in them should lie the right to aid the people against the consuls, nor should any senator be permitted to take this magistracy. And so they chose two 'tribunes of the people', Gaius Licinius and Lucius Albinus. These appointed three others to be their colleagues.

B. O. FOSTER (1919)

HANNIBAL CROSSES THE ALPS [1]

Hannibal reached the Alps without being molested by the Gauls who inhabited those regions. Then, though report – which customarily exaggerates uncertain danger – had already taught them what to expect, still, the near view of the lofty mountains, with their snows almost merging in the sky; the shapeless hovels perched on crags; the frost-bitten flocks and beasts of burden; the shaggy, unkempt men; animals and inanimate objects alike stiff with cold, and all more dreadful to look upon than words can tell, renewed their consternation.

As their column began to mount the first slopes, mountaineers were discovered posted on the heights above, who, had they lain concealed in hidden valleys, might have sprung out suddenly and attacked them with great rout and slaughter. Hannibal gave the command to halt, and sent forward some Gauls to reconnoitre. When informed by them that there was no getting by that way, he encamped in the most extensive valley to be found, in a wilderness of rocks and precipices. He then employed these same Gauls to insinuate themselves into the councils of the mountaineers (whose speech and customs did not differ greatly from their own), and in this way learned that his enemies guarded the pass only by day, and at night dispersed, every man to his own home.

As soon as it was light, he advanced up the hills, as though he hoped to rush the defile by an open attack in the daytime. Then, having spent the day in feigning a purpose other than his real one, he en-

1. 218 B.C.

trenched a camp on the spot where he had halted. But no sooner did he perceive that the mountaineers had dispersed from the heights and relaxed their vigilance, than, leaving for show more fires than the numbers of those who remained in camp demanded: leaving, too, the baggage and the cavalry and a great part of the infantry, he put himself at the head of some light-armed soldiers – all his bravest men – and, marching swiftly to the head of the defile, occupied those very heights which the enemy had held.

With the ensuing dawn the Carthaginians broke camp, and the remainder of their army began to move. The natives, on a signal being given, were already coming in from their fastnesses to occupy their customary post, when they suddenly perceived that some of their enemies were in possession of the heights and threatened them from above, and that others were marching through the pass. Both facts presenting themselves at the same time to their eyes and minds kept them for a moment rooted to the spot. Then, when they saw the helter-skelter in the pass and the column becoming embarrassed by its own confusion – the horses especially being frightened and unmanageable – they thought that whatever they could add themselves to the consternation of the troops would be sufficient to destroy them, and rushed down from the cliffs on either side, over trails and trackless ground alike, with all the ease of habit. Then indeed the Carthaginians had to contend at one and the same time against their foes and the difficulties of the ground, and the struggle amongst themselves, as each endeavoured to outstrip the rest in escaping from danger, was greater than the struggle with the enemy. The horses occasioned the greatest peril to the column. Terrified by the discordant yells, which the woods and ravines redoubled with their echoes, they quaked with fear; and if they happened to be hit or wounded, were so maddened that they made enormous havoc not only of men but of every sort of baggage. Indeed the crowding in the pass, which was steep and precipitous on both sides, caused many – some of them armed men – to be flung down to a great depth; but when beasts of burden with their packs went hurtling down, it was just like the crash of falling walls.

Dreadful as these sights were, still Hannibal halted for a little while and held back his men, so as not to augment the terror and confusion. Then, when he saw that the column was being broken in two, and there was danger lest he might have got his army over to no avail, if it were stripped of its baggage, he charged down from the higher ground and routed the enemy by the very impetus of the attack, though he added to the disorder amongst his own troops. But the flurry thus occasioned quickly subsided, as soon as the roads were cleared by the flight of the mountaineers; and the whole army was presently brought over the pass, not only without molestation but almost in silence. Hannibal then seized a stronghold which was the chief place in that region, together with the outlying hamlets, and with the captured food and flocks supported his troops for three days. And in those three days, being hindered neither by the natives, who had been utterly cowed at the outset, nor very greatly by the nature of the country, he covered a good deal of ground.

They came next to another canton, thickly settled for a mountain district. There, not by open fighting, but by his own devices, trickery and deception, Hannibal was all but circumvented. The elder head-men of the strongholds waited on him, as a deputation, and said that, taught by other men's misfortunes – a useful warning – they preferred to experience the friendship of the Carthaginians rather than their might; they were ready, therefore, to carry out his orders, and they requested him to accept provisions and guides and also hostages as a guarantee of good faith. Hannibal, neither blindly trusting nor yet repulsing them – in case rejection should make them openly hostile – returned a friendly answer, accepted the proffered hostages, and used the supplies which they had brought down, themselves, to the road. But he drew up his column, before following their guides, by no means as though for a march through a friendly country. The van was made up of elephants and cavalry; he himself, with the main strength of the infantry, came next, looking warily about him and watching everything.

When they had got to a narrow place, which was overhung on one side by a ridge, the tribesmen rose up on every quarter from their ambush and assailed them, front and rear, fighting hand to hand and at long range, and rolling down huge boulders on the marching troops. The rear-guard bore the brunt of the attack, and, as the infantry faced about to meet it, it was very evident that if the column had not been strengthened at that point, it must have suffered a great disaster in this pass. Even so, they were in the utmost peril and came near destruction. For while Hannibal was hesitating to send his infantry down into the defile – since he had no troops left to secure the rear of the infantry as he himself secured that of the horse – the mountaineers rushed in on his flank, and breaking through the column, established themselves in the road, so that Hannibal spent one night without cavalry or baggage.

On the following day, since by now the barbarians were attacking with less vigour, his forces were re-united and surmounted the pass; and though they suffered some casualties, still they lost more baggage animals than men. From this point on the mountaineers appeared in smaller numbers, and, more in the manner of brigandage than warfare, attacked sometimes the van, sometimes the rear, whenever the ground afforded an advantage or the invaders, pushing on too far ahead or lagging behind, gave opportunity. The elephants could be induced to move but very slowly along the steep and narrow trails; but wherever they went they made the column safe from its enemies, who were unaccustomed to the beasts and afraid of venturing too near them.

On the ninth day they arrived at the summit of the Alps, having come for the most part over trackless wastes and by roundabout routes, owing either to the dishonesty of their guides, or – when they would not trust the guides – to their blindly entering some valley, guessing at the way. For two days they lay encamped on the summit. The soldiers, worn with toil and fighting, were permitted to rest; and a number of baggage animals which had fallen among the rocks made their way to the camp by following the tracks of the army. Exhausted and discouraged as the soldiers were by many hardships, a snowstorm – for the constellation of the Pleiades was now setting – threw them into a great fear. The ground was everywhere covered deep with snow when at dawn they began to march, and as the column moved slowly on, dejection and despair were to be read in every countenance. Then Hannibal, who had gone on before the standards, made the army halt on a certain promontory which commanded an extensive prospect, and pointing out Italy to them, and just under the Alps the plains about the Po, he told them that they were now scaling the ramparts not only of Italy, but of Rome itself; the rest of the way would be level or downhill; and after one or at the most two battles, they would have in their hands and in their power the citadel and capital of Italy.

The column now began to make some progress, and even the

enemy had ceased to annoy them, except to make a stealthy raid as occasion offered. But the way was much more difficult than the ascent had been, as indeed the slope of the Alps on the Italian side is in general more precipitous in proportion as it is shorter. For practically every road was steep, narrow, and treacherous, so that neither could they keep from slipping, nor could those who had been thrown a little off their balance retain their footing, but came down one on top of the other, and the beasts on top of the men.

They then came to a much narrower cliff, and with rocks so perpendicular that it was difficult for an unencumbered soldier to manage the descent, though he felt his way and clung with his hands to the bushes and roots that projected here and there. The place had been precipitous before, and a recent landslip had carried it away to the depth of a good thousand feet. There the cavalry came to a halt, as though they had reached the end of the road, and as Hannibal was wondering what it could be that held the column back, word was brought to him that the cliff was impassable. Going then to inspect the place himself, he thought that there was nothing for it but to lead the army round, over trackless and untrodden steeps, however circuitous the detour might be.

But that way proved to be insuperable; for above the old, untouched snow lay a fresh deposit of moderate depth, through which, as it was soft and not very deep, the men in front found it easy to advance; but when it had been trampled down by the feet of so many men and beasts, the rest had to make their way over the bare ice beneath and the slush of the melting snow. Then came a terrible struggle on the slippery surface, for it afforded them no foothold, while the downward slope made their feet the more quickly slide from under them; so that whether they tried to pull themselves up with their hands, or used their knees, these supports themselves would slip, and down they would come again! Neither were there any stems or roots about, by which a man could pull himself up with foot or hand – only smooth ice and thawing snow, on which they were continually rolling. But the baggage animals, as they went over the snow, would sometimes even cut into the lowest crust, and, pitching forward and striking out with their hoofs, as they struggled to rise, would break clean through it, so that numbers of them were caught fast, as if entrapped, in the hard, deep-frozen snow.

At last, when men and beasts had been worn out to no avail, they encamped upon the ridge, after having, with the utmost difficulty, cleared enough ground even for this purpose, so much snow were they obliged to dig out and remove. The soldiers were then set to work to construct a road across the cliff – their only possible way. Since they had to cut through the rock, they felled some huge trees that grew near at hand, and lopping off their branches, made an enormous pile of logs. This they set on fire, as soon as the wind blew fresh enough to make it burn, and pouring vinegar over the glowing rocks, caused them to crumble. After thus heating the crag with fire, they opened a way in it with iron tools, and relieved the steepness of the slope with zigzags of an easy gradient, so that not only the baggage animals but even the elephants could be led down. Four days were consumed at the cliff, and the animals nearly perished of starvation; for the mountain tops are all practically bare, and such grass as does grow is buried under snow. Lower down one comes to valleys and sunny slopes and rivulets, and near them woods, and places that begin to be fitter for man's habitation. There the beasts were turned out to graze, and the men, exhausted with toiling at the road, were allowed to rest. Thence they descended in three days' time into the plain, through a region now that was less forbidding, as was the character of its inhabitants.

Such were the chief features of the march to Italy, which they accomplished five months after leaving New Carthage in Spain – as certain authorities state – having crossed the Alps in fifteen days. The strength of Hannibal's forces on his entering Italy is a point on which historians are by no means agreed. Those who put the figures highest give him a hundred thousand foot and twenty thousand horse; the lowest estimate is twenty thousand foot and six thousand horse.

B. O. FOSTER (1929)

Hannibal had conceived a hope that the consuls would give him an opportunity of fighting in a place that was formed by nature for a cavalry action, in which arm he was invincible. He therefore drew out his men in battle array and ordered the Numidians to make a sally and provoke the enemy. This caused the camp of the Romans to be once more the scene of strife amongst the soldiers and dissension between the consuls.[2] Paulus cast in Varro's teeth the recklessness of Sempronius and Flaminius; Varro retorted that Fabius was a specious example for timid and slothful generals, and called on gods and men to witness that it was through no fault of his that Hannibal had by now acquired as it were a prescriptive right to Italy, for he was kept in fetters by his colleague – and the soldiers, enraged as they were and eager to fight, were deprived of swords and arms. Paulus rejoined that if anything untoward should befall the Roman infantry, recklessly abandoned to an ill-advised and rash engagement, he would himself be guiltless of all blame, but would share in all the consequences; let Varro, he said, see to it that, where tongues were bold and ready, hands – when it came to fighting – were no less so.

While they wasted time, quarrelling rather than consulting, Hannibal withdrew the rest of his troops – whom he had kept in line till far on in the day – into his camp, and sent the Numidians across the river to attack the men from the smaller Roman camp who were fetching water. They had hardly come out upon the other bank when their shouts and tumult sent that unorganized rabble flying. So they rode on till they came to the party that was stationed in front of the rampart, and almost to the very gates. So wholly outrageous, however, did it seem that by now even a Roman camp should be terrorized by

1. 216 B.C. Cannae was a village on the south bank of the Aufidus (Ofanto) in Apulia.

2. The aristocratic tradition, which Livy supports, was hostile to Varro, who was represented as a radical anti-senatorial demagogue and compared to the democratic leader Gaius Flaminius, who in the previous year had fallen into Hannibal's ambush at Lake Trasimene. Quintus Fabius Maximus Cunctator favoured a strategy of exhaustion.

irregular auxiliaries, that only one thing kept the Romans from cross-ing the river forthwith and giving battle – the fact that Paulus happened then to be in command.

The next morning, therefore, Varro (whom the lot had made commander for that day) hung out the signal, without saying a word of the matter to his colleague; making his troops fall in, he led them over the river. Paulus followed him, for he could more easily disapprove of the plan than deprive it of his help. Once across, they joined to their own the forces which they had kept in the smaller camp, and marshalled their battle-line as follows: on the right wing – the one nearer the river – they placed the Roman cavalry, and next them the Roman foot; the left wing had on the outside the cavalry of the allies; and nearer the centre, in contact with the Roman legions, the infantry of the allies. The slingers and other light-armed auxiliaries were formed up in front. The consuls had charge of the wings, Varro of the left, Paulus of the right; and Servilius Geminus was entrusted with the centre.

Hannibal crossed the river at break of day, after sending ahead of him the slingers from the Balearic Islands and the other light-armed troops, and posted each corps in line of battle, in the order in which he had brought it over. The Gallic and Spanish horse were next the river, on the left wing, facing the Roman cavalry; the right wing was assigned to the Numidian horse; the centre was composed of infantry, so arranged as to have the Africans at both ends, and between them Gauls and Spaniards. The Africans might have passed for an array of Romans, equipped as they were with arms captured partly at the Trebia but mostly at Lake Trasimene.[1] The Gauls and the Spaniards had shields of almost the same shape; their swords were different in use and in appearance, those of the Gauls being very long and point-less, whilst the Spaniards, who attacked as a rule more by thrusting then by striking, had pointed ones that were short and handy. These tribes were more terrifying to look on than the others, because of the size of their bodies and the display they made of them. The Gauls were naked from the navel up; the Spaniards had formed up wearing crimson-bordered linen tunics that shone with a dazzling whiteness. The total number of the infantry who then took their place in line was forty thousand, of the cavalry ten thousand. The generals com-

1. 218 and 217 B.C. respectively.

manding on the wings were Hasdrubal on the left, Maharbal on the right; Hannibal himself, with his brother Mago, had the centre.

The sun – whether they had so placed themselves on purpose or stood as they did by accident – was, very conveniently for both sides, on their flanks, the Romans looking south, the Carthaginians north. A wind – which those who live in those parts call Volturnus – beginning to blow against the Romans carried clouds of dust right into their faces and prevented them from seeing anything.

With a shout the auxiliaries rushed forward, and the battle began between the light-armed troops. Then the Gallic and Spanish horse which formed the left wing engaged with the Roman right in a combat very unlike a cavalry action. For they had to charge front to front, there being no room to move out round the flank, for the river shut them in on one side and the ranks of infantry on the other. Both parties pushed straight ahead, and as the horses came to a standstill, packed together in the throng, the riders began to grapple with their enemies and drag them from their seats. They were fighting on foot now, for the most part; but sharp though the struggle was, it was soon over, and the defeated Roman cavalry turned and fled.

Towards the end of the cavalry engagement the infantry came into action. At first they were evenly matched in strength and courage, as long as the Gauls and Spaniards maintained their ranks; but at last the Romans, by prolonged and frequent efforts, pushing forward with an even front and a dense line, drove in the wedge-like formation which projected from the enemy's line, for it was too thin to be strong; and then, as the Gauls and Spaniards gave way and fell back in confusion, pressed forward and, without once stopping, forced their way through the crowd of fleeing, panic-stricken enemy, till they reached first the centre and ultimately – for they met with no resistance – the African supports. These had been used to form the two wings, which had been drawn back, while the centre, where the Gauls and Spaniards had been stationed, projected somewhat. When this wedge was first driven back far enough to straighten the front, and then, continuing to yield, even left a hollow in the centre, the Africans had already begun a flanking movement on either side; and as the Romans rushed incautiously in between, they enveloped them, and presently, extending their wings crescent-wise, even closed in on their rear. From this moment the Romans, who had gained one battle to no purpose, gave over the pursuit and slaughter of the Gauls and Spaniards and began a new fight with the Africans. In this they were at a twofold disadvantage: they were shut in, while their enemies ranged on every side of them; they were tired, and faced troops that were fresh and strong.

By this time the Roman left, where the cavalry of the allies had taken position facing the Numidians, was also engaged, though the fighting was at first only sluggish. It began with a Carthaginian trick. About five hundred Numidians, who, in addition to their customary arms and missiles, carried swords concealed under their breastplates, pretended to desert. Riding over from their own side, with their bucklers at their backs, they suddenly dismounted and threw down bucklers and javelins at the feet of their enemies. Being received into the midst of their ranks they were conducted to the rear and ordered to fall in behind. And while the battle was getting under way at every point, they kept quite still; but no sooner were the minds and eyes of all absorbed in the struggle, than they snatched up the shields which lay strewn about everywhere amongst the heaps of slain, and assailing the Romans from behind and striking at their backs and hamstrings, effected a great slaughter and a terror and confusion that were even greater. And now in one place there was a panic rout and in another an obstinate though hopeless struggle; and at this juncture Hasdrubal, who commanded in that part of the field (the Carthaginian right), withdrew the Numidians from the centre – since they fought only half-heartedly against men who met them face to face – and dispatching them in pursuit of the scattered fugitives, sent in the Spanish and Gallic cavalry to help the Africans, who were now almost exhausted, though more with slaying than with fighting.

In the other part of the field (the centre) Paulus, although he had received a severe wound from a sling at the very outset of the battle, nevertheless repeatedly opposed himself to Hannibal, with his men in close formation, and at several points restored the situation. He was guarded by Roman cavalry, who finally let their horses go, as the consul was growing too weak even to control his horse. At this Hannibal, being told by someone that the consul had ordered his troopers to dismount, is said to have exclaimed: 'How much better if he had handed them over to me in fetters!' The dismounted horsemen fought as men no longer doubting that the enemy must win.

They were beaten, but chose rather to die where they stood than to run away; and the victors, angry that their victory was thus delayed, cut them down when they could not rout them. But they routed them at last, when only a few were left, exhausted with fighting and with wounds. The survivors were now all dispersed, and those who could attempted to regain their horses and escape.

Gnaeus Cornelius Lentulus, a military tribune, as he rode by, caught sight of the consul Paulus sitting on a stone and covered with blood. 'Lucius Aemilius Paulus,' he cried, 'on whom the gods ought to look down in mercy, as the only man without guilt in this day's disaster, take this horse, while you have still a little strength remaining, and I can attend you and raise you up and guard you. Do not make this battle calamitous by a consul's death! Even without that, there are tears and grief enough.'

To this the consul answered, 'All honour, Cornelius, to your courage! But do not waste in unavailing pity the little time you have to escape the enemy. Go, and tell the senators in public session to fortify the city of Rome, and garrison it strongly before the victorious enemy draws near: in private say to Quintus Fabius that Lucius Aemilius Paulus has lived till this hour and now dies remembering his precepts. As for me, let me breathe my last in the midst of my slaughtered soldiers! – so that I shall not either be brought to trial for a second time after being consul, or else stand forth as the accuser of my colleague, blaming another in defence of my own innocence.' While they were speaking, there came up with them first a crowd of fleeing Romans, and then the enemy, who overwhelmed the consul – without knowing who he was – beneath a rain of missiles. Cornelius Lentulus, thanks to his horse, escaped in the confusion. The rout was now everywhere complete. Seven thousand men escaped into the smaller camp, ten thousand into the larger, and about two thousand into the village of Cannae itself. These last were immediately cut off by Carthalo and his cavalry, for the village was not fortified. The other consul, whether by accident or by design, had not joined any throng of fugitives, but fled to Venusia with some fifty horsemen.

It is said that forty-five thousand five hundred foot and two thousand seven hundred horse were slain, in an almost equal proportion of citizens and allies. In the number were the quaestors of both consuls, Lucius Atilius and Lucius Furius Bibaculus, and twenty-nine military tribunes, some former consuls, others former praetors or aediles – amongst others are mentioned Gnaeus Servilius Geminus and Marcus Minucius, who had been Master of the Horse in the preceding years and consul several years before – and besides these, eighty senators or men who had held offices which would have given them the right to be elected to the Senate, but had volunteered to serve as soldiers in the legions. The prisoners taken in this battle are said to have numbered three thousand foot-soldiers and fifteen hundred horsemen.

Such was the battle of Cannae, a calamity as memorable as that suffered at the Allia,[1] and though less grave in its results – because the enemy failed to follow up his victory – yet for the slaughter of the army even more grievous and disgraceful. For the flight at the Allia, though it betrayed the city, saved the army: at Cannae the consul who fled was accompanied by a mere fifty men; the other, dying, had almost the entire army with him.

In the two Roman camps the crowd was half-armed and destitute of leaders. The men in the larger camp sent a messenger bidding those in the smaller one to come over to them in the night, while the enemy, exhausted by the fighting and by the feasting that had followed on their triumph, were sunk in sleep. They would then set out in one body for Canusium. This plan some were for totally rejecting. Why, they asked, did not those who summoned them come themselves to the smaller camp, where they could just as well effect a junction? Clearly because the ground between was covered with enemies and they preferred to expose to such danger the persons of others rather than their own. Others were not so much displeased with the plan as wanting in resolution.

Then said the military tribune Publius Sempronius Tuditanus: 'So you would rather be captured by the greediest and most cruel of foes, and be priced at so much a head by those who ask, "Are you a Roman citizen or a Latin ally?" in order that from the insults and misery you Romans suffer, the Latins may be privileged to go free?" Never!" each man will answer, if you are indeed fellow citizens of Lucius Aemilius Paulus the consul, who preferred an honourable death to life with ignominy, and of all those heroes who lie heaped around him! But

1. Probably the modern Fosso Bettina, a stream flowing into the Tiber 11 miles north of Rome, where the Romans were defeated by the invading Gauls (c. 390 B.C.).

before daylight surprises us and the enemy blocks our way in greater force, let us break out through these men that are clamouring in disorder and confusion at our gates. With a sword and a stout heart a man may pass through enemies, be they never so thick. In close formation you may scatter this loose and unorganized force as though there were nothing in your way. Follow me, then, as many of you as desire safety for yourselves and for the commonwealth!' Uttering these words he grasped his sword, and, forming a column, strode away through the midst of the enemy; and when the Numidians hurled missiles at their right sides, which were unprotected, they shifted their shields to the right and so got through, about six hundred of them, to the larger camp; and thence, after being joined by the other great body of men, they made their way at once without loss to Canusium. These things the conquered did rather by the prompting of courage – natural or fortuitous – than in consequence of any plan of their own or any man's authority.

Hannibal's officers crowded round him with congratulations on his victory. The others all advised him, now that he had brought so great a war to a conclusion, to rest himself and to allow his weary soldiers to rest for the remainder of that day and the following night. But Maharbal, the commander of the cavalry, held that no time should be lost. 'No!' he cried, 'realize what has been accomplished by this battle: in five days you shall banquet in the Capitol! Follow after; I will go ahead of you with the cavalry, so that the Romans may know that you are there before they know that you are coming!' To Hannibal the idea was too joyous and too vast for his mind at once to grasp it. And so, while praising Maharbal's goodwill, he declared that he must have time to consider his advice. Then said Maharbal, 'Truly the gods do not bestow on the same man all their gifts; you know how to gain a victory, Hannibal: you know not how to use one!'

That day's delay is generally believed to have saved the city and the empire.

Adapted from B. O. FOSTER (1929)

THE DEFEAT OF HANNIBAL

*After maintaining his army for fifteen years in Italy, he is driven out,
followed to North Africa, and finally defeated at the battle of Zama.[1]*

Over twenty thousand of the Carthaginians and their allies were slain
on that day. About the same number were captured, together with
one hundred and thirty-two military standards and eleven elephants.
Of the victors, about fifteen hundred fell.

Hannibal, escaping with a few horsemen in the midst of the confusion, fled to Hadrumetum.[2] He had tried every expedient both before and during the engagement before he withdrew from the fray.
And even by Scipio's admission and that of all the military experts he
had achieved this distinction, that he had drawn up his line that day
with extraordinary skill: the elephants in the very front, that their
haphazard charge and irresistible strength might prevent the Romans
from following their standards and keeping their ranks – these were
the tactics upon which they based most of their hopes; then the
auxiliaries in front of the line of Carthaginians, so that men who were
brought together from the offscouring of all nations and held not by
loyalty but by their pay might have no way of escape open to them –
and that at the same time, as they met the first fiery attack of the
enemy, they might exhaust them and, if they could do no more,
might blunt the enemy's swords by their own wounds; next in order
the soldiers in whom lay all his hopes, the Carthaginians and Africans,
that (being equal to the Romans in everything else) they might have
the advantage in fighting with strength undiminished against the
weary and the wounded; then, removed to the last line and separated
by an open space as well, the Italian troops, of whom it was uncertain
whether they were allies or enemies. Having produced this as his last
masterpiece, Hannibal after his flight to Hadrumetum was called
away – returning to Carthage in the thirty-sixth year after he had left
it as a boy. Thereupon, in the Senate House, he admitted that he had
been defeated not only in a battle but also in the war, and that there
was no hope of safety except in successfully suing for peace.

F. G. MOORE (1949)

1. The battle (202 B.C.) was probably fought in a plain called Draa-el-Metnan
2. Now Sousse.

PROPERTIUS

SEXTUS PROPERTIUS, probably born as Assisium (Assisi) between 54 and 48 B.C., died at an uncertain date after 16 B.C. He was the most stormy, and unhappy in love, of the Roman elegiac poets. The Civil Wars took his property from him and left a mark on his mind. But his mother secured him a good education at Rome, and he passed into the circle of Maecenas. Therein he resembled other war-victims, Virgil and Horace – though Horace seems to have disliked him, and Propertius' pro-Augustan feelings took longer to mature than theirs. His passionate first book, often known as *Cynthia Monobiblos* – Cynthia is the name he gives his beloved – is almost contemporary with the *Georgics*.[1] Though Catullus and Gallus (whose works are lost) had written elegies before him, he claimed to be the Romanizer of Callimachus and his Alexandrian technique; he also owes debts to the popular Greek anthologist Meleager, compiler of *The Garland*. But his subjective elegy may be a Roman invention. Finally, in Book IV, like Virgil before him and Ovid after him, he offers his personal interpretation of that rich mine of poetical material contained in Italian myths and cults.

Propertius was much read in ancient literary circles,[2] but he left little mark on medieval poetry. Then, however, Petrarch mentioned him and also copied him, as did Tasso and Ariosto; and so Propertius returned to the main stream of western European culture.[3] Goethe was called by Schiller the 'German Propertius'. 'The Elegies of Propertius,' wrote Goethe, 'of which I have read the greater part in Knebel's translation, have produced an agitation (Erschütterung) in my nature, such as works of this kind are wont to cause: a desire to produce something similar, which I must evade, as at present I have quite other things in view.'

But a reaction had set in; Gibbon, and nineteenth-century scholars after him, could only see a chilly and pedantic over-elaboration. Paley, however, edited him in English (1853, 1872), and W. A. Sellar (1892)

1. *Cynthia* was probably written between 33 and 28 B.C.; his last Book (IV) between 21 and 16.

2. But the eminent critic Quintilian (see p. 333) preferred his less colourful, more fastidious, peace-loving contemporary Tibullus. His first Book, inspired by his love for 'Delia', seems to date from about 26 B.C.

3. He appears in a Jesuit reading list of 1599.

246

detected a revival in his reputation. A. E. Housman, at Oxford, neglected Greats in favour of the text of Propertius. Since then he has reminded critics both of Rembrandt and of Rossetti; T. S. Eliot and Ezra Pound have noted his mock-modest irony; and Pound has written his long poem – not a translation but an adaptation – *Homage to Sextus Propertius* (1917).

> Annalists will continue to record Roman reputations,
> Celebrities from the Trans-Caucasus will belaud Roman celebrities
> And expound the distentions of Empire,
> But for something to read in normal circumstances,
> For a few pages brought down from the forked hill unsullied,
> I ask a wreath which will not crush my head.
> And there is no hurry about it;
> I shall have, doubtless, a boom after my funeral,
> Seeing that long standing increases all things regardless of quality.

The present age finds Propertius the most interesting of the three surviving Roman elegiac poets. In any attempt to separate classics from romantics (however these words are defined), he, like Baudelaire, remains on both sides of the line. Cyril Connolly, listing 'writers' writers' as opposed to 'dons' writers', places Propertius – along with Lucretius and Catullus – at the head of the list. Yet he has few successful translators.

CUPID [1]

Had he not hands of rare device, whoe'er
    First painted love in figure of a boy?
He saw what thoughtless beings lovers were,
    Who blessings lose, whilst lightest cares employ.

Nor added he those airy wings in vain
    And bade o'er human hearts the godhead fly;
For we are tossed upon a wavering main;
    Our gale, inconstant, veers around the sky.

Nor without cause he grasps those barbed darts,
    The Cretan quiver o'er his shoulder cast;
Ere we suspect a foe, he strikes our hearts;
    And those inflicted wounds for ever last.

For me are fixed those arrows, in my breast;
    But sure his wings are shorn, the boy remains.
For never takes he flight nor knows he rest;
    Still, still I feel him warring through my veins.

CHARLES ELTON (1778-1853)

TWO REQUESTS

O you who are beautiful, you who were born
To hurt me, to be loved, to be beautiful,
O you alone born to be all these things, please
Let me come and see you more often.

My poetry shall make your beauty famous
More than any other woman's in the whole world.
Please, Calvus [2] and Catullus, have mercy and let me
Write even better poems than you did!

JACK LINDSAY (1927)

1. For another version, with additional couplets, see below, p. 253.
2. An orator and poet, friend of Catullus, with whom he is grouped by
Horace and Ovid as well as Propertius.

SUSCEPTIBILITY

You know, Demophoon, that yesterday
I looked at many girls, in fact at girls everywhere,
And every one I loved. And you know also
That I consequently get into much trouble.

If I enter a street and walk along,
I'm sure to come out the other end in love.
And the theatres! They were opened to slay me:
I'm in love again
If a girl lifts her arms, white arms tenderly outspread,
Or sings and is made lovely with a song.

You want to know, Demophoon,
Why any girl can catch my eye.
Love has never heard
That silly word Why.

Some men slash their arms with holy knives
Or cut themselves upon the thigh
At the goading of the Phrygian flutes –
    Apparently they like it.

We've all a madness
Somewhere in us awry,
And in my case
It's wanting an infinity of wives.

Though I go blind with minstrel Thamyras,[1] my grudging friend,
I'll keep my eye for beautiful girls till the very end.

JACK LINDSAY (1927)

1. A legendary Thracian bard who challenged the Muses to a trial of skill,
lost, and was struck blind for his presumption.

LOVE AND PEACE

Love is a god of peace, and peace is adored by lovers.
I'll have no wars save wars of love. That is all.
I own no lust for murderous gold,
I ask no jewels to bubble through wine,
No fat Campanian fields are mine,
No thousand yokes....
Your ruin tossed me no bronzes, Corinth.[1]

Ah, young earth stubborn in Prometheus' hands!
Too roughly he shaped our hearts.
He made our bodies straight,
Careless how the mind might sprawl,
Darkly looking out of eyes at fate.
And now the tempests throw us anywhere.
Any foe will do. War, War! For death we cry.

There's no coin you can carry on the ships of Hell;
You fool, you will be naked there,
Victor flung with victim.... One death alone is good:
When those who have loved life well
In fullness die.

My joy is this:
Song I loved in youth, and fingers twined
In music's dances.

My joy be this:
With coronals of wine to tangle my mind,
Spring-roses tangled round my head.

And when dull years bring age upon my kiss
And on my hair,
Then I shall learn all the things I never had time to learn –
About gods, and the coming and going of spring,

1. Corinthian bronze had great prestige: it was believed to contain gold or silver.

And how the moon is pared and how it grows round again,
Whither all the winds go proudly, over the sea,
What is the east wind's quarry, how clouds are filled
With misty water, whether a day will be
When all earth's citadels shall overturn,
How it is colour, curving, drinks the rain,
Why the sun's horses are at times caparisoned black,
Why Pindus quaked, why with his oxen and wain
Bootes is so slow,
Why the Pleiades are a bush of briary fire,
Why the ocean doesn't push waves up over the sands,
And why the seasons are four,
If there are dark gods and writhing giants on the rack,
Snakes for hair, wheels, tumbling rocks, and thirst
Amid water, Three-throats bellowing at the door,
Tityos cramped in over nine acres of mire: [1]
The truth of all these stories, all man has told
Flaming beyond the pyre.

These are some of the things
I'll settle before I die.

But all of you who are so mad on battle,
Get off and bring the standards of Crassus [2] home.

JACK LINDSAY (1927)

GONE

The girl I loved has left me. She has left me.

Do you tell me, friend, I have no cause for distress?
There are no enemies save those we love. ...
Kill me and my anger would be less.

1. Three-throats is Cerberus; Tityos was pegged down in Hades, covering
nine acres, while vultures tore at his liver, because he had assaulted the goddess
Latona. Propertius in this passage refers also to the other mythical punishments
inflicted for rebellion against divine authority.
2. The triumvir Crassus had lost his army and his standards to the Parthians
at Carrhae (Haran) in 53 B.C.

O can I see her leaning on another,
Who was mine, who was mine, so lately?
Then I could say 'You are mine' to her aloud. ...
But love's king of yesterday becomes by fate
Tomorrow's Fool. That is the way of love.
Great kings have lain in the dust, very great Lords;
There was an old city called Thebes,
And Troy had towers once.
Think of the gifts I gave and the songs I made!
Yet all that time I had her, she would never say the words
'I love you'.

JACK LINDSAY (1927)

GONE TO CLITUMNUS

I hate your leaving me in Rome. Yet, Cynthia,
    I am glad you will be buried in the country.
The farm-lands are quite chaste. They harbour no seducers
    To flatter you and turn your mind to vice.
No rivals will be fighting under your bedroom window
    And you will lose no sleep from importunate calls.
Alone, without me, you will gaze at the lonely hills,
    The cattle, and some peasant's poor domain.
There you will find no theatres to corrupt your morals,
    No temples (where you have so often sinned).
There you will watch the bulls ploughing, hour after hour,
    And see the vines barbered by skilful hands.
At the rude shrine you will burn an occasional candle
    When, at the rural altar, falls a kid,
And then shorten your dress to join the dancing chorus,
    But catch no possible lover's roving eye.
I myself shall go hunting – changing my allegiance
    From Venus to Diana, chaste and fair.
I quite look forward to the kill, hanging up antlers
    On pine-trees, telling hounds just what to do.
Of course I shall not try to challenge horrid lions,
    Or, face to face, encounter rustic boars.

No, I shall think it very bold to catch a delicate
    Hare, or neatly shoot a sitting bird,
Among the woods where the Clitumnus hides its lovely
    Springs, and white oxen bathe in the cool stream.
Whenever you have any wild ideas, darling,
    Remember, in a few dawns I'll be there.
Neither the lonely woods will be enough to keep me
    Nor all the streams wandering through moss-grown rocks,
But I shall make them constantly cry 'Cynthia!' –
    For every absent man has enemies.

GILBERT HIGHET (1957)

CYNTHIA IS DEAD

Yes: bending over my pillow, I saw Cynthia –
    Interred that day beside the highway's roar.
Still sleepless, brooding on my mistress' funeral,
    I loathed the chilly empire of my bed.
Her hair was just the same as at her burial,
    Her eyes the same; her dress scorched down one side;
The fire had eaten at her favourite beryl ring;
    Her lips had tasted Lethe, and were pale.
She spoke, in a voice panting with life and passion: her hands
    Quivered meanwhile, the frail knuckles snapped.

GILBERT HIGHET (1957)

THE GOD OF LOVE

He was a genius deft and wise
Who pictured Love in boyish guise.
He knew how senseless lovers are
To let small frets great pleasures mar.
A god with human heart he drew;
Tempestuous wings he gave him too,
Well knowing that we lovers toss
On waters where wild currents cross,

And neither can we ever know
The quarter whence the wind will blow.
A quiver from each shoulder hangs,
And shafts he holds with barbed fangs,
Because he strikes us unaware
That any enemy is there.
Once hit we're never free from pain;
In me his arrows still remain,
His image haunts me everywhere.
But he has lost his wings, I swear,
For from my heart he ne'er takes flight
But wars upon me day and night.
What boots it, Love, with me to stay
Whose life-blood has been drained away?
Since a boy's form you manifest
A girl should tempt you to her breast,
'Twere meeter that your poisoned dart
Should rankle in a virgin heart.
'Tis not myself your chastenings try
But the mere ghost that once was I.
If to destroy this ghost you please,
Who will indite you songs like these,
That humbly glorify your name
Since Cynthia's beauties they proclaim:
Her taper hands, her graceful tread,
Her jet black eyes, her golden head?

S. G. TREMENHEERE (1931)

OVID

PUBLIUS OVIDIUS NASO was born in 43 B.C. at Sulmo (Sulmona) in central Italy, moved in smart Roman society, and died in about A.D. 17 in exile at Tomis (Constanţa) on the Black Sea, where he had been sent for 'a poem and a mistake' – by Augustus, *ce poltron*, declared Voltaire, *qui osa exiler Ovide*. Ovid was the latest, wittiest, most talented story-teller, and emotionally least *engagé*, of Latin elegists. His elegiac poetry comprises: *The Amores*, *The Heroines* (*Heroides*; mostly epistles purporting to be addressed by legendary women to their absent husbands), *Cosmetics* (*Medicamina Faciei*), *The Art of Love* (*Ars Amatoria*), *The Cures of Love* (*Remedia Amoris*), *The Calendar* (*Fasti*), *Tristia*, *Letters from Pontus*, *Ibis* (a curse), *The Nut Tree*; and others now lost – and lost, also, is his successful tragedy, the *Medea*. His major work, not in elegiac couplets but in epic hexameters, is the *Metamorphoses*, a collection of many myths and legends about changes of shape.

Ovid was a deliberate modern who lacked the principles of the war-worn older generation – Virgil's high purpose and Horace's acceptance of Augustan morality; though a Christian Father, Lactantius, could quote him as believing in a single divine creator. But what has captivated many generations is his glorious skill as a teller of tales. The twelfth and thirteenth centuries were an 'Ovidian period' – 77 copies of Ovid have been noted in twelfth-century library catalogues, as against 72 of Virgil (more than twice as many as any other poet). Ovid at that time contributed very greatly both to the modern idea of *l'homme moyen sensuel* and to the ideal of Romantic Love – though himself, paradoxically, was almost clinical in his observation of Love's Passion. Troubadours and Minnesänger found inspiration in him; there are four medieval French versions of the *Art of Love*, and a thirteenth-century German paraphrase of the *Metamorphoses*. The following century witnessed French, then Italian and German, translations of the same work, and an Italian *Heroides*; then, from the 1470s and 1480s, the originals were repeatedly published in Italy. Tasso and Guarini testify to Ovid's spell, and so do innumerable paintings and sculptural groups – Titian's 'Ariadne on Naxos', Bernini's Daphne and Apollo group, Cellini's Perseus at Florence. Fashionable French society enjoyed a translation of the *Heroides* by Saint-Gelais (1505).

In Chaucer's *House of Fame* one of the pillars is dedicated to *Venus clerk Ovyde.* The *Metamorphoses* were translated into English from the French by Caxton in 1480, and many sixteenth-century versions followed.[1] The most influential of them was Arthur Golding's *Metamorphoses* (1565–7). English poetry now took on a markedly Ovidian colouring, and, as Francis Meres wrote (1598), 'the sweet witty soul of Ovid lives in mellifluous and honey-tongued Shakespeare, witness his *Venus and Adonis*, his *Lucrece*, his sugared sonnets among his private friends' – and his Cleopatra, with her many debts to the Dido of the *Heroides*. It has also been suggested that Shakespeare (though his 'small Latine', on any reckoning, was inferior to the Ovidian and Virgilian lore of Spenser's *Faery Queene*) made at least occasional references to the original.

The Augustan eighteenth century had completely absorbed Ovid's influence. He was Goethe's favourite Roman poet; and Keats was yet another who found in him an inexhaustible source of material. The fresh Ovidian countryside had its nineteenth-century admirers; but now there had come a time when his high-society cleverness began to seem less praiseworthy, and indeed barely respectable. But Paul Valéry wrote three poems on his theme of Narcissus; James Joyce significantly began his Latin with the *Metamorphoses*; Edward Field and Ezra Pound have used the myths of Icarus and Glaucus; and now there are signs of an Ovidian revival at Cambridge. European thought and art have seldom been able to do without classical mythology, and classical mythology has always meant Ovid.

1. e.g. *Art of Love* (anonymous, 1513), *Heroides* (G. Turberville, 1567), *Ibis* (T. Underdowne, 1569), *Tristia* (W. Churchyard, 1572), *Amores* (Marlowe, 1590 and 1597), and *Remedia Amoris* (T. Heywood, 1598).

THE METAMORPHOSES

ALL THINGS CHANGE

All things do change; but nothing sure doth perish. This same
    sprite
Doth fleet, and frisking here and there doth swiftly take his flight
From one place to another place, and entereth every wight,
Removing out of man to beast, and out of beast to man;
But yet it never perisheth nor never perish can.
And even as supple wax with ease receiveth figures strange,
And keeps not aye one shape, nor bides assurèd aye from change,
And yet continueth always wax in substance; so I saw
The soul is aye the selfsame thing it was, and yet astray
It fleeteth into sundry shapes. ...
In all the world there is not that that standeth at a stay.
Things ebb and flow, and every shape is made to pass away.
The time itself continually is fleeting like a brook:
For neither brook nor lightsome time can tarry still. But look!
As every wave drives other forth, and that that comes behind
Both thrusteth and is thrust itself, even so the times by kind
Do fly and follow both at once, and evermore renew,
For that that was before is left, and straight there doth ensue
Another that was never erst.
   Now have I brought a work to end which neither Jove's fierce
    wrath,
Nor sword, nor fire, nor fretting age with all the force it hath
Are able to abolish quite. Let come that fatal hour
Which, saving of this brittle flesh, hath over me no power,
And at his pleasure make an end of my uncertain time;
Yet shall the better part of me assured be to climb
Aloft above the starry sky; and all the world shall never
Be able for to quench my name; for look! how far so ever
The Roman Empire by the right of conquest shall extend,
So far shall all folk read this work; and time without all end,

If poets as by prophecy about the truth may aim,
My life shall everlastingly be lengthened still by fame.
                                    ARTHUR GOLDING (1565-7)

THE AGES OF MANKIND

The golden age was first; when man, yet new,
No rule but uncorrupted reason knew;
And, with a native bent, did good pursue.
Unforced by punishment, unawed by fear,
His words were simple, and his soul sincere:
Needless was written law, where none oppressed;
The law of man was written in his breast;
No suppliant crowds before the judge appeared;
No court erected yet, nor cause was heard;
But all was safe, for conscience was their guard.
The mountain trees in distant prospect please,
Ere yet the pine descended to the seas,
Ere sails were spread, new oceans to explore;
And happy mortals, unconcerned for more,
Confined their wishes to their native shore.
No walls were yet, nor fence, nor moat, nor mound;
Nor drum was heard, nor trumpet's angry sound:
Nor swords were forged; but, void of care and crime,
The soft creation slept away their time.
The teeming earth, yet guiltless of the plough,
And unprovoked, did fruitful stores allow:
Content with food, which nature freely bred,
On wildings and on strawberries they fed;
Cornels and bramble-berries gave the rest,
And falling acorns furnished out a feast.
The flowers, unsown, in fields and meadows reigned;
And western winds immortal spring maintained.
In following years the bearded corn ensued
From earth unasked, nor was that earth renewed.
From veins of valleys milk and nectar broke,
And honey sweating through the pores of oak.

But when good Saturn, banished from above,
Was driven to hell, the world was under Jove.
Succeeding times a silver age behold,
Excelling brass, but more excelled by gold.
Then Summer, Autumn, Winter did appear;
And Spring was but a season of the year.
The sun his annual course obliquely made,
Good days contracted, and enlarged the bad.
Then air with sultry heats began to glow,
The wings of winds were clogged with ice and snow;
And shivering mortals, into houses driven,
Sought shelter from the inclemency of heaven.
Those houses then were caves, or homely sheds,
With twining osiers fenced, and moss their beds.
Then ploughs, for seed, the fruitful furrows broke,
And oxen laboured first beneath the yoke.

To this next came in course the brazen age:
A warlike offspring prompt to bloody rage,
Not impious yet – Hard steel succeeded then;
And stubborn as the metal were the men.
Truth, Modesty, and Shame the world forsook:
Fraud, Avarice, and Force their places took.
Then sails were spread to every wind that blew;
Raw were the sailors, and the depths were new:
Trees, rudely hollowed, did the waves sustain,
Ere ships in triumph ploughed the watery plain.

Then landmarks limited to each his right:
For all before was common as the light.
Nor was the ground alone required to bear
Her annual income to the crooked share:
But greedy mortals, rummaging her store,
Digged from her entrails first the precious ore,
Which next to hell the prudent gods had laid;
And that alluring ill to sight displayed.
Thus cursèd steel, and more accursèd gold,
Gave mischief birth, and made that mischief bold:
And double death did wretched man invade,
By steel assaulted, and by gold betrayed.

Now (brandished weapons glittering in their hands)
Mankind is broken loose from moral bands;
No rights of hospitality remain:
The guest, by him who harboured him, is slain:
The son-in-law pursues the father's life;
The wife her husband murders, he the wife.
The step-dame poison for the son prepares;
The son inquires into his father's years.
Faith flies, and Piety in exile mourns;
And Justice, here oppressed, to heaven returns.

JOHN DRYDEN (1693)

THE ONE-EYED GIANT POLYPHEMUS PROPOSES TO THE SEA-NYMPH GALATEA

'My palace, in the living rock, is made
By nature's hand; a spacious pleasing shade;
Which neither heat can pierce, nor cold invade.
My garden filled with fruits you may behold,
And grapes in clusters, imitating gold;
Some blushing bunches of a purple hue:
And these, and those, are all reserved for you.
Red strawberries in shades expecting stand,
Proud to be gathered by so white a hand;
Autumnal cornels latter fruit provide,
And plums, to tempt you, turn their glossy side;
Not those of common kinds but such alone
As in Phaeacian orchards [1] might have grown:
Nor chestnuts shall be wanting to your food
Nor garden-fruits, nor wildings of the wood;
The laden boughs for you alone shall bear;
And yours shall be the product of the year.

'The flocks you see are all my own; beside
The rest that woods and winding valleys hide,
And those that folded in the caves abide.

1. The mythical land of Alcinous and Nausicaa, to which Odysseus came after he was shipwrecked.

Ask not the numbers of my growing store;
Who knows how many, knows he has no more.
Nor will I praise my cattle; trust not me,
But judge yourself, and pass your own decree;
Behold their swelling dugs; the sweepy weight
Of ewes, that sink beneath the milky freight;
In the warm folds their tender lambkins lie;
Apart from kids, that call with human cry.
New milk in nut-brown bowls is duly served
For daily drink; the rest for cheese reserved.
Nor are these household dainties all my store:
The fields and forests will afford us more;
The deer, the herd, the goat, the savage boar:
All sorts of venison; and of birds the best:
A pair of turtles taken from the nest.
I walked the mountains, and two cubs I found,
Whose dam had left them on the naked ground;
So like, that no distinction could be seen;
So pretty, they were presents for a queen;
And so they shall! I took them both away,
And keep, to be companions of your play.

JOHN DRYDEN (1693)

THE FALL OF PHAETON

*The mortal youth Phaeton visits, in the Palace of the Sun,
his father Phoebus Apollo, who vows he will grant any request:*

The youth, transported, asks without delay
To guide the Sun's bright chariot for a day . . .

Meanwhile the restless horses neighed aloud,
Breathing out fire, and pawing where they stood.
Tethys, not knowing what had passed, gave way,
And all the waste of heaven before them lay.
They spring together out, and swiftly bear
The flying youth through clouds and yielding air;
With wingy speed outstrip the eastern wind,

And leave the breezes of the morn behind.
The youth was light, nor could he fill the seat,
Or poise the chariot with its wonted weight:
But as at sea the unballast vessel rides,
Cast to and fro, the sport of winds and tides,
So in the bounding chariot tossed on high,
The youth is hurried headlong through the sky.
Soon as the steeds perceive it, they forsake
Their stated course, and leave the beaten track.
The youth was in a maze, nor did he know
Which way to turn the reins, or where to go;
Nor would the horses, had he known, obey.
Then the Seven Stars first felt Apollo's ray
And wished to dip in the forbidden sea.
The folded Serpent next the frozen pole,
Still and benumbed before, began to roll,
And raged with inward heat, and threatened war,
And shot a redder light from every star;
Nay, and 'tis said, Boötes, too, that fain
Thou wouldst have fled, though cumbered with thy wain.

The unhappy youth then, bending down his head,
Saw earth and ocean far beneath him spread:
His colour changed, he startled at the sight,
And his eyes darkened by too great a light.
Now could he wish the fiery steeds untried,
His birth obscure, and his request denied:
Now would he Merops for his father own,
And quit his boasted kindred to the Sun.

So fares the pilot, when his ship is tossed
In troubled seas, and all its steerage lost,
He gives her to the winds, and in despair
Seeks his last refuge in the gods and prayer.

What could he do? his eyes, if backward cast,
Find a long path he had already passed;
If forward, still a longer path they find:
Both he compares, and measures in his mind;
And sometimes casts an eye upon the east,
And sometimes looks on the forbidden west.

The horses' names he knew not in the fright:
Nor would he loose the reins, nor could he hold them tight.
    Now all the horrors of the heavens he spies,
And monstrous shadows of prodigious size
That, decked with stars, lie scattered o'er the skies.
There is a place above, where Scorpio, bent
In tail and arms, surrounds a vast extent;
In a wide circuit of the heavens he shines,
And fills the space of two celestial signs.
Soon as the youth beheld him, vexed with heat,
Brandish his sting, and in his poison sweat,
Half dead with sudden fear he dropped the reins;
The horses felt them loose upon their manes,
And, flying out through all the plains above,
Ran uncontrolled where'er their fury drove;
Rushed on the stars, and through a pathless way
Of unknown regions hurried on the day.
And now above, and now below they flew,
And near the earth the burning chariot drew.
    The clouds disperse in fumes, the wondering Moon
Beholds her brother's steeds beneath her own;
The highlands smoke, cleft by the piercing rays,
Or, clad with woods, in their own fuel blaze.
Next o'er the plains, where ripened harvests grow,
The running conflagration spreads below.
But these are trivial ills; whole cities burn,
And peopled kingdoms into ashes turn.

    The astonished youth, where'er his eyes could turn,
Beheld the universe around him burn:
The world was in a blaze; nor could he bear
The sultry vapours and the scorching air,
Which from below as from a furnace flowed.
And now the axle-tree beneath him glowed:
Lost in the whirling clouds, that round him broke,
And white with ashes, hovering in the smoke,
He flew where'er the horses drove, nor knew
Whither the horses drove, or where he flew.

The ground, deep cleft, admits the dazzling ray,
And startles Pluto with the flash of day.
The seas shrink in, and to the sight disclose
Wide, naked plains, where once their billows rose;
Their rocks are all discovered, and increase
The number of the scattered Cyclades.
The fish in shoals about the bottom creep,
Nor longer dares the crooked dolphin leap;
Gasping for breath, the unshapen phocae die,
And on the boiling wave extended lie.
Nereus, and Doris with her virgin train,
Seek out the last recesses of the main;
Beneath unfathomable depths they faint,
And secret in their gloomy regions pant.
Stern Neptune thrice above the waves upheld
His face, and thrice was by the flames repelled.

The Earth at length, on every side embraced
With scalding seas, that floated round her waist,
When now she felt the springs and rivers come
And crowd within the hollow of her womb,
Uplifted to the heavens her blasted head,
And clapped her hands upon her brows, and said
(But first, impatient of the sultry heat,
Sunk deeper down, and sought a cooler seat:)
'If you, great king of gods, my death approve,
And I deserve it, let me die, by Jove!
If I must perish by the force of fire,
Let me transfixed with thunderbolts expire.
See, whilst I speak, my breath the vapours choke!
(For now her face lay wrapped in clouds of smoke.)
See my singed hair, behold my faded eye
And withered face, where heaps of cinders lie!
And does the plough for this my body tear?
This the reward for all the fruits I bear,
Tortured with rakes, and harassed all the year?
That herbs for cattle daily I renew,
And food for man, and frankincense for you?
But grant me guilty; what has Neptune done?

The wavy empire, which by lot was given,
Why does it waste, and further shrink from heaven?
If I nor he your pity can provoke,
See your own heavens, the heavens begin to smoke!
Should once the sparkles catch those bright abodes,
Destruction seizes on the heavens and gods;
Atlas becomes unequal to his freight,
And almost faints beneath the glowing weight.
If heaven, and earth, and sea together burn,
All must again into their chaos turn.
Apply some speedy cure, prevent our fate,
And succour nature, e'er it be too late.'
She ceased; for, choked with vapours round her spread,
Down to the deepest shades she sunk her head.

    Jove called to witness every power above,
And even the god whose son the chariot drove,
That what he acts he is compelled to do,
Or universal ruin must ensue.
Straight he ascends the high ethereal throne,
From whence he used to dart his thunder down,
From whence his showers and storms he used to pour,
But now could meet with neither storm nor shower.
Then aiming at the youth, with lifted hand,
Full at his head he hurled the forky brand
In dreadful thunderings. Thus the almighty sire
Suppressed the raging of the fires with fire.

    At once from life and from the chariot driven,
The ambitious boy fell thunder-struck from heaven.
The horses started with a sudden bound,
And flung the reins and chariot to the ground:
The studded harness from their necks they broke;
Here fell a wheel, and here a silver spoke,
Here were the beam and axle torn away;
And, scattered o'er the earth, the shining fragments lay.
The breathless Phaëton, with flaming hair,
Shot from the chariot, like a falling star,
That in a summer's evening from the top
Of heaven drops down, or seems at least to drop;

Till on the Po his blasted corpse was hurled,
Far from his country, in the western world.

JOSEPH ADDISON (1672–1719)

THE CREATION

All frontiers fixed, the time had come to give
To every part its share of things that live;
And constellations that for long had been
Merged in the mass, their godlike forms unseen,
To heavenly habitations soon were gone,
And stars, like brilliant bubbles, rose and shone;
Birds beat the air, the beasts had earth to roam,
And flickering fish in water found a home.
  There wanted yet, to dominate the whole,
A more capacious mind, a loftier soul;
So man was formed, of elements conveyed
Direct from heaven, some think, by him who made
Order prevail in chaos – him I call
The cosmic architect, who fashioned all.
Or did the stuff of earth, so close akin
To heaven above that shared its origin,
And fresh from recent contact, still retain
Some molecules of fine ethereal grain?
Such earth, with water mixed, so some declare,
Prometheus shaped the form of gods to wear,
In attitude of rule, that while the race
Of creatures else looks down, man lifts his face
(For so his maker willed) and turns his eye
To starry heights above, and sweeps the sky.
Thus clothed with shapes of life unknown till then,
Earth's formless clay was moulded into men.

A. E. WATTS (1954)

RUMOUR [1]

Where three worlds meet, there lies a central space,
Of earth and sky and sea the meeting-place;
Where all that is, though worlds away, comes plain
To eye and ear: 'tis Rumour's hill-domain,
Her own devising, pierced on every side
With loops and entries, ever standing wide;
Her chosen fastness, by no portals closed,
But open day and night, the whole composed
Of echoing bronze, a sounding-chamber, stirred
By every breath, repeating all that's heard.
Nowhere within is peace or silence found;
And yet no shouting, but a low-voiced sound,
Like that of distant waves, goes murmuring round;
Or like the noise, when Jove's loud rattling shakes
The pitchy clouds, which dying thunder makes.
Through crowded halls, in ceaseless ebb and flow,
The feather-pated people come and go,
Rumours in thousands, talking each to each,
Truth mixed with lies, an endless hum of speech;
While some in vacant ears their gossip pour,
And some go off with tales heard just before;
And every tale with false accretion swells,
As each new sponsor adds to what he tells.
Credulity and random error here
Consort with baseless joy and panic fear;
Subversive treason shows a sudden face,
And whispers fly, whose author none can trace.
Whate'er befalls, the goddess sees, with eye
Searching for news, in earth and sea and sky.

A. E. WATTS (1954)

1. Compare Virgil's account (p. 161).

THE FLOOD

There was such wickedness once on earth that Justice fled to the sky, and the king of the gods determined to make an end of the race of men.

Then Jupiter let loose the South Wind, and the South Wind came with drenching wings. He veiled his terrible face in pitchy darkness; his beard was heavy with the storm and his hair was streaked grey with rain. Clouds sat upon his forehead; water poured from his feathers and the folds of his garments. He squeezed in his fist the hanging masses of cloud, and there was a crash. Thick vapours fell from the air, and Iris, the messenger of Juno, dressed in rainbow colours, carried water to feed the clouds.

The crops were battered to the ground and farmers wept for their fallen hopes; for all the year's work had turned out to have been useless.

Jupiter's anger was not confined to his province of the sky. Neptune, his sea-blue brother, sent the waves to help him. He summoned the rivers, and when they had entered the palace of their lord, he said: 'No need for many words. Just pour out the whole of your strength. That is what I want. Open all your doors, let nothing stop you, but give free rein to your flowing streams!' So he commanded, and they went away. Then the springs ran unchecked and the rivers rolled unbridled to the seas. Neptune smote the earth with his trident and the earth shivered and shook, giving free passage to the waters under the earth. The rivers broke their bounds and went rushing over the lowlands, dragging along with them fields of corn and orchards, men and beasts together, houses and religious buildings with all their holy images. If there was any house left which could stand up against the flood without crashing down, yet its roof was under water and its turrets were hid by the waves eddying above. Soon there was no telling land from sea. The whole world was sea, except that this sea had no shores.

You could see the men, one getting up on to a hill, another sitting in his curved boat, using oars now in the very place where he had been ploughing only a moment before. Another man is sailing over corn fields or over the roof of some great submerged house; yet another is catching fish among the topmost boughs of an elm. Perhaps their anchors grapple the green grass of meadows, or the curved keels scrape over vines growing under water. And where the light-limbed goats used to crop the turf, now ugly-looking seals go flopping about.

Under the water the sea-nymphs Nereides are staring in amazement at woods, houses, and cities. The forests are now full of dolphins who dash about in the tops of the trees and beat their tails against the swaying trunks. You might see a wolf swimming with a flock of sheep, yellow lions carried away by the water, and tigers too. The wild boar, though he is strong as a thunderbolt, cannot help himself, nor is the stag's fleet foot any use to him. He too is swept away; and the birds, after they have wandered far and looked everywhere for a place to alight, fall into the sea too weak to move their wings.

The sea, in its boundless power, had flattened out the smaller hills, and waves, never seen there before, were lapping round the crests of mountains. Nearly all the men perished by water; and those who escaped the water, having no food, died of hunger.

There is a place called Phocis, a rich land while there was any land, but at that time it was part of the sea, just a huge plain of hurrying water. There is a mountain there whose twin peaks seem to aim at the stars. It is called Parnassus and its summit is above the clouds. All the country round was under water, but Deucalion with his wife, in a little boat, got to this mountain and landed. There was no man more good or more devoted to fair dealing than Deucalion, and there was no more reverent woman than his wife, Pyrrha.

Now when Jupiter saw that the whole earth had become one lake of running water, and that from so many thousands of men and women only this one man and this one woman were left, and that both of them were innocent, both good decent folk, then he dispersed the clouds, made the north wind roll away the rain, and unveiled again the whole vault of heaven. The sea no longer raged. The ruler of the deep laid aside his three-pronged spear and calmed the waters. He called for sea-blue Triton, and soon Triton's head rose out of the deep and his shoulders all overgrown with barnacles. Neptune told him to blow on his horn of shell the signal for retreat to waves and rivers. He took up his bugle, a spiral shell, twisted at the mouthpiece and opening out wide at the other end. When he draws in his breath and blows into this bugle the sound goes out from the middle of the sea to the ends of the world. So now as soon as the shell had touched the lips and dripping beard of the god and the blast had been blown calling the retreat, the sound was heard by all the waters of earth and sea, and they obeyed, one and all. Now the sea has shores again, streams run brimming their channels, rivers go back to their beds, and the hills begin to appear. The earth emerges; land grows as water shrinks away, and as time passes woods appear below the naked summits of the hills, though mud still sticks to the leaves of the trees.

So the world came back again. But when Deucalion saw it all empty, and all the countries lying desolate in a tremendous silence, tears came into his eyes and he spoke thus to Pyrrha: 'My sister, my wife, you, the only woman left, once it was our family, our birth, and our wedding that brought us together, but now our dangers are another bond. We two are all the inhabitants of all the lands that the sun looks on when it rises and when it sets. The sea has the rest. And even now we cannot be sure that we are safe. The terror of those clouds still sticks in my mind. Poor creature, what would you feel like now, if you had been preserved from fate without me? How would you endure terror, if you were alone? Who then would be trying to console you? As for me I am sure that if you had been drowned I should go after you and be drowned too. Oh how I wish that I had the skill of Prometheus, my father, and could get all the people back again and pour life into moulded clay! As it is the whole race of mankind is comprised in us two, and we seem to have been preserved just as specimens of humanity. Such was the will of heaven.'

So he spoke, weeping, and then they decided to pray to the powers above, and ask for help from the holy oracle. Together they went straight away to the waters of Cepheus, which were not yet running clear, but they knew where the shallows were and so passed through them. They took water from the stream and sprinkled it on their heads and garments; then they went to the shrine of the holy goddess and saw the roof of the shrine shining with foul sea-slime, and the altars with no fire burning on them. When they reached the steps of the temple, they both fell on their faces and reverently kissed the ice-cold stones. Then they spoke: 'If the powers of heaven can feel anything or be at all moved by the prayers of the just, if the anger of the gods is not inflexible, then tell us, O Themis, what skill there is by which we can repair the ruin of the race. Lend thine aid, O most merciful one, to the drowned!'

Moved with compassion, the goddess gave her answer: 'Go forth from the temple. Veil your heads and unloose the girdles of your garments. Then scatter behind you on the ground the bones of your venerable mother.'

For a long time they stood still in amazement, till Pyrrha first broke the silence, and said that she could not do what the goddess had bidden them. Her lips trembled as she begged for pardon; but how could she dare to wound her mother's ghost by throwing her bones about? All the time they pondered within themselves and revolved in their minds the difficult words of the goddess's reply, so dark to understand.

Finally Deucalion found soothing words to calm his wife. 'Oracles,' he said, 'are good things and could never tell us to do anything bad. Now, either my usual intelligence has gone astray, or else "our venerable mother" is the earth. And by "bones" I think the oracle must mean the stones that are in the body of the earth. It is stones that we are told to scatter behind us.'

Pyrrha was certainly impressed by her husband's interpretation, but still they hardly dared to hope, so mistrustful were they both of the commands of heaven. Still, there was no harm in trying, so they went out of the temple, veiled their heads, girded up their tunics, and, as they had been told, scattered stones behind them as they went. Antiquity is our evidence for what happened next. Otherwise I doubt whether anyone would believe it. For the stones began to lose their hardness. Little by little they grew soft, and as they softened they began to take a new shape. They went on growing; something less hard than stone was stirring within them, something like humanity, although it was not quite clear yet, but more like pieces of sculpture that have only just been begun, which are more or less like what they are meant to be, but are not yet quite rounded off. All the earth and mud which stuck to the stones became flesh; the solid core became bones; veins in the mineral were still veins, but now they had blood in them. And in a short time, by the power of the gods, all the stones which Deucalion had sown grew up into men, and women sprang from the stones which Pyrrha scattered.

So we human beings are a hard stubborn race, well used to labour; and that is how we prove that this story of our birth is true.

REX WARNER (1950)

In the hill-country of Phrygia there is an oak, growing close beside
a linden tree, and a low wall surrounds them both. I have seen the spot
myself, for Pittheus sent me on a mission to that land, where his
father Pelops once was king. Not far off is a stagnant pool: once it was
habitable country, but now it has become a stretch of water, haunted
by marsh birds, divers and coots. Jupiter visited this place, disguised
as a mortal, and Mercury, the god who carries the magic wand, laid
aside his wings and accompanied his father. The two gods went to a
thousand homes, looking for somewhere to rest, and found a thousand homes bolted and barred against them.

However, one house took them in: it was, indeed, a humble dwelling roofed with thatch and reeds from the marsh; but a good-hearted
old woman, Baucis by name, and her husband Philemon, who was
the same age as his wife, had been married in that cottage in their
youth, and had grown grey in it together. By confessing their poverty
and accepting it contentedly, they had eased the hardship of their lot.
It made no difference in that house whether you asked for master or
servant – the two of them were the entire household: the same people
gave the orders and carried them out. So, when the heaven-dwellers
reached this humble home and, stooping down, entered its low doorway, the old man set chairs for them, and invited them to rest their
weary limbs; Baucis bustled up anxiously to throw a rough piece of
cloth over the chairs, and stirred up the warm ashes on the hearth,
fanning the remains of yesterday's fire, feeding it with leaves and
chips of dried bark, and blowing on it till it burst into flames. Then
the old woman took down finely split sticks and dry twigs which
were hanging from the roof, broke them into small pieces, and pushed
them under her little pot. Her husband had brought in some vege-
tables from his carefully-watered garden, and these she stripped of
their outer leaves. Philemon took a two-pronged fork and lifted down
a side of smoked bacon that was hanging from the blackened rafters;
then he cut off a small piece of their long-cherished meat, and boiled
it till it was tender in the bubbling water.

Meanwhile the old couple chattered on, to pass the time, and kept
their guests from noticing the delay. There was a beechwood bowl

there, hanging from a nail by its curved handle, which was filled with warm water, and the visitors washed in this, to refresh themselves. On a couch with frame and legs of willow-wood lay a mattress, stuffed with soft sedge grass. Baucis and Philemon covered this with the cloths which they used to put out only on solemn holidays – even so, the stuff was old and cheap, a good match for the willow couch. Then the gods took their places for the meal. Old Baucis tucked up her dress and, with shaky hands, set the table down in front of them. One of its three legs was shorter than the others, but she pushed a tile in below, to make it the same height. When she had inserted this, and so levelled the sloping surface, she wiped over the table with some stalks of fresh mint. Then she placed upon the board the mottled berry which honest Minerva loves, wild cherries picked in the autumn and preserved in lees of wine, endives and radishes and a piece of cheese, and eggs lightly roasted in ashes not too hot; all these were set out in clay dishes and, after they had been served, a flagon with a raised pattern, just as much silver as their dinner service, was set on the table, and beechwood cups, lined inside with yellow wax. After a short while, the hearth provided them with food piping hot, and the wine, which was of no great age, was sent round again. Then it was set aside for a little, to make way for dessert, which consisted of nuts, a mixture of figs and wrinkled dates, plums and fragrant apples in shallow baskets, and black grapes, just gathered. A shining honey comb was set in the midst of these good things and, above all, there was cheerful company, and bustling hospitality, far beyond their means.

As the dinner went on, the old man and woman saw that the flagon, as often as it was emptied, refilled itself of its own accord, and that the wine was automatically replenished. At the sight of this miracle, Baucis and Philemon were awed and afraid. Timidly stretching out their hands in prayer, they begged the gods' indulgence for a poor meal, without any elaborate preparations. They had a single goose, which acted as guardian of their little croft: in honour of their divine visitors, they were making ready to kill the bird, but with the help of its swift wings it eluded its owners for a long time, and tired them out, for age made them slow. At last it seemed to take refuge with the gods themselves, who declared that it should not be killed. 'We are gods,' they said, 'and this wicked neighbourhood is going to be punished as it richly deserves; but you will be allowed to escape this disaster. All you have to do is to leave your home, and climb up the steep mountainside with us.' The two old people both did as they were told and, leaning on their sticks, struggled up the long slope.

When they were a bowshot distant from the top, they looked round and saw all the rest of their country drowned in marshy waters, only their own home left standing. As they gazed in astonishment, and wept for the fate of their people, their old cottage, which had been small, even for two, was changed into a temple: marble columns took the place of its wooden supports, the thatch grew yellow, till the roof seemed to be made of gold, the doors appeared magnificently adorned with carvings, and marble paved the earthen floor. Then Saturn's son spoke in majestic tones: 'Tell me, my good old man, and you, who are a worthy wife for your good husband, what would you like from me?' Philemon and Baucis consulted together for a little, and then the old man told the gods what they both wished. 'We ask to be your priests, to serve your shrine; and since we have lived in happy companionship all our lives, we pray that death may carry us off together at the same instant, so that I may never see my wife's funeral, and she may never have to bury me.' Their prayer was granted. They looked after the temple as long as they lived.

Then, one day, bowed down with their weight of years, they were standing before the sacred steps, talking of all that had happened there, when Baucis saw Philemon beginning to put forth leaves, and old Philemon saw Baucis growing leafy too. When the tree-tops were already growing over their two faces, they exchanged their last words while they could, and cried simultaneously: 'Good-bye, my dear one!' As they spoke, the bark grew over and concealed their lips. The Bithynian peasant still points out the trees growing there side by side, trees that were once two bodies.

MARY M. INNES (1955)

ELEGIAC POEMS

WHEN OVID WAS YOUNG

I dearly loved the poets of the time;
Each poet was a god in my esteem.
Oft did I hear sage Macer [1] read his birds
And serpents, and the help each herb affords;
And oft Propertius, my companion dear,
With amorous raptures did present my ear.
Heroic Ponticus, iambic Battus
With pleasing strains did often recreate us,
And tuneful Horace oft my ear delighted
With curious ditties on his harp recited.
Virgil I only saw; and hasty fate
Tibullus' friendship did anticipate.
He followed Gallus, and Propertius him;
I was the fourth man in the rank of time.
As I my elders, so my juniors me
Adored; my Muse grew famous suddenly.
Thrice and no more had I shaven off my beard,
When first my youthful strains the people heard.
My mistress, in Corinna masked, did move
My wits; each village now could chant our love.
Much did I write, but what I faulty knew
Into the fault-correcting fires I threw.
And at my exile cast I in the flame,
Vexed with the Muses, many a work of fame.
My tender heart oft piercèd through with love
Each light occasion instantly did move.
But when I was from Cupid's passions free,
My Muse was mute and wrote no elegy.

JOHN GOWER (c. 1640)

1. Quintilian (see p. 333) coupled his name with that of Lucretius. Ponticus and Battus are, and perhaps were, obscure.

You bid me write to amuse the tedious hours,
And save from withering my poetic powers.
Hard is the task, my friend, for verse should flow
From the free mind, not fettered down by woe.
Restless amidst unceasing tempests tossed,
Whoe'er has cause for sorrow, I have most.
Would you bid Priam laugh, his sons all slain,
Or childless Niobe from tears refrain,
Join the gay dance, and lead the festive train?
Does grief or study most befit the mind,
To this remote, this barbarous nook confined?
Could you impart to my unshaken breast
The fortitude by Socrates possessed,
Soon would it sink beneath such woes as mine:
For what is human strength to wrath divine?
Wise as he was, and Heaven pronounced him so,
My sufferings would have laid that wisdom low.
Could I forget my country, thee and all,
And even the offence to which I owe my fall,
Yet fear alone would freeze the poet's vein,
While hostile troops swarm o'er the dreary plain.

Ill fares the bard in this unlettered land,[1]
None to consult, and none to understand.
The purest verse has no admirers here,
Their own rude language only suits their ear.
Rude as it is, at length familiar grown,
I learn it, and almost unlearn my own.
Yet to say truth, even here the Muse disdains
Confinement, and attempts her former strains,
But finds the strong desire is not the power,
And what her taste condemns the flames devour.
A part, perhaps, like this, escapes the doom,

1. The Dobruja, in which Ovid was exiled.

And, though unworthy, finds a friend at Rome;
But oh the cruel art, that could undo
Its votary thus! would that could perish too!
WILLIAM COWPER (1731–1800)

MYSELF

Take me, and I your slave will be
   As long as life endure:
Constant in my fidelity
   And in your service sure.

Mine is no name of ancient might
   Nor have I lands untold;
My father's but a simple knight
   And careful with his gold.

But Phoebus and the Muses nine
   Come ever to my call,
And Bacchus, finder of the vine,
   And Love, who gives me all.

My life is pure and free from stain,
   My heart is sound and true.
No gallant I, of conquests vain,
   But faithful still to you.
F. A. WRIGHT (1869–1946)

ADVICE TO WOMEN

Maidens, give ear and you shall hear
   What is your chiefest duty,
Pray listen well and I will tell
   You how to keep your beauty.

'Tis care that makes the barren earth
   Produce the ripened grain.
'Tis care that brings tree-fruit to birth
   With grafting and much pain.

Things that are cared for always please,
   And now each man's a dandy,
A girl must be as spruce as he
   And have her powder handy.

F. A. WRIGHT (1869–1946)

THE ART OF LOVE

Yield to rebuff: yielding will win the day;
Just play whatever part she'd have you play:
Like what she likes, decry what she decries,
Say what she says, deny what she denies.
Laugh when she laughs. She weeps? Be sure you weep.
Let her dictate the rules your face must keep.
When, at her whim, you throw the ivory dice,
Throw ill; if she does, bid her throw them twice;
At dominoes claim not the forfeit due;
Make sure the deuces always fall to you.

Her birthday hold a day of strict taboo:
All giving-days must be black days for you.
Vain all your schemes to dodge: a woman's stealth
Can always fleece a lover of his wealth.
Some vulgar salesman calls while you are by
And spreads his wares before her spendthrift eye;
She'll ask your judgement, as a connoisseur,
Then kiss you, then suggest you buy for her –
One thing for years her soul will satisfy,
Just what she needs, and now's the time to buy.
No use to plead you have no cash in sight:
You'll sign – and curse the day you learned to write.
Now she will beg towards her birthday-cake,
Born when it suits her whim the date to fake,
Now feign a loss and shed a touching tear –
A precious earring fallen from her ear.
She borrows much, but won't repay, of course:
You lose, and get no credit for your loss.

Ten tongues, ten months – still could I not convey
The unholy tricks that all such women play.

Yet there are cultured girls, a breed most rare,
And girls not cultured but who wish they were.
Both should be praised in song: a pleasing voice
Can make the meanest poetry sound choice.
Burn midnight oil: both may accept an ode
To her, in lieu of a small gift bestowed.

But what you mean to do in any case,
Contrive she asks, then do it as a grace.

L. P. WILKINSON (1955)

UNFAIR

So, must I always be accused of new offences?
    Although I win, I hate these endless fights!
If, in the marble theatre, I should glance round,
    At once you see a woman to complain of;
Or if some handsome girl looks silently towards me,
    You notice secret messages in her eyes.
If I admire one, you tear out my hair by the roots;
    If not, you think I am concealing my guilt.
If I don't look lovesick, you call me cold to you;
    If I do, I'm dying for another woman.
In fact, I wish I had committed some real sin,
    For guilty men accept their punishment;
But with your random charges and your vain suspicions,
    You make your anger seem pointless and cheap.

GILBERT HIGHET (1957)

PART III

THE EARLY EMPIRE

PHAEDRUS

GAIUS JULIUS PHAEDRUS, born in Macedonia about 15 B.C. as a slave, came to Rome, was freed by Augustus, offended but survived Tiberius' chief minister Sejanus, and died in about A.D. 50. He was confident of immortality as Romanizer (with improvements) of the traditional Greek fables collectively known by the name of Aesop.[1] Many of his fables are about animals, others are jokes, anecdotes, and short stories. The five books that have survived, together with additions included in Perotti's epitome (about 1465), include well over a hundred fables of his authorship, and others are known from prose paraphrases bearing the name 'Romulus'. Though Phaedrus, in the manner of other best-sellers, was ignored by contemporary critics, it was he who converted the fable from an incidental *genre* (Ennius, Lucilius, and Horace had attempted it) into an independent Roman literary form.

The moralizing fable was popular in the Middle Ages, but Avianus [2] was more widely read than Phaedrus, and the latter's poems were not published until 1596 (at Autun). La Fontaine was 'mainly Phaedrus transmuted from silver to gold', and Lessing, though critical in his appreciation, composed German versions of Phaedrus' fables and planned to edit them. Heine felt that the people in the streets of Paris were familiar, since he recognized them all from a picture-book of animals. 'The Wolf and the Lamb' and 'The Fox and the Sour Grapes' are eternally familiar; and today Phaedrus has an interest for anthropologists and sociologists since so many of his stories are derived from ancient folklore.

A new, sharp twist has now been given to the beast fable by George Orwell's *Animal Farm*.

1. Aesop was believed to have been a slave at Samos in the sixth century B.C.
2. *c.* A.D. 400, follower of Babrius (? second century), who wrote in Greek.

THE WOLF AND THE LAMB

By thirst incited, to the brook
The Wolf and Lamb themselves betook.
The Wolf high up the current drank,
The Lamb far lower down the bank.
Then, bent his ravenous maw to cram,
The Wolf took umbrage at the Lamb.
  'How dare you trouble all the flood,
And mingle my good drink with mud?'
'Sir,' says the Lambkin, sore afraid,
'How should I act, as you upbraid?
The thing you mention cannot be,
The stream descends from you to me.'
Abashed by facts, says he, 'I know
'Tis now exact six months ago
You strove my honest fame to blot' –
'Six months ago, sir, I was not.'
'Then 'twas the old ram thy sire,' he cried,
And so he tore him, till he died.
  To those this fable I address
Who are determined to oppress,
And trump up any false pretence,
But they will injure innocence.

                              CHRISTOPHER SMART (1765)

THE BATTLE OF THE MICE AND WEASELS

The routed Mice upon a day
Fled from the Weasels in array;
But in the hurry of the flight,
What with their weakness and their fright
Each scarce could get into his cave:
Howe'er, at last their lives they save.
But their commanders (who had tied
Horns to their heads in martial pride,

Which as a signal they designed
For non-commissioned mice to mind)
Stick in the entrance as they go,
And there are taken by the foe,
Who, greedy of the victim, gluts
With mouse-flesh his ungodly guts.
　　Each great and national distress
Must chiefly mighty men oppress;
While folks subordinate and poor
Are by their littleness secure.

CHRISTOPHER SMART (1765)

THE KING OF THE BEASTS

When in alliance with the strong,
The weak are sure to suffer wrong.
　　A Lion, in a royal whim,
Took other beasts to hunt with him.
A stag entangled in their toil,
He into three divides the spoil;
Then in these words the lordly beast
His humble company addressed:
'This portion I as strongest claim;
This, because Lion is my name;
And as for the remaining share,
To touch it, let me see who dare!'
Thus, as it ever will befall,
The greedy tyrant seized on all.

SIR BROOKE BOOTHBY (1809)

THE FOX AND THE CROW

Who in deceitful praise takes pleasure,
His folly will repeat at leisure.
    Perched o'er his head, sly Reynard sees
In a Crow's beak a tempting cheese;
When thus the cunning Fox began:
'O Crow, more fair than any swan!
If like thy form thy voice should be,
What bird can be compared to thee!'
To sing the flattered fool would try:
The cheese came tumbling from on high;
Voracious Reynard snapt it up,
And laughing, left his hungry dupe,
Who on an empty stomach rued
That flattery is but hollow food.

SIR BROOKE BOOTHBY (1809)

THE FROG AND THE OX

    When little folks will ape the great,
'Tis easy to foresee their fate.
    A Frog a well fed Ox had seen,
And, envying much his goodly mien,
She puffed and swelled her wrinkled hide;
And to her brood in triumph cried,
'Well! do I equal him in size?'
'Ah, no!' a little one replies.
Again her stretched-out sides dilate;
The difference still, they said, was great.
One effort more, in fate's despite,
She desperate made with all her might:
'Twas all in vain. The reptile, curst
With envy and ambition, burst.

SIR BROOKE BOOTHBY (1809)

SHE-GOATS AND BEARDS

The she-goats won a grant of beards from Jove.
Sore were the he-goats, murmuring loud that shes
Should reach the level of their dignity.
The God replied: 'Leave them for idle boast
The trappings and insignia of your state,
If rivals of your strength they may not be.'

J. P. POSTGATE (1922)

SENECA

LUCIUS ANNAEUS SENECA, Seneca the Younger (son of a historian and authority on rhetoric) was born in about 5 B.C. at Corduba (Cordova) in Spain, served Claudius[1] and his former pupil Nero as chief minister, and died in A.D. 65 at Nero's request.

Almost all Roman Republican tragedy is lost, but we have nine of Seneca's plays: *Agamemnon, Hercules (Furens), Hercules Oetaeus, Medea, Oedipus, Phaedra, Phoenician Women, Thyestes, Trojan Women*.[2] T.S. Eliot has said that Seneca's Stoical characters all seem to talk with the same voice, and at the top of it. Because of this ranting, his tragedies, despite brilliant rhetoric and occasional lyric beauty, seem to contain so much 'bad theatre' that they may never have been staged, or at least never staged except in Nero's private theatre; the matter is still disputed. Yet their impact on European drama has been incalculably great: 'If you seek Seneca's memorial', says F.L. Lucas, 'look round on the tragic stage of England, France, and Italy.' Already in *c.* 1315 there was a remarkable Italian imitation (the *Eccerinis* of Albertino Mussato); the following century witnessed translations in Spain (*c.* 1400) and Italy (1497) (where his tragedies had been printed at Ferrara). Then came the influential English *Ten Tragedies* in 'fourteeners' by J.Heywood, A. Nevyle, J.Studely, and T.Newton (1559–1581). There is very much of Seneca in the ghosts, tyrants, traitors, fatalists, and madmen of *Macbeth, Hamlet*, and *Lear* – as, earlier, in the exuberance of *Gorboduc*, of Marlowe's *Tamburlaine*, of *Titus Andronicus*; and Ben Jonson surprises us by equating 'him of Cordova dead' with Aeschylus and Euripides – to whom Seneca owes his themes, but very little of his psychology.

His prose works include a work on natural phenomena (*Naturales Quaestiones*), 124 moralizing letters written for publication and addressed to his friend Lucilius, and thirteen ethical treatises (of which ten are miscalled dialogues). The moral enlightenment and humanity of these works are largely based on Stoicism. They earned Seneca a forged correspondence with St Paul – in which Jerome and Augustine believed – and the approbation of such widely differing people as Calvin, who started his career with an edition of the essay *On Clemency*; Queen

1. He wrote a satire, in verse and prose, making fun of Claudius' death and deification.
2. The *Octavia*, about recent events, is believed to be by another hand.

Elizabeth, who read him with her tutor Ascham; Erasmus, who edited him; and Montaigne, who started life as a Stoic and read for preference Seneca and Plutarch – Seneca's only rival as a practical illustrator of morality for the western world. R. Whytinton (1547) and A. Golding (1577) translated two of Seneca's treatises into English (certain French, Spanish, and Italian versions date from the previous century); and Lodge produced a bad rendering of all Seneca's prose works in 1614.

Rhetorical Silver Latin Prose was not Seneca's creation, but it finds fullest expression in his epigrammatic and paradoxical brevity. It was he who inspired both the 'loose' and the 'curt' reactions against conventional Ciceronian English in c. 1600. Thoroughly Senecan, in many respects, are the fashionable philosophical epigrams of which, for example, Francis Bacon's more elaborate *Essays* are largely constructed; and Bacon acknowledged the debt in their dedication. 'We have scarce the idea of any other model,' said the third Earl of Shaftesbury; and Milton recommends the *Naturales Quaestiones* for schools.

Three hundred years later such favourable assessments would have become unlikely. Wordsworth admired Seneca's idealistic sentiments, but Macaulay compared their perusal to an unrelieved diet of anchovy sauce. When Swinburne eulogized Ben Jonson's 'high and pure atmosphere of feeling and thought', he was praising Seneca, from whom the passage Swinburne praised was borrowed. De Quincey and Sainte Beuve are among Seneca's avowed nineteenth-century admirers, and he inspired F. W. Farrar's extensively read *Seekers after God*. H. J. Rose, in his *History of Latin Literature* (1936), finds that the disparity between Seneca's sentiments and his life makes 'the gorge of the reader rise'. To-day, in Britain and America at least, he is chiefly studied for his influence on later European literatures. He has suffered extremes of popularity and neglect.

MESSENGER: A loathsome spring stands under shade, and slothful
    course doth take,
    With water black: even such as is: of irksome Stygian lake
    The ugly wave, whereby are wont to swear the gods on high.
    Here all the night the grisly ghosts and gods of death to cry
    The fame reports: with clinking chains resounds the wood eke
      where
    The sprites cry out: and everything that dreadful is to hear
    May there be seen: of ugly shapes from old sepulchres sent
    A fearful flock doth wander there, and in that place frequent
    Worse things than ever yet were known: aye, all the wood full oft
    With flame is wont to flash, and all the higher trees aloft
    Without a fire do burn: and oft the wood beside all this
    With triple barking roars at once: full oft the palace is
    Affright with shapes, nor light of day may on the terror quell.
    Eternal night doth hold the place, and darkness there of hell
    In midday reigns: from hence to them that pray, out of the ground
    The certain answers given are, what time with dreadful sound
    From secret place the fates be told, and dungeon roars within
    While of the God breaks out the voice.

                            Whereto when entered in
    Fierce Atreus was, that did with him his brother's children trail,
    Decked are the altars: who, alas! may it enough bewail?
    Behind the infants' backs anon he knit their noble hands,
    And eke their heavy heads about he bound with purple bands:
    There wanted there no frankincense, nor yet the holy wine,
    Nor knife to cut the sacrifice, besprinkt with leavens fine.
    Kept is all the order due, lest such a mischief great
    Should not be ordered well.
CHORUS: Who doth his hand on sword then set?
MESSENGER: He is himself the priest, and he himself the deadly verse
    With prayer dire from fervent mouth doth sing and oft rehearse.
    And he at the altar stands himself, he them assigned to die
    Doth handle, and in order set, and to the knife apply:
    He lights the fires, no rights were left of sacrifice undone.

The wood then quaked, and all at once from trembling ground
  anon
The Palace becked, in doubt which way the poise thereof would
  fall,
And shaking as in waves it stood: from there and therewithal
A blazing star that foulest train drew after him doth go:
The wines that in the fires were cast with changèd liquor flow,
And turn to blood: and twice or thrice the attire fell from his head,
The ivory bright in temples seemed to weep and tears to shed.
The sight amazed all other men, but steadfast still alway
Of mind, unmovèd, Atreus stands, and even the gods doth fray
That threaten him, and all delay forsaken bye and bye
To the altar turns, and therewithal aside he looks awry.
As hungry tiger wonts that doth in Ganges woods remain
With doubtful pace to range and roam between the bullocks twain,
Of either prey full covetous, and yet uncertain where
She first may bite, and roaring throat now turns the one to tear
And then to the other straight returns, and doubtful famine holds:
So Atreus dire between the babes doth stand and them beholds.

JASPER HEYWOOD (1560)

DEATH IS NOTHING

After death nothing is, and nothing death:
The utmost limits of a gasp of breath.
Let the ambitious zealot lay aside
His hopes of heaven; whose faith is but his pride.
Let slavish souls lay by their feat,
Nor be concerned which way or where
After this life they shall be hurled:
Dead, we become the lumber of the world,
And to that mass of matter shall be swept
Where things destroyed with things unborn are kept:
Devouring time swallows us whole,
Impartial death confounds body and soul.
For Hell, and the foul Fiend that rules

The everlasting fiery gaols,
Devised by rogues, dreaded by fools,
With his grim grisly dog that keeps the door,
Are senseless stories, idle tales,
Dreams, whimsies, and no more.

JOHN WILMOT, EARL OF ROCHESTER (1647–80)

MODERATION IN VICTORY

*Agamemnon opposes the demand of Pyrrhus, son of Achilles,
that King Priam's daughter Polyxena should be sacrificed on
Achilles' tomb.*

But why now stain a noble warrior's shade
With murder? Nay, thou must learn first of all
What conquerors may inflict, and conquered suffer.
A violent power no ruler wields for long,
A moderate lasts and lives. The loftier
Fortune exalts and lifts the might of man,
The lowlier should her favourite bear himself,
And fear the change of chance and dread the gods,
Too kindly grown. That greatness in a moment
Falls, I have learnt by conquest. What! does Troy
Make *us* now proud and wanton? We Greeks stand,
There where she fell. I do confess, sometimes
I have in pride of power dealt haughtily:
But all that arrogance is cured in me,
By what in others breeds it – Fortune's favour.
'Tis thou, dead Priam, that makest me at once
Both proud and fearful. Can I believe my power
More than an empty glittering name, a false
Circlet about my brows? Swift chance will snatch
All this away nor need a thousand ships
Nor ten years' war, maybe. Ah, not on all
So slowly do the threats of Fortune fall!

F. L. LUCAS (1922)

I'm glad to learn, from visitors of yours who come here, that you live on friendly terms with your slaves. That squares with your sensible outlook no less than with your philosophy. 'They're slaves.' Perhaps, but still fellow men. 'They're slaves.' But they share your roof. 'They're slaves.' Friends, rather – humble friends. 'They're slaves.' Well, fellow slaves, if you reflect that Fortune has an equal power over them and you. That's why I laugh at those who think it derogatory to dine with their slaves: why, except that insolent convention has surrounded the master at the dinner-table with a throng of standing slaves? He eats more than he can hold, with inordinate appetite he loads a distended stomach which has forgotten a stomach's function, only to disgorge more laboriously than he gorged: but his unlucky slaves are not allowed to stir a lip even to speak. Every whisper's hushed with the rod, not even accidental noises – cough, sneeze, or hiccup – are exempt from stripes. Any sound that breaks the silence is paid for with bitter pain. They stand the whole night through fasting and dumb. The result is that those who mayn't talk before the master's face talk of the master behind his back. But those who might talk not only before their masters but with them, whose lips were not sewn up, were ready to bow their necks to the sword in his cause, to divert the danger that threatened him upon their own heads. They talked at table, but were silent on the rack.

To the same supercilious temper belongs that well-worn saw, 'In every slave a foe.' No, we don't find slaves our foes; we make them so. For the moment I waive all mention of other cruelties and inhumanities – of the fact that we treat them in ways which would be an abuse even of beasts of draught, let alone human beings. Whenever we take our place at table, should we drop saliva, there's a man to wipe it away; another goes down and gathers up the leavings of a drunken diner. Another carves rare and costly birds. His trained hand wheels with unerring passes about breast and rump as he whips off the daintiest cuts – an unhappy being, whose whole life is summed up in the nice dismemberment of a capon; though he is unhappier who teaches that art at pleasure's behest than he who is driven by necessity to learn it. Yet another's entrusted with the revision of the dinner-list.

This poor creature's on his feet all the time, waiting to see whose powers of flattery, insatiate maw, or unbridled tongue merit another invitation for the morrow. Further there are the caterers, men with delicate knowledge of their master's palate, who can tell the very dish to fillip him by its flavour, or interest him by its appearance, or set him up when squeamish by its novelty, who have learnt what he has taken a dislike to just through over-indulgence, and what he's hungry for on the day in question.

As for dining with any of these, he wouldn't stand it: he thinks it a blow to his dignity to approach the same table with his slave. Heaven mend him! How many potential masters he has in their ranks! I've seen Callistus' master standing at Callistus' front door: [1] I have seen him – the man who had stuck a ticket on Callistus and exposed him for sale among slaves who were the joke of the market – refused admittance when others were passing in: the ex-slave once thrust into the first batch of the sales – the batch the auctioneer tries his voice on – showed his gratitude; in his turn he rejected him as unfit to darken his doors. His master sold Callistus, but how many things did Callistus sell to his master! So do you please reflect that the man you call your slave was born of the same seed, has the same good sky above him, breathes as you do, lives as you do, dies as you do! You may see him free, he may see you a slave – the odds are level.

At the time of Varus' disaster [2] Fortune brought low by scores men of the most brilliant ancestry, and in a fair way to climb into the Senate through the Army. One of them she made a shepherd, another a lodge-keeper: so pray despise a man in a state of life you may pass into even as you despise him! I don't want to launch myself upon an endless topic and start a debate on the treatment of slaves, toward whom we behave with the greatest arrogance, cruelty, and despitefulness. This, however, sums up my doctrine: treat your inferior with whom you live, as you'd have your superior treat you. Whenever the thought of the powers you wield over your slave comes into your head, let it come into your head also that your master wields the same powers over you.

1. Callistus was a freed slave who gained enormous power as Private Secretary to the emperor Claudius.
2. Publius Quinctilius Varus, ambushed and killed by Arminius in Germany in A.D. 9.

'But I have no master,' you object. You're hearty for your years: you will, perhaps. Have you forgotten how old Hecuba was when her slavery began – how old were Croesus, Darius' mother,[1] Plato, Diogenes in the like case? Treat your slave with kindness, with courtesy too; let him share your conversation, your deliberations, and your company. General cry of horror from the exquisite brigade! 'Of all the infamous humiliations!' I shall catch these same gentlemen kissing the hands of other people's slaves. Surely you must see how completely our forefathers freed masters from the odium and slaves from the reproach of their respective positions? The master they called 'father of the family', the slaves 'familiars', a term which still survives even on the stage in interludes. They instituted a feast day on which masters were to take meals with their slaves – and not then only, but then at least. They allowed them to bear office in the household and exercise jurisdiction, conceiving the household in fact as a petty body politic.

'Well? Shall I admit all slaves to my table?' No more so than all free men. But you're mistaken if you imagine that I shall exclude some on the ground of a degraded employment – take, for example, your muleteer or your byreman: I shan't judge them by employment but by character. A man gives himself his character: his employment chance bestows. Let some dine with you because they merit it, others that they may: for if any servile trait, the result of mean association, clings to them, the company of men of gentler training will soon knock that out. There's no reason, my dear Lucilius,[2] why you should look for a friend only at the Bar or in the House: if you keep your eyes about you you'll find one at home too. Good material often lies idle for want of an artist to shape it: put yours to the test, and you'll learn by experiment. The man who sets out to buy a horse by looking at saddle and bit instead of the animal itself, is a fool: he's a prince of fools who judges a man either by his coat or his rank in life – which we wear like a coat.

'He's a slave.' True, but perhaps free in spirit. 'He's a slave.' Will he be the worse off for that? Show me who isn't: one's the slave of animal passion, another of avarice, another of ostentation, all men of

---

1. The mother of King Darius III of Persia was captured by Alexander.
2. Seneca's *Moral Letters* and other works were addressed to Gaius Lucilius, provincial official and dilettante, born at Pompeii.

hope, all men of fear. I'll point you out an ex-consul in bonds to a little old woman, a millionaire to a chit of a housemaid; I will show you sprigs of the aristocracy who are chattels of a ballet-dancer: no slavery's more degrading than voluntary bondage. Hence your dainty persons needn't frighten you out of showing yourself companionable to your slaves instead of arrogantly superior: they should show you homage rather than fear.

Here some objector'll say that I'm inviting the slave to assume the cap of freedom, and ousting the master from the seat of pride, in asserting that slaves should show homage rather than fear to their master. 'Is that really what he says? Homage? The tribute of the free dependant – the suitor of the levée?' Such an objector'll be forgetting that what's enough for God isn't too little for a human master. True homage implies love: love and fear can't be combined. So I think you're quite right in not wanting your slaves to be afraid of you, and resorting only to verbal chastisement: the whip's for the correction of dumb things.

We aren't invariably injured by what displeases us; yet our spoilt-child existence drives us into our tantrums, and makes everything that isn't all we fancied call up a gust of anger. We put on a royal temperament. Despots, forgetting their own strength and others' weakness, will break into a white heat of fury over a pretended injury. From the risk of a real one they, above all men, are secured by their position. This they know quite well, but will grumble till they've marked down a chance for mischief: the grievance is just an excuse for aggression.

I don't want to keep you any longer, for you need no urging. A good character among its other points has this: content with itself, and so permanency. Moral evil is unstable: it changes often, not for a better shape but for another.

E. PHILLIPS BARKER (1932)

NOISY LODGINGS

I can't for the life of me see that absolute quiet is as necessary to the studious recluse as it seems. Here am I in the middle of a roaring babel. My lodgings are right over a bath!

Now imagine every sort of outcry that can revolt the ear. When the more athletic bathers take their dumb-bell exercise, I hear grunts as they strain or affect to strain, hissings and raucous gasps as they expel their breath after holding it: when I run against some sedentary soul, who is content with the mere humble massage, I catch the smack of the hand as it meets his shoulders, with a different note according as it alights flat or hollowed. But if a tennis-professional comes along and starts scoring the strokes, all's up. Next add the quarrelsome rowdy and the thief caught in the act and the man who loves his own voice in a bath: after that, the people who jump into the plunge-bath with a mighty splash. Besides those whose voices are the real unvarnished thing, if nothing else, you must imagine the re-mover of superfluous hair emitting from time to time a thin falsetto howl to advertise his presence, and never silent except when he's re-moving the superfluous hair and making some one else do the howl-ing in his stead. Then there is the cordial-seller with a whole gamut of yells, and the sausage-vendor, and the puff-pastry-man, and all the eating-house hawkers crying their wares each with a distinctive melody of his own.

'O man of iron,' you cry, 'or deaf as a post, to keep your reason unshaken among such a motley assortment of clamorous discords, though brother Chrysippus [1] is half-killed by the mere iteration of "good day"!' But I take my oath I think no more of that kind of din than of the plash of waves or falling water, though I hear that one nation changed the site of their capital simply and solely because they couldn't endure the roar of a cataract on the Nile. It seems to me that the articulate voice is more distracting than mere noise. The former draws your thoughts to itself, the latter only fills your ears and beats a tattoo on them. Among the noises which buzz about me without causing distraction I count carriages rolling by, the carpenter who lodges in the block and the blacksmith down the street, or the fellow who has his pitch by the Sweating Standard [2] and keeps trying his clack-boards and clarinets, but only blares away without playing a tune.

I still find an intermittent noise more troublesome than one which

1. The second founder of Stoicism (third century B.C.).
2. Perhaps this *Meta Sudans* was a conical fountain ; *metae* were originally the conical columns which were turning points of the Roman Circus.

is continuous. But by this time I've so steeled myself against all these things that I hear with equanimity even a rowing-master barking out the time to his crew. For I force my mind to be self-absorbed and deaf to all outside distractions: all may be clatter without, provided there be no turmoil within, provided that desire and fear refrain from quarrelling, avarice and extravagance keep truce and leave each other alone. Silence the whole parish, and what good is it if your emotions are obstreperous?

> By night's calm stillness lulled all things reposed.[1]

Wrong! There's no 'calm stillness' unless it's some act of Reason that lulls us: night breeds vexation of spirit instead of removing it, and only brings a change of anxieties. Men may sleep, but their dreams are as troublous as their waking hours. The true tranquillity is that into which the mind morally fit unfolds itself. Look at the man whose quest of sleep hushes a spacious mansion, upon whose ears not a sound must jar, and so all his host of servants are struck mute and those who come near him walk on tip-toe. Why, he's tossing to and fro, trying to snatch a fitful doze amid feverish thoughts, and grumbling at noises he never heard.

Why, think you? The noise is in his soul. Here lies the peacemaker's task, here's the mutiny to crush, for you mustn't suppose that the soul's at peace because the body's in bed. Sometimes rest is far from restful. That's why we should be spurred to action, and given some honest occupation to keep our hands full whenever we are victims of the inaction that wearies of itself. Great commanders, when they see their men getting out of hand, break them in by a spell of hard work and keep them employed with campaigning: busy men have never the time to grow restive, and if there's one thing more certain than another it is that the maladies bred by inaction are purged by action. Often it seems that we have retired through weariness of public life and disgust at some ill-starred or uncongenial post, and yet the advertising instinct sometimes breaks out again in the very retreat into which apprehension or waning interest has thrown us. The respite was due not to its elimination but to fatigue, or even pique at the perversity of things.

1. A quotation from the translation by Varro of Atax (southern France, first century B.C.) of the *Argonautica* of Apollonius Rhodius.

Of self-indulgence I say the same. Sometimes it has to all appearance quitted the field: we declare for the frugal life: from that moment it gives us no peace, and in the midst of our asceticism goes nosing after the pleasures it had merely discarded but not renounced, with a zest proportioned to the greater secrecy of its movements. Indeed, all distempers are milder when undisguised: even physical ailments are taking the turn towards health when they break covert and make a demonstration in force. Thus you may feel sure that avarice, snobbery, and the other maladies of the human mind are never more malignant than when they abate for the moment in a feigned convalescence. We seem to be fancy-free, yet are not. For if we're honest, if we've really sounded the retreat, if we really despise the vanities, then, as I was saying just now, nothing will distract us; men and birds may carol in chorus, but no such carolling will break the train of thoughts which are what thoughts should be, and have already acquired substance and certitude.

The character which responds to the stimulus of a cry or of accidental environment is erratic and has not yet attained inward detachment. It harbours that spice of uneasiness and fear which makes the man friend Virgil describes all eyes and ears:

> And I, whom erst no hail of darts dismayed,
> Nor massed adverse array of Greece in arms,
> Blench at a breath, start at a sound, in fear
> Alike for that I lead and that I bear.[1]

Here we have first the philosophic adept, unaffrighted by hurtling darts, the shock of shields as the packed battalions meet, or the crash of a city's overthrow: the other is the untaught laic: he fears for his belongings, aghast at every crack or rustle, prostrated by any solitary cry – which he takes for a view-halloo, half dead with fright at the least movement: his packs make a coward of him. Pick any one you like of the happy prosperous with their many appendages and many burdens, and you'll see the man

> in fear
> Alike for that he leads and that he bears.

So you mustn't be sure of your equilibrium until no clamour affects

1. *Aeneid*, Book II, 726 ff. Aeneas was leading his son Ascanius, and carrying his father Anchises, from the ruins of Troy.

you, no voice shakes your hold on yourself, whether it coax or threaten or boom emptily round you in meaningless uproar.

'Yes? and isn't it sometimes more convenient to be free from noise?' I admit it. That's why I shall shortly make a move. I wanted to test and train myself. Why stay longer on the rack, when Ulysses discovered such a simple antidote for his ship's company even against the Sirens? [1]

E. PHILLIPS BARKER (1932)

THE GREAT FIRE OF LYONS

Our friend Liberalis is distressed today. News has come of the utter destruction of Lyons by fire. It's a catastrophe which might shock any one, to say nothing of a man devoted to his native place. As a result he finds himself deserted by the equanimity which he cultivated (of course) in view of what he regarded as realizable fears.

I'm not surprised, however, that such an unexpected and almost unheard-of disaster as this should have seemed as much beyond fear as it was without precedent. Many cities have been ravaged by fire, but none wholly destroyed: for even when buildings are fired by an enemy the flames die out in many places: they may be rekindled repeatedly but seldom are so omnivorous as to leave nothing for the crowbar. An earthquake has scarcely ever proved so violent and destructive as to overthrow whole towns. There has never been an outbreak so furious that nothing survived to be fuel for a second conflagration. But here a single night has laid low a host of architectural splendours, any one of which might have made a separate city famous: in the depth of peace has fallen a stroke not to be dreaded in war itself. Unbelievable! Everywhere the sword slumbers, over all the world is diffused the sense of safety, and behold Lyons, Gaul's cynosure, is not! Whenever fortune strikes down a community she allows a premonitory dread. Greatness always takes some time to fall. But here was a mighty city; a night passes, and no city at all! In short it was gone in less time than I take to tell it. Liberalis can face his personal troubles steadfast and unbowed; under all this he droops.

And he has good reason to be shaken. A bolt from the blue is

1. He plugged their ears with beeswax, as Circe had suggested.

specially crushing: unfamiliarity lends weight to misfortune, and there was never a man whose grief was not heightened by surprise. So nothing must be unforeseen to us. At every turn we must dispatch our thoughts ahead and imagine not only the usual but the possible. For what is there which fortune doesn't pluck down in its bloom when she chooses? – which she doesn't assail and demolish the more for the lustre of its outward show? Can anything be untoward and difficult for her? She doesn't always follow the same road or exert all her force in her assaults: sometimes she raises our own hands against us, sometimes is content with her own powers and contrives traps that need no agent. There's no moment's truce: amid our very pleasures causes of pain arise. In the midst of peace up springs war, and the bulwarks of security are transformed into engines of alarm: the friend becomes an adversary, the ally an enemy. Summer calm is plunged in sudden storms fiercer than those of winter. We see no foe, yet we suffer the ills of war, and if all else fails excessive prosperity finds the instruments of its own destruction. Illness assails the most ascetic, phthisis the most robust, punishment falls on the utterly guiltless, hubbub breaks in on the recluse.

Chance chooses some new means to impress its power on the apparently unmindful. The fabric raised by many men's successive labours and heaven's signal favour is rent and scattered by a day. Nay, to say 'day' suggests too long a respite from the hurrying forces of calamity. An hour, an instant suffices for the overthrow of empires. It would be some stay for our feebleness, some alleviation of our lot, if the fall were always as slow as the rise: but as it is, the stages of growth make their appearance slowly, to ruin the pace is headlong. Whether for an individual or a society there's no fixity: the destinies of men and of cities equally roll on their way. Amid the most peaceful surroundings terror springs up, and, with never a storm in the offing to produce it, mischief sallies from the least looked-for corner.

Kingdoms which stood firm through civil war, or the assaults of a foreign foe, come crashing down with never a finger laid on them. How few States have carried their prosperity far!

It follows that we must take everything into account and fortify our souls against any possibility. Reflect upon exile, the pains of sickness, war, shipwreck. Chance may tear you from your country, or your country from you, may hound you into the wilderness; the very space that's crowded to suffocation may become itself a wilderness. The terms on which human life is lived must be kept in view as a whole: we must mentally anticipate not merely all that happens with some frequency, but all that may happen at the extreme estimate, unless we want to be crushed and dazed by the infrequent as if it were the unknown: we must not conceive fortune by halves.

How often have cities of Asia or Greece fallen at a single earthquake shock! How many towns have been swallowed up in Syria or Macedonia! What repeated havoc that destroyer has wrought in Cyprus! How often has Paphos [1] crashed down upon its own ruins! Again and again news reaches us of a whole city's downfall, and yet how small a fraction of mankind are we, who receive such news so often! So let us face the assaults of chance erect, and be sure that whatever happens is not so bad as rumour's exaggeration makes it.

A capital has perished by fire – a wealthy city, the jewel of the provinces which formed at the same time its setting and its foil, yet perched upon a single hill-top, and that of no great extent. Why, all, all those cities of whose magnificence and renown you now hear – time will sweep away their very traces! There have been glorious cities in Greece: see how their very foundations have perished utterly, till nothing is left to witness their bare existence. It's not only things made with hands that decay, nor only structures raised by human skill and industry that the ages overturn: mountains crumble away, whole districts have been known to subside; landmarks once far out of sight of the sea now lie beneath its waters. The fury of volcanic fires has sapped the hills on which they once gleamed, and levelled what once were soaring peaks, the mariner's beacon and comfort.

Yes, even the works of nature herself suffer: then mustn't we contemplate the downfall of cities with resignation? Fall they will! This is the end that awaits them one and all, whether a subterranean explosion of imprisoned air shakes off its incubus, or the accumulated fury of the caverned torrent overwhelms its barriers, or a volcanic outburst rips the solid earth-crust, or age, the inevitable, storms their bastions piecemeal, or malaria banishes their populations, and they moulder, deserted, under the rust of disuse. It would be waste of time

1. Near the western extremity of Cyprus: it contained a famous temple of Aphrodite.

to count all ways by which doom can come. One thing I know, and it's this: all the works of mortal hand lie under sentence of mortality: we live among things doomed.

E. Phillips Barker (1932)

GOD IN MAN

You couldn't be better employed, or more for your own good, if, as your letter tells me, you're moving steadily towards the true sanity, for which it's foolish to pray, seeing that you have but your own consent to win. We needn't lift our hands to heaven, we need wheedle no sacristan into letting us approach the ear of some graven image, as if by so doing we made ourselves more audible. *God's near you, with you, in you.*

Yes, Lucilius, within us a holy spirit has its seat, our watcher and guardian in evil and in good. As we treat him so he treats us. The good man, in fact, is never without God. Can any one rise superior to Fortune without his aid? Isn't he the source of every generous and exalted inspiration? In every good man

Dwells nameless, dimly seen, a god.[1]

If you're confronted by some dense grove of aged and giant trees shutting out every glimpse of sky with screen upon screen of branches, the towering stems, the solitude, the sense of strangeness in a dusk so deep and unbroken, where no roof is, will make deity real to you. Again, the cavern that holds a hill-side poised on its deep-tunnelled galleries of rock, hollowed into that roomy vastness by nature's tools, not man's, will strike some hint of sanctity into your soul. We render homage to the sources of great rivers. The vast stream that bursts suddenly from hiding has its altars; hot springs are worshipped; there are lakes hallowed by their dark inscrutable waters and unplumbed depth.

So, if you see a man undismayed by dangers, untroubled by desires, happy in adversity, calm in the midst of storm, eyeing mankind from

1. *Aeneid*, Book VIII, 352.

above and the gods on their own plane, won't you be touched with awe before him? Won't you say, 'Here's a thing too great and sublime for any credible comparison between it and the puny body in which it dwells'? Into that body a divine force has descended. The splendid and disciplined soul, which leaves the little world unheeded and smiles at the objects of all our hopes and fears, draws its driving power from heaven. So great a creation can't stand without divinity for its stay. Hence more than half its substance dwells in the being from which it descends. Sunbeams, it's true, touch the earth, yet belong to the body that emits them. Thus a spirit, great and holy, sent down to give us a nearer knowledge of the divine, lives among us but cleaves to the fountain of its existence: from this it is pendent, on this its gaze is fixed, thither it strives, and moves among our concerns as a superior.

What spirit is this? The soul whose lustre proceeds from the good that's in it and no other. Is there greater folly than to praise a man for what doesn't belong to him? Greater madness than his whose admiration is given to that which may in a twinkling be transferred elsewhere? It isn't the golden bit that makes the thoroughbred. When the lion with a gilded mane is released from his cage – a manhandled beast, bullied into a meek acceptance of his finery – isn't it a different thing from the enlargement of his unbroken brother of the wilds? The latter is a bounding fury, as nature intended him to be, a thing of rugged beauty, seen only to be feared, which is his glory. The other cowed creature of gold-leaf is contemptible beside him.

No one should boast of anything but what's his own. We're loud in admiration of the vine that loads its branches with fruit and drags its very props to the ground by the weight of the grapes it bears: would any one prefer a vine hung with bunches and leaves of gold? Fruitfulness is the vine's peculiar virtue. So in a man, too, praise is due only to what belongs to him. Suppose he has handsome servants, a beautiful house, plenty of land under corn, plenty of money out at interest; all these are no part of him: they're his environment. Praise in him what can neither be removed nor bestowed, what's inseparable from his humanity.

And what, you ask, is that? His spirit, and Reason as perfected in that spirit. For man's a creature of Reason. So his good is consummated if he fulfils the end he's born to. And what does this Reason demand of him? A very easy thing – to live in accord with his own nature. But it's made hard by the universal insanity: we jostle each other into vices. How is a recall to health of spirit possible for those whom no one seeks to check and every one pushes on?

E. PHILLIPS BARKER (1932)[1]

1. I have taken the liberty of modernizing one or two archaisms.

LUCAN

MARCUS ANNAEUS LUCANUS, born at Corduba (Cordova) in Spain in A.D. 39, died in A.D. 65 at the orders of his former friend and jealous fellow-poet Nero – to whose autocracy a gradually increasing aversion can be detected in his work. His epigrammatic, spectacular epic *The Civil War* (*Bellum Civile*), though it inevitably owes much to Virgil, attempts something different since, rejecting divine interventions, it deals with fairly recent history – the struggle between Pompey and Caesar. The poem is often known as the *Pharsalia* after their decisive battle – though its hero has sometimes been said to be neither of those two men, but Cato.

In the Middle Ages Lucan was often honoured as a historian and philosopher rather than a poet.[1] In French heroic poetry, however, he was copied more often than the less ebullient Virgil. Dante, too, quotes him fifty times and he is one of the *Inferno*'s four 'lords of highest song' – the others are Homer, Horace, and Ovid – to whom Dante is presented by Virgil.[2] The *Pharsalia* was first printed at Rome in 1469 and rendered into Italian in 1492. In an England which appreciated its rich grandiose rhetoric, Christopher Marlowe translated the first book (1593), and several English versions of all ten books appeared within the first half of the seventeenth century. Corneille's theme *La Mort de Pompée* is one to which Lucan had devoted some of his finest lines. Brébeuf burlesqued him in *Lucain Travesti* (1656). Nicholas Rowe's English translation (1703–18) was denounced by Richard Bentley as inaccurate and diffuse, but described by Samuel Johnson as uniquely 'exhibiting the genius and spirit of the original'.

Byron considered that the *Pharsalia* was insufficiently admired; and Shelley called it 'a poem of wonderful genius and transcending Virgil'. He admired its tilts against tyranny, and the power of its imaginative, sombre, rhetorical poetry. In *A Defence of Poetry* (March 1821), it is true, he saw its writer as a 'mock-bird', but in *Adonais*, written so soon after-

---

1. But Otloh of St Emmeram was punished for reading him, by a dream in which he was beaten by a monster.

2. Boccaccio, however, based his *Theseid* on the *Thebaid* of Lucan's younger contemporary, Statius.

wards, Lucan is one of the 'inheritors of unfulfilled renown' whom the
death of Keats evokes in his mind:

> Chatterton
> Rose pale, his solemn agony had not
> Yet faded from him; Sidney, as he fought
> And as he fell and as he lived and loved
> Sublimely mild, a Spirit without spot,
> Arose; and Lucan, by his death approved:
> Oblivion as they rose shrank like a thing reproved.

In 1834 Désiré Nisard charged Lucan with a decadent distortion of
literary standards comparable to Victor Hugo's. In the following year
Macaulay concedes the failure of 'what were meant for bold poetical
flights', but added: 'I know no declamation in the world, not even
Cicero's best, which equals some passages in the *Pharsalia*.'

Lucan is still read in schools and universities, yet 'the art of understanding Lucan,' as A. E. Housman observed, 'makes no steady and
continuous progress, and relapse accompanies advance.' This is partly
because our century, with its unusual distaste for the purple patch, is
ill-fitted to recognize at least some of his great qualities. Nevertheless,
in the opinion of Robert Graves, this failure of contact is only temporary:
since Lucan's 'modernist traits – impatience with craftsmanship, digres-
sive irrelevances, emphasis on the macabre, lack of religious conviction,
turgid hyperbole, inconsistency, appeal to violence – have been re-
discovered by this new, disagreeable world'.

Thee, Pompey, thy past deeds by turns infest,
And jealous glory burns within thy breast:
Thy famed piratic laurel seems to fade
Beneath successful Caesar's rising shade:
His Gallic wreaths then viewest with anxious eyes
Above thy naval crowns triumphant rise.
Thee, Caesar, thy long labours past incite,
Thy use of war, and custom of the fight;
While bold ambition prompts thee in the race,
And bids thy courage scorn a second place.
Superior power, fierce faction's dearest care,
One could not brook, and one disdained to share.
Justly to name the better cause were hard,
While greatest names for either side declared:
Victorious Caesar by the gods was crowned,
The vanquished party was by Cato owned.
Nor came the rivals equal to the field:
One to increasing years began to yield,
Old age came creeping in the peaceful gown,
And civil functions weighed the soldier down:
Disused to arms, he turned him to the laws,
And pleased himself with popular applause;
With gifts and liberal bounty sought for fame,
And loved to hear the vulgar shout his name;
In his own theatre rejoiced to sit,
Amidst the noisy praises of the pit.
Careless of future ills that might betide,
No aid he sought to prop his failing side,
But on his former fortune much relied.
Still seemed he to possess and fill his place;
But stood the shadow of what once he was.
So in the field, with Ceres' bounty spread,
Uprears some ancient oak his reverend head;
Chaplets and sacred gifts his boughs adorn,
And spoils of war by mighty heroes worn.

1. For other estimates of Caesar, see above, p. 124, and below, p. 408.

But the first vigour of his root now gone,
He stands dependent on his weight alone;
All bare his naked branches are displayed,
And with his leafless trunk he forms a shade:
Yet, though the winds his ruin daily threat,
As every blast would heave him from his seat;
Though thousand fairer trees the field supplies,
That rich in youthful verdure round him rise:
Fixed in his ancient state he yields to none,
And wears the honours of the grove alone.

But Caesar's greatness, and his strength, was more
Than past renown, and antiquated power;
'Twas not the fame of what he once had been,
Or tales in old records and annals seen;
But 'twas a valour, restless, unconfined,
Which no success could sate, nor limits bind;
'Twas shame, a soldier's shame, untaught to yield,
That blushed for nothing but an ill-fought field;
Fierce in his hopes he was, nor knew to stay,
Where vengeance or ambition led the way;
Still prodigal of war whene'er withstood,
Nor spared to stain the guilty sword with blood;
Urging advantage he improved all odds,
And made the most of fortune and the gods;
Pleased to o'erturn whate'er withheld his prize,
And saw the ruin with rejoicing eyes.
Such while earth trembles, and heaven thunders loud,
Darts the swift lightning from the rending cloud;
Fierce through the day it breaks, and in its flight
The dreadful blast confounds the gazer's sight;
Resistless in its course delights to rove,
And cleaves the temples of its master Jove:
Alike where'er it passes or returns,
With equal rage the fell destroyer burns;
Then with a whirl, full in its strength, retires,
And recollects the Force of all its scattered fires.

NICHOLAS ROWE (1703–18)

Not far away for ages past had stood
An old unviolated sacred wood,
Whose gloomy boughs, thick interwoven, made
A chill and cheerless everlasting shade:
There nor the rustic gods nor satyrs sport,
Nor Fauns and Silvans with the nymphs resort:
But barbarous priests some dreadful power adore,
And lustrate every tree with human gore.
If mysteries in times of old received
And pious ancientry be yet believed,
There nor the feathered songster builds her nest,
Nor lonely dens conceal the savage beast:
There no tempestuous winds presume to fly;
E'en lightnings glance aloof, and shoot obliquely by.
No wanton breezes toss the dancing leaves,
But shivering horror in the branches heaves.
Black springs with pitchy streams divide the ground,
And, bubbling, rumble with a sullen sound.
Old images of forms misshapen stand,
Rude and unknowing of the artist's hand;
With hoary filth begrimed, each ghastly head
Strikes the astonished gazer's soul with dread.
No gods, who long in common shapes appeared,
Were e'er with such religious awe revered:
But zealous crowds in ignorance adore,
And still, the less they know, they fear the more.
Oft (as fame tells) the earth in sounds of woe
Is heard to groan from hollow depths below;
The baleful yew, though dead, has oft been seen
To rise from earth, and spring with dusky green;
With sparkling flames the trees unburning shine,
And round their boles prodigious serpents twine.
The pious worshippers approach not near,
But shun their gods, and kneel with distant fear:

The priest himself, when or the day or night
Rolling have reached their full meridian height,
Refrains the gloomy paths with wary feet,
Dreading the demon of the grove to meet:
Who, terrible to sight, at that fixed hour
Still treads the round about his dreary bower.

NICHOLAS ROWE (1703–18)

THE DELPHIC ORACLE

But while every nation and every leader prepared for the coming struggle, careless of the future, Appius Claudius Pulcher alone shrank from taking arms until he had asked advice from Heaven. He approached the Delphic Oracle, which had been closed to the public for many years, and consulted the god Apollo. The town of Delphi stands on Mount Parnassus, the only mountain that showed above the waters during Deucalion's flood [1]; even so one of its twin peaks was submerged. These peaks rise exactly midway between the eastern and western limits of the world and are sacred to Apollo and Dionysus, whom the Theban Bacchantes regard as respectively the immortal and the mortal aspects of the god celebrated in their triennial festival. Delphi was once the lair of the serpent Python, whom Juno sent to persecute Leto when Jupiter had got her with child. Leto's son Apollo came here soon afterwards to avenge her and, though not yet a practised archer, shot Python dead. At that time the Oracle belonged to Jupiter's aunt Themis; but Apollo, understanding that a vapour which rose from the Delphic chasm made anyone who inhaled it speak divine truth, seized it from her for his own prophetic use.

Which of the immortal Gods, I wonder, has condescended to leap down from Heaven and ensconce himself in those dark subterranean grottoes, with the weight of the mountain piled upon him? He must be very powerful, because he knows every link in the eternal chain of events, and has a divine share in the secret knowledge of things to come; and also very obliging, because he makes revelations to all mankind. It is doubtful, of course, whether this god merely predicts

1. For the story of Deucalion, see above, p. 268.

the future or whether he directs it by his oracular declarations. Perhaps a large element of the divine is embedded in the earth and acts as its ruler, incidentally supporting our terrestrial globe as it floats on empty space; and that, though closely associated with Jupiter on high, this essence seeps up from the chasm at Delphi. There the priestess inhales it, and when it reaches her heart she bellows prophecies for all to hear; very much as the flames in the crater of Etna send lava boiling over its lip; or as the Giant Typhoeus, who lies everlastingly buried under the Island of Ischia, scorches the rocks of Campania in his struggles to escape.

Every honest visitant may approach this holy spot, but it is protected against defilement by criminals. Moreover, no wicked requests are whispered here, since prayer is banned – the god merely announces irrevocable doom. He shows favour to the just; indeed, he has often allotted new homes to the entire population of cities which have had to be abandoned – Tyre, for instance. He has also encouraged others to fight in self-defence, as he did for the Athenians before the Battle of Salamis; and ended famines by disclosing the remedy, or epidemics by explaining their origin. The world suffers no heavier loss than when, at times, the Delphic Oracle is closed because certain great ones, afraid of the future, have stopped the god's mouth. His priestesses alone do not regret the ban, since the oracular frenzy – which is both a gift and a punishment – shortens their lives; the vehemence of the inspiration proving too much for flesh and blood to endure indefinitely.

When Appius came to consult the Oracle, intent on learning the secrets of Rome's destiny, no priestess had occupied the sacred tripod for many years and silence therefore reigned on the towering crag. However, he ordered the priest to open the Temple and usher the Pythoness into Apollo's sacred presence. Her name was Phemonoë, and she was strolling idly from the Castalian Spring towards the laurel grove when he caught hold of her, dragged her to the shrine, and pushed her inside; but, being afraid to enter the innermost sanctuary, she tried to discourage Appius' curiosity by prevarication. 'Appius,' she said, 'why do you take it upon yourself to demand the truth? Responses no longer come from the chasm; it is as though the god lay buried far below. Perhaps the spirit of inspiration has deserted the oracular vent, and found an outlet in some distant country; or perhaps, when the Gauls sacked and burned this Temple, the ashes drifted into the chasm, blocking Apollo's path. It may even be that the Gods themselves have silenced the Oracle, on the ground that the Sibylline verses entrusted to you Romans should be sufficient for your purposes. Or is it that Apollo, who forbids criminals to enter this Temple, has found no living person worthy of his confidences?'

Phemonoë was clearly not telling the truth; her very agitation suggested that the god must still be at work. So the priest tied one laurel wreath, bound with white wool, above her brow in the form of a fillet, and used a similar one to secure the long tresses behind. But Phemonoë, as yet unwilling to seat herself on a tripod in the innermost sanctuary, came to a sudden halt just beyond the Temple threshold, pretending to be possessed. What she said was uttered neither wildly nor incoherently, as it would have been had the god taken possession of her; and this new subterfuge wronged the oracular credit of Apollo even more than Appius. The sound of her voice, which did not echo tremendously through the Temple vaults; the laurel wreaths, which stayed on her head instead of being tossed off by the bristling of her hair; and the failure of the Temple threshold to shake or the laurel grove to quiver – all these signs convinced Appius that she shrank from submitting to Apollo's power. He shouted angrily: 'You impious creature, I have come to inquire about the fate of this distracted world. Unless you stop speaking in your natural voice and go down at once to the chasm for true inspiration, the gods whose Oracles you are taking in vain will punish you – and so will I!'

Appius' violence terrified her into action. She approached the lip of the great chasm and seated herself on the tripod. Then for the first time she experienced the divine afflatus, still active after so many centuries, and Apollo genuinely possessed her at last. He forced his way into her heart, masterful as ever, driving out her private thoughts and draining her body of all that was mortal, so that he could possess it wholly. She went blundering frantically about the shrine, with the God mounted on the nape of her neck, knocking over the tripods that stood in her path. The hair rose on her scalp, and when she tossed her head the wreaths went flying across the bare floor. Apollo's fury was so fierce that fire seemed to boil from her mouth. He whipped her, goaded her, darted flames into her intestines; but at the same time kept her on the curb and prevented her from disclosing as much as she knew. Countless centuries crowded tormentingly in her breast; rival secrets contended within her for utterance. She understood all that was or would be, from the beginning of the world to its very end, and could have revealed the laws that govern the Ocean or the number of sands on every shore in existence. But just as the Sibyl of Cumae (a Euboean colony) disliked being made the repository of so many national destinies, and therefore haughtily chose that of Rome for sole revelation – so Phemonoë went through a distressing search among the fates of far more important men than Appius before she finally came upon his own. As soon as she recognized it, her mouth foamed frenziedly; she groaned, gasped, uttered weird sounds, and made the huge cave re-echo with her dismal shrieks. In the end Apollo forced her to intelligible speech, and here is the response she gave:

> Appius, you shall avoid the tremendous perils of warfare,
> Taking your solitary ease in Euboea, that haven of refuge.

This was all, because Apollo cut short the prophecy.

I wonder why the divine oracles, capable of universal truth, especially the Oracle of Apollo, from whom the Gods hide no single secret, were disinclined to reveal the closing chapter in this fatal history – the fall of generals, the death of kings, the ruin of so many nations, which Rome's civil war implied. Was it that the Gods themselves had not yet decided on this catastrophe, that the stars were equally doubtful whether or not Pompey should be killed, and that therefore the fate of multitudes could not yet be confidently predicted? Or was the silence due to policy: a decision to let Fortune have her own way and – because a Brutus once took heroic vengeance on the tyrannical King Tarquin – to give no warning that might deter another man of the same name from curtailing the mad ambitions of Julius Caesar?

The Priestess ran full tilt against the Temple doors, broke them open and rushed out. She was still in a prophetic ecstasy, not having been able to expel the god, who continued to prevent her from telling Appius the full story. Her eyes rolled wildly as she gazed at the sky, and her expression changed continuously: never placid, but varying between alarm and menace. Her cheeks were alternately scarlet and deathly pale, and this was a paleness which induced rather than registered fear. As yet she felt no relief after her labours, but was shaken by heavy sobs, as the sea goes on roaring hoarsely even when a northerly gale has dropped; and before her spirit could be restored to the light of common day, a spell of unconsciousness intervened. Apollo was washing her mind with Lethe water, to make her forget the fateful secrets she had learned during his effulgent visitation. The spirit of divine truth departed and returned whence it had come; Phemonoë collapsed on the floor, and was revived with difficulty.

The oracle, however, being mbiguous, deceived Appius into thinking that he stood in no danger of immediate death. Though none could yet foresee who would be master of the world, he cheerfully decided to make himself master of Chalcis in Euboea. The fool never thought to ask what god, except Death alone, could assure his escape from the shock of war and the widespread suffering that this would entail. He was fated to take his 'solitary ease in Euboea, that haven of refuge' by being buried in a sequestered but famous tomb near the asbestos quarries of Carystos. It faces across the narrow sea towards Rhamnos in Attica – a town sacred to Nemesis, the goddess who punishes human ambition. In between lie the so-called 'Hollows of Euboea', where the sea is disturbed by the rapid, constantly-shifting current from the straits: the same current that sets the ships of Chalcis adrift and swings them across to Aulis in Boeotia – the fatal shore whence Agamemnon's fleet once sailed to Troy.

ROBERT GRAVES (1956)

POMPEY AND HIS WIFE

When Pompey saw that Caesar had assembled his main forces and that a clash was imminent,[1] he decided to send his beloved wife Cornelia away to Lesbos, where she would be spared the alarms of war. Tender-hearted husbands are like that: anxiety for his wife's safety made even Pompey shrink from an immediate engagement. If there was one thing in existence which he wanted to protect from the catastrophe threatening Rome and the whole world, it was Cornelia. He had already come to his decision, but could not bring himself to give the order for her removal, preferring to put off the inevitable and snatch what pleasure he might before fate intervened.

One night, Cornelia awoke in the grey dawn and clasped him to

1. For Caesar's account of the subsequent battle, see above, p. 110.

her, searching for his lips; but he turned from her in distress and she was shocked to find that his cheeks were wet with tears. Asked what ailed him, he sighed deeply and explained: 'Darling, I could once tell you that you were dearer to me than life; but life was then still sweet. The sad day which we have postponed too long, or which we should have postponed yet longer, has come at last. Caesar and his entire army are here and we must meet him in battle; I am therefore sending you to Lesbos, where you will be safe. Please do not renew your entreaties; I have already fought with myself to keep you at my side, but the answer is "no"! It will not be a protracted separation. The coming battle is bound to prove decisive – one of two great men must topple to a fall. But I am much mistaken in your love for me if the spectacle of civil war does not horrify you; so please be content to wait until my messengers bring news of the dangers I have faced.

'The truth is that, since fighting may break out at any moment, I am ashamed to sleep peacefully beside you, or to rise from your embraces while trumpets announce the doom of this distracted world. How can I face the horror of civil war unless I share it by voluntary self-denial? Now you must go off and conceal yourself where you can be safer than any distant king or remote tribe, and not feel so crushed by the weight of your anxiety as if you had stayed with me. And should Heaven have decided to wreck my army, I want the better part of me to survive; I expect you to prepare a pleasant retreat in which we can hide together from Caesar's vengeance.'

The shock was so overpowering that Cornelia turned quite numb, and some time elapsed before she could find words to frame her reproaches.

Then Cornelia sprang out of bed in frantic grief, intent on beginning her new life of anguish without the least delay. Though they had been faithful lovers for many years, she deliberately wasted her last chance of hugging him to her breast, or caressing his head. They parted in such haste and sorrow that neither could bear to say 'good-bye'. It was the saddest day that she or he had ever known – or ever would know, because every grief which followed fell upon hearts already dulled by misfortune.

Cornelia swayed, but was caught by her attendants as she collapsed and carried in their arms down to the shore. There she threw herself at full length on the sand, clutching at it; but they finally got her aboard. She suffered far more than when, as Pompey's loyal companion, she had said good-bye to the shores of her native land with Caesar's men pressing hard on their heels; this second flight had to be made all alone.

She slept fitfully the next night; it was the first that she had spent without him since their marriage. The coldness and silence of his side of the bed frightened her; she felt defenceless and deserted. If ever she drowsed off for a moment, she would forget the day's events and stretch out her hands in the darkness; but wake to find them cheated. The fact was that, though burning with love for Pompey, she could not bring herself to curl up and occupy the whole bed, but always kept his place vacant. She feared that she had lost him for ever; and the reality proved to be even worse. It would not be long now before they met again, as miserable shades.

ROBERT GRAVES (1956)

LUCAN'S EPITAPH

Cordova bore me, Nero slew. My lyre
The duel sang of son-in-law and sire.
Not mine the long-drawn period's delays
Of crawling verses, mine the short sharp phrase.
If thou wouldst shine, dart with the lightning's flight:
A style is striking only if it smite.

J. P. POSTGATE (1922)

PETRONIUS

CURIOUSLY enough, the identity of the founder of the European novel is disputed. He is most often identified with GAIUS(?) PETRONIUS 'ARBITER', who set the fashions of Nero's court and, on losing the emperor's favour, elegantly put an end to his life in A.D. 65. However, another candidate is Titus Petronius Niger, consul in the same reign (A.D. 63) – but it has also been suggested, though without general acceptance, that the author lived one or even two hundred years later. Whoever he was, we have a substantial part of his picaresque novel. We know it as the *Satyricon*; he may have called it the *Satirae*, 'Satires'. Like a well-known branch of satire,[1] it includes both prose and poetry – lyric and mock-epic; perhaps there is a mockery of epic in the whole theme. Another conventional form, that of the novelettish Greek prose-romance, is given a satirical twist by the disreputability of Petronius' 'heroes'; and tribute is paid to the short-story tradition [2] by a number of almost self-contained tales or incidents. The most familiar of these describes the *Dinner of Trimalchio*, the self-made man living on the Bay of Naples. It is a Symposium far removed from Plato's.

A manuscript of the *Dinner* was discovered at Trav (now in Yugoslavia) in 1650 and published at Padua in 1664, other surviving portions of the work having been printed at Milan some 180 years earlier. Dryden and Voltaire were both admirers of Petronius; one of his stories, *The Widow of Ephesus*, supplied Lafontaine with a theme. To Alexander Pope:

> Fancy and art in gay Petronius please:
> The scholar's learning, with the courtier's ease.

'In his way of representing life,' says J. Wight Duff, 'Petronius is in the company of Rabelais,[3] Fielding, and Smollett. Now one thinks of Gil Blas as a parallel, now of some of Dumas' adventurers ... the same sort of sensual delight in good food animates Anatole France. ... Enough of Petronius has survived to prove his mastery of some qualities

---

1. Named Menippean after its Hellenistic exponent Menippus of Gadara.
2. These popular short, sharp stories were known as Milesian Tales, after Aristides of Miletus (first century B.C.).
3. But his model had been the Greek Lucian, who lived in the second century A.D.

felt to be most enjoyable in the modern novel, such as his humour of situation and dialogue, often as pronounced as in Dickens, his restrained irony of attitude, not tragic as in Hardy, but verging towards Meredith's comic spirit. ....'

Cyril Connolly places Petronius, with Tacitus, in the forefront of those Latin prose-authors who have a message not only for modern scholars but for modern writers.

Everyone had now sat down except Trimalchio, who had the first place kept for him. A donkey in Corinthian bronze stood on the sideboard, with panniers holding olives, white in one side, black in the other. Two dishes hid the donkey; Trimalchio's name and their weight in silver was engraved on their edges. There were also dormice rolled in honey and poppy-seed, and supported on little bridges soldered to the plate. Then there were hot sausages laid on a silver grill, and under the grill damsons and seeds of pomegranate.

While we were engaged with these delicacies, Trimalchio was conducted in to the sound of music, propped on the tiniest of pillows. A laugh escaped the unwary. His head was shaven and peered out of a scarlet cloak, and over the heavy clothes on his neck he had put on a napkin with a broad stripe and fringes hanging from it all round. On the little finger of his left hand he had an enormous gilt ring, and on the top joint of the next finger a smaller ring which appeared to me to be entirely gold, but was really set all round with iron cut out in little stars. Not content with this display of wealth, he bared his right arm, where a golden bracelet shone, and an ivory bangle clasped with a plate of bright metal. Then he said, as he picked his teeth with a silver quill, 'It was not convenient for me to come to dinner yet, my friends, but I gave up all my own pleasure; I did not like to stay away any longer and keep you waiting. But you will not mind if I finish my game?' A boy followed him with a table of terebinth wood and crystal pieces, and I noticed the prettiest thing possible. Instead of black and white counters they used gold and silver coins.

Trimalchio kept passing every kind of remark as he played, and we were still busy with the hors d'œuvres when a tray was brought in with a basket on it, in which there was a hen made of wood, spreading out her wings as they do when they are sitting. The music grew loud: two slaves at once came up and began to hunt in the straw. Peahens' eggs were pulled out and handed to the guests. Trimalchio turned his head to look, and said, 'I gave orders, my friends, that peahens' eggs should be put under a common hen. And upon my oath I am afraid they are hard-set by now. But we will try whether they are still fresh enough to suck.' We took our spoons, half-a-pound in weight at least, and hammered at the eggs, which were balls of fine meal. I was on the point of throwing away my portion. I thought a peachick had already formed. But hearing a practised diner say, 'What treasure have we here?' I poked through the shell with my finger, and found a fat becafico rolled up in spiced yolk of egg.

Trimalchio had now stopped his game, and asked for all the same dishes, and in a loud voice invited any of us who wished to take a second glass of mead. Suddenly the music gave the sign, and the light dishes were swept away by a troop of singing servants. An entrée-dish happened to fall in the rush, and a boy picked it up from the ground. Trimalchio saw him, and directed that he should be punished by a box on the ear, and made to throw down the dish again. A chairman followed and began to sweep out the silver with a broom among the other rubbish. Then two long-haired Ethiopians with little wine-skins, just like the men who scatter sand in an amphitheatre, came in and gave us wine to wash our hands in, for no one offered us water.

When I was unable to eat any more I turned to my neighbour to get as much news as possible. I began to seek for far-fetched stories, and to inquire who the woman was who kept running about everywhere.

'She is Trimalchio's wife Fortunata,' he said, 'and she counts her money by the bushel. And what was she a little while ago? You will pardon me if I say that you would not have taken a piece of bread from her hand. Now, without why or wherefore, she is queen of Heaven, and Trimalchio's all in all. In fact, if she tells him that it is dark at high noon, he will believe it. He is so enormously rich that he does not know himself what he has; but this lynx-eyed woman has a plan for everything, even where you would not think it. She is temperate, sober, and prudent, but she has a nasty tongue, and henpecks him on his own sofa. Whom she likes, she likes; whom she dislikes, she dislikes. Trimalchio has estates wherever a kite can fly in a day, is millionaire of millionaires. There is more plate lying in his steward's room than other people have in their whole fortunes. And his slaves! My word! I really don't believe that one out of ten of them knows his master by sight. Why, he can knock any of these young louts into a nettle-bed if he chooses. You must not suppose either that he buys anything. Everything is home-grown: wool, citrons, pepper; you can have cock's milk for the asking. Why, his wool was not growing of fine enough quality. He bought rams from Tarentum and sent them into his flocks with a smack behind. He had bees brought from Athens to give him Attic honey on the premises; the Roman-born bees, incidentally, will be improved by the Greeks. Within the last few days, I may say, he has written for a cargo of mushroom spawn from India.

And he has not got a single mule which is not the child of a wild ass. You see all the cushions here: every one has purple or scarlet stuffing. So high is his felicity. But do not look down on the other freedmen who are his friends. They are very juicy people. That one you see lying at the bottom of the end sofa has his eight hundred thousand. He was quite a nobody. A little time ago he was carrying loads of wood on his back. People do say – I know nothing, but I have heard – that he pulled off a goblin's cap and found a fairy hoard. If God makes presents I am jealous of nobody. Still he has a fine opinion of himself. So he has just put up a notice on his hovel: "This attic, the property of Caius Pompeius Diogenes, to let from the 1st of July, the owner having purchased a house."

'That person there, too, who is lying in the freedman's place is well pleased with himself. I do not blame him. He had his million in his hands, but he has had a bad shaking. I believe he cannot call his hair his own. No fault of his I am sure; there is no better fellow alive; but it is the damned freedmen who have pocketed everything. You know how it is: the company's pot goes off the boil, and the moment business takes a bad turn your friends desert you. You see him in this state: and what a fine trade he drove! He was an undertaker. He used to dine like a prince: boars cooked in a cloth, wonderful sweet things, game, chefs, and confectioners! There used to be more wine spilt under the table than many a man has in his cellars. He was a fairy prince, not a mortal. When his business was failing, and he was afraid his creditors might guess that he was going bankrupt, he advertised a sale in this fashion: "Gaius Julius Proculus will offer for sale some articles for which he has no further use." '

Phileros had been talking, but Ganymede broke in: 'You go talking about things which are neither in heaven nor earth, and none of you care all the time how the price of food pinches. I swear I cannot get hold of a mouthful of bread today. And how the drought goes on!

There has been a famine for a whole year now. Damn the magistrates, who play "Scratch my back, and I'll scratch yours" in league with the bakers. So the little people come off badly; for the jaws of the upper classes are always keeping carnival. I do wish we had the bucks I found here when I first came out of Asia. That was life. If the flour was any but the finest, they beat those vampires into a jelly, until they put the fear of God into them.

'I remember Safinius: he used to live then by the old arch when I was a boy. He was more of a mustard-pot than a man: used to scorch the ground wherever he trod. Still he was straight; you could trust him, a true friend: you would not be afraid of him to play at *morra* with him in the dark.[1] How he used to dress them down in the senate-house, every one of them! Never using roundabout phrases, making a straightforward attack. And when he was pleading in the courts, his voice used to swell like a trumpet. Never any sweating or spitting: I imagine he had a touch of the Asiatic style. And how kindly he returned one's greeting, calling every one by name quite like one of ourselves!

'So at that time food was dirt-cheap. You could buy a larger loaf for twopence than you and your better half together could get through. One sees a bun bigger now. Lord, things are worse every day. This town goes downhill like the calf's tail. But why do we put up with a magistrate not worth three pepper-corns, who cares more about putting twopence in his purse than keeping us alive? He sits grinning at home, and pockets more money a day than other people have for a fortune. I happen to know where he came by a thousand in gold. If we had any spunk in us he would not be so pleased with himself.

'Nowadays people are lions in their own houses, and foxes out of doors. I have already eaten my rags, and if these prices keep up, I shall have to sell my cottages. Whatever is to happen if neither the gods nor man will take pity on this town? As I hope to have joy of my children, I believe all these things come from Heaven. For no one now believes that the gods are gods. There is no fasting done, no one cares a button for religion: they all shut their eyes and count their own goods. In old days the mothers in their best robes used to climb the hill with bare feet and loose hair, pure in spirit, and pray Jupiter to

1. For this game, see above, p. 41, n.

send rain. Then it used promptly to rain by the bucket: it was now or never: and they all came home, wet as drowned rats. As it is, the gods are gouty in the feet because we are sceptics. So our fields lie baking –'

'Oh, don't be so gloomy,' said Echion, the old clothes dealer. ' "There's ups and there's downs", as the country bumpkin said when he lost his spotted pig. What is not today, will be tomorrow: so we trudge through life. I engage you could not name a better country to call one's own, if only the men in it had sense. It has its troubles now like others. We must not be too particular when there is a sky above us all. If you were anywhere else, you would say that roast pork walked in the streets here. Just think, we are soon to be given a superb spectacle lasting three days; not simply a troupe of professional gladiators, but a large number of them freedmen. And our good Titus has a big imagination and is hot-blooded: it will be one thing or another, something real anyway. I know him very well, and he is all against half-measures. He will give you the finest blades, no running away, butchery done in the middle, where the whole audience can see it. And he has the wherewithal; he came into thirty million when his father came to grief. If he spends four hundred thousand, his estate will never feel it, and his name will live for ever.

'My nose prophesies a good meal from Mammaea, two shillings each for me and mine.[1] If he does, he will put Norbanus quite in the shade. You know he will beat him hands down. After all, what has Norbanus ever done for us? He produced some decayed twopenny-halfpenny gladiators, who would have fallen flat if you breathed on them; I have seen better ruffians turned in to fight the wild beasts. He shed the blood of some mounted infantry that might have come off a lamp; dunghill cocks you would have called them: one a spavined mule, the other bandy-legged, and the holder of the bye, just one corpse instead of another, and hamstrung. One man, a Thracian, had some stuffing, but he too fought according to the rule of the schools. In short, they were all flogged afterwards. How the great crowd roared at them, "Lay it on"! They were mere runaways, to be sure. "Still," says Norbanus, "I did give you a treat." Yes, and I clap my

1. Mammaea is a candidate for local office who pays for a good dinner for Echion and his fellow guildsmen.

hands at you. Reckon it up, and I give you more than I got. One good turn deserves another.

'Now, Agamemnon,[1] you look as if you were saying, "What is this bore chattering for?" Only because you have the gift of tongues and do not speak. You do not come off our shelf, and so you make fun of the way we poor men talk. We know you are mad with much learning. But I tell you what; can I persuade you to come down to my place some day and see my little property? We shall find something to eat, a chicken and eggs; it will be delightful, even though the weather this year has made everything grow at the wrong time – we shall find something to fill ourselves up with.

'My little boy is growing into a follower of yours already. He can do simple division now; if he lives, you will have a little servant at your heels. Whenever he has any spare time, he never lifts his nose from the slate. He is clever, and comes of a good stock, even though he is too fond of birds. I killed three of his goldfinches just lately, and said a weasel had eaten them. But he has found some other hobby, and has taken to painting with great pleasure. He has made a hole in his Greek now, and begins to relish Latin finely, even though his master is conceited and will not stick to one thing at a time. The boy comes asking me to give him some writing to do, though he does not want to work.

'I have another boy who is no scholar, but very inquiring, and can teach you more than he knows himself. So on holidays he generally comes home, and is quite pleased whatever you give him. I bought the child some books with red-letter headings in them a little time ago. I want him to have a smack of law in order to manage the property. Law has bread and butter in it. He has dipped quite deep enough into literature. If he is restless, I mean to have him learn a trade, a barber or an auctioneer, or at least a barrister, something that he can carry to the grave with him. So I drum it into him every day: "Mark my words, Primigenius, whatever you learn, you learn for your own good. Look at Phileros, the barrister: if he had not worked, he would not be keeping the wolf from the door today. It is not so long since he used to carry things round on his back and sell them, and now he makes a brave show even against Norbanus. Yes, education is a treasure, and culture never dies."'

1. A down-at-heels literary professor.

Later, Niceros told this story:

'While I was still a slave, we were living in a narrow street; the house now belongs to Gavilla. There it was God's will that I should fall in love with the wife of Terentius the inn-keeper; you remember her, Melissa of Tarentum, a pretty round thing. But I swear it was no base passion: I did not care about her in that way, but rather because she had a beautiful nature. If I asked her for anything it was never refused me; if she made twopence I had a penny; whatever I had I put into her pocket, and I was never taken in. Now one day her husband died on the estate. So I buckled on my shield and greaves, and schemed how to come at her: and as you know, one's friends turn up in tight places.

'My master happened to have gone to Capua to look after some silly business or other. I seized my opportunity, and persuaded a guest in our house to come with me as far as the fifth milestone. He was a soldier, and as brave as Hell. So we trotted off about cock-crow; the moon shone like high noon. We got among the tombstones: my man went aside to look at the epitaphs. I sat down with my heart full of song and began to count the graves. Then when I looked round at my friend, he stripped himself and put all his clothes by the roadside. My heart was in my mouth, but I stood like a dead man. He made a ring of water round his clothes and suddenly turned into a wolf.

'Please do not think I am joking; I would not lie about this for any fortune in the world. But as I was saying, after he had turned into a wolf, he began to howl, and ran off into the woods. At first I hardly knew where I was, then I went up to take his clothes; but they had all turned into stone. No one could be nearer dead with terror than I was. But I drew my sword and went slaying shadows all the way till I came to my love's house. I went in like a corpse, and nearly gave up the ghost; the sweat ran down my legs, my eyes were dull, I could hardly be revived. My dear Melissa was surprised at my being out so late, and said, "If you had come earlier you might at least have helped us; a wolf got into the house and worried all our sheep, and let their blood like a butcher. But he did not make fools of us, even though he got off; for our slave made a hole in his neck with a spear."

'When I heard this, I could not keep my eyes shut any longer, but at break of day I rushed back to my master Gaius's house like a defrauded publican, and when I came to the place where the clothes were turned into stone, I found nothing but a pool of blood. But when I reached home, my soldier was lying in bed like an ox, with a doctor looking after his neck. I realized that he was a werewolf, and I never could sit down to a meal with him afterwards, not if you had killed me first. Other people may think what they like about this; but may all your guardian angels punish me if I am lying.'

We were all dumb with astonishment, but Trimalchio said, 'I pick no holes in your story; by the soul of truth, how my hair stood on end! For I know that Niceros never talks nonsense: he is very dependable, and not at all a chatterbox.'

Then the host, Trimalchio, embarked on his reminiscences:

'I won't keep you a moment – I built five ships, got a cargo of wine – which was worth its weight in gold at the time – and sent them to Rome. You may think it was a put-up job; every one was wrecked, truth and no fairy-tales. Neptune gulped down thirty million in one day. Do you think I lost heart? Lord! no, I no more tasted my loss than if nothing had happened. I built some more, bigger, better, and more expensive, so that no one could say I was not a brave man. You know, a huge ship has a certain security about her. I got another cargo of wine, bacon, beans, perfumes, and slaves. Fortunata did a noble thing at that time; she sold all her jewellery and all her clothes, and put a hundred gold pieces into my hand. They were the leaven of my fortune. What God wishes soon happens. I made a clear ten million on one voyage. I at once bought up all the estates which had belonged to my patron. I built a house, and bought slaves and cattle; whatever I touched grew like a honey-comb. When I came to have more than the whole revenues of my own country, I threw up the game: I retired from active work and began to finance freedmen.

'I was quite unwilling to go on with my work when I was encouraged by an astrologer who happened to come to our town, a little Greek called Serapa, who knew the secrets of the Gods. He told me things that I had forgotten myself; explained everything from needle and thread upwards; knew my own inside, and only fell short of telling me what I had had for dinner the day before. You would have thought he had always lived with me. You remember, Habinnas? – I believe you were there? – "You fetched your wife from you know where. You are not lucky in your friends. No one is ever as grateful to you as you deserve. You are a man of property. You are nourishing a viper in your bosom," and, though I must not tell you this, that even now I had thirty years four months and two days left to live.

'Moreover I shall soon come into an estate. My oracle tells me so. If I could only extend my boundaries to Apulia I should have gone far enough for my lifetime. Meanwhile I built this house while Mercury watched over me. As you know, it was a tiny place; now it is a palace. It has four dining-rooms, twenty bed-rooms, two marble colonnades, an upstairs dining-room, a bed-room where I sleep myself, this viper's boudoir, an excellent room for the porter; there is plenty of spare room for guests. In fact when Scaurus came he preferred staying here to anywhere else, and he has a family place by the sea. There are plenty of other things which I will show you in a minute. Take my word for it: if you have a penny, that is what you are worth; by what a man hath shall he be reckoned. So your friend who was once a worm is now a king.'

MICHAEL HESELTINE (1930)

THE SIMPLE LIFE

Small house and quiet roof tree, shadowing elm,
Grapes on the vine and cherries ripening,
Red apples in the orchard, Pallas' tree
Breaking with olives, and well-watered earth,
And fields of kale and heavy creeping mallows
And poppies that will surely bring me sleep.
And if I go a-snaring for the birds
Or timid deer, or angling the shy trout,
'Tis all the guile that my poor fields will know.
Go now, yea, go, and sell your life, swift life,
For golden feasts. If the end waits me too,
I pray it find me here, and here shall ask
The reckoning from me of the vanished hours.

HELEN WADDELL (1929)

ENQUIRY

Sister art to Phoebus, Lady Moon?
   Then, I pray you, take to him my prayer.
   'God of Delphi, of Sicilian marble
   I have built a fane to worship there,
I have sung a shining song and piped it
   On a slender reed, and all for thee.
Dost thou hear me? Art a god, Apollo?
Tell me then – a man whose purse is hollow,
Will find the wherewithal to fill it – where?'
               HELEN WADDELL (1929)

TANTALUS [1]

Unhappy Tantalus! Forced on by desire,
He cannot drink though deep in water,
Nor pluck the hanging fruit above.
Let this be the image of a mighty rich man
Who amasses all things but has his fears,
And digests hunger with a dried-up mouth.
               PAUL DINNAGE (1953)

1. Tantalus stole the food of the gods and gave it to mortals; so this was his eternal punishment in Hell.

PART IV

THE IMPERIAL PEACE

QUINTILIAN

MARCUS FABIUS QUINTILIANUS was born at Calagurris (Calahorra) in northern Spain between A.D. 35 and 40; it is not known when he died. A lawyer by upbringing and profession, appointed by Vespasian as the first State-paid professor of rhetoric at Rome, he retired between 88 and 90, became tutor to Domitian's grandnephews, and wrote his major work *On the Training of an Orator* (*Institutio Oratoria*) in twelve books.

This sensible, experienced, and moderate restatement of the classical system of education and more especially of higher education – a system based, curiously as it seems to us, on tuition in public speaking – transmitted a tradition which was not seriously modified until St Augustine and St Jerome; and it exercised a major influence on the Renaissance. Petrarch's copy, though incomplete, appealed to his interest in the training of a dominant élite. His fellow-Florentine Poggio Bracciolini, during an interval in the Council of Constance (1415–17), came upon a complete copy in a tower of the monastery at St Gallen in Switzerland. Quintilian then became the staple diet of pioneer humanist schools such as that of Vittorino da Feltre (1378–1446) at Mantua, with its emphasis on character-training – which ultimately led to Dr Arnold – and the more literary academy of the Veronese Guarino (1374–1460) at Ferrara. The book was first printed in 1470 at Rome, and translated into Italian in 1566.

Interest in Quintilian has been threefold: it has been directed towards his rhetorical theory and practice, his general views on education – recommended by Milton – and the literary criticism (advice to his pupils on suitable reading) which is the most widely read portion of his work, receiving sympathetic appreciation, for example, in Alexander Pope's *Essay on Criticism*.

Quintilian is indispensable to our understanding of Roman writers because he reveals to us their educational and cultural background, beliefs and aims. 'The men of antiquity,' observed Giacomo Leopardi, 'devoted to the art of style an infinitely greater amount of study than we give to it; they understood a thousand secrets whose existence we do not even suspect or which we comprehend with difficulty when explained by Cicero or Quintilian.' Later in the same nineteenth century Quintilian shared with Catullus and Lucretius the unusual distinction (among Latin writers) of praise from Theodor Mommsen. More recently, British classical scholars have been well to the fore in interpreting Quintilian; but our critics do not often share Pope's admiration of his literary comments.

I prefer that a boy should begin with Greek, because Latin, being in general use, will be picked up by him whether we will or no; while the fact that Latin learning is derived from Greek is a further reason for his being first instructed in the latter. I do not however desire that this principle should be so superstitiously observed that he should for long speak and learn only Greek, as is done in the majority of cases. Such a course gives rise to many faults of language and accent; the latter tends to acquire a foreign intonation, while the former through force of habit becomes impregnated with Greek idioms, which persist with extreme obstinacy even when we are speaking the other tongue. The study of Latin ought therefore to follow at no great distance and in a short time proceed side by side with Greek. The result will be that, as soon as we begin to give equal attention to both languages, neither will prove a hindrance to the other.

Some hold that boys should not be taught to read till they are seven years old, that being the earliest age at which they can derive profit from instruction and endure the strain of learning. Those however who hold that a child's mind should not be allowed to lie fallow for a moment are wiser. Chrysippus,[1] for instance, though he gives the nurses a three years' reign, still holds the formation of the child's mind on the best principles to be a part of their duties. Why, again, since children are capable of moral training, should they not be capable of literary education? I am well aware that during the whole period of which I am speaking we can expect scarcely the same amount of progress that one year will effect afterwards. Still, those who disagree with me seem in taking this line to spare the teacher rather than the pupil. What better occupation can a child have so soon as he is able to speak? And he must be kept occupied somehow or other. Or why should we despise the profit to be derived before the age of seven, small though it be? For though the knowledge absorbed in the previous years may be but little, yet the boy will be learning something more advanced during that year in which he would otherwise have been occupied with something more elementary. Such progress each successive year increases the total, and the time gained during child-

1. See above, p. 297, n.

hood is a clear profit to the period of youth. Furthermore as regards the years which follow I must emphasize the importance of learning what has to be learnt *in good time*. Let us not therefore waste the earliest years: there is all the less excuse for this, since the elements of literary training are solely a question of memory, which exists even in small children – but it is specially retentive at that age.

I am not however so blind to differences of age as to think that the very young should be forced on prematurely or given real work to do. Above all things we must take care that the child, who is not yet old enough to love his studies, does not come to hate them and dread the bitterness which he has once tasted, even when the years of infancy are left behind. His studies must be made an amusement: he must be questioned and praised and taught to rejoice when he has done well; sometimes too, when he refuses instruction, it should be given to some other to excite his envy, at times also he must be engaged in competition and should be allowed to believe himself successful more often than not, while he should be encouraged to do his best by such rewards as may appeal to his tender years.

Still, all our pupils will require some relaxation, not merely because there is nothing in this world that can stand continued strain – and even unthinking and inanimate objects are unable to maintain their strength, unless given intervals of rest – but because study depends on the good will of the student, a quality that cannot be secured by compulsion. Consequently if restored and refreshed by a holiday they will bring greater energy to their learning and approach their work with greater spirit of a kind that will not submit to be driven. I approve of play in the young; it is a sign of a lively disposition; nor will you ever lead me to believe that a boy who is gloomy and in a continual state of depression is likely to show alertness of mind in his work, lacking as he does the impulse most natural to boys of his age. Such relaxation must not however be unlimited: otherwise the refusal to give a holiday will make boys hate their work, while excessive indulgence will accustom them to idleness.

There are moreover certain games which have an educational value for boys, as for instance when they compete in posing each other with all kinds of questions which they ask turn and turn about. Games too reveal character in the most natural way, at least that is so if the teacher will bear in mind that there is no child so young as to be unable to learn to distinguish between right and wrong, and that the character is best moulded when it is still guiltless of deceit and most susceptible to instruction: for once a bad habit has become engrained, it is easier to break than bend. There must be no delay, then, in warning a boy that his actions must be unselfish, honest, self-controlled; and we must never forget the words of Virgil:

> So strong is custom formed in early years.

I disapprove of flogging – although it is the regular custom and meets with the acquiescence of Chrysippus – because in the first place it is a disgraceful form of punishment and fit only for slaves, and is in any case an insult, as you will realize if you imagine its infliction at a later age. Secondly if a boy is so insensible to instruction that reproof is useless, he will, like the worst type of slave, merely become hardened to blows. Finally there will be absolutely no need of such punishment if the master is a thorough disciplinarian.

H. E. BUTLER (1921)

THE PROPER USE OF TIME

Any one of the various branches of knowledge which I have mentioned will, as a rule, be found to be comprised in a few volumes – a fact which shows that instruction does not require an indefinite amount of time to be devoted to it. The rest depends entirely on practice, which at once develops our powers and maintains them, once developed. Knowledge increases day by day; and yet how many books is it absolutely necessary to read in our search for its attainment – for example of facts from the historians or of eloquence from the orators, or, again, for the opinions of the philosophers and the lawyers? That is to say, if we are content to read merely what is useful without attempting the impossible task of reading everything.

But it is ourselves that make the time for study short: for how little time we allot to it! Some hours are passed in the futile labour of ceremonial calls, others in idle chatter, others in staring at the shows of the theatre, and others again in feasting. To this add all the other various forms of amusement – the insane attention devoted to the cultivation of the body, journeys abroad, visits to the country, anxious calculation of loss and gain, the allurements of lust, wine-bibbing, and those remaining hours which are all too few to gratify our souls on fire with passion for every kind of pleasure. If all this time were spent on study, life would seem long enough and there would be plenty of time for learning, even though we should take the hours of daylight only into our account, without asking any assistance from the night – of which a considerable space is superfluous even for the heaviest sleeper.

As it is, we count not the years which we have given to study, but the years we have lived. And indeed even although geometricians, musicians, and grammarians, together with the professors of every other branch of knowledge, spend all their lives (however long) in the study of one single science, it does not therefore follow that we require several lives more if we are to learn more. For they do not spend all their days even to old age in learning these things, but – being content to have learned these things and nothing more – exhaust their length of years not in acquiring, but in imparting knowledge.

H. E. BUTLER (1922)

CICERO

It is our orators, above all, who enable us to match our Roman eloquence against that of Greece. For I would set Cicero against any one of their orators without fear of refutation. I know well enough what a storm I shall raise by this assertion, more especially since I do not propose for the moment to compare him with Demosthenes; for there would be no point in such a comparison, as I consider that Demosthenes should be the object of special study, and not merely studied, but even committed to memory. I regard the excellences of these two orators as being for the most part similar, that is to say, their judgement, their gift of arrangement, their methods of division, preparation and proof, as well as everything concerned with invention. In their actual style there is some difference. Demosthenes is more concentrated, Cicero more diffuse; Demosthenes makes his periods shorter than Cicero, and his weapon is the rapier, whereas Cicero's periods are longer, and at times he employs the bludgeon as well.

Nothing can be taken from the former, nor added to the latter; the Greek reveals a more studied, the Roman a more natural art.

As regards wit and the power of exciting pity, the two most powerful instruments where the feelings are concerned, we have the advantage. Again, it is possible that Demosthenes was deprived by national custom of the opportunity of producing powerful perorations, but against this may be set the fact that the different character of the Latin language debars us from the attainment of those qualities which are so much admired by the adherents of the Attic school. As regards their letters, which have in both cases survived, and dialogues, which Demosthenes never attempted, there can be no comparison between the two. But, on the other hand, there is one point in which the Greek has the undoubted superiority: he comes first in point of time, and it was largely due to him that Cicero was able to attain greatness. For it seems to me that Cicero, who devoted himself heart and soul to the imitation of the Greeks, succeeded in reproducing the force of Demosthenes, the copious flow of Plato, and the charm of Isocrates.

But he did something more than reproduce the best elements in each of these authors by dint of careful study; it was to himself that he owed most of, or rather all, his excellences, which spring from the extraordinary fertility of his immortal genius. For he does not, as Pindar says, 'collect the rain from heaven, but wells forth with living water,' since Providence at his birth conferred this special privilege upon him, that eloquence should make trial of all her powers in him. For who can instruct with greater thoroughness, or more deeply stir the emotions? Who has ever possessed such a boon of charm? He seems to obtain as a gift what in reality he extorts by force, and when he wrests the judge from the path of his own judgement, the latter seems not to be swept away, but merely to follow. Further, there is such weight in all that he says that his audience feel ashamed to disagree with him, and the zeal of the advocate is so transfigured that it has the effect of the sworn evidence of a witness, or the verdict of a judge. And at the same time all these excellences, of which scarce one could be attained by the ordinary man even by the most concentrated effort, flow from him with every appearance of spontaneity, and his style, although no fairer has ever fallen on the ears of men, none the less displays the utmost felicity and ease.

It was not, therefore, without good reason that his own contemporaries spoke of his 'sovereignty' at the bar, and that for posterity the name of Cicero has come to be regarded not as the name of a man, but as the name of eloquence itself. Let us, therefore, fix our eyes on him, take him as our pattern, and let the student realize that he has made real progress if he is a passionate admirer of Cicero.

H. E. BUTLER (1922)

HINTS FOR COUNSEL

The litigant should be made to repeat his statements at least once, not merely because certain points may have escaped him on the occasion of his first statement – as is extremely likely to happen if, as is often the case, he is a man of no education – but also that we may note whether he sticks to what he originally said. For a large number of clients lie, and hold forth not as if they were instructing their advocate in the facts of the case, but as if they were pleading with a judge. Consequently we must never be too ready to believe them, but must test them in every way, try to confuse them and draw them out. For just as doctors have to do more than treat the ailments which meet the eye, and need also to discover those which lie hid – since their patients often conceal the truth – so the advocate must look out for more points than his client discloses to him. After he considers that he has given a sufficiently patient hearing to the latter's statements, he must assume another character and adopt the role of his opponent, urging every conceivable objection that a discussion of the kind which we are considering may permit. The client must be subjected to a hostile cross-examination and given no peace: for by inquiring into everything, we shall sometimes come upon the truth where we least expect it.

In fact, the advocate who is most successful in getting up his case is he who is incredulous. For the client promises everything: the people, he says, will bear witness to the truth of what he says, he can produce documentary evidence at a moment's notice, and there are some points which he says his opponent will not deny. It is therefore necessary to look into every document connected with the case, and, where the mere sight of them is not sufficient, they must be read through. For very frequently they are either not at all what the client alleged them to be, or contain less, or are mixed up with elements that may damage our case, or prove more than is required and are likely to detract from their credibility just because they are so extravagant. Further, it will often be found that the thread is broken or the seal tampered with or the signatures unsupported by witnesses. And unless you discover such facts at home, they will take you by surprise in court and trip you up, doing you more harm by forcing you to abandon them than they would have done had they never been promised you.

H. E. BUTLER (1922)

MARTIAL

Marcus Valerius Martialis, born at Bilbilis (Calatayud) in Spain in about A.D. 40, came to Rome in his twenties, lived a poor, uncomfortable life there, became a little more prosperous when he was getting on in years, and died in about 104. He is the greatest epigrammatist of the ancient world, and has imprinted his definition of the term on subsequent European literatures.

> What is an epigram? A dwarfish whole,
> Its body brevity, and wit its soul.[1]

For many of his 1,561 surviving poems have that amusing point or sting, often satirical, which had been rare in the more contemplative Greek epigram and has again, today, been generally supplanted by a more emotional aim. Martial's sort of epigram was what Silver Latin taste wanted – though he lacks its typical rhetoric. Italian and German translations – the former already more than a century old – were published in 1544, and Clément Marot (the first writer of French sonnets), who died in the same year, imitated numerous epigrams of Martial.[2] A specially commissioned Jesuit collection appeared in 1558 and ran into eighteen editions, and certain of his poems were translated into English by T. Kendall (*Flowers of Epigrams*, 1577). Martial was often quoted in critical essays, such as Ben Jonson's *Discoveries*; Milton referred to his prose prefaces in justification of his own to *Samson*. Herrick and Cowley knew Martial's epigrams. At their briefest, they are the single couplets of which one series is entitled 'presents for guests' (*Xenia*) – a title borrowed by Goethe and Schiller for the *Xenien* in which (without Martial's variety of metre) they mocked their literary enemies. Lessing's essay on the epigram is centred on Martial's work. 'No other poet in any language,' says H. W. Garrod, 'has the same never-failing grace and charm and brilliance, the same arresting ingenuity, an equal facility and finish.' He has also been called the laureate of t iviality. But this does too little justice to his not unprofound pungency, kindness of heart, appreciation of natural beauty, and sensitive knowledge of human behaviour.

1. Samuel Taylor Coleridge.
2. His versions were printed in 1596.

OLD AGE

At length my friend (while Time, with still career,
Wafts on his gentle wing his eightieth year)
Sees his past days safe out of Fortune's power,
Nor dreads approaching fate's uncertain hour;
Reviews his life, and in the strict survey
Finds not one moment he could wish away,
Pleased with the series of each happy day.
Such, such a man extends his life's short space,
And from the goal again renews the race;
For he lives twice, who can at once employ
The present well, and even the past enjoy.

ALEXANDER POPE (1737) [1]

THE POET

He unto whom thou art so partial,
Oh, reader! is the well-known Martial,
The Epigrammatist: while living,
Give him the fame thou wouldst be giving:
So shall he hear, and feel, and know it –
Post-obits rarely reach a poet.

LORD BYRON (1821)

AN EXPLANATION

Philaenis weeps with just one eye.
    Queer, is it not?
You wish you knew the reason why?
    That's all she's got.

PAUL NIXON (1911)

1. A loose adaptation, revised; he had written the first in 1717.

THE QUALITY OF A BOOK

Good work you'll find, some poor, and much that's worse;
It takes all sorts to make a book of verse.

PLAGIARISM

A rumour says that you recite
As *yours* the verses that *I* write.
Friend, if you'll credit them to me
I'll send you all my poems free;
But if as yours you'd have them known,
Buy them, and they'll become your own.

BADLY READ

The verse is mine; but friend, when you declaim it,
It seems like yours, so grievously you maim it.

SELF-PRAISE

You're rich and young, as all confess,
And none denies your loveliness;
But when we hear your boastful tongue
You're neither pretty, rich, nor young.

UNTRUSTWORTHY

When Linus begged a loan, his friend,
A prudent soul, declined to lend –
But *gave* him half, because he found
That saved ten shillings in the pound.

DEFINITION OF A DEBTOR

You disappoint no creditor, you say?
True, no one ever thought that you would pay.

UNPRODUCTIVE

You blame my verse; to publish you decline;
Show us your own, or cease to carp at mine.

THE NEED FOR LEISURE

'Your trifling all is vain,
Sing me a nobler strain!'
  Thus you implore me;
Then grant the ease I crave,
Such as Maecenas gave
  To bards before me.

So shall I weave a song
That through the ages long
  May never perish;
Nay, for the funeral flame
Cannot consume a fame
  That all men cherish.

Dully the oxen toil
On harsh and barren soil
  That yields no treasure.
But fat and fruitful earth
Turns weariness to mirth
  And toil to pleasure.

THE ADVANTAGE

You ask me how my farm can pay,
    Since little it will bear.
It pays me thus – 'Tis far away,
    And you are never there.

EDUCATION

Long have you pondered what employ
Or training you should give your boy.
Firstly, a cultured education
Today is reckoned sheer damnation;
All classic authors are a curse,
Bacon is ruin, Milton worse;
If he loves rhyme, he must forgo it:
Good Lord! he might become a poet!
If art be naught and money all –
Why, train him for the Music Hall,
Or if he's dull of intellect
Make him a tout or architect.

RECIPROCITY

Why don't I send my book to you
Although you often urge me to?
The reason's good, for if I did
You'd send me yours – which God forbid!

REFUSAL

Present you with my books? Not I indeed.
I know you want to sell them, not to read.

SCALE

Your few quatrains are not amiss,
Your couplets too are neat; for this
   You earn a mild regard,
But little fame, for many men
Can write good verses now and then –
   To make a book is hard.

PRAISE OF THE PAST[1]

All save the ancient poets you decry,
   The living cannot gain your approbation;
Excuse me – 'tis not worth my while to die,
   Even to earn your valued admiration.

BIRTHDAY PRESENT

Quintus, a little birthday gift I planned,
   But you refuse and nothing will persuade you;
Well, reconcile my wish and your command
   By giving me the gift I should have made you.

AN EXCUSE

The rich feign wrath – a profitable plan;
'Tis cheaper far to hate than help a man.

F. A. POTT (before 1924)[2]

BOW-LEGGED

As your legs are as curved as the moon's horns when new,
Then your bath should be shaped like a drinking-horn too.

1. For Horace on this same theme, see above, p. 203.
2. An adaptation.   The preceding versions also are his.

BLACK AND WHITE

Moll's teeth are black, while Susan's white have grown.
The reason: Sue's are bought, but Moll's her own.

F. A. WRIGHT (1924)

HER OWN WORK

A candid epitaph: Chloe inters
Seven husbands, and then signs the work as hers.

E. V. RIEU (1924)

MARRIAGE

Why not marry money? 'Tis more in my way
To love and to cherish than love and obey.
For a match to be equal, in person and purse
A man's better half should be rather the worse.

TO AN UNFRIENDLY CRITIC

Sour critic, who can here no merit find,
May you, unenvied, envy all mankind!

A. L. FRANCIS and H. F. TATUM (1924)

NO CHANGE

Once a surgeon, Dr Baker
Then became an undertaker,
Not so much his trade reversing,
Since for him it's just re-hearsing.

T. W. MELLUISH (1955)

THE RESULT

Rome's quoting, praising, singing out my verses,
In every hand and pocket there's my book:
A chap there blushes, blenches, coughs, and curses –
That's how I want my rhymes to make 'em look!

PRETTY GOOD

Oh Atticus, how prettily you plead,
Speak, write those poems and stories we all read;
A pretty pundit, singer, dancer, writer,
Pretty at tennis, pretty as first-nighter.
You're pretty good at pretty little, aren't ye,
My Atticus, the world's worst dilettante?

INHERITANCE

The light-heaped pyre lay ready for the match,
Numa's wife, weeping, incense-bearing, hovered:
Grave, bier, and undertaker ... here's the catch –
He'd made me heir – but blast him, he recovered!

HIRE PURCHASE

Spiv-suited, Zoilus laughs himself quite sick
At my old clothes – but Z., they're not on tick.

THE PRICE OF FRIENDSHIP

The man, this dining pal of yours,
How trust you his fidelity?
He's out for oysters, mullets, boars –
If I serve these, he's true to me.

STUART PIGGOTT (1955)

PLINY

Pliny the younger, Gaius Plinius Caecilius Secundus, was born at Comum (Como) in A.D. 61 or 62, was adopted by his uncle Pliny the elder (the encyclopaedic scientist),[1] and died before 114. Among contemporaries Pliny the younger was well known for his forensic speeches (now lost). His formal oration in praise of Trajan, the *Panegyricus* (one of the very few post-Ciceronian pagan speeches that have come down to us), enjoyed a great reputation in antiquity. To us his chief interest lies in his ten books of letters. One book, the last, contains correspondence exchanged between Pliny and Trajan; it includes a memorable statement of policy concerning the Christians. The remaining 247 letters (to 105 recipients) were written or edited (unlike Cicero's letters) for publication. They are early and highly civilized representatives of a literary form which is one of Rome's most distinctive gifts to Europe. In the Middle Ages Seneca's moralizing kind of epistle was more popular; but during the Renaissance Pliny greatly pleased Politian and Erasmus. The greater part of his letters were printed at Venice in 1471, but the first complete edition of his works was the Aldine volume of 1508. A. Fleming published an English translation of selected passages in 1576.

'Some of the more elaborate of these letters,' says J.W. Mackail, 'would fall quite naturally into place among the essays of *The Spectator* or *The Rambler*; in many others the combination of thin and lucid commonsense with a vein of calculated sensibility can hardly be paralleled till we reach the age of Rousseau. In his descriptive pieces there is an accent which hardly recurs till the age of Thomson's *Seasons* and of Gray's *Letters*.' Pope's Letters, too, are in the Plinian tradition; and his friend the Earl of Orrery translated the whole collection. But Pliny's greatest English translator (though his version is a loose one) was William Melmoth (1746), considered by some contemporaries superior to his original. Pliny could be called, like Madame Sévigné, 'garrulous but with art'. One of his nineteenth-century admirers was Sainte-Beuve. Much of what Pliny has to say – for instance about nature – strikes a modern enough note, if the reader can overcome the barrier which separates twentieth-century taste from any and every literary letter.

1. Before his adoption Pliny the younger's name was Publius Caecilius Secundus.

THE ERUPTION OF VESUVIUS AND DEATH OF
THE ELDER PLINY

To Tacitus

Your request that I would send you an account of my uncle's end, so that you may transmit a more exact record of it to posterity, deserves my acknowledgements; for if his death shall be celebrated by your pen, the glory of it, I am aware, will be rendered for ever deathless. For although he perished, as did whole peoples and cities, in the destruction of a most beautiful region, and by a misfortune memorable enough to promise him a kind of immortality; although he has himself composed many and lasting works; yet, I am persuaded, the mentioning of him in your immortal writings will greatly contribute to the perpetuation of his name. Happy I esteem those whom Providence has gifted with the ability either to do things worthy of being written, or to write in a manner worthy of being read; but most happy they, who are blessed with both talents! In which latter class my uncle will be placed both by his own writings and by yours. The more willingly do I undertake, indeed solicit, the task you set me.

He was at that time with the fleet under his command at Misenum.[1] On the 24th of August, at about one in the afternoon, my mother requested him to observe a cloud of very unusual size and appearance. He had sunned himself, then taken a cold bath, and after a leisurely luncheon was engaged in study. He immediately called for his shoes and went up an eminence from which he might best view this uncommon spectacle. It was not at that distance discernible from what mountain this cloud issued, but it was found afterwards to be Vesuvius. I cannot give you a more exact description of its shape than by comparing it to that of an umbrella pine-tree. For it shot up a great height in the form of a trunk, which extended itself at the top into several branches; because, I imagine, a momentary gust of air blew it aloft, and then failing, forsook it; thus causing the cloud to expand laterally as it dissolved – or possibly the downward pressure of its own weight produced this effect. It was at one moment white, at another dark and spotted, as if it had carried up earth or cinders.

1. See below, p. 392, n.

My uncle, true savant that he was, considered the phenomenon to be important and worth a nearer view. He ordered a light vessel to be got ready, and gave me the opportunity, if I thought proper, to accompany him. I replied I would rather study; and, as it happened, he had himself given me a theme for composition. As he was coming out of the house he received a note from Rectina, the wife of Bassus, who was in the utmost alarm at the imminent danger (his villa stood just below us, and there was no way to escape but by sea); she earnestly entreated him to save her from such deadly peril. He changed his first design and what he began in a scientific, he pursued in a heroic frame of mind. He ordered large galleys to be launched, and went himself on board one, with the intention of assisting not only Rectina, but many others; for the villas stand extremely thick upon that beautiful coast. Hastening to the place from which others were flying, he steered his direct course to the point of danger, and with such freedom from fear as to be able to make and dictate his observations upon the successive motions and configurations of the dreadful volcano.

And now cinders, which grew thicker and hotter the nearer he approached, fell into the ships, then pumice-stones too, with stones blackened, scorched, and cracked by fire; then the sea ebbed suddenly from under them, while the shore was blocked up by landslips from the mountains. After considering a moment whether he should retreat he said to the captain who was urging that course, 'Fortune befriends the brave! Take me to Pomponianus.' Pomponianus was then at Stabiae, distant by half the width of the bay (for, as you know, the shore, curving gently in its sweep, forms here a receptacle for the sea). He had already embarked his baggage; for though at Stabiae the danger was not yet near, it was full in view, and certain to be extremely near, as soon as it spread; and he resolved to fly as soon as the contrary wind should cease. It was entirely favourable, however, for carrying my uncle to Pomponianus. He embraced, comforted, and encouraged his alarmed friend, and in order to soothe the other's fears by his own unconcern, desired to be conducted to a bathroom; and after having bathed, he sat down to supper with great cheerfulness, or at least (which is equally heroic) with all the appearance of it.

In the meanwhile Mount Vesuvius was blazing in several places with spreading and towering flames, the refulgent brightness of which the darkness of the night set in high relief. But my uncle, in order to soothe apprehensions, kept saying that some fires had been left alight by the terrified country people, and what they saw were only deserted villas on fire in the abandoned district. After this he retired to rest, and it is most certain that his rest was a most genuine slumber; for his breathing, which (as he was pretty fat) was somewhat heavy and sonorous, was heard by those who attended at the door of his bedroom. But the court which led to his apartment now lay so deep under a mixture of pumice-stone and ashes that, if he had continued longer in his bedroom, the way out would have been blocked. On being aroused, he came out, and returned to Pomponianus and the others, who had sat up all night. They consulted together as to whether they should hold out in the house, or wander about in the open. For the house now tottered under repeated and violent concussions, and seemed to rock to and fro as if torn from its foundations. In the open air, on the other hand, they dreaded the falling pumice-stones, light and porous though they were. Yet this, by comparison, seemed the lesser danger of the two – a conclusion which my uncle arrived at by balancing reasons, and the others by balancing fears. They tied pillows upon their heads with napkins; and this was their only defence against the showers that fell round them.

It was now day everywhere else, but there a deeper darkness prevailed than in the most obscure night: relieved, however, by many torches and other illuminations. They thought proper to go down upon the shore to observe from close at hand if they could possibly put out to sea, but they found the waves still running extremely high, and against them. There my uncle, having thrown himself down upon a disused sail, repeatedly called for, and drank, draughts of cold water. Soon after, flames and a strong smell of sulphur (their forerunner) dispersed the rest of the company in flight; him they only aroused. He raised himself up with the assistance of two of his slaves, but instantly fell; some unusually gross vapour, as I conjecture, having obstructed his breathing and blocked his windpipe, which was not only naturally weak and constricted, but chronically inflamed. When day dawned again (the third from the last which he beheld) his body was found entire and uninjured, and still fully clothed as in life; its posture was that of a sleeping rather than a dead man.

Meanwhile my mother and I were at Misenum. But this has no connexion with history, and your inquiry went no farther than concerning my uncle's death. I will therefore put an end to my letter. Suffer me only to add that I have faithfully related to you what I was either an eye-witness of myself, or heard at the time, when report speaks most truly. You will select what is most suitable to your purpose; for there is a great difference between a letter, and a history – between writing to a friend, and writing for the public.

Adapted from WILLIAM MELMOTH (1746) [1]

EDUCATION FOR COMO

To Tacitus

I rejoice that you have safely arrived in Rome; for though I am always desirous to see you, I am more particularly so now. I propose to stay a few days longer at my Tusculum estate in order to finish a little work which I have upon my hands. For I am afraid, should I put a stop to this design now that it is so nearly completed, I should find it difficult to resume it. Meanwhile, that I may strike while the iron is hot, I send this letter, like an *avant-courier*, to request a favour of you – which I mean shortly to ask in person. But before I inform you what my request is, I must let you into the occasion of it.

Being lately at my native place, a young lad, son to one of my fellow-townsmen, made me a visit. 'Do you go to school?' I asked him. 'Yes,' said he. 'And where?' He told me, 'At Milan.' 'And why not here?' 'Because' (said his father, who was present, and had in fact brought the boy with him), 'we have no teachers.' 'How is that?' said I; 'surely it is very important to you who are fathers' (and very opportunely several of the company were so) 'that your sons should receive their education here, rather than anywhere else. For where can they be placed more agreeably than in their own country, or maintained in more modest habits and at less expense than at home and under the eye of their parents? Upon what very easy terms might you, by a general contribution, procure teachers, if you would only apply towards raising a salary for them what you now spend on your sons' lodging, journeys, and whatever one has to pay for when abroad (which means, paying for everything!).

1. Melmoth's translations have been amended by W.M.L.Hutchinson (1915) and again by the present editor.

'Why, I, who have as yet no children myself, am ready to give a third part of any sum you shall think proper to raise for this purpose, for the benefit of our town, which I regard as a daughter or a parent. I would take upon myself the whole expense, were I not apprehensive that my benefaction might hereafter be abused and perverted to private ends; as I have observed to be the case in several places where teachers are engaged by the local authorities. The single means to prevent this mischief is to leave the choice of the professors entirely to the parents, who will be all the more careful to make a right decision, since they will be obliged to share the expense of maintaining them. For though they may be careless in disposing of another's bounty, they will certainly be cautious how they apply their own; and will see that none but those who deserve it shall receive my money, when they must at the same time receive theirs too. Let my example then encourage you to unite enthusiastically in this project; and be assured, the greater the sum my share shall amount to, the more agreeable it will be to me. You can undertake nothing more advantageous to your children, nor more acceptable to your country. They will by this means receive their education where they receive their birth, and be accustomed from their infancy to inhabit and love their native soil.

'I hope you will be able to procure professors of such distinguished abilities that the neighbouring towns will be glad to draw their learning from here; and as you now send your children to foreigners for education, may foreigners hereafter flock here for their instruction.'

I thought it proper to give you a fairly full description of the origins of this affair, so that you may better appreciate how agreeable it will be to me, if you undertake the office I request. I entreat you, therefore, with all the earnestness a matter of so much importance deserves, to look out, amongst the great number of men of letters which the reputation of your genius brings to you, teachers to whom we may apply for this purpose. It must, however, be understood that I cannot make a binding agreement with any of them. For I would leave it entirely free to the parents to judge and choose as they shall think proper: all the share I pretend to claim is that of contributing my care and my money. If therefore any one shall be found who relies upon his own talents, he may come here; but under the proviso that the said reliance is all he can count upon, so far as I am concerned.

Adapted from WILLIAM MELMOTH (1746)

FLOATING ISLANDS

To Gallus

Those works of art or nature which are usually the motives of our travels by land or sea are often overlooked and neglected if they lie within our reach – whether it be that we are naturally less inquisitive concerning those things which are near us, while we push ourselves forward in pursuit of remote objects; or because the easiness of gratifying a desire is always sure to damp it; or, perhaps, we defer from time to time viewing what we know we have an opportunity of seeing when we please. Whatever the reason be, it is certain there are several rarities in and near Rome which we have not only never seen, but even never so much as heard of: and yet if they had been the produce of Greece, or Egypt, or Asia, or any other country which offers us a rich display of wonders, we would long since have heard about them, read about them, and surveyed them ourselves.

For myself at least, I confess, I have lately become acquainted with one of these curiosities, to which I was an entire stranger before. My wife's grandfather asked me to look round his estate near Ameria.[1] As I was walking over his grounds I was shewn a lake that lies below them, called Vadimon, and given at the same time an incredible account of it. So I went close up to this lake. It is exactly circular; there is not the least break or bend in the circle, but all is regular and just as if it had been hollowed and cut out by the hand of art. The colour of its water is a whitish-blue, verging upon green, and somewhat cloudy; it has the odour of sulphur and a strong medicinal taste, and possesses the property of cementing fractures. Though it is but of moderate extent, yet the winds have a great effect upon it, throwing it into violent commotions.

No vessels are permitted to sail here, as its waters are held sacred; but several grassy islands swim about it, covered with reeds and rushes, and whatever other plants the more prolific neighbouring marsh and the borders of the lake produce. No two islands are alike in size or shape; but the edges of all of them are worn away by their frequent collision against the shore and one another. They have all the

1. In south-western Umbria; the modern Amelia.

same depth, and the same buoyancy; for their shallow bases are formed like the hull of a boat. This formation is distinctly visible from every point of view; the hull lies half above and half below the water. Sometimes the islands cluster together and seem to form one entire little continent; sometimes they are dispersed by veering winds; at times, when it is calm, they desert their station and float up and down separately.

You may frequently see one of the larger islands sailing along with a lesser joined to it, like a ship with its long boat; or perhaps, seeming to strive which shall outswim the other; then again all are driven to one spot of the shore of which they thus form a prolongation. In one place or another they are constantly diminishing or restoring the area of the lake, only ceasing to contract it anywhere, when they occupy the centre. Cattle have often been known, while grazing, to advance upon those islands as upon the border of the lake, without perceiving that they are on moving ground, till, being carried away from shore, they are alarmed by finding themselves surrounded with water, as if they had been put on board ship; and when they presently land wherever the wind drives them ashore, they are no more conscious of disembarking than they had been of embarking. This lake empties itself into a river, which after running a little way above ground sinks into a cavern and pursues a subterraneous course, and if anything is thrown in brings it up again where the stream emerges.

I have given you this account because I imagined it would be as new and agreeable to you as it was to me; since I know you take the same unique pleasure as myself in contemplating the works of nature.

Adapted from WILLIAM MELMOTH (1746)

GHOST STORIES

To Sura

The present recess gives me an opportunity to learn something, and you to tell it. I am extremely eager to know your sentiments concerning ghosts. Do you believe they actually exist and have their own proper shapes and a measure of divinity, or are only the false impressions of a terrified imagination?

What particularly inclines me to give credit to their existence is a story which I heard of Curtius Rufus.[1] When he was in low circumstances and unknown in the world, he attended the newly-appointed governor of Africa into that province. One afternoon as he was walking in the public portico he was extremely daunted by the appearance of a woman who seemed to him of a size and beauty more than human. She told him she was the Genius that presided over Africa, and was come to inform him of the future events of his life: – that he should go back to Rome, where he should hold office, and return to that province as governor, and there should die. Every circumstance of this prophecy was actually accomplished. It is said further that, upon his arrival at Carthage, as he was coming out of the ship, the same figure accosted him upon the shore. It is certain, at least, that being seized with a fit of illness, though there were no symptoms in his case that led his attendants to despair, he instantly gave up all hope of recovery – judging, it would seem, of the truth of the future part of the prediction, by that which had already been fulfilled; and of the misfortune which threatened him, by the success which he had experienced.

To this story, let me add another as remarkable as the former, but attended with circumstances of greater horror; which I will give you exactly as it was related to me. There was at Athens a large and spacious, but ill-reputed and sickness-ridden house. In the dead of the night a noise, resembling the clashing of iron, was frequently heard. If you listened more attentively, it sounded like the rattling of fetters. At first it seemed at a distance, but approached nearer by degrees. Immediately afterward a phantom appeared in the form of an old man, extremely meagre and squalid, with a long beard and bristling hair, rattling the chains on his feet and hands. The poor inhabitants consequently passed sleepless nights in the most dismal terrors imaginable. This, as it broke their rest, threw them into ill-health, which, as their horrors of mind increased, proved in the end fatal to them. For even in the daytime, though the spectre did not appear, yet the memory of it made such a strong impression upon their imaginations

1. A self-made man who won an honorary Triumph from Claudius by discovering a silver mine while governor of Upper Germany. The recipient of the letter, Lucius Licinius Sura, was a close friend of Trajan, who like him came from Spain.

that it still seemed to be before their eyes, and their terror remained when the cause of it was gone. By this means the house was at last deserted, as being judged by everybody to be absolutely uninhabitable; so that it was now entirely abandoned to the ghost. However, in hopes that some tenant might be found who was ignorant of this great calamity which attended it, a bill was put up, giving notice that it was either to be let or sold.

It happened that Athenodorus the philosopher came to Athens at this time, and reading the bill noticed the price. The extraordinary cheapness raised his suspicion; nevertheless, when he heard the whole story, he was so far from being discouraged, that he was more strongly inclined to rent it, and, in short, actually did so. When night approached, he ordered a bed to be prepared for him in the fore-part of the house, and after calling for a light, his pen, and his tablets, he directed all his people to retire within. But that his mind might not, for want of employment, be open to the vain terrors of imaginary noises and apparitions, he applied himself to writing with all his faculties. The first part of the night passed in the usual silence. Then began the clanking of iron fetters. However, he neither lifted up his eyes, nor laid down his pen, but closed his ears by concentrating. The noise increased and advanced nearer, till it seemed at the door, and at last in the very room. He looked round and saw the apparition exactly as it had been described to him: it stood before him, beckoning with its finger. Athenodorus made a sign with his hand that it should wait a little, and bent again to his writing, but the ghost rattled its chains over his head as he wrote. He looked round, and saw it beckoning as before. Upon this he immediately took up his lamp and followed it. The ghost slowly stalked along, as if encumbered with its chains; and having turned into the courtyard of the house, suddenly vanished – and Athenodorus was alone. He marked the spot with a handful of grass and leaves. The next day he went to the magistrates, and advised them to order that spot to be dug up. There they found bones commingled and intertwined with chains; for the body had mouldered away by long lying in the ground, leaving them bare, and corroded by the fetters. The bones were collected, and buried at the public expense. So the ghost was duly laid, and the house was haunted no more.

This story I believe from the reports of others; I can myself affirm to others what I now relate. I have a freedman named Marcus, who has some tincture of letters. One night his younger brother, who was sleeping in the same bed with him, saw, as he thought, somebody sitting on the couch, and dreamt that this person put a pair of shears to his head, and actually cut off the hair from the very crown of it. When morning came, they found the boy's crown was shorn, and the hair lay scattered about on the floor. After a short interval, a similar occurrence gave credit to the former. A slave-boy of mine was sleeping amidst several others in their quarters, when two persons clad in white came in (as he tells the story) through the windows, cut off his hair as he lay, and withdrew the same way they entered. Daylight revealed that this boy too had been shorn, and that his hair was likewise spread about the room. Nothing remarkable followed, unless it were that I escaped prosecution; prosecuted I should have been, if Domitian (in whose reign these things happened) had lived longer. For an information lodged by Carus [1] against me was found in his files. Hence it may be conjectured, since it is customary for accused persons to let their hair grow, that this cutting of my servants' hair was a sign I should defeat the peril that hung over me.

So do please apply your learning to this question. It deserves your prolonged and profound consideration; and I am not myself an unworthy recipient of your abundant knowledge. And though you should, after your manner, argue on both sides, yet I hope you will throw your weightiest reasons into one scale – rather than dismiss me in suspense and uncertainty, for I am consulting you on purpose to determine my doubts.

Adapted from WILLIAM MELMOTH (1746)

THE CHRISTIANS

From Pliny, Governor of Bithynia, to The Emperor Trajan [2]

It is my usual custom, my lord, to refer to you all matters about which I am in doubt. For who can better guide me when I hesitate or inform

1. Mettius Carus was one of the most notorious of Domitian's informers.
2. In A.D. 110–11 Pliny was sent by Trajan to govern Bithynia and Pontus (northern Anatolia) with special powers as the emperor's own representative; the finances of the Greek cities were in disorder.

me in my ignorance? I have never taken part in any examinations of Christians: for that reason I do not know the usual nature and extent of punishment or investigation. I have been in considerable doubt as to whether age should be taken into consideration, whether all persons, however young they are, should be treated in the same way as those of riper years, whether repentance should win pardon, whether a man who has avowedly been a Christian should not benefit by his having ceased to be one, whether the mere profession unaccompanied by criminal acts should be punished, or only criminal acts connected with the profession. In the meantime, in the case of those reported to me as being Christians, I have followed this practice. I asked the people themselves whether they were Christians. If they admitted it, I asked them a second and a third time, after threatening them with capital punishment: if they persisted, I ordered them to be led away for execution. For I did not doubt that, whatever the nature of their profession, at any rate their obstinacy and intractable doggedness deserved to be punished. There were others just as crazed whom I listed for sending to Rome because they were Roman citizens.

Presently through the very handling of such cases, as often happens, charges of this offence began to spread and more varieties turned up. An anonymous document was brought before me containing many people's names. When those who denied that they were or had been Christians called upon the gods, following my dictation, and worshipped your image (which for this reason I had ordered to be brought in with statues of other gods) with incense and wine, and, what is more, cursed Christ – and it is said that those who are really Christians cannot be compelled to do any of these things – I considered that I should let them go. Others, whose names were given by informers, said that they were Christians and presently denied it; at least they had been once, but had ceased to be, some three years before, some more than that – some even twenty years ago. All in this category also worshipped your image and the statues of the gods and cursed Christ. Moreover they declared that the limit of their guilt or mistake had been that they had been accustomed to congregate on a fixed day before daybreak, and sing a hymn antiphonally to Christ as if he were a god; and bind themselves by an oath not with a view to some crime, but not to commit theft, robbery, or adultery, not to break their word, not to repudiate a trust when called upon. When they had done this, it was their custom to depart and meet together again to take food, but perfectly ordinary and harmless; this actual practice they had given up after my edict, whereby according to your orders I had forbidden the existence of brotherhoods. All the more essential did I consider it to make inquiries (even under torture) of two maid-servants who were styled deaconesses, as to the truth. I discovered nothing except a cult that was irregular and extravagant. Because of this I adjourned any examination and had recourse to seeking your advice.

The business seemed to me to merit consultation, particularly because of the number of people involved. For many of every age and rank, and even of both sexes, are called and will be called into peril. It is not only cities, but also villages and the countryside, that the infection of this cult has pervaded; this it seems possible to stop and put right. Anyhow there is sufficient evidence that people are beginning to throng the temples which lately were almost deserted, to attend again the long suspended religious rites, and that there is again a sale of food for sacrifices, which up till now very rarely found a purchaser. From this it is easy to surmise what a crowd of people there are who could be reformed, granted an opportunity for repentance.[1]

L. A. and R. W. L. WILDING (1955)

REPLY ABOUT THE CHRISTIANS [2]

Trajan to Pliny

You have followed the correct procedure, dear Secundus, in investigating the cases of those who were accused in your court of being Christians. It is not possible to lay down a rule that can be universally applicable, in a set form of words. They are not to be hunted out; any who are accused and convicted should be punished, with the proviso that if a man says that he is not a Christian and makes it obvious by his actual conduct, namely by worshipping our gods, then, however suspect he may have been with regard to the past, he should gain

1. For Tacitus' account of the Christians under Nero, see below, p. 399.
2. Trajan's letter, though not countenancing deliberate persecution, was execrated by the early Christian Fathers; conversely Trajan was honoured in the fourth century by Roman pagans.

pardon from his repentance. No anonymous lists that are submitted should carry weight in any charges. That would be the worst of precedents and out of keeping with the spirit of our age.

L. A. and R. W. L. WILDING (1955)

JUVENAL

DECIMUS JUNIUS JUVENALIS was born at Aquinum (Aquino) in about
A.D. 50, and was trained as a rhetorician, as his works abundantly show;
he died sometime after 127. The 'harsh, wild laughter' of this greatest of
Roman satirists has come down to us in sixteen poems. They deal with
the following subjects: philosopher-hypocrites, the humiliations of poor
men at Rome (and poor writers in particular), the faults of women, the
despicable character of the (deceased) emperor Domitian, the evils of
pride of birth and false friendship, misguided ambitions, people's brutality to each other, the unfair privileges of soldiers, and the bad effects
parents can have on their children.

> Whatever mankind does, their hope, fear, rage, and pleasure,
> Their business and their sport, are the hotch-potch of my book.
> And when was there a richer crop of vices?

Juvenal, adding to the heritage of Ennius, Lucilius, and Horace an
elevated personal conception of the satirist's task, is the true founder of
this *genre* as a continuous European tradition. From A.D. 1000 library
catalogues show a marked increase in the copies of Juvenal in circula-
tion; [1] in a recent compilation the twelfth-century figure, 29, is only
exceeded by Virgil, Horace, Ovid, and Persius (32) (Juvenal's almost
untranslatable satirical predecessor of Neronian date). The poems of
Juvenal were admired by Boccaccio and first printed (from an inferior
text) in *c.* 1467–9, probably at Rome; an Italian translation dates from
1480. François Pitheu discovered a good text at Lorsch, near Mainz, in
c. 1573.[2] In 1599 the Archbishop of Canterbury forbade the further
activity in this field of certain young English rebel poets – including
John Donne – who numbered Juvenal among their models. Satire became more fully understood after a study by Casaubon in 1605. A well-
known English version was published by Holyday in 1673, and twenty
years later Dryden translated some of the poems – and also vigorously
adapted him to questions of the day. High, also, among the products of
this neo-classical art of adaptation rank the French satires of Nicolas

---

1. Vilgardus, a tenth-century student of Ravenna, pleaded that his heresy
was due to a demon in the shape of Juvenal (as well as to others resembling
Virgil and Horace).

2. His brother published it about twelve years later.

Boileau (1636–1711) and Samuel Johnson's *London* and *The Vanity of Human Wishes* – masterpieces earning him ten and fifteen guineas – based on Juvenal's third and tenth satires respectively. 'Rousseau and Marat quoted him on the title-pages of their pamphlets (what fitter prophet for a bourgeois revolution?); Burke in the House of Commons when recommending compromise with the American colonists. Hugo admired him as a political rebel, Flaubert fell in love with his style. Byron, in *English Bards and Scotch Reviewers*, devoured him whole.' [1] His most famous English translation is that of William Gifford (1802).

Juvenal's bitter eloquence, rather than his ethics, has attracted imitators. During the past century verse-satirists have become ever fewer; Roy Campbell is a rare example. What Juvenal needs most 'is one or two good modern verse translations and adaptations. ... We do not live as yet in an age like that which he described. Those who believe that it is approaching – men like Aldous Huxley, Arthur Koestler, and George Orwell – are the heirs of Juvenal today.' [2]

1. *Times Literary Supplement*, 12 November 1954.
2. Gilbert Highet (1954), to whom the verses quoted above are owed.

Of all the vows, the first and chief request
Of each is to be richer than the rest:
And yet no doubts the poor man's draught control,
He dreads no poison in his homely bowl.
Then fear the deadly drug, when gems divine
Enchase the cup, and sparkle in the wine.

Will you not now the pair of sages praise,
Who the same end pursued, by several ways?
One pitied, one contemned the woeful times:
One laughed at follies, one lamented crimes.[1]
Laughter is easy; but the wonder lies,
What stores of brine supplied the weeper's eyes!
Democritus could feed his spleen, and shake
His sides and shoulders till he felt them ache;
Though in his country town no Lictors were,
Nor rods nor axe nor Tribune did appear;
Nor all the foppish gravity of show
Which cunning magistrates on crowds bestow.
What had he done, had he beheld on high
Our Praetor seated, in mock majesty?
His chariot rolling o'er the dusty Place
While, with dumb pride and a set formal face,
He moves in the dull ceremonial track,
With Jove's embroidered coat upon his back:[2]
A suit of hangings had not more oppressed
His shoulders than that long, laborious vest.
A heavy gewgaw (called a crown), that spread
About his temples, drowned his narrow head,
And would have crushed it with the massy freight
But that a sweating slave sustained the weight –

1. There was a tradition that the Greek philosopher and atomist Democritus could not restrain his laughter, and that Heraclitus could not restrain his tears, at the spectacle of human life.

2. This is the *Pompa Circensis*, the procession which preceded the races in the Circus.

A slave in the same chariot seen to ride,
To mortify the mighty madman's pride.
Add now the imperial Eagle, raised on high,
With golden beak (the mark of majesty),
Trumpets before, and on the left and right
A cavalcade of nobles, all in white:
In their own natures false and flattering tribes,
But made his friends by places and by bribes.

In his own age, Democritus could find
Sufficient cause to laugh at human kind.
Learn from so great a wit: a land of bogs
With ditches fenced, a heaven fat with fogs,[1]
May form a spirit to sway the State,
And make the neighbouring monarchs fear their fate.
He laughs at all the vulgar cares and fears,
At their vain triumphs, and their vainer tears;
An equal temper in his mind he found,
When Fortune flattered him, and when she frowned.
'Tis plain from hence that what our vows request
Are hurtful things, or useless at the best.
Some ask for envied power: which public hate
Pursues, and hurries headlong to their fate:
Down go the titles: and the statue crowned
Is by base hands in the next river drowned.

JOHN DRYDEN (1693)

CRIME

Would it not make a modest author dare
To draw his table-book within the square,
And fill with notes, when lolling at his ease
Maecenas-like the happy rogue he sees
Borne by six wearied slaves in open view,
Who cancelled an old will, and forged a new –

1. Democritus came from the Thracian town of Abdera, which was pro-
verbial for the stupidity of its inhabitants.

Made wealthy at the small expense of signing
With a wet seal, and a fresh interlining?

The lady, next, requires a lashing line,
Who squeezed a toad into her husband's wine:
So well the fashionable Medicine thrives,
That now 'tis practised even by country wives –
Poisoning without regard of fame or fear:
And spotted corpse are frequent on the bier.
Wouldst then to honours and preferments climb,
Be bold in mischief, dare some mighty crime,
Which dungeons, death, or banishment deserves:
For Virtue is but drily praised, and starves.
Great men to great crimes owe their plate embossed,
Fair palaces, and furniture of cost,
And high commands: a sneaking sin is lost.

JOHN DRYDEN (1693)

THE POOR DEPENDANT

For, first, of this be sure: when'er your lord
Thinks proper to invite you to his board,
He pays, or thinks he pays, the total sum
Of all your pains, past, present, and to come.
Behold the meed of servitude! the great
Reward their humble followers with a treat,
And count it current coin: – they count it such,
And, though it be but little, think it much.
    If, after two long months, he condescend
To waste a thought upon a humble friend,
Reminded by a vacant seat, and write,
'You, Master Trebius, sup with me tonight;'
'Tis rapture all! Go now, supremely blest,
Enjoy the meed for which you broke your rest,
And, loose and slipshod, ran your vows to pay,
What time the fading stars announced the day;

Or at that earlier hour, when, with slow roll,
Thy frozen wain, Boötes, turned the pole;
Yet trembling, lest the levée should be o'er,
And the full court retiring from the door!

And what a meal at last! such ropy wine,
As wool, which takes all liquids, would decline;
Hot, heady lees, to fire the wretched guests,
And turn them all to corybants, or beasts.
At first, with sneers and sarcasms, they engage,
Then hurl the jugs around, with mutual rage;
Or, stung to madness by the household train,
With coarse stone pots a desperate fight maintain;
While streams of blood in smoking torrents flow,
And my lord smiles to see the battle glow!

Not such his beverage: he enjoys the juice
Of ancient days, when beards were yet in use,
Pressed in the Social War! [1] – but will not send
One cordial drop to cheer a fainting friend.
Tomorrow, he will change, and, haply, fill
The mellow vintage of the Alban hill,
Or Setian; [2] wines which cannot now be known,
So much the mould of age has overgrown
The district, and the date; such generous bowls,
As Thrasea and Helvidius, [3] patriot souls!
While crowned with flowers, in sacred pomp, they lay,
To FREEDOM quaffed, on Brutus' natal day.

Before your patron, cups of price are placed,
Amber and gold, with rows of beryls graced:
Cups you can only at a distance view,
And never trusted to such guests as you!
Or, if they be – a faithful slave attends,
To count the gems, and watch your fingers' ends.

---

1. 91–88 B.C.; so it was nearly two hundred years old!
2. Augustus liked the wine of Setia, in Latium, best of Italian wines.
3. Thrasea Paetus and his son-in-law Helvidius Priscus were both Republicans and Stoics who lost their lives for their political views, under Nero and Vespasian respectively.

You'll pardon him; but lo! a jasper there,
Of matchless worth, which justifies his care:
For Virro, like his brother peers, of late
Has stripped his fingers to adorn his plate;
And jewels now emblaze the festive board,
Which decked with nobler grace the hero's[1] sword
Whom Dido prized above the Libyan lord.
From such he drinks: to you the slaves allot
The Beneventine cobbler's four-lugged pot,[2]
A fragment, a mere shard, of little worth,
But to be trucked for matches . . . . and so forth.

   If Virro's veins with indigestion glow,
They bring him water cooled in Scythian snow:
What! did I late complain a different wine
Fell to thy share? A different water's thine!

    Gaetulian slaves [3] your vile potations pour,
Or the course paws of some huge, raw-boned Moor,
Whose hideous form the stoutest would affray,
If met, by moonlight, near the Latian way:
On him a youth, the flower of Asia, waits,
So dearly purchased that the joint estates
Of Tullus, Ancus, would not yield the sum,
Nor all the wealth of all the kings of Rome!

   Mark with what insolence another thrusts
Before your plate the impenetrable crusts,
Black, mouldy fragments, which defy the saw,
The mere despair of every aching jaw!
While manchets of the finest flour are set
Before your lord; but be you mindful, yet,
And taste not, touch not: of the pantler [4] stand
In trembling awe, and check your desperate hand.
Yet, should you dare – a slave springs forth, to wrest
The sacred morsel from you. 'Saucy guest!'

1. Aeneas.
2. Called 'Vatinian' after a cobbler of Beneventum, a friend of Nero, who
was long-nosed like the pots.
3. From the Sahara.
4. butler.

He frowns, and mutters, 'wilt thou ne'er divine
What's for thy patron's tooth, and what for thine?
Never take notice from what tray thou'rt fed,
Nor know the colour of thy proper bread?'
    Was it for this, the baffled client cries,
The tears indignant starting from his eyes,
Was it for this I left my wife ere day,
And up the bleak Esquilian urged my way,
While the wind howled, the hail-storm beat amain,
And my cloak smoked beneath the driving rain?
    But lo, a lobster introduced in state,
Stretches, enormous, o'er the bending plate!
Proud of a length of tail, he seems to eye
The humbler guests with scorn, as, towering by,
He takes the place of honour at the board,
And crowned with costly pickles, greets his lord!
A crab is yours, ill garnished and ill fed,
With half an egg – a supper for the dead!

    Does Virro ever pledge you? ever sip
The liquor touched by your unhallowed lip?
Or is there one of all your tribe so free,
So desperate, as to say – 'Sir, drink to me'?
O, there is much that never can be spoke
By a poor client in a threadbare cloak!
    But should some godlike man, more kind than fate,
Some god, present you with a knight's estate,
Heavens, what a change! how infinitely dear
Would Trebius then come! How great appear,
From nothing! Virro, so reserved of late,
Grows quite familiar: 'Brother, send your plate,
Dear brother Trebius! you were wont to say
You liked this trail,[1] I think – Oblige me, pray.' –
O Riches! – this 'dear brother' is your own,
To you this friendship, this respect is shown.

    You champ on spongy toadstools; hateful treat!
Fearful of poison in each bit you eat:

1. giblets.

He feasts secure on mushrooms, fine as those
Which Claudius, for his special eating, chose,
Till one more fine, provided by his wife,
Finished at once his feasting, and his life!

    Apples as fragrant, and as bright of hue,
As those which in Alcinoüs' garden grew,
Mellowed by constant sunshine; or as those,
Which graced the Hesperides, in burnished rows;
Apples, which you may smell, but never taste,
Before your lord and his great friends are placed;
While you enjoy mere windfalls: such stale fruit
As serves to mortify the raw recruit,
When, armed with helm and shield, the lance he throws,
And trembles at the shaggy master's blows.

    You think, perhaps, that Virro treats so ill
To save his gold: no, 'tis to vex you still:
For, say, what comedy such mirth can raise
As hunger, tortured thus a thousand ways?
No (if you know it not), 'tis to excite
Your rage, your frenzy, for his mere delight;
'Tis to compel you all your gall to show,
And gnash your teeth in agonies of woe.
You deem yourself (such pride inflates your breast)
Forsooth a freeman, and your patron's guest;
He thinks you a vile slave, drawn by the smell
Of his warm kitchen there; and he thinks well.

    Your palate still beguiles you: Ah, how nice
That smoking haunch! Now we shall have a slice!
NOW that half hare is coming! Now a bit
Of that young pullet! Now – and thus you sit,
Thumbing your bread in silence; watching still,
For what has never reached you, never will!

    No more of freedom! 'tis a vain pretence:
Your patron treats you like a man of sense:
For, if you can, without a murmur, bear,
You well deserve the insults which you share.
Anon, like voluntary slaves, you'll throw
Your humbled necks beneath the oppressor's blow,

Nay, with bare backs, solicit to be beat,
And merit SUCH A FRIEND, and SUCH A TREAT!

WILLIAM GIFFORD (1802)

THE EVILS OF ROME

What should I do at Rome? I have not learnt
The art of lying. If a book be bad,
I cannot praise and ask to take it home.
I am ignorant of the movements of the stars.
I neither will nor can promise a son
His father's death. The entrails of a frog
Never did I inspect. Others possess
More skill than I to convey to a wife
Presents and messages from a paramour.
From me no thief can expect aid; and so
No Governor will appoint me to his staff.
'Tis just as though I were a poor maimed trunk
With crippled hands, of no use any more.
Who nowadays is courted, save a man
Privy to some guilt, whose mind seethes and burns
With things hid that must never be disclosed?
He neither thinks he owes you anything,
Nor ever will he bestow on you a gift,
Who has made you sharer of an innocent secret.
The beloved friend of Verres [1] will be he
Who can impeach Verres at any hour
That best may please him. Let not all the sands
Of shady Tagus, sweeping with their gold
Down to the sea, be prized by you so high
That for them you should lose your sleep, and gloomily
Accept gifts which one day you must abandon,
And evermore be feared by your great friend.

Did ever anyone with too little money,
And no match for the fortune of his bride,

1. The extortionate governor of Sicily, denounced by Cicero.

Find favour as a son-in-law here at Rome?
What poor man ever is left a legacy,
Or ever gets appointed by the aediles
As their assessor? All penurious Romans
Should have marched out in a body long ago.

    Nowhere is it an easy task to rise
For that man whose domestic poverty
Obstructs his merits. But for such at Rome,
It is a harder struggle than elsewhere.
A big rent for a miserable lodging;
A big sum spent on filling your slaves' bellies;
For your own frugal dinner a big price.
You feel ashamed to dine off earthenware;
Yet you would find it no disgrace at all
If suddenly transported to a Marsian
Or Sabine table, where you'd be content
To wear a cape of coarse Venetian blue.

    Who is afraid, or ever was afraid
Of his house tumbling down at cool Praeneste
Or at Volsinii mid its wooded hills,
At humble Gabii, or upon the steep
Precipices of Tibur?[1] But this city
That we inhabit, for the most part rests
On slender props: for that is how the landlord
Tries to prevent us falling to the ground.
He fills in some old gaping crack, then bids us
Sleep secure when the crash has almost come.
There only let me live, where are no fires,
No scares by night. Already Ucalegon[2]
Is calling out for water, and carrying down
His furniture; already your third floor
Is filled with smoke; of all this you know nothing.
For if the alarm begins on the ground-floor,

1. Palestrina, Bolsena, Castiglione, Tivoli.
2. i.e. 'the man next door'. At the burning of Troy (*Aeneid*, II, 311) 'already Ucalegon's house is burning next door' (in Greek his name meant 'Don't Care').

The last to burn will be the man who has naught
To shelter him from the rain, except the tiles,
Where come the gentle doves to lay their eggs.

Here many a sick man dies for want of sleep
(No doubt his ailing state was caused by food
Lying undigested on a burning stomach);
For in what hired room is sleep possible?
To sleep in Rome, one must be rich indeed.
Here is the fountain-head of all our maladies.
The passage through the narrow winding streets
Of four-wheeled vehicles, the shouts and lowing
When a herd's brought to a standstill, would make sleep
Impossible for a Drusus, or for sea-calves.[1]
When social duties summon the rich man,
The crowd makes way for him, as he is carried swiftly
In a huge Liburnian litter above their heads,[2]
Writing or reading as he goes, or sleeping;
For in a litter with the window shut
Slumber is easy. Yet he will arrive
Before me. Hurry as I may, I am blocked
By a surging crowd in front, while a vast mass
Of people crushes on to me from behind.
One with his elbow punches me, another
With a hard litter-pole: one bangs a beam
Against my head, a wine-cask someone else.
With mud my legs are plastered; from all sides
Huge feet trample upon me, and a soldier's
Hobnails are firmly planted on my toes.
See you the smoke that rises from that throng
Seeking its dole? A hundred guests are there,
Each followed by a kitchener of his own.
Corbulo [3] himself could scarcely bear the weight

1. They were regarded as exceptionally heavy sleepers. The point of 'Drusus' is uncertain; it might refer to Claudius (a Drusus by birth), who was very somnolent.

2. Liburnians (from Croatia) were used in Rome as sedan-bearers.

3. A famous general in the time of Claudius and Nero, described by Tacitus as a heavy man.

Of all those monstrous vessels, all those pans
Poised on his crown, which that poor little slave
Is carrying with head held erect, fanning
The flame as he runs along. Newly-patched tunics
Are torn to shreds. Up comes a dray, whereon
Is quivering a long tree-trunk, then a wagon
Hauling a pine. Threateningly they nod
Over the heads of the people. If the axle
Of that cart loaded with Ligurian marble
Should break, and pour its mountainous mass of rock
Down on the crowd, what's left then of their bodies?
Who can identify the limbs, the bones?
The crushed plebeian's corpse vanishes utterly
Just like his soul. Meanwhile his folk at home,
Unwitting of his doom, are washing dishes,
Blowing up fires with puffed cheeks, clattering
The greasy strigils,[1] laying towels ready,
Filling the flasks with oil. While thus his slaves
Are variously busied, he himself
Already is sitting on the banks of Styx,
A novice, shuddering at the grim ferryman,
With no hope of a passage in his boat
Across the muddy flood, no coin, poor ghost,
Between his teeth to tender for a fare.

Consider now these other various perils
That threaten us by night. That roof, from which
A tile may crash down on my skull, how high
It seems above us! How many times are cracked
Or broken crocks flung from the window! Look
With what a heavy blow they dint and bruise
The pavement! It may well be you'll be deemed
An easy-going fool, improvident
Of sudden accidents, if you should go out
To dinner intestate; for you have indeed
As many dangers to your life to fear

1. A curved instrument of metal, bone, or wood, used for scraping the body
after bathing.

As that night there are wakeful windows open
Beneath which you must pass. You can but hope,
And silently put up this piteous prayer
That they may be content to pour down on you
Nothing worse than great pailfuls of their slops.

To these many more reasons I could add
For my departure. But the mules are ready;
The sun sinks; I must start. The muleteer
Has long been signalling to me with his whip.
So farewell! Don't forget me. And every time
That, eager to recruit your health, you escape
From Rome to your Aquinum, send for me,
And I will come from Cumae to your Ceres
Helvina and your Diana.[1] In my thick boots
I'll visit your chilly country to hear your satires,
Unless they think me unworthy of that honour.

R. C. TREVELYAN (1940)

THE SAME

Most sick men here die from insomnia (of course
Their illness starts with food undigested, clogging
The burning stomach) – for in any rented room
Rest is impossible. It costs money to sleep in Rome.
There is the root of the sickness. The movement of heavy waggons
Through narrow streets, the oaths of stalled cattle-drovers
Would break the sleep of a deaf man or a lazy walrus.

GILBERT HIGHET (1957)

1. Juvenal's friend, who has here been telling him of the horrors of Rome, has earlier said that he is leaving to settle at Cumae in Campania. Ceres' epithet Helvina is unexplained; presumably she was worshipped under this name at Juvenal's native town Aquinum.

TACITUS

PUBLIUS (or GAIUS) CORNELIUS TACITUS is of uncertain name origin, and race.[1] Born in about A.D. 55, he held office in the black years of Domitian – whose persecution of senators drove iron into his soul – and the consulship under Nerva in 97; he was governor of Asia (western Anatolia) some fifteen years afterwards; he may or may not have survived Trajan (d. 117).

Tacitus was a distinguished public speaker, and his earliest extant work is often believed to be the *Dialogue on Orators* (discussing the decline of contemporary oratory). His historical monographs the *Agricola* (*De Vita Julii Agricolae*) and the *Germania* (*De Origine et Situ Germanorum*) were both published in about 98. The former is a eulogistic biography of his father-in-law – with descriptions of Britain, including cryptic references to Scotland; the *Germania* is an ethnographical and geographical study of central Europe.

His first major historical work, generally known as the *Histories* (its original title is uncertain), told the story of Rome from the death of Nero to the death of Domitian (A.D. 68–96). We have about a third of this work, describing the Civil Wars of 68–70. The book that we call the *Annals*, as indicated by its manuscript heading 'From the death of the divine Augustus', starts at A.D. 14. It carried the tale to the death of Nero; but his last two years, and portions of earlier reigns, are missing.

Missing, too, are the works of Tacitus' predecessors and models – if the latter term can be used of so markedly individual a writer. Tacitus' story is our earliest account, our most reliable account (despite all the prejudices of his complex soul), and indeed – in Latin – our only extensive, account, of this decisive period in the history of the western world. His haunting studies of Tiberius and his contemporaries, and of the Claudian and Neronian courts, are the supreme productions of Roman history.

Owing to the astonishing and abrupt astringency of his style he left no followers, and enjoyed little fame in antiquity or the Middle Ages.[2] His existence today depends upon a tenuous thread. We are dependent upon a single manuscript for Books I–VI of the *Annals*, and upon another

1. Possibly his family came from the south of France; possibly his father was imperial paymaster for the Rhine armies.

2. There was one great Latin historian after Tacitus, namely Ammianus Marcellinus (born *c.* 330 at Antioch), who wrote a history of the years from A.D. 96 to 378.

single manuscript for the other surviving half (Books xi–xvi) and for the five extant books of the *Histories*. Boccaccio seems to have known one of them, but it was not until the later fifteenth century that Tacitus' fame at last began to grow to sensational dimensions; his belief in the potentialities of the human spirit, even throughout the grimmest adversity, was a mighty contribution to humanism. The second of the two manuscripts, with the *Germania*, was published at Venice in about 1470, the *Agricola* in about 1482, and a complete edition of his surviving works at Rome in 1515. In 1581 came the first political commentary on Tacitus, by Charles Pascal. There were sixteenth-century translations, first into Spanish, then into Italian, French, and English (*Agricola* and *Histories* by Sir Henry Savile 1591, *Germania* and *Annals* by R. Greenway 1598). One of his greatest editors was Justus Lipsius (in the Low Countries, 1547–1606), author of an edition of Tacitus which was frequently reprinted: Lipsius offered to repeat any passage with a dagger at his chest, to be plunged into his body if his memory failed. Montaigne admired Tacitus – and so did Machiavelli. Partly because of this latter influence, Venetians early in the next century regarded Tacitus as too subversive for the publication of Boccalini's *Commentaries* to be permissible. Ben Jonson in *Sejanus His Fall* (acted 1603, published 1605) acknowledges his debt to the *Annals*.[1] Milton denounced the Frenchman Saumaize for interpreting Tacitus as a supporter of autocracy. Tacitus' influence is apparent in Corneille's *Othon*, in Racine's *Britannicus*, in Crébillon's *Rhadamiste et Zénobie*, in the writings of the French Revolutionaries and their forerunners (Rousseau and Mirabeau translated him), and in Alfieri's *Ottavia*. Napoleon wanted to correct his 'inaccuracies'. The French and English versions of Dureau de la Malle (1790) and Arthur Murphy (1793), though they seem inexact today, long remained the standard translations.

By 1837 the total number of English versions, to date, was at least 35; the total in all languages at least 393. 'There are a dozen plays on Nero,' notes M. Hadas; 'Sienkiewicz' *Quo Vadis*, and such contemporary novelists as Feuchtwanger in his Josephus stories and Robert Graves in his Claudius series, have long sections which are but adaptations of Tacitus.' Yet such is the difficulty of Tacitus' prose (not to speak of textual corruptions) that scholars have declared that he 'never has been translated, and probably never will be', and that he is 'the despair of the translator'.[2]

---

1. As well as to the other principal historical sources, Suetonius and the Greek Dio Cassius.
2. Church and Brodribb (1876), and Tyrrell (1908).

Who the first inhabitants of Britain were, whether natives or immigrants, remains obscure; one must remember we are dealing with barbarians. But physical characteristics vary, and that very variation is suggestive. The reddish hair and large limbs of the Caledonians proclaim a German origin, the swarthy faces of the Silures,[1] the tendency of their hair to curl and the fact that Spain lies opposite, all lead one to believe that Spaniards crossed in ancient times and occupied the land. The peoples nearest to the Gauls are correspondingly like them. Perhaps the original strain persists, perhaps it is climatic conditions that determine physical type in lands that converge from opposite directions on a single point. On a general estimate, however, we may believe that it was Gauls who took possession of the neighbouring island. In both countries you will find the same ritual, the same religious beliefs. There is no great difference in language, and there is the same hardihood in challenging danger, the same subsequent cowardice in shirking it. But the Britons show more spirit; they have not yet been softened by protracted peace. The Gauls, too, we have been told, had their hour of military glory; but then came decadence with peace, and valour went the way of lost liberty. The same fate has befallen such of the Britons as have long been conquered; the rest are still what the Gauls used to be.

Their strength is in their infantry. Some tribes also fight from chariots. The nobleman drives, his dependants fight in his defence. Once they owed obedience to kings; now they are distracted between the jarring factions of rival chiefs. Indeed, nothing has helped us more in war with their strongest nations than their inability to co-operate. It is but seldom that two or three States unite to repel a common danger; fighting in detail they are conquered wholesale. The climate is objectionable, with its frequent rains and mists, but there is no extreme cold. Their day is longer than is normal in the Roman world. The night is bright and, in the extreme North, short, with only a brief interval between evening and morning twilight. If no clouds block the view, the sun's glow, it is said, can be seen all night long. It does not set and rise, but simply passes along the horizon. The reason

1. In South Wales and Monmouthshire.

must be that the ends of the earth, being flat, cast low shadows and cannot raise the darkness to any height; night therefore fails to reach the sky and its stars. The soil can bear all produce, except the olive, the vine and other natives of warmer climes, and it is fertile. Crops are slow to ripen, but quick to grow – both facts due to one and the same cause, the extreme moistness of land and sky. Britain yields gold, silver, and other metals, to make it worth conquering. Ocean, too, has its pearls, but they are dusky and mottled. Some think that the natives are unskilful in gathering them. Whereas in the Red Sea the oysters are torn alive and breathing from the rocks, in Britain they are collected as the sea throws them up. I find it easier to believe in a defect of quality in the pearls than of greed in us.

The Britons themselves submit to the levy, the tribute, and the other charges of Empire with cheerful readiness, provided that there is no abuse. *That* they bitterly resent; for they are broken in to obedience, not to slavery. The deified Julius, the first Roman to enter Britain with an army, did indeed intimidate the natives by a victory and secure a grip on the coast.[1] But though perhaps he hinted to posterity how the island might be won, it was not his to bequeath. After him came the Civil Wars, with the leading men of Rome fighting against their country. Even when peace returned, Britain was long out of mind. The deified Augustus spoke of this as 'policy', Tiberius called it 'precedent'. Gaius Caesar (Caligula) unquestionably planned an invasion of Britain; but his quick fancies shifted like a weathercock, and his vast efforts against Germany ended in farce. The deified Claudius was responsible for reviving the plan.

HAROLD MATTINGLY (1948)

THE GERMANS

For myself I accept the view that the peoples of Germany have never been tainted by intermarriage with other peoples, and stand out as a nation peculiar, pure, and unique of its kind. Hence the physical type, if one may generalize at all about so vast a population, is everywhere the same – wild, blue eyes, reddish hair, and huge frames that excel only in violent effort. They have no corresponding power to endure

1. For Caesar's own account of his invasions, see above, p. 96.

hard work and exertion, and have little capacity to bear thirst and heat; but their climate and soil *have* taught them to bear cold and hunger.

When not engaged in warfare, they spend some little time in hunting, but more in idling, abandoned to sleep and gluttony. All the heroes and grim warriors dawdle their time away, while the care of house, hearth, and fields is left to the women, old men, and weaklings of the family. The warriors themselves lose their edge. They are so strangely inconsistent. They love indolence, but they hate peace. It is usual for States to make voluntary and individual contributions of cattle or agricultural produce to the chiefs. These are accepted as a token of honour, but serve also to relieve essential needs. The chiefs take peculiar pleasure in gifts from neighbouring States, such as are sent not only by individuals, but by the community as well – choice horses, splendid arms, metal discs and collars; the practice of accepting money payments they have now learnt – from us.

It is a well-known fact that the peoples of Germany never live in cities, and will not even have their houses set close together. They live apart, dotted here and there, where spring, plain, or grove has taken their fancy. Their villages are not laid out in Roman style, with buildings adjacent or interlocked. Every man leaves an open space round his house, perhaps as a precaution against the risk of fire, perhaps because they are such inexpert builders. They do not even make any use of little stone blocks or tiles; what serves their every purpose is ugly timber, both unimpressive and unattractive. They smear over some parts of their houses with an earth that is so pure and brilliant that it looks like painting or coloured mosaics. They have also the habit of hollowing out caves underground and heaping masses of refuse on the top. In these they can escape the winter's cold and store their produce. In such shelters they take the edge off the bitter frosts; and, should an invader come, he ravages the open country, but the secret and buried stores may pass altogether unnoticed or escape detection, simply because they have to be looked for.

A man is bound to take up the feuds as well as the friendships of father or kinsman. But feuds do not continue unreconciled. Even homicide can be atoned for by a fixed number of cattle or sheep, and the satisfaction is received by the whole family. This is much to the advantage of the community, for private feuds are peculiarly dangerous side by side with liberty.

No nation abandons itself more completely to banqueting and entertainment than the German. It is accounted a sin to turn any man away from your door. The host welcomes his guest with the best meal that his means allow. When supplies run out, the host takes on a fresh role; he directs and escorts his guest to a new hostelry. The two go on, uninvited, to the nearest house. It makes no difference; they are welcomed just as warmly. No distinction is ever made between acquaintance and stranger as far as the right to hospitality is concerned. As the guest takes his leave, it is usual to let him have anything he asks for; the host, too, is no more shy in asking. They take delight in presents, but ask no credit for giving them and admit no obligation in receiving them. There is a pleasant courtesy in the relations between host and guest.

As soon as they rise from their sleep, which is often protracted well into the day, they wash in water that is usually warm; can one wonder, where winter holds such sway? After washing, they breakfast; each has his special place and his special table. Then they sally forth in arms to business or, as often as not, to banquets. Drinking bouts, lasting a day and night, are not considered in any way disgraceful. Such quarrels as inevitably arise over the cups are seldom settled by mere hard words, more often by blows and wounds. None the less, they often make banquets an occasion for discussing such serious affairs as the reconciliation of enemies, the forming of marriage alliances, the adoption of new chiefs, and even the choice of peace or war. At no other time, they feel, is the heart so open to frank suggestions or so quick to warm to a great appeal. The Germans are neither canny nor cunning, and take advantage of the occasion to unbosom themselves of their most secret thoughts; every soul is naked and exposed. The next day comes reconsideration, and so due account is taken of both occasions. They debate at a time which cuts out pretence, they decide at a time that precludes mistake.

For drink they extract a juice from barley or grain, which is fermented to make something not unlike wine. The Germans who live nearest the Rhine can actually get wine in the market. Their food is plain – wild fruit, fresh game, or curdled milk. They satisfy their hunger without any elaborate service or appetizers. But they show no corresponding self-control in drinking. You have only to indulge their intemperance by supplying all that they crave, and you will gain as easy a victory through their vices as through your own arms.

HAROLD MATTINGLY (1948)

TIBERIUS WITHDRAWS TO CAPRI

Now, after long consideration and frequent postponements, Tiberius at last left for Campania. His ostensible purpose was the dedication of temples to Jupiter and Augustus at Capua and Nola respectively. But he had decided to live away from Rome. Like most historians, I attribute his withdrawal to the intrigues of his chief minister Sejanus. Yet, since he maintained this seclusion for six years after Sejanus' execution, I often wonder whether it was not really caused by a desire to hide the cruelty and immorality which his actions made all too conspicuous. It was also said that in old age he became sensitive about his appearance. Tall and abnormally thin, bent, and bald, he had a face covered with sores and often plaster. His retirement at Rhodes had accustomed him to unsociability and secretive pleasures.

According to another theory he was driven away by the bullying of his mother the Augusta (Livia); to share control with her seemed intolerable, to dislodge her impracticable – since that control had been given him by her. For Augustus had considered awarding the empire to his universally loved grand-nephew Germanicus. But his wife had induced him to adopt Tiberius instead.[*] The Augusta harped accusingly on this obligation – and exacted repayment.

Tiberius left with only a few companions – one senator and ex-consul,[†] one distinguished non-senator [‡] – and Sejanus. The rest were literary men, mostly Greeks whose conversation diverted him. The astrologers asserted that the conjunction of heavenly bodies under which he had left Rome precluded his return. This proved fatal to many who deduced, and proclaimed, that his end was near. For they did not foresee the unbelievable fact that his voluntary self-exile would last eleven years. Time was to show how narrow is the dividing-line between authentic prediction and imposture: truth is sur-

[*] Tiberius was made to adopt his nephew Germanicus.
[†] Marcus Cocceius Nerva the jurist.   [‡] Curtius Atticus.

rounded by mystery. For the assertion proved authentic – though he came to adjacent points of the countryside or on the coast, and often approached the city's very walls. But the prophets' foreknowledge was limited: for he lived to a great age.

A dangerous accident to Tiberius at this time stimulated idle gossip, and gave him reason for increased confidence in Sejanus' friendship and loyalty. While they were dining at a villa called The Cave – in a natural cavern between the sea at Amyclae and the hills of Fundi – there was a fall of rock at the cave-mouth. Several servants were crushed, and amid the general panic the diners fled. But Sejanus braced himself across Tiberius on hands and knees, keeping off the falling boulders. That is how the soldiers who rescued them found him. The incident increased Sejanus' power. Tiberius believed him disinterested, and listened trustingly to his advice, however disastrous.

Towards the family of the late Germanicus and his widow Agrippina the elder, Sejanus adopted the role of judge. Agents suborned as accusers were to direct their main onslaught against Germanicus' eldest son Nero Caesar, heir to the throne, who though youthfully unpretentious often forgot the care which the circumstances demanded. His ex-slaves and dependants, impatient for power, urged him to show vigour and confidence. Rome and the armies wanted it, they said, and no counter-strokes would be risked by Sejanus, whose targets were youthful timidity and senile passivity.

Nero Caesar listened. His intentions were harmless. But he sometimes made thoughtless, disrespectful remarks. Spies noted, reported, and exaggerated these, and he was given no opportunity to explain. People began to show disquiet in various ways. They avoided him, or turned away after greeting him, or, very often, broke off conversations abruptly. Sejanus' partisans stood and watched, sneering. Tiberius treated Nero Caesar grimly, or smiled insincerely – the young man seemed equally guilty whether he spoke or remained silent. Even night-time was not safe. For whether he slept, or lay awake, or sighed, his wife told her mother, and the mother reported it to Sejanus. Sejanus even made an accomplice of the young man's brother Drusus Caesar – tempting him with supreme power if only he could eliminate his already undermined elder brother. Drusus Caesar's degraded character was animated by power-lust and the usual hatred between brothers – also jealousy, because his mother

Agrippina preferred Nero Caesar. But Sejanus' cultivation of Drusus Caesar did not exclude plans to begin his destruction too, since the youth, as he knew, was hot-headed and could be trapped.

Tiberius was dedicating the temples in Campania. He issued an edict forbidding the disturbance of his privacy, and troops were posted in the towns to prevent crowds. He detested these towns, and indeed the whole mainland. So he took refuge on the island of Capri, separated from the tip of the Sorrento promontory by three miles of sea. Presumably what attracted him was the isolation of Capri. Harbourless, it has few roadsteads even for small vessels; sentries can control all landings. In winter the climate is mild, since hills on the mainland keep off gales. In summer the island is delightful, since it faces west and has open sea all round. The bay it overlooks was exceptionally lovely, until Vesuvius' eruption transformed the landscape.*

Here in Capri, in twelve spacious, separately named villas, Tiberius settled. His former absorption in State affairs ended. Instead he spent the time in secret orgies, or idle, malevolent thoughts. But his abnormally credulous suspicions were unabated. Sejanus, who had encouraged them even at Rome, whipped them up, and now openly disclosed his designs against Agrippina and Nero Caesar. Soldiers attached to them reported with a historian's precision their correspondence, visitors, and doings private and public. Agents advised them to take refuge with the armies of Germany, or, in the Forum – at its most crowded time of day – to grasp the statue of the divine Augustus and appeal to Senate and public.

The next year began deplorably. A distinguished gentleman outside the Senate called Titius Sabinus was dragged to gaol because he had been Germanicus' friend. Sabinus had maintained every attention to Germanicus' widow and children, visiting their home, escorting them in public – of their crowds of followers he was the only survivor. Decent men respected this, but spiteful people hated him. His downfall was planned by four ex-praetors ambitious for the consulship. For the only access to this lay through Sejanus; and only crimes secured Sejanus' goodwill.

The four arranged that, with the others present as witnesses, one of

* This was an area of Greek colonization, and tradition records that Capri had been occupied by the Teleboi.

them, Latinius Latiaris * (who knew Sabinus slightly) should trap him with a view to prosecution. So Latiaris, after some casual remarks, complimented Sabinus on his unshaken adherence, in its misfortunes, to the family he had supported in its prosperity – and he commented respectfully about Germanicus, sympathetically about Agrippina. Sabinus burst into tearful complaints; for misery is demoralizing. Latiaris then openly attacked Sejanus as cruel, domineering, and ambitious – and did not even spare Tiberius. These exchanges of forbidden confidences seemed to cement a close friendship. So now Sabinus sought out Latiaris' company, frequenting his house and unburdening his sorrows to this outwardly reliable companion.

The four partners next considered how to make these conversations available to a larger audience. The meeting-place had to appear private. Even if they stood behind the doors, they risked being seen or heard or detected by some chance suspicion. So the three senators wedged themselves between roof and ceiling. In this hiding-place – as undignified as the trick was despicable – they applied their ears to chinks and holes. Meanwhile Latiaris had found Sabinus out of doors and, pretending to have fresh news to report, escorted him home to Sabinus' bedroom. There Latiaris dwelt on the unfailing subject of past and present distresses, introducing some fresh terrors too. Sabinus embroidered at greater length on the same theme; once grievances find expression, there is no silencing them. Acting rapidly, the accusers wrote to Tiberius and disclosed the history of the trap and their own deplorable role. At Rome there was unprecedented agitation and terror. People behaved secretively even to their intimates, avoiding encounters and conversation, shunning the ears both of friends and strangers. Even voiceless, inanimate objects – ceilings and walls – were scanned suspiciously.

In a letter read in the Senate on 1 January Tiberius, after the customary New Year formalities, rounded upon Sabinus, alleging that he had tampered with certain of the emperor's ex-slaves and plotted against his life. The letter unequivocally demanded retribution. This was hastily decreed. The condemned man was dragged away, crying (as loudly as the cloak muffling his mouth and the noose round his neck allowed) that this was a fine New Year ceremony – this year's sacrifice was to Sejanus! But wherever his eye rested or his words

* The others were Marcus Porcius Cato, Petilius Rufus, and Marcus Opsius.

carried, there was a stampede: all roads and public places were evacuated and deserted. Some, however, reappeared and showed themselves again: alarmed because they had displayed alarm. For it seemed that no day would be free of convictions when, at a season in which custom forbade even an ominous word, sacrifices and prayers were attended by manacles and nooses. Tiberius had incurred this indignation deliberately, people said – it was a purposeful, premeditated action to show that the newly elected officials who opened the religious year could also open the death-cells.

The emperor wrote again, thanking the Senate for punishing a public danger, and adding that he had grave anxieties and reasons to suspect disaffected persons of plotting. He mentioned no names. But Nero Caesar and Agrippina were undoubtedly meant. If I did not propose to record each event under its own year, I should have liked to anticipate and recount immediately the fates of the four criminal plotters against Sabinus – partly in the reign of Gaius (Caligula), and partly also under Tiberius. For Tiberius, unwilling though he was for others to destroy his villainous agents, frequently wearied of them and, when new recruits became available, eliminated their distasteful predecessors. However, this punishment of guilty men – and other similar cases – I shall describe at the proper time.

Gaius Asinius Gallus, of whose children Agrippina was aunt, now proposed that the emperor should indicate his fears to the Senate, and permit their removal. Now of all his self-ascribed virtues Tiberius cherished none more dearly than dissimulation. So he greatly disliked disclosing what he had suppressed. However Sejanus calmed him, not from affection for Gallus, but to let the emperor's hesitations take their course. For, as Sejanus knew, Tiberius reached decisions slowly, but once the outburst occurred there was a rapid transition from grim words to terrible action.

MICHAEL GRANT (1956)

TWO POISONING CASES

Agrippina the younger [1] had long decided to murder her husband, the Emperor Claudius. Now she saw her opportunity. Her agents were

1. Daughter of Germanicus and Agrippina the elder, and mother of Nero, whom Claudius had adopted as heir in preference to his own son Britannicus.

ready. But she wanted advice about poisons. A sudden, drastic effect would give her away. A gradual, wasting recipe might make Claudius, faced with death, love his son again. What was needed was something subtle that would upset the emperor's faculties but produce a deferred fatal effect. An expert in such matters was selected – a woman called Locusta, recently sentenced for poisoning, but with a long career of imperial service ahead of her. By her talents, a preparation was supplied. It was administered by a eunuch * who habitually served the emperor and tasted his food.

Later, the whole story became known. Contemporary writers stated that the poison was sprinkled on a particularly succulent mushroom. But because Claudius was torpid – or drunk – its effect was not at first apparent; and an evacuation of his bowels seemed to have saved him. Agrippina was horrified. But when the ultimate stakes are so alarmingly large, immediate disrepute is brushed aside. She had already secured the complicity of the emperor's doctor Xenophon; and now she called him in. The story is that, while pretending to help Claudius to vomit, he put a feather dipped in a quick poison down his throat. Xenophon knew that major crimes, though hazardous to undertake, are profitable to achieve.

The Senate was summoned. Consuls and priests offered prayers for the emperor's safety. But meanwhile his already lifeless body was being wrapped in blankets and poultices. Moreover, the appropriate steps were being taken to secure the accession of Agrippina's son Nero. First Agrippina, with heart-broken demeanour, clutched to her bosom Britannicus (Claudius' son by his previous marriage) – as though to draw comfort from him. He was the very image of his father, she declared. By various devices she prevented him from leaving his room, and likewise detained his sisters, Claudia Antonia and Octavia. Blocking every approach with guards, Agrippina issued frequent encouraging announcements about the emperor's health, to maintain the army's morale and await the propitious moment forecast by the astrologers.

At last, at midday on 13 October, the palace gates were suddenly thrown open. Attended by Sextus Afranius Burrus, commander of the Guard, out came Nero to the battalion which, in accordance with regulations, was on duty. At a word from its commander, he was

* His name was Halotus.

389

cheered and put in a litter. Some of the men are said to have looked round hesitantly and asked where Britannicus was. However, as no counter-suggestion was made, they accepted the choice offered them. Nero was then conducted into the Guards' camp. There, after saying a few words appropriate to the occasion – and promising gifts on the generous standard set by his father – he was hailed as emperor. The army's decision was followed by senatorial decrees. The provinces, too, showed no hesitation.

Claudius was voted divine honours, and his funeral was modelled on that of the divine Augustus – Agrippina imitating the grandeur of her great-grandmother Livia, the first Augusta. But Claudius' will was not read, in case his preference of stepson to son should create a public impression of unfairness and injustice.

(*A few months pass.*)

Nero was worried. As the day of his stepbrother Britannicus' fourteenth birthday approached, he pondered on the violent behaviour of his mother Agrippina – also on Britannicus' character, lately revealed by a small indication which had gained him wide popularity. During the amusements of the Saturnalia the young men had thrown dice for who should be king, and Nero had won. To the others he gave various orders causing no embarrassment. But he commanded Britannicus to get up and come into the middle and sing a song. Nero hoped for laughter at the boy's expense, since Britannicus was not accustomed even to sober parties, much less to drunken ones. But Britannicus composedly sang a poem implying his displacement from his father's home and throne. This aroused sympathy – and in the frank atmosphere of a nocturnal party, it was unconcealed. Nero noticed the feeling against himself, and hated Britannicus all the more.

Though upset by Agrippina's threats, he could not find a charge against his stepbrother or order his execution openly. Instead, he decided to act secretly – and ordered poison to be prepared. Arrangements were entrusted to a colonel of the Guard * who was in charge of the notorious convicted poisoner Locusta. It had earlier been ensured that Britannicus' attendants should be unscrupulous and disloyal. His tutors first administered the poison. But it was evacuated, being either too weak or too diluted for prompt effectiveness. Impatient at the slowness of the murder, Nero browbeat the colonel and

* Julius Pollio.

ordered Locusta to be tortured. They thought of nothing but public opinion, he complained; they safeguarded themselves and regarded his security as a secondary consideration. Then they swore that they would produce effects as rapid as any sword-stroke; and in a room adjoining Nero's bedroom, from well-tried poisons, they concocted a mixture.

It was the custom for young imperial princes to eat with other noblemen's children of the same age at a special, less luxurious table, before the eyes of their relations; that is where Britannicus dined. A selected servant habitually tasted his food and drink. But the murderers thought of a way of leaving this custom intact without giving themselves away by a double death. Britannicus was handed a harmless drink. The taster had tasted it; but Britannicus found it too hot, and refused it. Then cold water containing the poison was added. Speechless, his whole body convulsed, he instantly ceased to breathe.

His companions were horrified. Some, uncomprehending, fled. Others, understanding better, remained rooted in their places, staring at Nero. He still lay back unconcernedly – and he remarked that this often happened to epileptics; that Britannicus had been one since infancy; soon his sight and consciousness would return. Agrippina tried to control her features. But their evident consternation and terror showed that, like Britannicus' sister Octavia, she knew nothing. Agrippina realized that her last support was gone. And here was Nero murdering a relation. But Octavia, young though she was, had learnt to hide sorrow, affection, every feeling. After a short silence the banquet continued.

Britannicus was cremated the night he died. Indeed, preparations for his inexpensive funeral had already been made. As his remains were placed in the imperial mausoleum, there was a violent storm. It was widely believed that the gods were showing their fury at the boy's murder – though even his fellow-men generally condoned it, arguing that brothers were traditional enemies and that the empire was indivisible.

MICHAEL GRANT (1956)

Nero had come to the conclusion that wherever his mother Agrippina was she was intolerable. He decided to kill her. His only doubt was whether to employ poison, or the dagger, or violence of some other kind. Poison was the first choice. But a death at the emperor's table would not look fortuitous after Britannicus had died there. Yet her criminal conscience kept her so alert for plots that it seemed impracticable to corrupt her household. Moreover, she had strengthened her physical resistance by a preventive course of antidotes. No one could think of a way of stabbing her without detection. Besides, there was the danger that the selected assassin might shrink from carrying out his dreadful orders.

However, a scheme was put forward by Anicetus, an ex-slave who commanded the fleet at Miseno in Campania.[1] In Nero's boyhood Anicetus had been his tutor; he and Agrippina hated each other. A ship could be made, he now said, with a section which would come loose at sea and hurl Agrippina into the water without warning. Nothing is so productive of surprises as the sea, remarked Anicetus; if a shipwreck did away with her, who could be so unreasonable as to blame a human agency instead of wind and water? Besides, when she was dead the emperor could allot her a temple and altars and the other public tokens of filial duty.

This ingenious plan found favour. The time of year, too, was suitable, since Nero habitually attended the festival of Minerva at Baiae. Now he enticed his mother there. 'Parents' tempers must be borne!' he kept announcing. 'One must humour their feelings.' This was to create the general impression that they were friends again, and to produce the same effect on Agrippina. For women are naturally inclined to believe welcome news.

As she arrived from Anzio,[2] Nero met her at the shore. After welcoming her with outstretched hands and embraces, he conducted her to Bauli, a mansion on the bay between Cape Miseno and the waters of Baiae. Some ships were standing there. One, more sumptuous than the rest, was evidently another compliment to his mother, who had

1. Roman naval base on the northern headland of the Bay of Naples. The fashionable resort of Baiae lay about three miles along the coast.
2. Birthplace of Nero as well as of Caligula.

formerly been accustomed to travel in warships manned by the imperial navy. Then she was invited out to dinner. The crime was to take place on the ship under cover of darkness. But an informer, it was said, gave the plot away; Agrippina could not decide whether to believe the story, and preferred a sedan-chair as her conveyance to Baiae.

There her alarm was relieved by Nero's attentions. He received her kindly, and gave her the place of honour next himself. The party went on for a long time. They talked about various things; Nero was boyish and intimate – or confidentially serious. When she left, he saw her off, gazing into her eyes and clinging to her. This may have been a final piece of shamming – or perhaps even Nero's brutal heart was affected by his last sight of his mother, going to her death.

But heaven seemed determined to reveal the crime. For it was a quiet, star-lit night and the sea was calm. The ship began to go on its way. Agrippina was attended by two of her friends. One of them, Crepereius Gallus, stood near the tiller. The other, Acerronia, leant over the feet of her resting mistress, happily talking about Nero's remorseful behaviour and his mother's re-established influence. Then came the signal. Under the pressure of heavy lead weights, the roof fell in. Crepereius was crushed, and died instantly. Agrippina and Acerronia were saved by the raised sides of their couch, which happened to be strong enough to resist the pressure. Moreover, the ship held together.

In the general confusion, those in the conspiracy were hampered by the many who were not. But then some of the oarsmen had the idea of throwing their weight on one side, to capsize the ship. However, they took too long to concert this improvised plan, and meanwhile others brought weight to bear in the opposite direction. This provided the opportunity to make a gentler descent into the water. Acerronia ill-advisedly started crying out, 'I am Agrippina! Help, help the emperor's mother!' She was struck dead by blows from poles and oars and whatever ship's gear happened to be available. Agrippina herself kept quiet and avoided recognition. Though she was hurt – she had a wound in the shoulder – she swam until she came to some sailing-boats. They brought her to the Lucrine lake,[1] from which she was taken home.

1. Between Baiae and the great commercial port of Pozzuoli (Puteoli) on the way to Naples.

There she realized that the invitation and special compliment had been treacherous, and the collapse of her ship planned. The collapse had started at the top, like a stage-contrivance. The shore was close by, there had been no wind, no rock to collide with. Acerronia's death and her own wound also invited reflection. Agrippina decided that the only escape from the plot was to profess ignorance of it. She sent an ex-slave Agerinus to tell her son that by divine mercy and his lucky star she had survived a serious accident. The messenger was to add, however, that despite anxiety about his mother's dangerous experience Nero must not yet trouble to visit her – at present rest was what she needed. Meanwhile, pretending unconcern, she cared for her wound and physical condition generally. She also ordered Acerronia's will to be found and her property sealed. Here alone no pretence was needed.

To Nero, awaiting news that the crime was done, came word that she had escaped with a slight wound – after hazards which left no doubt of their instigator's identity. Half-dead with fear, he insisted she might arrive at any moment. 'She may arm her slaves! She may whip up the army, or gain access to the Senate or Assembly, and incriminate me for wrecking and wounding her and killing her friends! What can I do to save myself?' Could his chief advisers Burrus and Seneca [1] help? Whether they were in the plot is uncertain. But they were immediately awakened and summoned.

For a long time neither spoke. They did not want to dissuade and be rejected. They may have felt matters had gone so far that Nero had to strike before Agrippina, or die. Finally, Seneca ventured so far as to turn to Burrus and ask if the troops should be ordered to kill her. He replied that the Guard were devoted to the whole imperial house and to the memory of Agrippina's father Germanicus; they would commit no violence against his offspring. Anicetus, he said, must make good his promise. Anicetus unhesitatingly claimed the direction of the crime. Hearing him Nero cried that this was the first day of his reign – and the magnificent gift came from a former slave! 'Go quickly!' he said. 'And take men who obey orders scrupulously!'

Agrippina's messenger arrived. When Nero was told, he took the initiative, and staged a fictitious incrimination. While Agerinus de-

---

1. Burrus was joint commander of the Praetorian Guard. For Seneca, see above, p. 288.

livered his message, Nero dropped a sword at the man's feet and had him arrested as if caught red-handed. Then he could pretend that his mother had plotted against the emperor's life, been detected, and – in shame – committed suicide.

Meanwhile Agrippina's perilous adventure had become known. It was believed to be accidental. As soon as people heard of it they ran to the beach, and climbed on to the embankment, or fishing-boats nearby. Others waded out as far as they could, or waved their arms. The whole shore echoed with wails and prayers and the din of all manner of inquiries and ignorant answers. Huge crowds gathered with lights. When she was known to be safe, they prepared to make a show of rejoicing.

But a menacing armed column arrived and dispersed them. Anicetus surrounded her house and broke in. Arresting every slave in his path, he came to her bedroom door. Here stood a few servants – the rest had been frightened away by the invasion. In her dimly lit room a single maid waited with her. Agrippina's alarm had increased as nobody, not even Agerinus, came from her son. If things had been well there would not be this terribly ominous isolation, then this sudden uproar. Her maid vanished. 'Are you leaving me, too?' called Agrippina. Then she saw Anicetus. Behind him were a naval captain and lieutenant.* 'If you have come to visit me,' she said, 'you can report that I am better. But if you are assassins, I know my son is not responsible. He did not order his mother's death!' The murderers closed round her bed. First the captain hit her on the head with a truncheon. Then, as the lieutenant was drawing his sword to finish her off, she cried out: 'Strike here!' – pointing to her womb. Blow after blow fell, and she died.

So far accounts agree. Some add that Nero inspected his mother's corpse and praised her figure; but that is contested. She was cremated that night, on a dining-couch, with meagre ceremony. While Nero reigned, her grave was not covered with earth or enclosed, though later her household gave her a modest tomb beside the road to Miseno, on the heights where Julius Caesar's mansion overlooks the bay beneath. During the cremation one of her former slaves, Mnester, stabbed himself to death. Either he loved his patroness, or he feared assassination.

* Their names were Herculeius and Obaritus.

This was the end which Agrippina had anticipated for years. The prospect had not daunted her. When she asked astrologers about Nero, they had answered that he would become emperor, but kill his mother. Her reply was, 'Let him kill me – provided he becomes emperor!' But Nero only understood the horror of his crime when it was done. For the rest of the night, witless and speechless, he alternately lay paralysed and leapt to his feet in terror – waiting for the dawn which he thought would be his last. Hope began to return to him when at Burrus' suggestion the colonels and captains of the Guard came and cringed to him, with congratulatory handshakes for his escape from the unexpected menace of his mother's evil activities. Nero's friends crowded to the temples. Campanian towns nearby followed their lead and displayed joy by sacrifices and deputations.

Nero's insincerity took a different form. He adopted a gloomy demeanour, as though sorry to be safe and mourning for his parent's death. But the features of the countryside are less adaptable than those of men; and Nero's gaze could not escape the dreadful view of that sea and shore. Besides, the coast echoed (it was said) with trumpet blasts from the neighbouring hills – and wails from his mother's grave. So Nero departed to Naples.

MICHAEL GRANT (1956)

THE GREAT FIRE

Nero's excesses were overtaken by disaster. Whether it was accidental or caused by the emperor's criminal act is uncertain – both versions have supporters. Now started the most terrible and destructive fire which Rome had ever experienced. It began in the Circus, where it adjoins the Palatine and Caelian hills. Breaking out in shops selling inflammable goods, and fanned by the wind, the conflagration instantly grew and swept the whole length of the Circus. There were no walled mansions or temples, or any other obstructions which could arrest it. First, the fire swept violently over the level spaces. Then it climbed the hills – but returned to ravage the lower ground again. It outstripped every counter-measure. The ancient city's narrow winding streets and irregular blocks encouraged its progress.

Terrified, shrieking women, helpless old and young, people intent on their own safety, people unselfishly supporting invalids or waiting for them, fugitives and lingerers alike – all heightened the confusion. When people looked back, menacing flames sprang up before them or outflanked them. When they escaped to a neighbouring quarter, the fire followed – even districts believed remote proved to be involved. Finally, with no idea where or what to flee, they crowded on to the country roads, or lay in the fields. Some who had lost everything – even their food for the day – could have escaped, but preferred to die. So did others, who had failed to rescue their loved ones. Nobody dared fight the flames. Attempts to do so were prevented by menacing gangs. Torches, too, were openly thrown in, by men crying that they acted under orders. Perhaps they had received orders. Or they may just have wanted to plunder unhampered.

Nero was at Anzio. He only returned to the city when the fire was approaching the mansion he had built to link the Gardens of Maecenas to the Palatine. The flames could not be prevented from overwhelming the whole of the Palatine, including his palace. Nevertheless, for the relief of the homeless, fugitive masses he threw open the Field of Mars, including Agrippa's public buildings, and even his own Gardens. Nero also constructed emergency accommodation for the destitute multitude. Food was brought from Ostia and neighbouring towns, and the price of corn was cut.* Yet these measures, for all their popular character, earned no gratitude. For a rumour had spread that, while the city was burning, Nero had gone on his private stage and, comparing modern calamities with ancient, had sung of the destruction of Troy.

By the sixth day enormous demolitions had confronted the raging flames with bare ground and open sky, and the fire was finally stamped out.† But before panic had subsided, or hope revived, flames broke out again in the more open regions of the city. Here there were fewer casualties; but the destruction of temples and pleasure arcades was even worse. This new conflagration caused additional ill-feeling because it started on Tigellinus' [1] estate.‡ For people believed that Nero was ambitious to found a new city to be called after himself.

* To less than ¼ sesterce a pound.   † At the foot of the Esquiline Hill.
‡ In the Aemilian district.
1. Tigellinus, a former horse-dealer, was Nero's chief adviser and Commander of the Guard.

Of Rome's fourteen districts only four remained intact. Three were levelled to the ground. The other seven were reduced to a few scorched and mangled ruins. To count the mansions, blocks, and temples destroyed would be difficult. They included shrines of remote antiquity,★ the precious spoils of countless victories, Greek artistic masterpieces, and authentic records of old Roman genius. All the splendour of the rebuilt city did not prevent the older generation from remembering these irreplaceable objects. It was noted that the fire had started on 19 July, the day on which the Senonian Gauls had captured and burnt the city (390 B.C.).†

But Nero profited by his country's ruin to build a new palace. Its wonders were not so much customary and commonplace luxuries like gold and jewels, but lawns and lakes and faked rusticity – woods here, open spaces and views there. With their cunning, impudent artificialities, Nero's architects and contractors ‡ outbid Nature.

They also fooled away an emperor's riches. For they promised to dig a navigable canal from Lake Avernus to the Tiber estuary, over the stony shore and mountain barriers. The only water to feed the canal was in the Pontine marshes. Elsewhere, all was precipitous or waterless. Moreover, even if a passage could have been forced, the labour would have been unendurable and unjustified. But Nero was eager to perform the incredible; so he attempted to excavate the hills adjoining Lake Avernus. Traces of his frustrated hopes are visible today.

In parts of Rome unfilled by Nero's palace, construction was not – as after the burning by the Gauls – without plan or demarcation. Street-fronts were of regulated dimensions and alignment, streets were broad, and houses spacious. Their height was restricted, and their frontages protected by colonnades. Nero undertook to erect these at his own expense, and also to clear debris from building-sites before transferring them to their owners. He announced bonuses, in proportion to rank and resources, for the completion of houses and blocks

★ Among the losses were Tullius' temple of the Moon, the Great Altar and holy place dedicated by Evander to Hercules, the temple vowed by Romulus to Jupiter and Stayer, Numa's sacred residence, and Vesta's shrine containing Rome's household gods.

† Others elaborately calculated that the two fires were separated by the same number of years, months, and days.

‡ Their names were Severus and Celer.

before a given date. Rubbish was to be dumped in the Ostian marshes by corn-ships returning down the Tiber.

A fixed proportion of every building had to be massive, untimbered stone from Gabii or Alba (these stones being fireproof). Furthermore, guards were to ensure a more abundant and extensive public water-supply, hitherto diminished by irregular private enterprise. Householders were obliged to keep fire-fighting apparatus in an accessible place; and semi-detached houses were forbidden – they must have their own walls. These measures were welcomed for their practicality; and they beautified the new city. Some, however, believed that the old town's configuration had been healthier, since its narrow streets and high houses had provided protection against the burning sun, whereas now the shadowless open spaces radiated a fiercer heat.

So much for human precautions. Next came attempts to appease heaven. After consultation of the Sibylline books, prayers were addressed to Vulcan, Ceres, and Proserpina; Juno, too, was propitiated.[1] But neither human resources, nor imperial munificence, nor appeasement of the gods, eliminated sinister suspicions that the fire had been instigated. To suppress this rumour, Nero fabricated scapegoats – and punished with every refinement the notoriously depraved Christians (as they were popularly called). Their originator, Christ, had been executed in Tiberius' reign by the governor of Judaea, Pontius Pilatus. But in spite of this temporary setback the deadly superstition had broken out afresh, not only in Judaea (where the mischief had started) but even in Rome. All degraded and shameful practices collect and flourish in the capital.

First, Nero had self-acknowledged Christians arrested. Then, on their information, large numbers of others were condemned – not so much for incendiarism as for their anti-social tendencies. Their deaths were made farcical. Dressed in wild animals' skins, they were torn to pieces by dogs, or crucified, or made into torches to be ignited after dark as substitutes for daylight. Nero provided his Gardens for the spectacle, and exhibited displays in the Circus, at which he mingled with the crowd – or stood in a chariot, dressed as a charioteer. Despite

1. By women who had been married – first on the Capitol, then at the nearest sea-board, where water was taken to sprinkle her temple and statue. Women with husbands living also celebrated ritual banquets and vigils.

their guilt as Christians, and the ruthless punishment it deserved, the victims were pitied. For it was felt that they were being sacrificed to one man's brutality rather than to the national interest.

MICHAEL GRANT (1956)

THE EMPIRE AFTER NERO'S DEATH

I am now coming to an epoch teeming with calamities, drenched in bloodshed, shattered by fighting. Even peace was full of horrors. Four emperors met violent deaths. There were three civil wars, foreign wars in greater number – and wars that were civil and foreign at the same time.* Italy, too, was smitten with catastrophes unknown for many centuries or wholly unprecedented. The supremely fertile coast of Campania had its cities engulfed and overwhelmed by Vesuvius. Rome itself was ravaged by fires. Her most antique shrines were destroyed; the Capitol itself was gutted – by Roman hands. Sacred rites were profaned. Adultery proliferated in high places. Exiles were thick upon the sea, and its rocks were polluted with murdered corpses.

In the capital there were grimmer brutalities. Birth, wealth, acceptance of office, refusal of office – all of these were indiscriminately labelled as crimes. But the surest path to ruin was a fine record. The rewards gained by informers were in proportion to the horrors they committed. Consulships and priesthoods were among their loot; others became imperial agents, or by their influence behind the scenes caused ruin far and wide, amid execration and terror. Bribery made slaves betray their masters, ex-slaves their patrons. Even if men had no enemies, they were destroyed – by their friends.

And yet this period was not completely unproductive of goodness: there was no lack of glorious examples. Refugees were helped by their mothers, exiles by their wives. Men's relatives, sons-in-law, bravely, intrepidly supported them; slaves showed loyalty that even torture

---

* During this period (A.D. 68–96) there was success in the East, disaster in the West. Illyricum revolted. The Gallic provinces wavered. Britain was conquered – but at once abandoned. The Sarmatian and Suebian tribes rose. The Dacians gained glory from their battles against us – whether they were victories or defeats. Even the Parthians were almost provoked to war by the fabrications of a man who pretended to be Nero.

could not undermine. Famous men met their dooms with courage, dying worthily of the admired deaths of old.

Besides this accumulation of disasters upon humanity, the heavens and the earth displayed their portents. Warnings were brought by thunderbolts. There were prophecies of the future – some helpful, others grim; some ambiguous, others clear. For never have there been more terrible Roman disasters, more unmistakable proofs that it is not our safety which interests the gods but our punishment.

Before beginning my allotted task, I ought to indicate the circumstances that prevailed in Rome at that time – and the temper of the armies, the attitudes of the provincials, and the factors that made for strength and weakness throughout the world. I shall try to describe not only the actual succession of events – which is frequently due to chance – but their underlying causes too.

Nero's end [1] was at first received with joyful demonstrations. Yet it roused mixed emotions both in the capital – among the senators, populace, and garrison – and in the army and its commanders in the field. For the State secret was out: emperors could be made outside Rome. Nevertheless, the senators were happy; and their ruler being both new and absent, they instantly exploited their freedom to the full. The principal non-senators were almost as pleased as the Senate. Optimism was also felt by the more respectable sections of the public, including those associated with the aristocratic families – and also by the dependants and former slaves of those in exile. But there was depression and hungry gossip among the riff-raff – the circus- and theatre-addicts – and among the more disreputable slaves and the ruined men whom Nero had discreditably maintained.

The metropolitan garrison, schooled in loyalty to the Caesars, had been induced to abandon Nero by ingeniously exercised pressure rather than by their own inclinations. Now, however, they understood the situation – the bonus promised in Galba's name was not forthcoming; the services and rewards of peace were insignificant compared to those of war; and they were forestalled, in Galba's favour, by the army that had made him emperor. Their rebellious feelings were whipped up by Gaius Nymphidius Sabinus, Commander of the Guard; for he was criminally intriguing to win the empire for

1. The Senate and people of Rome had risen against him in summer, A.D. 68, in favour of Galba, governor of Nearer Spain.

himself. Though the attempt cost Nymphidius his life, and so the seditious movement lost its leader, many soldiers had a guilty conscience. Besides, there was abundant comment on Galba's meanness and senility. The men had once respected and admired his strictness. Now, in their reaction against old-fashioned discipline, they found it infuriating; for Nero's fourteen-year reign had taught them to love emperors' defects just as they had once revered their merits. Besides, there was Galba saying: 'I choose my soldiers; I do not buy them' – a praiseworthy sentiment from a national viewpoint, but perilous for himself; and it did not fit into the picture.

Galba was old and ineffective, and his advisers Titus Vinius and Cornelius Laco were his ruin. The one was an utterly degraded character, the other completely lazy. Vinius' crimes and Laco's inertness provoked disgust – which recoiled on Galba. His advance on Rome had been slow and bloody. He had killed Cingonius Varro, consul designate, as an accomplice of Nymphidius, and the ex-consul Petronius Turpilianus as one of Nero's generals. Dying unheard, undefended, they passed for innocent men.

After his massacre of thousands of unarmed soldiers, Galba's entrance into the capital made a sinister impression; it inspired even the perpetrators with forebodings. A brigade had been brought from Spain. Another that Nero had raised from the navy remained in Rome. There were many other units too.* The capital was full of strange troops; here was abundant revolutionary material. But the soldiers were not particularly inclined towards any one leader: whoever was daring enough would have them at his disposal.

MICHAEL GRANT (1956)

THE PSYCHOLOGY OF CIVIL WAR

Certain writers have recorded (I find) that these two armies of Otho and Vitellius,[1] afraid of fighting or disgusted by their leaders (whose

---

* These had come from Germany, Britain, and Illyricum. Selected by Nero, they had been dispatched to the Dariel Pass over the Caucasus for the campaign he was planning against the Albani. But he had recalled them to suppress the rebellion of Vindex.

1. Otho had murdered and succeeded Galba on 15 January A.D. 69, but

shameful criminality was becoming more notorious every day), considered the possibility of stopping the war and discussing matters together, or allowing the Senate to select an emperor. That, it was said, was why Otho's generals advised delay; among their number Suetonius Paulinus was the one who particularly hoped to be chosen, since he was the senior ex-consul and a distinguished commander who had won great prestige in his British campaigns.[1]

Now I will grant that a few soldiers may privately have preferred peace to fighting, and a good, blameless emperor to utterly depraved ruffians. But I do not believe that a man with the sense of Paulinus, living in times so corrupt, can have believed that public opinion was so enlightened, or that the men whose love of war had broken the peace would become so peace-loving that they stopped the war. There was no possibility, in my view, that armies differing so strongly in speech and customs should come to such an agreement, or that generals and commanders who were mostly well aware of their own extravagant, penurious, and criminal records would tolerate any emperor except a completely degraded rascal who was at their disposal owing to the services they had done him.

Lust for power is ancient and ingrained in the human soul. It had grown to full stature, and broken out, when the Empire became great. After the conquest of the world and the elimination of rival cities and monarchs, Romans had become free to covet the safe possession of wealth. Then started the first quarrels between patricians and plebeians. Next came trouble-making tribunes, overbearing consuls; the capital and the Forum witnessed our first essays in civil war.

Later, freedom had been forcibly eliminated by the humble proletarian Marius and the merciless nobleman Sulla: in its place they put tyranny. After them came Pompey, not a better man than they, but a better hypocrite. Thereafter, what men always competed for was autocratic power. The Roman citizens in their brigades at Pharsalia

Vitellius, governor of Lower Germany, who had been hailed emperor on 2 January, marched south against him. Before his arrival his generals won the battle of Bedriacum (22 miles east of Cremona) against Otho, who committed suicide.

1. He had invaded Anglesey and stamped out Druidism there, and then suppressed the revolt of Boudicca (Boadicea) (A.D.61).

and Philippi [1] did not lay down their weapons; much less were the armies of Otho and Vitellius likely to put an end to the war spontaneously. The same divine anger, the same human mania, the same incentives to crime, drove them into battle. True, each of these wars was practically ended by a single blow; but that was because of the worthlessness of the emperors.

MICHAEL GRANT (1956)

VITELLIUS' MARCH ON ROME AFTER THE VICTORY [2]

Every day Vitellius behaved more sluggishly – and aroused greater contempt. Stopping to enjoy the attractions of every town and mansion on the way, he gradually approached Rome with his ponderous entourage. Following him were sixty thousand demoralized soldiers, and even more camp-followers; and petty camp-traders are more troublesome than any slave. With him, too, was a mass of generals and friends – a company whom even the strictest discipline could scarcely have reduced to order. This great gathering was swelled by senators and other gentlemen who came from Rome to meet them, some afraid, some to flatter: gradually everyone joined this throng, since, when the rest were going, nobody wanted to be left behind. The dregs of Rome's population flocked to Vitellius – men he already knew for their degrading compliance with his tastes: parasites, actors, charioteers, whose squalid friendship caused him remarkable pleasure. To accumulate supplies, cities were plundered; even the farmers were robbed, and their fields, ready for the harvest, were ravaged like enemy territory.

Among the soldiers, too, there were many bloodthirsty fights; for ever since the outbreak at Pavia the quarrel between the regulars and auxiliaries had persisted. Only when there were country-people for them to join in assaulting was there unity. The worst of the massacres was at the seventh milestone from Rome. There Vitellius was distributing cooked food to the army, like the rations handed out to gladia-

1. 48 and 42 B.C., resulting in the deaths of Pompey and of Caesar's assassins respectively.
2. See above, p. 403, n.

tors. The whole camp was packed with crowds of civilians from Rome. These played a townsman's joke on the unsuspecting troops by surreptitiously cutting their belts and then asking where their swords were. The troops were unused to being ridiculed and took it badly. Drawing their swords, they fell on the unarmed civilians. Among those killed was the father of one of the soldiers; he was walking with his son as he was cut down. When the corpse was recognized, and news of his death went round, the slaughter of harmless people ceased.

In Rome a panic was caused by the infiltration of the first soldiers to arrive. They mostly made for the Forum, wanting to look at the place where Galba had been killed. They themselves looked quite as formidable as the murderers, with their shaggy wild animals' skins and huge spears. Unaccustomed to the crowds they met, they ran clumsily into passers-by; and when someone they jostled knocked them down, or they fell on the slippery streets, the soldiers began cursing, and soon their fists and swords were at work. Even generals and colonels caused terror as they paraded through the streets with armed escorts.

Finely mounted and in full uniform, with general's sword and cloak, Vitellius approached the capital from the Milvian Bridge, driving senators and populace in front of him. But his associates deterred him from entering Rome as if it were a captured city; so he changed into official civilian dress and entered on foot, at the head of an orderly column. First came the Eagles of four brigades, with the standards of four others flanking them; then, after the infantry, twelve cavalry regiments following their colours; next paraded thirty-four battalions of auxiliary infantry, differentiated by the names of their home-countries or the style of their weapons. In front of the Eagles marched the divisional chiefs of staff and the colonels and senior company commanders in white uniform; the other company commanders, with shining arms and decorations, headed their companies. Every soldier's discs and chains glittered. It was a splendid sight; such an army deserved a better emperor than Vitellius.

So, at its head, Vitellius mounted the Capitol. There he embraced his mother and bestowed upon her the name of Augusta. Next day he addressed the senate and the public as though they belonged to a foreign country. He spoke pompously about himself, glorifying his own industry and moderation, though his crimes were familiar to his hearers and to all Italy, through which he had proceeded in a disgusting condition of indolence and extravagance. Yet the irresponsible public, without means to distinguish between truth and lies, yelled the usual well-trained applause and flattery. When Vitellius refused the name of Augustus they compelled him to accept it – though either decision was equally futile.[1]

MICHAEL GRANT (1956)

1. For after a very few months he succumbed to Vespasian, governor of Judaea.

SUETONIUS

GAIUS SUETONIUS TRANQUILLUS lived from about A.D. 69 to about 140; he was for a time the emperor Hadrian's secretary, but was dismissed, allegedly for an infringement of court etiquette involving the empress (c. 119–21). Suetonius gave an individual and picturesque turn to ancient methods of biography, and was as outstanding among Latin biographers as his moralizing contemporary Plutarch (so carefully studied by the humanists – and by Shakespeare) was among Greek writers in this field. Suetonius wrote a great many works, of which most are now lost. His most important writings were his thirty-three *Lives of Famous Men* (*De Viris Illustribus*, composed A.D. 103–13), of which a few surviving Lives of Poets (if later accretions are subtracted) may form part; and his *Lives of the Twelve Caesars* (*De Vita Caesarum*, published c. 121), which are extant.

Unlike most ancient historians he presents his wonderfully varied material indifferently and therefore indiscriminately – without suppression, prejudice, rhetoric, or integration; his accounts have been compared to the *procès verbal* of the French lawcourts, but seldom have cases been as exciting as his subject-matter.

Suetonius is the founder of modern biography; a direct line leads from his numerous ancient followers (for henceforward history took a biographical bias), through St Jerome's literary and historical writings, Einhard's *Life of Charlemagne* (815–21), William of Malmesbury's *History of the English Kings* (1127–8), and Petrarch's attentive interest, to the biographies of the Renaissance and today. French and Italian versions of Suetonius date from before 1381 and from 1438 respectively; his surviving works were twice printed in 1470, at Rome; and his *Twelve Caesars* found an English translator in Philemon Holland (1606), who is duly spirited but diffuse:

> Philemon with translations does so fill us,
> He will not let Suetonius be Tranquillus.

But Holland also, quite rightly, will not allow the superficial view that Suetonius was a mere scandal-monger; indeed, his version is dedicated to Lady Harington on the portentous ground 'that there is seated in your person a singular affection to advance good literature, with an extraordinarie respect of learned men.'

Caesar was a most skilful swordsman and horseman, and showed surprising powers of endurance. He always led his army, more often on foot than in the saddle, went bareheaded in sun and rain alike, and could travel for long distances at incredible speed in a gig, taking very little luggage. If he reached an unfordable river he would either swim or propel himself across it on an inflated skin; and often arrived at his destination before the messengers whom he had sent ahead to announce his approach.

It is a disputable point which was the more remarkable when he went to war: his caution or his daring. He never exposed his army to ambushes, but made careful reconnaissances; and refrained from crossing over into Britain until he had collected reliable information (from Gaius Volusenus) about the harbours there, the best course to steer, and the navigational risks. On the other hand, when news reached him that his camp in Germany was being besieged, he disguised himself as a Gaul and picked his way through the enemy outposts to take command on the spot.

He ferried his troops across the Adriatic from Brindisi to Dyrrhachium in the winter season, running the blockade of Pompey's fleet. And one night, when Mark Antony had delayed the dispatch of reinforcements despite repeated pleas, Caesar muffled his head with a cloak and secretly put to sea in a small boat, alone and incognito; forced the helmsman to steer into the teeth of a gale, and narrowly escaped shipwreck.

Religious scruples never deterred him for a moment. At the formal sacrifice before he launched his attack on Scipio and King Juba, the victim escaped; but he paid no heed to this most unlucky sign and marched off at once. He had also slipped and fallen as he disembarked on the coast of Africa, but turned an unfavourable omen into a favourable one by clasping the ground and shouting: 'Africa, I have tight hold of you!' Then, to ridicule the prophecy according to which it was the Scipios' fate to be perpetually victorious in Africa, he took about with him a contemptible member of the Cornelian branch of the Scipio family, nicknamed 'Salvito' – or 'Greetings! but off with him!' – the 'Greetings!' being an acknowledgement of his distinguished birth, the 'Off with him!' a condemnation of his disgusting habits.

Sometimes he fought after careful tactical planning, sometimes on the spur of the moment – at the end of a march, often; or in miserable weather, when he would be least expected to make a move. Towards the end of his life, however, he took fewer chances: having come to the conclusion that his consistent run of victories ought to sober him, now that he could not possibly gain more by winning yet another battle than he would lose by a defeat. It was his rule never to let enemy troops rally once he had routed them, and always therefore to assault their camp at once. If the fight were a hard-fought one, he used to send the chargers away – his own among the first – as a warning that those who feared to stand their ground need not hope to escape on horseback. This charger of his, an extraordinary animal with feet that looked almost human – each of its hoofs was cloven in five parts, resembling human toes – had been foaled on his own estate. When the soothsayers pronounced that its master would one day rule the world, Caesar carefully reared, and was the first to ride, the beast; nor would it allow anyone else to do so. Eventually he raised a statue to it before the Temple of Mother Venus.

If Caesar's troops gave ground, he would often rally them in person, catching individual fugitives by the throat and forcing them round to face the enemy again; even if they were panic-stricken – as when one standard-bearer threatened him with the sharp butt of his Eagle and another, whom he tried to detain, ran off leaving the Eagle in his hand.

Caesar's reputation for presence of mind is fully borne out by the instances quoted. After Pharsalus, he had sent his legions ahead of him into Asia and was crossing the Hellespont in a small ferry-boat, when Lucius Cassius with ten naval vessels approached. Caesar made no attempt to escape but rowed towards the flagship and demanded Cassius' surrender; Cassius gave it and stepped aboard Caesar's craft. Again, while attacking a bridge at Alexandria, Caesar was forced by a sudden enemy sortie to jump into a row-boat. So many of his men followed him that he dived into the sea, and swam two hundred yards until he reached the nearest Caesarean ship – holding his left hand above water the whole way to keep certain documents dry; and towing his cloak behind him with his teeth, to save this trophy from the Egyptians.

He judged his men by their fighting record, not by their morals or social position, treating them all with equal severity – and equal indulgence; since it was only in the presence of the enemy that he insisted on strict discipline. He never gave forewarning of a march or a battle, but kept his troops always on the alert for sudden orders to go wherever he directed. Often he made them turn out when there was no need at all, especially in wet weather or on public holidays. Sometimes he would say: 'Keep a close eye on me!', and then steal away from camp at any hour of the day or night, expecting them to follow. It was certain to be a particularly long march, and hard on stragglers.

If rumours about the enemy's strength were causing alarm, his practice was to heighten morale, not by denying or belittling the danger, but on the contrary by further exaggerating it. For instance, when his troops were in a panic before the battle of Thapsus, at the news of King Juba's approach, he called them together and announced 'You may take it from me that the King will be here within a few days, at the head of ten infantry legions, thirty thousand cavalry, a hundred thousand lightly armed troops, and three hundred elephants. This being the case, you may as well stop asking questions and making guesses. I have given you the facts, with which I am familiar. Any of you who remain unsatisfied will find themselves aboard a leaky hulk and being carried across the sea wherever the winds may decide to blow them.'

Though turning a blind eye to much of their misbehaviour, and never laying down any fixed scale of penalties, he allowed no deserter or mutineer to escape severe punishment. Sometimes, if a victory had been complete enough, he relieved the troops of all military duties and let them carry on as wildly as they pleased. One of his boasts was: 'My men fight just as well when they are stinking of perfume.' He always addressed them not with 'My men', but with 'Comrades ...', which put them into a better humour; and he equipped them splendidly. The silver and gold inlay of their weapons both improved their appearance on parade and made them more careful not to get disarmed in battle, these being objects of great value. Caesar loved his men dearly; when news came that Titurius' command had been massacred, he swore neither to cut his hair nor to trim his beard until they had been avenged.

By these means he won the devotion of his army as well as making it extraordinarily gallant. At the outbreak of the Civil War, every centurion in every legion volunteered to equip a cavalryman from his savings; and the private soldiers unanimously offered to serve under him without pay or rations, pooling their money so that nobody should go short. Throughout the entire struggle not a single Caesarean deserted, and many of them, when taken prisoners, preferred death to the alternative of serving with the Pompeians. Such was their fortitude in facing starvation and other hardships, both as besiegers or as besieged, that when Pompey was shown at Dyrrhachium the substitute for bread, made of grass, on which they were feeding, he exclaimed: 'I am fighting wild beasts!' Then he ordered the loaf to be hidden at once, not wanting his men to find out how tough and resolute the enemy were and so lose heart.

Here the Caesareans suffered their sole reverse, but proved their stout-heartedness by begging to be punished for the lapse; whereupon he felt called upon to console rather than upbraid them. In other battles, they beat enormously superior forces. Shortly before the defeat at Dyrrhachium, a single company of the Sixth Legion held a redoubt against four Pompeian legions, though almost every man had been wounded by arrow-shot – one hundred and thirty thousand arrows were afterwards collected on the scene of the engagement. This high level of courage is less surprising when individual examples are considered: here the centurion Cassius Scaeva, blinded in one eye, wounded in thigh and shoulder, and with no less than a hundred and twenty holes in his shield, continued to defend the approaches to the redoubt. Nor was his by any means an exceptional case. At the naval battle of Marseilles a private soldier named Gaius Acilius grasped the stern of an enemy ship and, when someone lopped off his right hand, nevertheless boarded her and drove the enemy back with the boss of his shield only – a feat rivalling that of the Athenian Cynaegirus (brother of the poet Aeschylus), who showed similar courage when maimed in trying to detain a Persian ship after the victory at Marathon.

Caesar's men did not mutiny once during the Gallic War, which lasted thirteen years. In the Civil Wars they were less dependable, but whenever they made insubordinate demands he faced them boldly and always brought them to heel again – not by appeasement but by sheer exercise of personal authority. At Piacenza, although Pompey's armies were as yet undefeated, he disbanded the entire Ninth Legion with ignominy, later recalling them to the Colours in response to their abject pleas; but with great reluctance and only after executing the ringleaders.

At Rome, too, when the Tenth Legion agitated for their discharge and bounty, and were terrorizing the City, Caesar defied the advice of his friends and at once confronted the mutineers in person. Again he would have disbanded them ignominiously, though the African war was still being hotly fought; but by addressing them as 'Citizens' he readily regained their affections. A shout went up: 'We are your soldiers, Caesar, not civilians!', and they clamoured to serve under him in Africa: a demand which he nevertheless disdained to grant. He showed his contempt for the more disaffected soldiers by withholding a third part of the prize-money and land which had been set aside for them.

ROBERT GRAVES (1956)

THE HABITS OF AUGUSTUS

In this character sketch, I need not omit his eating habits. He was frugal and, as a rule, preferred the food of the common people, especially the coarser sort of bread, whitebait, fresh hand-pressed cheese, and green figs of the second crop; and would not wait for dinner, if he felt hungry, but ate anywhere. The following are verbatim quotations from his letters:

'I had a snack of bread and dates while out for my drive today ...'

and:

'On the way back in my litter from King Numa's Palace on the Sacred Way, I munched an ounce of bread and a few hard-skinned grapes.'

and again:

'My dear Tiberius,
Not even a Jew fasts so scrupulously on his sabbaths,[1] as I have done today. Not until dusk had fallen did I touch a thing; and that

1. But Jews did not fast on the sabbath.

was at the baths, before I had my oil rub, when I swallowed two mouthfuls of bread.'

This failure to observe regular mealtimes often resulted in his dining alone, either before or after his guests; but he came to the dining hall nevertheless and watched them eat.

Augustus was also a habitually abstemious drinker. During the siege of Modena, according to Cornelius Nepos,[1] he never took more than three cups of wine-and-water at dinner. In later life, his limit was a pint; if he ever exceeded this, he would deliberately vomit. Raetian was his favourite, but he seldom touched wine between meals; instead, he would moisten his throat with a morsel of bread dunked in cold water; or a slice of cucumber or the heart of a young lettuce; or a sour apple off the tree, or from a store cupboard.

After luncheon, he used to rest for awhile without removing clothes or shoes; one hand shading his eyes, his feet uncovered. When dinner was over he would retire to a couch in his study, where he worked late until all the outstanding business of the day had been cleared off; or most of it. Then he went to bed and slept seven hours at the outside, with three or four breaks of wakefulness. If he found it hard to fall asleep again on such occasions, as frequently happened, he sent for readers or story-tellers; and on dropping off would not wake until the sun was up. He could not bear lying sleepless in the dark with no one by his side; and if he had to officiate at some official or religious ceremony that involved early rising – which he also loathed – would spend the previous night at a friend's house as near the venue as possible. Even so, he often needed more sleep than he got, and would doze off during his litter journeys through the City, if anything delayed his progress and the bearers set the litter down.

Augustus was remarkably handsome, and of very graceful gait even as an old man; but negligent of his personal appearance. He cared so little about his hair that, to save time, he would have two or three barbers working hurriedly on it together, and meanwhile read or write something, whether they were giving him a haircut or a shave. He always wore so serene an expression, both talking or in repose, that a Gallic chief once confessed to his compatriots: 'When granted

1. The biographer Octavian (the future Augustus) supported the consuls against Antony at Modena (Mutina) in 43 B.C.

an audience with the Emperor during his passage across the Alps, I would have carried out my plan of hurling him over a cliff, had not the sight of that tranquil face softened my heart; so I desisted.'

Augustus' eyes were clear and bright, and he liked to believe that they shone with a sort of divine radiance: it gave him profound pleasure if anyone at whom he glanced keenly dropped his head as though dazzled by looking into the sun. In old age, however, his left eye had only partial vision. His teeth were small, few, and decayed; his hair, yellowish and rather curly; his eyebrows met above the nose; he had ears of normal size, a Roman nose, and a complexion intermediate between dark and fair. Julius Marathus, Augustus' freedman and recorder, makes his height five foot seven inches; but this is an exaggeration, although, with body and limbs so beautifully proportioned, one did not realize how small a man he was, unless someone tall stood close to him.

His body is said to have been marred by blemishes of various sorts – a constellation of seven birthmarks on his chest and stomach, exactly corresponding with the Great Bear; and a number of hard, dry patches suggesting ringworm, caused by an itching of his skin and a too vigorous use of the scraper at the baths. He had a weakness in his left hip, thigh, and leg, which occasionally gave him the suspicion of a limp; but this was improved by the sand-and-reed treatment. Sometimes the forefinger of his right hand would be so numbed by cold that it hardly served to guide a pen, even when strengthened with a long horn finger-stall. He also suffered from bladder pains which, however, ceased to trouble him once he had passed gravel in his urine.

Augustus survived several dangerous illnesses at different periods. The worst was after his Cantabrian conquest,[1] when abscesses on the liver reduced him to such despair that he consented to try a remedy which ran counter to all medical practice: because hot fomentations afforded him no relief, his physician Antonius Musa successfully prescribed cold ones. He was also subject to certain seasonal disorders: in early spring a tightness of the diaphragm; and when the sirocco blew, catarrh. These so weakened his constitution that either hot or cold weather caused him great distress.

In winter, he wore no fewer than four tunics and a heavy woollen gown above his undershirt; and below that a woollen chest-protec-

1. Wars in northern Spain (26–25 B.C.).

tor; also underpants and woollen gaiters. In summer, he slept with the bedroom door open, or in the courtyard beside a fountain, having someone to fan him; and could not bear the rays even of the winter sun, but always wore a broad-brimmed hat to protect himself against glare, whether in the Palace grounds or elsewhere. He preferred to travel by litter, at night, and his bearers kept so leisurely a pace that they were two days in reaching Palestrina or Tivoli; yet, whenever it was possible to reach his destination by sea, he did so. Indeed, he pampered his health, especially by not bathing too often, and being usually content with an oil rub – or with a sweat-bath, after which he took a douche of water either warmed over a fire or allowed to stand in the sun until it had lost its chill. When hot brine, or sulphur water from the Anio springs, was prescribed for his rheumatism, he did no more than sit on a wooden bath-seat – calling it by the Spanish name *dureta* – and alternately dip his wrists and feet into the bath.

As soon as the Civil Wars were over, Augustus discontinued his riding and fencing exercises on the Campus Martius and used, instead, to play catch with two companions, or hand-ball with several. But soon he was content to go hacking, or take walks, muffled in a cloak or blanket, that ended with a sharp sprint across rough ground. Sometimes he went fishing as a relaxation; sometimes he played at dice, marbles, or nuts in the company of little boys, and was always on the look-out for ones with cheerful faces and cheerful chatter, especially Syrians and Moors – he loathed people who were dwarfish or in any way deformed, regarding them as freaks of nature and bringers of bad luck.

ROBERT GRAVES (1956)

THE ABERRATIONS OF CALIGULA

No parallel can be found for Caligula's far-fetched extravagances. He invented new kinds of baths, and the most unnatural dishes and drinks – bathing in hot and cold perfumes, drinking valuable pearls dissolved in vinegar, and providing his guests with golden bread and golden meat; and would remark that Caesar alone could not afford to be frugal. For several days in succession he scattered largesse from the roof of the Julian Basilica; and built Liburnian galleys, with ten banks of oars, jewelled poops, multi-coloured sails, and with huge baths, colonnades, and banqueting halls aboard – not to mention growing vines and apple-trees of different varieties. In these vessels he used to take early-morning cruises along the Campanian coast, reclining on his couch and listening to songs and choruses. Villas and country-houses were run up for him regardless of expense – in fact, Caligula seemed only interested in doing the apparently impossible – which led him to construct moles in deep, rough water far out to sea, drive tunnels through exceptionally hard rocks, raise flat ground to the height of mountains, and reduce mountains to the level of plains; and all at immense speed, because he punished delay with death. But why give details? Suffice it to record that, in less than a year, he squandered Tiberius' entire fortune of twenty-seven million gold pieces and an enormous amount of other treasure besides.

When bankrupt and in need of funds, Caligula concentrated on wickedly ingenious methods of raising funds by false accusations, auctions, and taxes. He ruled that no man could inherit the Roman citizenship acquired by any ancestor more remote than his father; and when confronted with certificates of citizenship issued by Julius Caesar or Augustus, rejected them as obsolete. He also disallowed all property returns to which, for whatever reason, later additions had been appended. If a leading-centurion had bequeathed nothing either to Tiberius or himself since the beginning of the former's reign, he would rescind the will on the ground of ingratitude; and voided those of all other persons who were said to have intended making him their heir when they died, but had not yet done so. This caused widespread alarm, and even people who did not know him personally would tell their friends or children that they had left him everything; but if they continued to live after the declaration he considered himself tricked, and sent several of them presents of poisoned sweetmeats. Caligula conducted these cases in person, first announcing the sum he meant to raise, and not stopping until he had raised it. The slightest delay nettled him, and he once passed a single sentence on a batch of more than forty men, charged with various offences, and then boasted to his wife Caesonia, when she woke from her nap, that he had done very good business since she dozed off.

He would auction whatever properties were left over from a theatrical show; driving up the bidding to such heights that many of those present, forced to buy at fantastic prices, found themselves ruined, and committed suicide by opening their veins. A famous occasion was when Aponius Saturninus fell asleep on a bench, and Caligula warned the auctioneer to keep an eye on the senator of praetorian rank who kept nodding his head. Before the bidding ended Aponius had unwittingly bought thirteen gladiators for a total of 90,000 gold pieces.

While in Gaul, Caligula did so well by selling the furniture, jewellery, slaves, and even the freedmen, of his condemned sisters [1] at a ridiculous over-valuation, that he decided to do the same with the furnishings of the Old Palace. So he sent to Rome, where his agents commandeered public conveyances, and even draught animals from the bakeries, to fetch the stuff north; which led to a bread shortage in the City, and to the loss of many law-suits, because litigants who lived at a distance were unable to appear in court and meet their bail. He then used all kinds of tricks for disposing of the furniture: scolding the bidders for their avarice, or for their shamelessness in being richer than he was, and pretending grief at this surrender of family property to commoners. Discovering that one wealthy provincial had paid the Imperial secretariat 2,000 gold pieces to be smuggled into a banquet, Caligula was delighted that the privilege of dining with him should be valued so highly, and, when next day the same man turned up at the auction, made him pay 2,000 gold pieces for some trifling object – but also sent him a personal invitation to dinner.

ROBERT GRAVES (1956)

NERO THE IMPERIAL ARTIST

Music formed part of Nero's childhood curriculum, and he early developed a taste for it. Soon after his accession, he summoned Terpnus, the greatest lyre-player of the day, to sing to him when dinner had ended, for several nights in succession, until very late. Then, little by little, he began to study and practise himself, and conscientiously undertook all the usual exercises for strengthening and developing the voice. He would lie on his back with a slab of lead on his chest, use

---

1. In A.D. 40 Caligula disgraced and exiled his sisters Agrippina the younger and Julia Livilla for an alleged conspiracy.

enemas and emetics to keep down his weight, and refrain from eating apples and every other food considered deleterious to the vocal chords. Ultimately, though his voice was still feeble and husky, he was pleased enough with his progress to nurse theatrical ambitions, and would quote to his friends the Greek proverb: 'Unheard melodies are never sweet.' His first stage appearance was at Naples, where, disregarding an earthquake which shook the theatre,[1] he sang his piece through to the end. He often performed at Naples, for several consecutive days too; and even while giving his voice a brief rest, could not stay away from the theatre, but went to dine in the orchestra – where he promised the crowd in Greek that, when he had downed a drink or two, he would give them something to make their ears ring. So captivated was he by the rhythmic applause of some Alexandrian sailors from a fleet which had just put in, that he sent to Egypt for more. He also chose a few young knights, and more than five thousand ordinary youths, whom he divided into claques to learn the Alexandrian method of applause – they were known, respectively, as 'Bees', 'Roof-tiles', and 'Brick-bats' – and provide it liberally whenever he sang.[2] It was easy to recognize them by their bushy hair, splendid dress, and the absence of rings on their left hands. The knights who led them earned five gold pieces a performance.

Appearances at Rome meant so much to Nero that he held the Neronia[3] again before the required five years elapsed. When the crowd clamoured to hear his heavenly voice, he answered that he would perform in the Palace gardens later if anyone really wanted to hear him; but when the Guards on duty seconded the appeal, he delightedly agreed to oblige them. He wasted no time in getting his name entered on the list of competing lyre-players, and dropped his ticket into the urn with the others. The Guards colonels carried his lyre as he went up to play, and a group of military tribunes and close friends accompanied him. After taking his place and briefly begging the audience's kind attention, he made Cluvius Rufus, the ex-Consul, announce the title of the song. It was the whole of the opera *Niobe*; and he sang on until two hours before dusk. Since this allowed the remaining com-

1. It collapsed just after the audience had dispersed.
2. The Bees made a loud humming noise. The Roof-tiles clapped with their hollowed hands; the Brick-bats, flat-handed.
3. Quinquennial Games with dramatic contests, inaugurated by him.

petitors no chance to perform, he postponed the award of a prize to the following year, which would give him another opportunity to sing. But since a year was a long time to wait, he continued to make frequent appearances. He toyed with the idea of playing opposite professional actors in public shows staged by magistrates: because one of the Praetors had offered him 12,500 gold pieces if he would consent. And he did actually appear in operatic tragedies, taking the parts of heroes and gods, sometimes even of heroines and goddesses, wearing masks either modelled on his own face, or on the face of whatever woman happened to be his current mistress. Among his performances were *Canace in Childbirth*, *Orestes the Matricide*, *Oedipus Blinded*, and *Distraught Hercules*. There is a story that a young recruit on guard in the wings recognized him in the rags and fetters demanded by the part of Hercules, and dashed boldly to his assistance.

Horses had been Nero's main interest since childhood; whatever his tutors might do, they could never stop his chatter about the chariot-races at the Circus. When scolded by one of them for telling his fellow-pupils about a Leek-Green charioteer who had the misfortune to get dragged by his team, Nero untruthfully explained that he had been discussing Hector's fate in the *Iliad*. At the beginning of his reign he used every day to play with model ivory chariots on a board, and came up from the country to attend all the races, even minor ones, at first in secret and then without the least embarrassment; so that there was never any doubt at Rome when he would be in residence. He frankly admitted that he wished the number of prizes increased, which meant that the contest now lasted until a late hour and the faction-managers no longer thought it worth while to bring out their teams except for a full day's racing. Very soon Nero set his heart on driving a chariot himself, in a regular race, and, after a preliminary trial in the Palace Gardens before an audience of slaves and loungers, made a public appearance in the Circus Maximus; on this occasion one of his freedmen replaced the magistrate who dropped the napkin as the starting signal.

However, these amateur incursions into the arts at Rome did not satisfy him, and he headed for Greece, as I mentioned above. His main reason was that the cities which regularly sponsored musical contests had adopted the practice of sending him every available prize for lyre-playing; he always accepted these with great pleasure, giving the delegates the earliest audience of the day and invitations to private dinners. They would beg Nero to sing when the meal was over, and applaud his performance to the echo, which made him announce: 'The Greeks alone are worthy of my genius; they really listen to music.' So he sailed off hastily and, as soon as he arrived at Cassiope, gave his first song recital before the altar of Jupiter Cassius; after which he went the round of all the contests.

He ordered those contests which normally took place only at long intervals to be held during his visit, even if it meant repeating them; and broke tradition at Olympia by introducing a musical competition into the athletic games. When Helius, his freedman–secretary, reminded him that he was urgently needed at Rome, he would not be distracted by official business, but answered: 'Yes, you have made yourself quite plain. I am aware that you want me to go home; you will do far better, however, if you encourage me to stay until I have proved myself worthy of my reputation.'

No one was allowed to leave the theatre during his recitals, however pressing the reason, and the gates were kept barred. We read of women in the audience giving birth, and of men being so bored with the music and the applause that they furtively dropped down from the wall at the rear, or shammed dead and were carried away for burial. Nero's stage fright and general nervousness, his jealousy of rivals, and his awe of the judges, were more easily seen than believed. Though usually gracious and charming to other competitors, whom he treated as equals, he abused them behind their backs, and often insulted them to their faces; and if any were particularly good singers, he would bribe them not to do themselves justice. Before every performance he would address the judges with the utmost deference: saying that he had done what he could, and that the issue was now in Fortune's hands; but that since they were men of judgement and experience, they would know how to eliminate the factor of chance. When they told him not to worry, he felt a little better, but still anxious; and mistook the silence of some for severity, and the embarrassment of others for disfavour, admitting that he suspected every one of them.

He strictly observed the rules, never daring to clear his throat and even using his arm, rather than a handkerchief, to wipe the sweat from his brow. Once, while acting in a tragedy, he dropped his sceptre and quickly recovered it, but was terrified of disqualification. The accompanist, however – who played a flute and made the necessary dumbshow to illustrate the words – swore that the slip had passed unnoticed, because the audience were listening with such rapt attention; so he took heart again. Nero insisted on announcing his own victories; which emboldened him to enter the competition for heralds. To destroy every trace of previous winners in these contests, he ordered all their statues and busts to be taken down, dragged away with hooks, and hurled into private privies. On several occasions he took part in the chariot-racing, and at Olympia drove a ten-horse team, a novelty for which he had censured King Mithridates in one of his own poems. On this occasion he was thrown from the chariot, and had to be helped in again; but, though he failed to stay the course and retired before the finish, the judges nevertheless awarded him the prize. On the eve of his departure, he presented the whole province with its freedom and conferred Roman citizenship as well as large cash rewards on the judges. It was during the Isthmian Games at Corinth that he stood in the middle of the stadium and personally announced these benefits.

Physical characteristics of Nero:

> Height: average.
> Body: pustular and malodorous.
> Hair: light blond.
> Features: pretty, rather than handsome.
> Eyes: dullish blue.
> Neck: squat.
> Belly: protuberant.
> Legs: spindling.

His health was amazingly good: for all his extravagant indulgence he had only three illnesses in fourteen years, and none of them serious enough to stop him from drinking wine or breaking any other regular habit. He did not take the least trouble to dress as an Emperor should, but always had his hair set in rows of curls and, when he visited Greece, let it grow long and hang down his back. He often gave audiences in an unbelted silk dressing-gown, slippers, and a scarf.

As a boy, Nero read most of the usual school subjects except philosophy which, Agrippina warned him, was no proper study for a future ruler. His tutor Seneca hid the works of the early rhetoricians from him, intending to be admired himself as long as possible. So Nero turned his hand to poetry, and would dash off verses without any effort. It is often claimed that he published other people's work as his own; but notebooks and loose pages have come into my possession, which contain some of Nero's best-known poems in his own handwriting, and have clearly been neither copied nor dictated. Many erasures and cancellations, as well as words substituted above the lines, prove that he was thinking things out for himself. Nero also took more than an amateur's interest in painting and sculpture.

His greatest weaknesses were his thirst for popularity and his jealousy of men who caught the public eye by any means whatsoever. Because he had swept the board of all public prizes offered for acting, and was also an enthusiastic wrestler – during his tour of Greece he had never missed a single athletic meeting – most people expected him to take part in the Classical events at the next Olympiad. He used to squat on the ground in the stadium, like the judges, and if any pair of competitors worked away from the centre of the ring, would push them back himself. Because of his singing and chariot-driving he had been compared to Phoebus Apollo; now, apparently, he planned to become a Hercules, for according to one story he had a lion so carefully trained that he could safely face it naked, before the entire amphitheatre; and then either kill it with his club or else strangle it.

Just before the end, Nero took a public oath that if he managed to keep his throne, he would celebrate the victory with a music festival, performing successively on water-organ, flute, and bagpipes; and when the last day came, would dance the role of Turnus in Virgil's *Aeneid*. He was supposed to have killed the actor Paris, because he considered him a serious professional rival.

ROBERT GRAVES (1956)

PART V

THE NORTH AFRICANS

APULEIUS

Lucius Apuleius was born at Madaurus (Mdaourouch in Algeria) in about A.D. 123. The date of his death is uncertain. Novelist, priest, and popular philosopher, poet and devotee of Isis, lawyer and lecturer, he was accused of magic: we possess his *Apologia*, conducted with the fantastic exuberance of the new era. The transformation of one 'Lucius' into an ass [1] (a theme perhaps borrowed, with the latitude inevitable in so brilliant a borrower, from a lost Greek novel) is recounted in the *Metamorphoses*, otherwise known as *The Golden Ass*. This is the supreme efflorescence of the ancient prose-romance – 'last child of the Greek genius' – and the only Latin novel that has come down to us complete.

It contains the elaborate folk-tale of the Fairy Bridegroom, *Cupid and Psyche*, which, in late antiquity and the Middle Ages, seemed more profoundly allegorical than it really was. Apuleius' gay story-telling delighted the Renaissance. *The Golden Ass* was first printed at Rome in 1469, and Spanish, Italian, French, and German translations were published within a few years of each other (1513–38). It inspired Raphael, and greatly appealed to the ebullience of the Elizabethan age, in which it was finely, if unreliably, translated by William Adlington (1566). La Fontaine gracefully told the tale of the Fairy Bridegroom in *Les Amours de Psyché et de Cupidon* (1673), and two centuries later its spirit – the 'perfumed personality' of Apuleius, as he calls it – was lusciously evoked by Walter Pater. The most readable modern version is that of Robert Graves, who prefaces it with a controversial explanation: 'I have made no attempt to bring out the oddness of the Latin by writing in a style, say, somewhere between Lyly's *Euphues* and Amanda Ros's *Irene Iddesleigh*; paradoxically, the effect of oddness is best achieved in convulsed times like the present by writing in as easy and sedate an English as possible.'

1. St Augustine remained unconvinced that Apuleius himself had not been turned into an ass.

Venus was jealous of the beautiful Psyche, who was told by an oracle that she must wed a terrible, inhuman, serpentine, all-powerful husband. She walks bravely to the doom of her wedding at the top of a high hill.

'Why do I delay? Why should I refuse him that is appointed to destroy all the world?' Thus ended she her words, and thrust herself with a strong gait amongst the people that followed: then they brought her to the appointed rock of the high hill, and set her thereon and so departed. The torches and lights were put out with the tears of the people, and every man gone home with bowed heads: the miserable parents, well nigh consumed with sorrow, closed themselves in their palace and gave themselves to everlasting darkness. Thus poor Psyche being left alone weeping and trembling on the highest top of the rock, there came a gentle air of softly breathing Zephyrus and carried her from the hill, with a meek wind, which retained her garments up, and by little and little brought her down into a deep valley, where she was laid in a soft grassy bed of most sweet and fragrant flowers.

Thus fair Psyche being sweetly couched amongst the soft and tender herbs, as in a bed of dewy grass and fragrant flowers, and having qualified the troubles and thoughts of her restless mind, was now well reposed: and when she had refreshed herself sufficiently with sleep, she rose with a more quiet and pacified mind, and fortuned to espy a pleasant wood environed with great and mighty trees, and likewise a running river as clear as crystal; in the middest and very heart of the woods, well nigh at the fall of the river, was a princely edifice, wrought and builded, not by the art or hand of man, but by the mighty power of a god: and you would judge at the first entry therein that it were some pleasant and worthy mansion for the powers of heaven. For the embowings above were curiously carven out of citron and ivory, propped and undermined with pillars of gold; the walls covered and seeled with silver; divers sorts of beasts were graven and carved, that seemed to encounter with such as entered in: all things were so curiously and finely wrought that it seemed either to be the work of some demigod, or God himself, that put all these beasts into silver. The pavement was all of precious stone, divided and cut one from another, whereon was carved divers kinds of pictures, in such sort that blessed and thrice blessed were they which might go upon such a pavement of gems and ornaments: every part and angle of the house was so well adorned by the precious stones and inestimable treasure there, and the walls were so solidly built up with great blocks of gold, that glittered and shone in such sort that the chambers, porches, and doors gave out the light of day as it had been the sun. Neither otherwise did the other treasure of the house disagree unto so great a majesty, that verily it seemed in every point a heavenly palace fabricated and builded for Jupiter himself wherein to dwell among men.

Then Psyche, moved with delectation, approached nigh, and taking a bold heart entered into the house led on by the beauty of that sight, and beheld everything there with great affection: she saw storehouses wrought exceeding fine, and replenished with abundance of riches, and, finally, there could nothing be devised which lacked there, but amongst such great store of treasure, this was more marvellous, that there was no closure, bolt, or lock, and no guardian to keep the same. And when with great pleasure she viewed all these things, she heard a voice without any body, that said: 'Why do you marvel, lady, at so great riches? Behold all that you see is at your commandment: wherefore go you into the chamber and repose yourself upon the bed, and desire what bath you will have, and we, whose voices you hear, be your servants, and ready to minister unto you according to your desire: in the mean season, when you have refreshed your body, royal meats and dainty dishes shall be prepared for you.'

Then Psyche perceived the felicity of divine providence, and according to the advertisement of the incorporeal voices she first reposed herself upon the bed, and then refreshed her body in the bath. This done, she saw the table garnished with meats, and a round chair to sit down, and gladly reposed herself beside the array for dining, which she thought was set very conveniently for her refreshment. Then straightway all sorts of wines like nectar were brought in, and plentiful dishes of divers meats, not by anybody but as it were by some divine spirit or breath, for she could see no person before her, but only hear words falling on every side, and she had only voices to serve her. After that all the rich services were brought to the table, one came in and sang invisibly, another played on the harp, and that, too, could not be seen; the harmony of a large concourse did so greatly thrill in her ears that, though there were no manner of person, yet seemed she in the midst of a great choir.

WILLIAM ADLINGTON (1566)[1]

CUPID'S PALACE AGAIN

'Why delay the coming of him who was born for the destruction of the whole world?'

She was silent, and with firm step went on the way. And they proceeded to the appointed place on a steep mountain, and left there the maiden alone, and took their way homewards dejectedly. The wretched parents, in their close-shut house, yielded themselves to perpetual night; while to Psyche, fearful and trembling and weeping sore upon the mountain-top, comes the gentle Zephyrus. He lifts her mildly, and, with vesture afloat on either side, bears her by his own soft breathing over the windings of the hills, and sets her lightly among the flowers in the bosom of a valley below.

Psyche, in those delicate grassy places, lying sweetly on her dewy bed, rested from the agitation of her soul and arose in peace. And lo! a grove of mighty trees, with a fount of water, clear as glass, in the midst; and hard by the water, a dwelling-place, built not by human hands but by some divine cunning. One recognized, even at the entering, the delightful hostelry of a god. Golden pillars sustained the roof, arched most curiously in cedar-wood and ivory. The walls were hidden under wrought silver: all tame and woodland creatures leaping forward to the visitor's gaze. Wonderful indeed was the craftsman, divine or half-divine, who by the subtlety of his art had breathed so wild a soul into the silver! The very pavement was distinct with pictures in goodly stones. In the glow of its precious metal the house is its own daylight, having no need of the sun. Well might it seem a place fashioned for the conversation of gods with men!

Psyche, drawn forward by the delight of it, came near, and, her courage growing, stood within the doorway. One by one, she admired the beautiful things she saw; and, most wonderful of all! no

1. Adapted by Stephen Gaselee (1915).

lock, no chain, nor living guardian protected that great treasure house. But as she gazed there came a voice – a voice, as it were unclothed of bodily vesture – 'Mistress!' it said, 'all these things are thine. Lie down, and relieve thy weariness, and rise again for the bath when thou wilt. We thy servants, whose voice thou hearest, will be beforehand with our service, and a royal feast shall be ready.'

And Psyche understood that some divine care was providing, and, refreshed with sleep and the bath, sat down to the feast. Still she saw no one: only she heard words falling here and there, and had voices alone to serve her. And the feast being ended, one entered the chamber and sang to her unseen, while another struck the chords of a harp, invisible with him who played on it. Afterwards the sound of a company singing together came to her, but still so that none was present to sight; yet it appeared that a great multitude of singers was there.

WALTER PATER (1885)

THE TRIALS OF PSYCHE

Venus, furious at her son Cupid's love for Psyche, imprisons him and imposes three Labours upon her.[1]

With this, Venus flew at poor Psyche, tore her clothes to shreds, pulled out handfuls of her hair, then grabbed her by the shoulders and shook her until she nearly shook her head off, giving her a terrible time. Next she called for quantities of wheat, barley, millet, lentils, beans, and the seeds of poppy and vetch, and mixed them all together into a huge heap. 'You look such a dreadful sight, slave,' she said, 'that the only way that you are ever likely to get a lover is by hard work. So now I'll test you myself, to find out whether you're industrious. Do you see this pile of seeds all mixed together? Sort out the different kinds, stack them in separate little heaps, and prove that you're quick-fingered by getting every grain in its right place before nightfall.' Without another word, she flew off to attend some wedding breakfast or other.

Psyche made no attempt to set about her stupendous task, but sat

1. The Three Labours are a universally familiar theme of fairy-stories and folk-tales (*märchen*); so are the Three Sisters, of whom Psyche is the Cinderella.

gazing dumbly at it, until a very small ant, one of the country sort, happened to pass and realized what was going on. Pity for Psyche as wife of the mighty God of Love set the little thing shrieking wild curses at the cruel mother-in-law and scurrying about to round up every ant in the district. 'Take pity on her, sisters, take pity on this pretty girl, you busy children of the generous Earth. She's the wife of Love himself and her life is in great danger. Quick, quick, to the rescue!'

They came rushing up as fast as their six legs would carry them, wave upon wave of ants, and began working furiously to sort the pile out, grain by grain. Soon they had arranged it tidily in separate heaps, and run off again at once. . . . .

As soon as the Goddess of Dawn had set her team moving across the sky, Venus called Psyche and said: 'Do you see the grove fringing the bank of that stream over there, with fruit bushes hanging low over the water? Shining golden sheep are wandering about in it, without a shepherd to look after them. I want you to fetch me a hank of their precious wool, and I don't care how you get it.'

Psyche rose willingly enough, but with no intention of obeying Venus' orders: she had made up her mind to throw herself in the stream and so end her sorrows. But a green reed, of the sort used in Pan's pipes, was blown upon by some divine breeze and whispered to her. 'Wait, Psyche, wait! I know what dreadful sorrows you have suffered, but you must not pollute these sacred waters by a suicide. And, another thing, you must not go into the grove, to risk your life among those dangerous sheep; not yet. The heat of the sun so infuriates the beasts that they kill any human being who ventures among them. Either they gore them with their sharp horns, or butt them to death with their stony foreheads or bite them with their poisonous teeth. Wait, Psyche, wait until the afternoon wears to a close, and the serene whispers of these waters lull them asleep. Hide meanwhile under that tall plane-tree who drinks the same water as I do, and as soon as the sheep calm down, go into the grove and gather the wisps of golden wool that you'll find sticking on every briar there.'

It was a simple, kindly reed, and Psyche took its advice, which proved to be sound: that evening she was able to return to Venus with a whole lapful of the delicate golden wool. Yet even her performance of this second dangerous task did not satisfy the Goddess, who frowned and told her with a cruel smile: 'Someone has been helping you again, that's quite clear. But now I'll put your courage and prudence to a still severer test. Do you see the summit of that high mountain over there? You'll find that a dark-coloured stream cascades down its precipitous sides into a gorge below and then floods the Stygian marshes and feeds the hoarse River of Wailing. Here is a little jar. Go off at once and bring it back to me brimful of ice-cold water fetched from the very middle of the stream at the point where it bursts out of the rock.'

She gave Psyche a jar of polished crystal and packed her off with renewed threats of what would happen if she came back empty-handed.

Psyche started at once for the top of the mountain, thinking that there at least she would find a means of ending her wretched life. As she came near she saw what a stupendously dangerous and difficult task had been set her. The dreadful waters of the Styx burst out from half-way up an enormously tall, steep, slippery precipice; cascaded down into a narrow conduit which they had hollowed for themselves in the course of centuries, and flowed unseen into the gorge below. On both sides of their outlet she saw fierce dragons crawling, never asleep, always on guard with unwinking eyes, and stretching their long necks over the sacred water. And the waters sang as they rolled along, varying the words every now and then: 'Be off! Be off!' and 'What do you wish, wish, wish? Look! Look!' and 'What are you at, are you at? Care, take care! Off with you, off with you, off with you! Death! Death!'

Psyche stood still as stone, her mind far away: the utter impossibility of escaping alive from the trap that Venus had set for her was so overwhelming that she could no longer even relieve herself by tears – that last comfort of women when things go wrong with them. But the kind, sharp eyes of Providence notice when innocent souls are in trouble. At her suggestion Jupiter's royal bird, the rapacious eagle, suddenly sailed down to her from Heaven. He gratefully remembered the ancient debt that he owed to Cupid for having helped him to carry Ganymede, the beautiful Phrygian prince, up to Heaven to become Jupiter's cup-bearer; and since Psyche was Cupid's wife he screamed down at her: 'Silly, simple, inexperienced Psyche, how can you ever hope to steal one drop of this frightfully sacred stream? Surely you have heard that Jupiter himself fears the waters of Styx, and that, just as you swear by the Blessed Gods, so they swear by the Sovereign Styx. But let me take that little jar.' He quickly snatched it from her grasp and soared off on his strong wings, steering a zigzag course between the two rows of furious fangs and vibrating three-forked tongues, until he reached the required spot. The stream was reluctant to give up its water and warned him to escape while he still could, but he explained that the Goddess Venus wanted the water and that she had commissioned him to fetch it; a story which carried some weight with the stream. He filled the jar with the water and brought it safely back to the delighted Psyche.

She returned with it to Venus but could not appease her fury even with this latest success. Venus was resolved to set a still more outrageous test, and said with a sweet smile that seemed to spell her complete ruin: 'You must be a witch, a very clever, very wicked witch, else you could never have carried out my orders so exactly. But I have still one more task for you to perform, my dear girl. Please take this box and go down to the Underworld to the death-palace of Pluto. Hand it to Queen Proserpine and say: "The Lady Venus' compliments, and will you please send this box back to her with a little of your beauty in it, not very much but enough to last for at least one short day. She has had to make such a drain on her own store, as a result of sitting up at night with her sick son, that she has none left." Then come back with the box at once, because I must use her make-up before I appear at the Olympic Theatre tonight.'

This seemed the end of everything, since her orders were to go down to the Underworld of Tartarus. Psyche saw that she was openly and undisguisedly being sent to her death. She went at once to a high tower, deciding that her straightest and easiest way to the Underworld was to throw herself down from it. But the tower suddenly broke into human speech: 'Poor child,' it said, 'do you really mean to commit suicide by jumping down from me? How rash of you to lose hope just before the end of your trials. Don't you realize that as soon as the breath is out of your body you will indeed go right down to the depths of Tartarus, but that once you take that way there's no hope of return? Listen to me. The famous Greek city of Lacedaemon is not far from here. Go there at once and ask to be directed to

Taenarus, which is rather an out-of-the-way place to find.[1] It's on a peninsula to the south. Once you get there you'll find one of the ventilation holes of the Underworld. Put your head through it and you'll see a road running downhill, but there'll be no traffic on it. Climb through at once and the road will lead you straight to Pluto's palace. But don't forget to take with you two pieces of barley bread soaked in honey water, one in each hand, and two coins in your mouth.

'When you have gone a good way along the road you'll meet a lame ass loaded with wood, and its lame driver will ask you to hand him some pieces of rope for tying up part of the load which the ass has dropped. Pass him by in silence. Then hurry forward until you reach the river of the dead, where Charon will at once ask you for his fee and ferry you across in his patched boat among crowds of ghosts. It seems that the God Avarice lives thereabouts, because neither Charon nor his great father Pluto does anything for nothing. (A poor man on the point of death is expected to have his passage-fee ready; but if he can't get hold of a coin, he isn't allowed to achieve true death, but must wander about disconsolately forever on this side of Styx.) Anyhow, give the dirty ruffian one of your coins, but let him take it from your mouth, not from your hand. While you are being ferried across the sluggish stream, the corpse of an old man will float by; he will raise a putrid hand and beg you to haul him into the boat. But you must be careful not to yield to any feeling of pity for him; that is forbidden. Once ashore, you will meet three women some distance away from the bank. They will be weaving cloth and will ask you to help them. To touch the cloth is also forbidden. All these apparitions, and others like them, are snares set for you by Venus; her object is to make you let go one of the sops you are carrying, and you must understand that the loss of even one of them would be fatal – it would prevent your return to this world. They are for you to give to Cerberus, the huge, fierce, formidable hound with three heads on three necks, all barking in unison, who terrifies the dead; though of course the dead have no need to be frightened by him because they are only shadows and he can't injure shadows.

1. Taenarus is the central peninsula of the Peloponnese (south of Lacedae-mon = Sparta); near its cape is a cave through which Heracles traditionally dragged Cerberus up from Hades.

'Cerberus keeps perpetual guard at the threshold of Proserpine's dark palace, the desolate place where she lives with her husband Pluto. Throw him one of your sops and you'll find it easy to get past him into the presence of Proserpine herself. She'll give you a warm welcome, offer you a cushioned chair and have you brought a magnificent meal. But sit on the ground, ask for a piece of common bread, and eat nothing else. Then deliver your message, and she'll give you what you came for.

'As you go out, throw the cruel dog the remaining sop as a bribe to let you pass; then pay the greedy ferryman the remaining coin for your return fare across the river, and when you're safely on the other bank follow the road back until you see once again the familiar constellations of Heaven. One last, important warning; be careful not to open or even look at the box you carry back; that hidden receptacle of divine beauty is not for you to explore.'

It was a kind and divinely inspired tower, and Psyche took its advice. She went at once to Taenarus where, armed with the coins and the two sops, she ran down the road to the Underworld. She passed in silence by the lame man with the lame ass, paid Charon the first coin, stopped her ears to the entreaties of the floating corpse, refused to be taken in by the appeal of the spinning women, pacified the dreadful dog with the first sop and entered Proserpine's palace. There she refused the comfortable chair and the tempting meal, sat humbly at Proserpine's feet, content with a crust of common bread, and finally delivered her message. Proserpine secretively filled the box, shut it, and returned it to her; then Psyche stopped the dog's barking with the second sop, paid Charon with the second coin, and returned from the Underworld, feeling in far better health and spirits than while on her way down there. When she saw the daylight again she offered up a prayer of praise for its loveliness. Though she was in a hurry to complete her errand she foolishly allowed her curiosity to get the better of her. She said to herself: 'I should be a fool to carry this little boxful of divine beauty without borrowing a tiny touch of it for my own use: I must do everything possible to please my beautiful lover.'

She opened the box, but it contained no beauty nor anything else, so far as she saw: but out crept a truly Stygian sleep, which seized her and wrapped her in a dense cloud of drowsiness. She fell prostrate and lay there like a corpse, the open box beside her.

Cupid, now recovered from his injury and unable to bear Psyche's absence a moment longer, flew out through the narrow window of the bedroom where his mother had been holding him a prisoner. His wings, invigorated by their long rest, carried him faster than ever before. He hurried to Psyche, carefully brushed away the cloud of sleep from her body and shut it up again in its box, then roused her with a harmless prick of an arrow. 'Poor girl,' he said, 'your curiosity has once more nearly ruined you! Hurry now and complete the task which my mother set you; and I'll see to everything else.' He flew off, and she sprang up at once to deliver Proserpine's present to Venus.

ROBERT GRAVES (1950)

THE GREAT GODDESS ISIS [1]

Not long afterwards I awoke in sudden terror. A dazzling full moon was rising from the sea. It is at this secret hour that the Moon-goddess, sole sovereign of mankind, is possessed of her greatest power and majesty. She is the shining deity by whose divine influence not only all beasts, wild and tame, but all inanimate things as well, are invigorated; whose ebbs and flows control the rhythm of all bodies whatsoever, whether in the air, on earth, or below the sea. Of this I was well aware, and therefore resolved to address the visible image of the goddess, imploring her help; for Fortune seemed at last to have made up her mind that I had suffered enough, and to be offering me a hope of release.

When I had finished my prayer and poured out the full bitterness of my oppressed heart, I returned to my sandy hollow, where once more sleep overcame me. I had scarcely closed my eyes before the apparition of a woman began to rise from the middle of the sea, with so lovely a face that the gods themselves would have fallen down in adoration of it. First the head, then the whole shining body gradually emerged and stood before me poised on the surface of the waves. Yes, I will try to describe this transcendent vision, for though human

1. Her Egyptian cult was the most powerful and widespread of the emotional mystery religions – promising initiates happiness in the after-life – which swept through the Graeco-Roman world during the first three centuries A.D.

speech is poor and limited, the Goddess herself will perhaps inspire me with poetic imagery sufficient to convey some slight inkling of what I saw.

Her long thick hair fell in tapering ringlets on her lovely neck, and was crowned with an intricate chaplet in which was woven every kind of flower. Just above her brow shone a round disc, like a mirror, or like the bright face of the moon, which told me who she was. Vipers rising from the left-hand and right-hand partings of her hair supported this disc, with ears of corn bristling beside them. Her many-coloured robe was of finest linen; part was glistening white, part crocus-yellow, part glowing red and along the entire hem a woven bordure of flowers and fruit clung swaying in the breeze. But what caught and held my eye more than anything else was the deep black lustre of her mantle. She wore it slung across her body from the right hip to the left shoulder, where it was caught in a knot resembling the boss of a shield; but part of it hung in innumerable folds, the tasselled fringe quivering. It was embroidered with glittering stars on the hem and everywhere else, and in the middle beamed a full and fiery moon.

In her right hand she held a bronze rattle, of the sort used to frighten away the God of the Sirocco; its narrow rim was curved like a sword-belt, and three little rods, which sang shrilly when she shook the handle, passed horizontally through it. A boat-shaped gold dish hung from her left hand, and along the upper surface of the handle writhed an asp with puffed throat and head raised ready to strike. On her divine feet were slippers of palm leaves, the emblem of victory.

All the perfumes of Arabia floated into my nostrils as the Goddess deigned to address me: 'You see me here, Lucius, in answer to your prayer. I am Nature, the universal Mother, mistress of all the elements, primordial child of time, sovereign of all things spiritual, queen of the dead, queen also of the immortals, the single manifestation of all gods and goddesses that are. My nod governs the shining heights of Heaven, the wholesome sea-breezes, the lamentable silences of the world below. Though I am worshipped in many aspects, known by countless names, and propitiated with all manner of different rites, yet the whole round earth venerates me.'

ROBERT GRAVES (1950)

The Golden Ass *is the last pagan masterpiece represented in this book: although, a century and a half later, there was to be an interesting revival of pagan poetry. But of the richly graceful nature poems of Tiberianus and the neo-Virgilian Eclogues of Nemesianus I have not found true enough reproductions, and I believe – with apologies to certain skilful, even brilliant* tours de force *– that the disturbing, nostalgic* Vigil of Venus *(like that earlier Hymn,* Horace's Carmen Saeculare*) is scarcely translatable. The closing years of the fourth century witnessed the* 'singular and isolated figure of Claudian, the posthumous child of the classical world' : [1] *his contemporaries were the Christian poets whose proper place is a medieval sequel to this collection.*

1. J. W. Mackail.

TERTULLIAN

QUINTUS SEPTIMUS FLORENS TERTULLIANUS, born in North Africa in about A.D. 160, lived at Carthage, died in about 225. Tertullian wrote at a time of passionate religious feeling and controversy, and in the land where they were most passionate of all and where many of the literary achievements of the age saw the light. A pagan by birth and a lawyer by career, he was converted to Christianity: he formulated the doctrine of the Trinity, and was the first Latin writer to claim that the Scriptures are the source of all wisdom ('Homer comes from Moses'). 'I can call the emperor *Master*,' said Tertullian, 'but I remain a free man of God before him.'

In the best-known of his more than thirty surviving works, the *Apologeticus*, he vigorously, indeed violently, defends his new faith in a language designed to convince Roman provincial administrators – though he wrote: 'nothing is more foreign to us than politics'. His later writings, composed after his adherence to the strict Montanist sect – which believed itself the recipient of a new activity of the Holy Spirit – show a greater austerity: his aim is no longer the reconciliation of classical culture with the new ideals, but its other-worldly rejection. The empire of the Caesars is forerunner of the empire of Christ; Tertullian is on his way from the world of Cicero to St Jerome's monastic withdrawal and eremitic mortification. But the journey was hard: Tertullian reluctantly allowed that Christian children must attend pagan schools, though he forbade Christians to teach in them – the traditional education was indefensible, but still indispensable.

Tertullian's works were first published at Basle in 1521. In 1584 François de Maulde (Modius) discovered at Fulda a manuscript of the *Apologeticus* embodying a variant textual tradition. This manuscript disappeared in the troubles of the next century, but not before its deviations had been published by de Jon (Junius) (1597). Havercamp (1718) suggested that they comprise a rewriting by Tertullian himself.

The 'zealous African's' grim expectations of last judgement, and 'of so many sage philosophers blushing in red-hot flames with their deluded scholars', moved Gibbon to an interruption: 'the humanity of the reader will permit me to draw a veil over the rest of this infernal description' – which, so far, he had judiciously mistranslated. This 'vehement, irate, witty, tender man, hater of shams and of culture, cultured himself', [1] has been compared with Thomas Carlyle, and his exaggerated paradoxes with those of Chesterton. A modern translator, T.R. Glover (1931), states his desire to render him 'with the full force possible – biting, stinging, gripping stuff – turning the reader into a listener and arguing at him. The grammar is different, the structure different, I know – but I hope there is something of the same passion, and for the same cause.'

1. E.K. Rand.

Then, again, you do not deal with us in accordance with your procedure in judging criminals. If the other criminals plead Not Guilty, you torture them to make them confess; the Christians alone you torture to make them deny. Yet, if it were something evil, we should deny our guilt, and you would use torture to force us to confess it.

A man shouts, 'I am a Christian.' He says what he is. You, sir, wish to hear what he is *not*. Presiding to extort the truth, you take infinite pains in our case, and ours alone, to hear a lie. 'I am,' says he, 'what you ask if I am; why torture me to twist the fact round? I confess, and you torture me. What would you do if I denied?' Clearly, when others deny, you do not readily believe them; if we have denied, you at once believe us. Let this topsy-turvy dealing of yours suggest to you the suspicion that there may be some hidden power which makes tools of you against the form, yes, against the very nature, of judicial procedure – against the laws themselves into the bargain.

For, unless I am mistaken, the laws bid evil men to be brought to light, not hidden; they enact that those confessing be condemned, not acquitted. This is laid down by decrees of the Senate, by rescripts of the emperors. This Empire of which you are ministers is the rule of citizens, not of tyrants. With tyrants torture was also used as penalty; with you, it is moderated and used for examination only. Maintain your law by it till the necessary confession is made. If it is forestalled by confession, it serves no purpose. It is the sentence that is called for then; the guilty man must cancel the penalty due by enduring it, not by being relieved of it. No, nobody desires to acquit him; it is not permissible to wish it; that is why no man is forced to deny his guilt. But the Christian, a man guilty of every crime, the enemy of gods, emperors, laws, morals, of all Nature together – so you conceive of him; and then you force him to deny the charge, in order to acquit him – a man you will not be able to acquit unless he has denied.

You are playing fast and loose with the laws. You want him to deny that he is guilty, in order to *make* him innocent – and quite against his will, too, by now; and even his past is not to count against him. What is the meaning of this confusion? this failure to reflect that more credence is to be given to a voluntary confession than to a forced

440

denial? to reflect that, when compelled to deny, he may not honestly deny; and, once acquitted, he may again after your tribunal laugh at your enmity, once more a Christian?

T. R. Glover (1931)

THE CIRCUS

Look at the populace coming to the show – mad already! disorderly, blind, excited already about its bets! The praetor is too slow for them; all the time their eyes are on his urn, in it, as if rolling with the lots he shakes up in it. The signal is to be given. They are all in suspense, anxious suspense. One frenzy, one voice! (Recognize their frenzy from their empty-mindedness.) 'He has thrown it!' they cry; every-one tells everybody else what every one of them saw, all of them on the instant. I catch at that evidence of their blindness; they do not see what was thrown – a handkerchief, they think; no! a picture of the devil hurled from heaven!

So it begins and so it goes on – to madness, anger, discord: to everything forbidden to the priests of peace. Next taunts or mutual abuse without any warrant of hate, and applause unsupported by affection. What of their own are they going to achieve who act there in that way – when they are not their own? Unless it be merely the loss of their self-control; they are plunged in grief by another's bad luck, high in delight at another's success. What they long to see, what they dread to see – neither has anything to do with them; their love is without reason, their hatred without justice. Or is it allowed us to love without cause any more than to hate without cause? God, at any rate, forbids us to hate even with cause, when He bids us love our enemies. God does not allow us to curse even with cause, when He teaches us to bless those who curse us. But what can be more merci-less than the circus, where men do not even spare their princes or their fellow-citizens? If any of these forms of madness, with which the circus rages, is anywhere permitted to saints, then it will be lawful in the circus also; but if nowhere, then neither in the circus.

Granted that you have there something that is sweet, agreeable, and innocent, some things that are excellent. No one mixes poison with gall and hellebore; no, it is into delicacies well made, well flavoured, and, for the most part, sweet things, that he drops the venom. So does the Devil; the deadly draught he brews, he flavours with the most agreeable, the most welcome gifts of God. So count all you find there – brave and honest, resounding, musical, exquisite – as so much honey dropping from a poisoned bit of pastry; and do not count your appetite for the pleasure worth the risk in the sweetness.

Let his own guests batten on sweets of that sort. The place, the time, the host who invites, are theirs. Our feast, our marriage-festival, is not yet. We cannot take our place at table with them, because they cannot with us. It is a matter of turn and turn about. Now they are happy, and we are afflicted. 'The world,' it says, 'will rejoice; you will be sad.' Then let us mourn while the heathen rejoice, so that, when they have begun to mourn, we may rejoice; lest, if we share their joy now, then we may be sharing their mourning too. You are too dainty, O Christian, if you long for pleasure in this world as well as the other – a bit of a fool into the bargain, if you think *this* pleasure. Philosophers have given the name 'pleasure' to quiet and tranquillity; in it they rejoice, take their ease in it, yes, glory in it. And you – why, I find you sighing for goal-posts, the stage, the dust, the arena. I wish you would tell me; cannot we live without pleasure, we who must die with pleasure? For what else is our prayer but that of the apostle 'to leave the world and be at home with the Lord'? Our pleasure is where our prayer is.

But what a spectacle is already at hand – the return of the Lord, now no object of doubt, now exalted, now triumphant! What exultation will that be of the angels, what glory that of the saints as they rise again! What the reign of the righteous thereafter! What a city, the New Jerusalem! Yes, and there are still to come other spectacles – that last, that eternal Day of Judgement, that Day which the Gentiles never believed would come, that Day they laughed at, when this old world and all its generations shall be consumed in one fire.

How vast the spectacle that day, and how wide! What sight shall wake my wonder, what my laughter, my joy and exultation! as I see all those kings, those great kings, welcomed (we were told) in heaven, along with Jove, along with those who told of their ascent, groaning in the depths of darkness! And the magistrates who persecuted the name of Jesus, liquefying in fiercer flames than they kindled in their rage against the Christians! those sages, too, the philosophers blushing before their disciples as they blaze together, the disciples whom they taught that God was concerned with nothing, that men have no souls at all, or that what souls they have shall never return to their former bodies! And then the poets trembling before the judgement-seat, not of Rhadamanthus, not of Minos, but of Christ whom they never looked to see! And then there will be the tragic actors to be heard, more vocal in their own tragedy; and the players to be seen, lither of limb by far in the fire; and then the charioteer to watch, red all over in the wheel of flame; and, next, the athletes to be gazed upon, not in their gymnasiums but hurled in the fire – unless it be that not even then would I wish to see them, in my desire rather to turn an insatiable gaze on them who vented their rage and fury on the Lord.

T. R. GLOVER (1931)

ST AUGUSTINE

AURELIUS AUGUSTINUS, St Augustine, was born at Tagaste (Souk-Ahras in Algeria) in A.D. 354 – far the greater part of Latin Christian literature is African – and died in 430. He was educated in north Africa, lived at Rome, taught rhetoric at Milan, became a convert from Manichaeism (partly through the influence of St Ambrose) in 386, and in 391 was ordained priest at Hippo Regius in north Africa, where he was bishop from 395 until his death. His surviving works are six times as long as Cicero's. They include *On Christian Doctrine*, the *Confessions* (in thirteen books, of which the first ten are autobiographical), *On the Trinity*, *On the Agreement of the Evangelists*, *On the City of God*, over 600 sermons (including 125 on the Fourth Gospel), 300 epistles, and much work on the text of the Bible (which was also the most noteworthy activity of his contemporary, St Jerome).

He admired Cicero, Virgil, and Horace – he felt the Roman empire had been worthy of none of them – not so much for writing well as for calling men back to first principles; Cicero's lost ethical treatise the *Hortensius* was, with writings of the Neo-Platonist philosophers, one of the great influences on his youthful years. Cicero had asserted that virtue is the result of human effort, that human nature is naturally good, and that free will prevails; whereas Augustine came to believe that virtue is the result of divine grace alone, that sin is original in human nature, and that the idea of free will is detestable. Yet he believed that the Christian must take his pick of the pagan heritage, just as the people of Israel had looted the Egyptians.

Augustine stood at a turning-point. His *City of God*, the work of thirteen years (*c.* 413–26), delivered a death-blow to paganism. Despite the official recognition of Christianity by the Roman State, he made a sweeping distinction between the earthly city, whose citizens aimed only at material benefits on earth, and the heavenly city, whose citizens lived on earth as pilgrims, 'like prisoners'. This powerful work – together with Boethius' *Consolation* and the *Etymologies* of Isidore of Seville – taught the Middle Ages nearly all they knew about the ancient world. Augustine bequeathed to the Christian future many Platonic, Neo-Platonic, and Stoic elements; and 'the whole dream and partial actuality of a Holy Roman Empire', it has been said, 'may have owed its stimulus to a misunderstanding of the *City of God*.'

Cicero's and Quintilian's educational ideals were now transformed into the Seven Liberal Arts: to Augustine these were grammar, logic, rhetoric, music, geometry, arithmetic, and philosophy. These Arts, and his willingness to accept a limited amount from paganism, exercised – with the many other fruits of his exceptionally vigorous intellect – an incalculable effect on many medieval centuries, on the Renaissance and on the Reformation. St Thomas Aquinas, Petrarch, Erasmus, Luther, Calvin, all preferred Augustine to any other early Father, and the *Pensées* of Pascal draw abundantly upon his thought. The *City of God* was first printed at Subiaco in 1467, and a complete edition of Augustine's works was published at Basle in 1506. His religious influence has lived on with overwhelming strength in Newman and modern thought.

In the frank introspection of the *Confessions* he was the forerunner of Montaigne and Rousseau. Proust is like him in his efforts to reproduce exactly, in turn, each successive mental state. One of the many minor heritages of Augustine, and other Fathers (and perhaps Tacitus too), has been the crop of popular nineteenth-century novels and twentieth-century films attributing Rome's fall to immoral paganism: Lord Lytton's *Last Days of Pompeii* (1834), Lewis Wallace's *Ben Hur* (1880), Sienkiewicz' *Quo Vadis* (1896).

You might ask what difference it makes under whose government a man lives – for his life lasts but a few days and then ceases and he is destined to die – provided that those who govern him do not compel him to acts of impiety or unrighteousness. But the Romans did no harm to the nations whom they conquered and brought under their own laws, except that they did these things at the cost of tremendous slaughter in wars. If only they could have imposed their laws by agreement, they would have brought about the same result more successfully (though then they would not have enjoyed the glory of triumph); and indeed they themselves actually lived under the laws which they imposed on the rest of the world. If this could have been done without invoking Mars and Bellona [1] and without giving Victory a place in the picture (for there must be battles if there is to be a victor), then without doubt the Romans would have been on one and the same plane with the rest of the world.

Particularly would this have been true if that most acceptable and equitable measure had been brought in earlier than in fact it was – I mean the extension of the fellowship of the State to all belonging to the Roman Empire, so that they became Roman citizens and the privileges of the few were granted to all alike. [2] But even so the landless populace would have depended for a livelihood on public funds; it would have been more acceptable, surely, if under a system of good State administration the means of that livelihood had been provided by agreement rather than extorted from defeated peoples.

For I simply do not see what contribution can be made to wholeness and goodness of character by the actual rankings which men give themselves – I mean, one set of men being the victors, another the vanquished. All that is achieved is an empty pride in worldly reputation; the men who have been fired with insatiable desire for glory and have conducted flaming wars have already reaped their reward. They gain no other advantages; their estates are not free from land-duty, they have no access to knowledge which others have not. There are

1. The goddess of war, often identified with Roma.
2. This step was not taken until A.D. 212 (by Caracalla), when its effects were little more than nominal.

many senators in other lands who have never set eyes on Rome. Take away vain-glory and what are all men except just plain men? If this obstinate age were to permit honour to run with character, even so worldly reputation ought not to count for much; it is just smoke without substance.

No: in dealing with this subject let us avail ourselves of the help which our Lord God has given us. Let us reflect upon the attractions despised and the sufferings borne, the cravings suppressed in the quest of worldly reputation by men who deserved to win it as the reward of all their high qualities. And then let us Christians draw a lesson even from this source and take it to heart and learn to stifle our own pride. It may be true that between the city in which it has been promised that we shall reign and the earthly city there is a great gulf – as wide as the distance between heaven and earth: and likewise between temporal felicity and everlasting life, and between vapid praise and real substantial glory, between the fellowship of angels and the fellowship of mortals, between the light of the sun and moon and the light of Him who made the sun and moon. Yet the citizens of so glorious a country must not imagine that they have done anything wonderful if to obtain that land they have done a little good or suffered a few evils, when the Romans wrought such heroic deeds and endured such trials on behalf of an empire which they had already won.

Why, there is even a faint shadowy resemblance between the Roman Empire and the heavenly city. The one gathers its citizens to the everlasting country by promising remission of sins; Romulus offered a place of refuge for the multitude from which Rome was later to be founded, and he attracted them by freeing them from punishment for all their former misdeeds of every kind.

R. H. BARROW (1940)

TEMPTATIONS

We repair the daily deteriorations of the body by eating and drinking, until the day when You will *destroy both the belly and the meats*, for You will kill our emptiness with a marvellous fullness, and You will clothe this corruptible with eternal incorruption. But for the present time the necessity is sweet to me, and I fight against that sweetness lest

I be taken capture by it. I wage daily war upon it by fasting, bringing my body again and again into subjection; but the pain this gives me is driven away by the pleasure (of eating and drinking). For hunger and thirst really are painful: they burn and kill, like fever, unless food comes as medicine for their healing. And since this medicine is ready to hand, from the comfort of Your gifts, in which earth and sea and sky serve our infirmity, this very infirmity is called delight.

This You taught me, that I should learn to take my food as a kind of medicine. But while I am passing from the pain of hunger to the satisfaction of sufficiency, in that very passage the snare of concupiscence lies in wait for me. For the passage is itself a pleasure, yet there is no other way to achieve sufficiency than that which necessity forces us to travel. And while we eat and drink for the sake of health, yet a perilous enjoyment runs at the heels of health and often enough tries to run ahead of it: so that what I say I am doing and really desire to do for my health's sake, I do in fact for the sake of the enjoyment. For there happens not to be the same measure for both: what suffices for health is too little for enjoyment; so that often it is not at all clear whether it is the necessary care of my body calling for more nourishment, or the deceiving indulgence of greed wanting to be served. Because of this uncertainty my wretched soul is glad, and uses it as a cover and an excuse, rejoicing that it does not clearly appear what is sufficient for the needs of health, so that under the cloak of health it may shelter the business of pleasure.

Day after day I fight against these temptations, and I call upon Thy right hand and to Thee refer my perplexities, for I have no clear guidance upon this matter. I hear the word of God commanding me: *Let not your hearts be overcharged with surfeiting and drunkenness and the cares of this life.* Drunkenness is far from me, and Thou wilt have mercy that it may never come near me; but over-eating has sometimes crept up on Thy servant: Thou wilt have mercy, that it may depart from me. *For no man can be continent unless Thou give it.*

The pleasures of the ear did indeed draw me and hold me more tenaciously, but You have set me free. Yet still when I hear those airs, in which Your words breathe life, sung with sweet and measured voice, I do, I admit, find a certain satisfaction in them, yet not such as to grip me too close, for I can depart when I will. Yet in that they are received into me along with the truths which give them life, such airs seek in my heart a place of no small honour, and I find it hard to know what is their due place. At times indeed it seems to me that I am paying them greater honour than is their due – when, for example, I feel that by those holy words my mind is kindled more religiously and fervently to a flame of piety because I hear them sung than if they were not sung: and I observe that all the varying emotions of my spirit have modes proper to them in voice and song, whereby, by some secret affinity, they are made more alive. It is not good that the mind should be enervated by this bodily pleasure. But it often ensnares me, in that the bodily sense does not accompany the reason as following after it in proper order, but, having been admitted to aid the reason, strives to run before and take the lead. In this matter I sin unawares, and then grow aware.

Yet there are times when through too great a fear of this temptation, I err in the direction of over-severity – even to the point sometimes of wishing that the melody of all the lovely airs with which David's Psalter is commonly sung should be banished not only from my own ears, but from the Church's as well: and that seems to me a safer course, which I remember often to have heard told of Athanasius, bishop of Alexandria, who had the reader of the psalm utter it with so little modulation of the voice that he seemed to be saying it rather than singing it. Yet when I remember the tears I shed, moved by the songs of the Church in the early days of my new faith; and again when I see that I am moved not by the singing but by the things that are sung – when they are sung with a clear voice and proper modulation – I recognize once more the usefulness of this practice.

Thus I fluctuate between the peril of indulgence and the profit I have found: and on the whole I am inclined – though I am not propounding any irrevocable opinion – to approve the custom of singing in church, that by the pleasure of the ear the weaker minds may be roused to a feeling of devotion. Yet whenever it happens that I am more moved by the singing than by the thing that is sung, I admit that I have grievously sinned, and then I should wish rather not to have heard the singing. See in what a state I am! Weep with me and weep for me, all you who feel within yourselves that goodness from which good actions come. Those of you who have no such feeling will not be moved by what I am saying. But do Thou, O Lord my

God, hear me and look upon me and see me and heal me, Thou in whose eyes I have become a question to myself; and that is my infirmity.

F. J. SHEED (1943)

THE BOYHOOD OF ST AUGUSTINE

And so, by frequently hearing the same words differently arranged in different sentences, I began to perceive what the things were, of which they were symbols; and, when I had broken in my mouth to these symbols, I could now use them to express my wants and exchange communication with those about me. Thus, though I was still subject to the authority of my parents and the control of my elders, I launched out on to the stormy sea of human society.

And what misery, what mockery I found there, O God, my God! This was the pattern of boyish virtue held up to me, to be obedient to my instructors, so that I might achieve worldly success and rise to great heights in the glib arts that minister to the honour of man and the wealth that is no true wealth. With this in mind I was sent to school to learn letters. Why they were useful I did not know, poor child, but if I was slow to learn, I was beaten. My elders, of course, approved of this, and many generations before mine had trodden down this painful path, which we were compelled to follow, since sweat and tears are multiplied for the sons of Adam. But we found men who prayed to you, Lord, and, learning from them, we came to feel – as well as we could at our age – that you are somebody great, who might, though not apparent to our senses, hear us and help us. So even as a boy I began to pray to you, my help and my refuge; to call upon you I burst the bonds of my tongue, and with all the strong emotion that a weak child can feel I prayed to you that I might not be beaten at school. But you did not hear me, which was a lesson in wisdom for me, and my elders and even my parents, who wanted no hurt to come to me, laughed at the floggings that hurt me so painfully.

Does any one, Lord, think lightly of racks and hooks and all such instruments of torture, to escape which men everywhere pray to you in terror? Is any one so imbued with lofty sentiments by his devotion to you, any one so stout hearted – or should I say, so unfeeling – that, though he loves the victims who shrink in anguish from such tortures, he laughs at them as lightly as our parents at the agonies inflicted upon us schoolboys by our masters? Certainly we feared them no less, and prayed to you no less earnestly that we might be spared them, and yet we continued to sin by writing or reading or thinking less about our lessons than we were required to do. For it was not memory or intelligence that we lacked, Lord: these it was your will that we should have in ample measure for our years. But we loved playing games, and for this we were punished by men who surely behaved in much the same way themselves. But the foolery of adults is called business; the business of children – for such it is – is punished, and no one pities the children or the adults or both. Can any good judge of things think it right that a boy should be beaten for playing a game of ball and so impeding his progress in the acquisition of knowledge, which will one day help him to play an uglier game? And what was there to choose between me and the master who beat me? For, if one of his colleagues defeated him on a point of pedantry, he was more tormented with envy than I was, when I lost a game of ball?

Nevertheless I was sinning, Lord, my God, ordainer and creator of all natural things, but of sin ordainer only. I was sinning, Lord, my God, by acting contrary to the commands of my parents and my teachers. For, whatever their intentions, it was possible for me in later life to make a good use of the learning which they wished me to acquire. And my disobedience did not come from a choice of something better but from a love of play. I loved the elation of winning a game, and I loved to have my ears tickled by the inventions of fiction, that only make them itch more violently, and more and more the same spirit of curiosity fired my eyes and I gazed avidly at the shows of the theatre, the games of grown up people.

I was initiated into the study of Greek at a very early age, and why it is that I hated it I have never really understood. For I loved Latin – the Latin, that is to say, of the grammar school, not that taught in the elementary school; for the elementary instruction in reading, writing, and arithmetic, was to me as much of a burden and a punishment as Greek at every stage. Now, what was the cause of this, if not sin and the vanity of life, the vanity of being flesh, as I was, and a spirit walking and not turning back? For surely this primary instruction, which gradually, but once and for all, formed in me the power of reading anything I find written and writing anything I want to write, was more reliable and therefore better than the later lessons, in which I was obliged to memorize the wanderings of Aeneas, (whoever Aeneas was), while I forgot my own wanderings; and to weep for the death of Dido, who killed herself for love, while meanwhile, wretched boy, I shed not a single tear for myself thus dying away from you, O God, my life.

Yet what is more wretched than a wretch who has not pity for himself but tears for the death of Dido? – tears for Dido dying because she loved Aeneas, none for himself dying because he does not love you, God, the light of my heart, the bread that feeds my soul, the power that is husband to my mind and to the bosom of my meditations. I did not love you; I was unfaithful to you, and in the midst of my infidelities I heard on all sides the cry, 'Well done! Well done!' For the friendship of this world is adulterous infidelity towards you, and its applause is intended to make a man ashamed not to be like everybody else. But for this I had no tears: my tears were for Dido 'destroyed, and by the sword a fatal journey gone', while I myself was going a fatal journey to the depths of your creation, away from you and down into the earth of my own earthiness. And if I was forbidden to read these books, I was sad at not being able to read what made me sad.

ANDREAS MAYOR (1954)

FRIENDSHIP

Time is not idle; its revolution is not without effect. Through our senses it works great changes in our minds. For me too time came and went and, as day succeeded day, gradually it implanted in me new hopes and new memories, and slowly I was patched together again with pleasures of the old familiar sort. My grief for my dead friend was displaced by them, but to it succeeded, if not fresh griefs, conduct which could not fail to cause them. For why was it that grief had pierced so easily to the depths of my being? Was it not simply that, in loving one subject to death as though he would never die, I had poured out my soul like water on the sand? And now what most restored and refreshed me was the comfort I found in new friends, with

whom I loved what after friendship I loved best: the great Mani-
chaean myth,[1] a huge lie from beginning to end, which gained access
through our itching ears to tickle and seduce our minds. This myth
did not die for me just because one of my friends had died.

But friendship itself had other greater charms: the talk and the
laughter together; the mutual kindnesses and compliances; the common study of favourite books; the shared enjoyment of frivolity or
seriousness; the occasional disagreement without hostility – like that of
a man with himself – which adds a spice to frequent and fundamental
agreement; the teaching and the learning that pass between one friend
and another; the happiness of meeting which follows the unpleasant-
ness of separation; the thousand and one welcome signs – a word, a
glance, an expression of the face, any little impulse – which spring
spontaneously from those who love and are loved, and act like tinder
to set their hearts ablaze and fuse them into one.

This it is that we prize in friendship, and prize so highly that our
human conscience feels guilty if we do not return love for love, demanding from the loved one no satisfaction beyond these instances of
affection. And this is why the death of a friend brings mourning and
the darkness of grief, turning joy to bitterness and drowning the heart
in tears, so that the lost life of the dead is the death of the living. Happy
is he who loves You, and his friend in You, and his enemy for Your
sake. For the only man who never loses those dear to him is he to
whom all are dear in Him who is never lost. And who is He but our
God, God who made the sky and the earth and fills them with His
presence, since by filling them He made them? No one loses You unless he leaves You, and if he leaves You, where does he go, where does
he escape to? Only from You gentle to You angry. For everywhere
he will find Your law operating to punish him; and Your law is
truth, and You are truth.

ANDREAS MAYOR (1954)

1. i.e. the widespread belief that the world contains evil because it was
created not by God but by a Demiurge ignorant of or hostile to God. Mani
called himself Apostle of Jesus Christ, but lived in Zoroastrian Persia, and is
often regarded as a Zoroastrian rather than a Christian heretic.

THE VANITY OF THE CLASSICS

What of my other studies? What use was it to me that, when I was only about twenty, I read by myself and understood the *Ten Categories* of Aristotle, which had fallen into my hands? It was a book whose very title had always inspired me with awe, for I had heard the professor who taught me rhetoric at Carthage and other eminent scholars almost burst their cheeks with pride when they mentioned it. I had thought it must be a great, a superhuman work. Well, I read it and I discussed the results of my solitary reading with others who had mastered it, they said, only with the help of lectures and diagrams and learned teachers, and they could add nothing to what I had discovered for myself. I understood perfectly clearly what they had to say about substances (for instance, a man) and the things that may be predicated of substances, such as a man's shape (quality), how tall he is (quantity), whose brother he is (relation); where he is placed; when he was born; whether he is standing or sitting; whether he is wearing shoes or wearing armour; whether he is doing anything or anything is being done to him. I understood, I say, how everything can be fitted into one or other of these nine categories, of which I have given a few examples, or into the category of substance itself.

But what use was this knowledge to me? Was it not rather a stumbling-block, since, believing as I did that everything that exists must somehow or other be included in these categories, I tried to apply the formula to Your mysterious simple, unchangeable nature, O my God? I supposed that You too are a subject, of which Your greatness and Your beauty are attributes, and that these qualities exist in You as they might in other subjects, in, for instance, material objects. But the truth is that, whereas You are essentially Your greatness and Your beauty, a material object is not great or beautiful by virtue of being matter, since it would be just as much matter if it were smaller and less beautiful. How utterly false my ideas of You were: the fantasies of my own wretchedness, not the solid truth of Your blessedness. For You had decreed that the earth should bear thorns and thistles for me and that I should gain my bread with toil, and your decree was being fulfilled.

So what use was it to me that I, the depraved slave of bad desires, read by myself and understood all the books of the so-called liberal arts that I could lay my hands on? I was delighted by them, and I did not know whence they derived what they had of truth and certainty. For my back was turned to the light and my face to the things lit by the light, so that my face saw the things lit by the light but received no light itself.

ANDREAS MAYOR (1954)

ALYPIUS AT A GLADIATORS' FIGHT

The whole place was seething with savage enthusiasm, but he shut the doors of his eyes and forebade his soul to go out into a scene of such evil. If only he could have blocked up his ears too. For in the course of the fight some man fell; there was a great roar from the whole mass of spectators which fell upon his ears; he was overcome by curiosity and opened his eyes, feeling perfectly prepared to treat whatever he might see with scorn and to rise above it. But he then received in his soul a worse wound than that man, whom he had wanted to see, received in his body. His own fall was more wretched than that of the gladiator which had caused all that shouting which had entered his ears and unlocked his eyes and made an opening for the thrust which was to overthrow his soul – a soul that had been reckless rather than strong and was all the weaker because it had trusted in itself when it ought to have trusted in you. He saw the blood and he gulped down savagery. Far from turning away, he fixed his eyes on it. Without knowing what was happening, he drank in madness, he was delighted with the guilty contest, drunk with the lust of blood. He was no longer the man who had come there but was one of the crowd to which he had come, a true companion of those who had brought him.

REX WARNER (1963)

LIST OF DATES

SOURCES AND ACKNOWLEDGEMENTS

(For acknowledgements for hitherto unpublished translations see p. ix.)

PLAUTUS

    p. 14 *Mostellaria* 431; p. 18 *ibid.* 532

TERENCE

    p. 25 *Adelphi* 26

CICERO

    p. 32 *De Re Publica* II, 5; p. 34 *De Officiis* III, 19; p. 42 *De Re Publica* I, 43

    p. 46 *Second Philippic* 55, 84 (from W. C. A. Ker, *Philippics*, Loeb Classical Library, William Heinemann Ltd, 1926)

    p. 50 *Epistulae ad Atticum* I, 18; p. 52 *Epistulae ad Familiares* V, 12; p. 54 *Epistulae ad Atticum* V, I, 3; p. 55 *ibid.* XIII, 52; p. 56 *Epistulae ad Familiares* IV, 5 (from L. P. Wilkinson, *Letters of Cicero*, Geoffrey Bles Ltd, 1949. Reproduced by permission of L. P. Wilkinson, Esq.)

    p. 59 *Epistulae ad Familiares* XI, 28

    p. 60 *Epistulae ad M. Brutum* I, 17 (from L. P. Wilkinson, *Letters of Cicero*, Geoffrey Bles Ltd, 1949. Reproduced by permission of L. P. Wilkinson, Esq.)

LUCRETIUS

    p. 65 *De Rerum Natura* III, 830

    p. 69 *De Rerum Natura* I, 62 (from Sir Robert Allison, *On the Nature of Things*, A. L. Humphrey, 1919)

    p. 69 *De Rerum Natura* III, 1 (from R. C. Trevelyan, *De Rerum Natura*, University Press, Cambridge, 1937)

    p. 70 *De Rerum Natura* V, 925 (from R. E. Latham, *The Nature of the Universe*, Penguin Books Ltd, 1951)

CATULLUS

    p. 86 *Poems* 72 and 85, 92; p. 87 *Poems* 50, 51

    p. 88 *Poems* 96; p. 89 *ibid.* 96, 101 (from H. W. Garrod in *Oxford Book of Latin Verse*, Oxford University Press, 1912)

    p. 90 *Poems* 17; p. 91 *ibid.* 27 (from H. MacNaghten, *The Poems of Catullus*, Gerald Duckworth & Co. Ltd, 1925)

    p. 91 *Poems* 51 (from E. A. Havelock, *The Lyric Genius of Catullus*, Basil Blackwell, 1939)

    p. 92 *Poems* 49 (from Jack Lindsay, *Catullus*, Sylvan Press Ltd, 1948)

    p. 93 *Poems* 85 (from J. M. and J. M. Todd, *Voices from the Past*, Phoenix House Limited, 1955)

    p. 93 *Poems* 76 (from L. A. and R. W. L. Wilding, *A Classical Anthology*, Faber and Faber Ltd, 1955)

    p. 93 *Poems* 63 (from P. Whigham, *Catullus*, Penguin Books Ltd, 1966)

ACKNOWLEDGEMENTS

CAESAR

p. 96 *De Bello Gallico* IV, 20 (from S. A. Handford, *The Conquest of Gaul*, Penguin Books Ltd, 1951)

p. 110 *De Bello Civili* III, 85

SALLUST

p. 118 *De Catilinae Conjuratione* 8; p. 120 *Bellum Jugurthinum* 41; p. 121 *De Catilinae Conjuratione* 5; p. 122 *ibid.* 36; p. 123 *ibid.* 53 (from J. C. Rolfe, *Sallust*, Loeb Classical Library, William Heinemann Ltd, 1920)

VIRGIL

p. 131 *Eclogues* VI, 13

p. 134 *Eclogues* IV, 1 (from E. V. Rieu, *The Pastoral Poems*, Penguin Books Ltd, 1949)

p. 136 *Georgics* II, 475

p. 139 *Georgics* IV, 1; p. 146 *ibid.* IV, 457 (from C. Day Lewis, *Georgics*, Jonathan Cape Ltd, 1940. Reproduced by permission of the publisher and O.U.P., Inc., New York)

p. 148 *Georgics* I, 287; p. 150 *ibid.* III, 477 (from L. A. S. Jermyn, *The Singing Calendar*, Basil Blackwell, 1947)

p. 153 *Aeneid* VI, 268 (from J. E. Flecker, *Collected Poems*, Martin Secker and Warburg Ltd, 1916)

p. 155 *Aeneid* VII, 511 (from R. Knox, *Aeneid*, Oxford University Press, 1924)

p. 156 *Aeneid* IV, 1 (from C. Day Lewis, *The Aeneid*, The Hogarth Press Ltd, 1952. Copyright 1952 by Cecil Day Lewis. Reprinted by permission of The Hogarth Press Ltd and Harold Matson Company)

p. 176 *Aeneid* VIII, 184 (from Rolfe Humphries' translation of *The Aeneid of Virgil*. Copyright 1951 by Charles Scribner's Sons. Reprinted with the permission of the author and the publisher)

HORACE

p. 183 *Odes* II, 10; I, 11; p. 184 *ibid.* I, 5: I, 9; p. 186 *ibid.* III, 29; p. 189 *ibid.* II, 8: II, 16; p. 191 *ibid.* IV, 3: IV, 9, 29; p. 192 *ibid.* III, 3, 37; p. 194 *ibid.* IV, 9: II, 14; p. 195 *ibid.* I, 22; p. 196 *Epodes* II, 1; p. 198 *Odes* II, 9; p. 199 *ibid.* III, 3; p. 200 *ibid.* II, 3, 9

p. 200 *Odes* IV, 7 (from A. E. Housman, *More Poems*, Jonathan Cape Ltd, 1936. Reproduced by permission of the publisher, the Society of Authors, and Henry Holt and Company, Inc. Copyright, in America. 1940, by Henry Holt and Company, Inc.)

p. 201 *Odes* III, 19 (from Sir Edward Marsh, *Odes*, Macmillan and Co. Ltd, 1941. Reproduced by permission of Christopher Hassall, Esq.)

p. 202 *Odes* I, 34 (from Lord Dunsany, *Odes*, William Heinemann Ltd, 1947. Reproduced by permission of Lord Dunsany)

p. 203 *Epistles* I, 1, 41: II, 1, 34; p. 204 *ibid.* II, 1, 76: II, 1, 139; p. 205 *Satires* I, 5, 1; p. 208 *ibid.* I, 10, 1

ACKNOWLEDGEMENTS

p. 210 *Satires* II, 6, 79; p. 211 *ibid.* I, 131 (from R. C. Trevelyan, *Translations from Horace, Juvenal and Montaigne*, Cambridge University Press, 1940. Reproduced by permission of Humphrey Trevelyan, Esq.)

p. 212 *Ars Poetica* I; p. 213 *ibid.* 14; p. 214 *ibid.* 38: 125; p. 215 *ibid.* 153: 263; p. 216 *ibid.* 291: 323: 333; p. 217 *ibid.* 408; p. 218 *ibid.* 445: 9: 23; p. 219 *ibid.* 38: 60; p. 220 *ibid.* 128: 263: 319: 333; p. 221 *ibid.* 342: 347: 361

LIVY

p. 224 *Preface*

p. 225 I, 8, 4; p. 228 II, 9, 1; p. 230 II, 32, 1; p. 232 XXI, 32, 6; p. 237 XXII, 44, 4 (from B. O. Foster, Loeb Classical Library, William Heinemann Ltd 1919–29)

p. 244 XXX, 35, 3 (from F. G. Moore, Loeb Classical Library, William Heinemann Ltd, 1949)

PROPERTIUS

p. 248 *Elegies* II, 12

p. 248 *Elegies* II, 25; p. 249 *ibid.* II, 22A; p. 250 *ibid.* III, 5; p. 251 *ibid.* II, 8 (from Jack Lindsay, *Some of Propertius' Love Poems*, Fanfrolico Press, 1927. Reproduced by permission of Jack Lindsay, Esq.)

p. 252 *Elegies* II, 19; p. 253 *ibid.* IV, 7 (from Gilbert Highet, *Poets in a Landscape*, Hamish Hamilton Ltd, 1957. Copyright 1957 by Gilbert Highet. Reproduced by permission of Hamish Hamilton Ltd and Alfred A. Knopf, Inc.)

p. 253 *Elegies* II, 10 (from S. G. Tremenheere, *Propertius*, Simpkin Marshall Ltd, 1931)

OVID

p. 257 *Metamorphoses* XV, 165, 177, 871; p. 258 *ibid.* I, 89; p. 260 *ibid.* XIII, 810; p. 261 *ibid.* II, 47, 154

p. 266 *Metamorphoses* I, 69; p. 267 XII, 39 (from A. E. Watts, *Metamorphoses*, University of California Press, 1954)

p. 268 *Metamorphoses* I, 264 (from Rex Warner, *Men and Gods*, William Heinemann Ltd, 1950 and Penguin Books Ltd, 1952)

p. 272 *Metamorphoses* VIII, 620 (from Mary M. Innes, *The Metamorphoses*, Penguin Books Ltd, 1955)

p. 275 *Tristia* IV, 10, 41; p. 276 *ibid.* V, 12

p. 277 *Amores* I, 3, 5; *De Medicamine Faciei* I (from F. A. Wright, *The Mirror of Love*, Routledge and Kegan Paul Ltd, 1923)

p. 278 *Ars Amatoria* II, 2, 197: I, 417: II, 281 (from L. P. Wilkinson, *Ovid Recalled*, Cambridge University Press, 1956)

p. 279 *Amores* II, 7 (from Gilbert Highet, *Poets in a Landscape*, Hamish Hamilton Ltd, 1957. Copyright 1957 by Gilbert Highet. Reproduced by permission of Hamish Hamilton Ltd and Alfred A. Knopf, Inc.)

ACKNOWLEDGEMENTS

PHAEDRUS

   p. 284 *Fables* I, 1 : IV, 6; p. 285 *ibid.* I, 5; p. 286 *ibid.* I, 13 : I, 24
   p. 287 *ibid.* IV, 16 (17 in some editions) (from J. P. Postgate, *Translators and Translations*, G. Bell and Sons Ltd, 1922)

SENECA

   p. 290 *Thyestes* 665; p. 291 *Troades* 397
   p. 292 *Troades* 255 (from F. L. Lucas, *Seneca and Elizabethan Tragedy*, University Press, Cambridge, 1922)
   p. 293 *Epistulae Morales* 47; p. 296 *ibid.* 56; p. 300 *ibid.* 91 (XIV, 3); p. 303 *ibid.* 41 (IV, 2) (from E. P. Barker, *Letters*, Oxford University Press, 1932)

LUCAN

   p. 308 *Bellum Civile* (*Pharsalia*) I, 120; p. 310 *ibid.* III, 399
   p. 311 *Bellum Civile* (*Pharsalia*) V, 65; p. 315 *ibid.* V, 722 (from Robert Graves, *Pharsalia*, Penguin Books Ltd, 1956)
   p. 317 *Epitaphium Lucani* (from J. P. Postgate, *Translators and Translations*, G. Bell and Sons Ltd, 1922)

PETRONIUS

   p. 320 *Satyricon* 31; p. 321 *ibid.* 37; p. 322 *ibid.* 44; p. 324 *ibid.* 45; p. 326 *ibid.* 61; p. 327 *ibid.* 76 (from Michael Heseltine, *Satyricon*, Loeb Classical Library, William Heinemann Ltd, 1922)
   p. 328 *Poems* 8 (Loeb edition); p. 329 *ibid.* 21 (from Helen Waddell, *Medieval Latin Lyrics*, Constable and Co. Ltd, 1929 and Penguin Books Ltd, 1952)
   p. 329 *Satyricon* 82 (from Paul Dinnage, *The Satyricon*, Neville Spearman Limited, 1953)

QUINTILIAN

   p. 335 *Institutio Oratoria* I, i, 12; p. 336 *ibid.* I, iii; p. 337 *ibid.* XII, xi, 16; p. 338 *ibid.* X, i, 105; p. 340 *ibid.* XII, 8 (from H. E. Butler, *Institutio Oratoria*, Loeb Classical Library, William Heinemann Ltd, 1920–2)

MARTIAL

   p. 343 *Epigrams* X, 23 : I, 1
   p. 343 *Epigrams* IV, 65 (from P. Nixon, *Martial*, Houghton Mifflin Company, 1911)
   p. 344 *Epigrams* I, 16 : I, 29 : I, 38 : I, 64 : I, 75; p. 345 *ibid.* II, 3 : I, 91 : I, 107; p. 346 *ibid.* II, 38 : V, 56 : V, 73 : VII, 77; p. 347 *ibid.* VII, 85 : VIII, 69; IX, 53 : III, 37 : II, 35; p. 348 *ibid.* V, 43 (from J. A. Pott and F. A. Wright, *Martial*, Routledge and Kegan Paul, Ltd, 1924)
   p. 348 *Epigrams* IX, 15 (from E. V. Rieu, *A Book of Latin Poetry*, Methuen and Co., 1925)
   p. 348 *Epigrams* VIII, 12 : I, 40 (from Francis and Tatum, *Martial*, Cambridge University Press, 1924. Reproduced by permission of W. W. Tatum, Esq.)
   p. 349 *Epigrams* VI, 60 : II, 7 : X, 97 : II, 58 : IX, 14

ACKNOWLEDGEMENTS

PLINY

p. 350 *Epistulae* VI, 16; p. 354 *ibid.* IV, 13; p. 356 *ibid.* VIII, 20; p. 357 *ibid.*
VII, 27

p. 360 *Epistulae* X, 96; p. 362 *ibid.* X, 97 (from L. A. and R. W. L. Wilding,
A Classical Anthology, Faber and Faber Ltd, 1955)

JUVENAL

p. 366 *Satires* X, 23; p. 367 *ibid.* I, 63; p. 368 *ibid.* V, 12; p. 371 *ibid.* V, 127.

p. 373 *Satires* III, 41: 160; p. 374 *ibid.* 190; p. 375 *ibid.* 232; p. 377 *ibid.* 315
(from R. C. Trevelyan, *Translations from Horace, Juvenal and Montaigne*,
Cambridge University Press, 1940. Reproduced by permission of
Humphrey Trevelyan, Esq.)

p. 377 *Satires* III, 232 (from Gilbert Highet, *Poets in a Landscape*, Hamish
Hamilton Ltd, 1957. Copyright 1957 by Gilbert Highet. Reproduced by
permission of Hamish Hamilton Ltd and Alfred A. Knopf, Inc.)

TACITUS

p. 380 *Agricola* 11; p. 381 *Germania* 4 (from H. Mattingly, *On Britain and
Germany*, Penguin Books Ltd, 1948)

p. 384 *Annals* IV, 57; p. 386 *ibid.* IV, 67; p. 388 *ibid.* XII, 66; p. 390 *ibid.* XIII,
15; p. 392 *ibid.* XIV, 3; p. 396 *ibid.* XV, 38 (from Michael Grant, *The Annals
of Imperial Rome*, Penguin Books Ltd, 1956)

p. 400 *Histories* I, 2; p. 402 *ibid.* II, 37; p. 404 *ibid.* II, 87

SUETONIUS

p. 408 *Divus Julius* 57; p. 412 *Augustus* 76; p. 415 *Gaius* 37; p. 417 *Nero* 20;
p. 421 *ibid.* 51 (from Robert Graves, *The Twelve Caesars*, Penguin Books
Ltd, 1957)

APULEIUS

p. 426 *Metamorphoses* IV, 34; p. 428 *ibid.* IV, 34

p. 429 *Metamorphoses* VI, 10; p. 430 *ibid.* VI, 11; p. 435 *ibid.* XI, 1, 3 (from
Robert Graves, *The Golden Ass*, Penguin Books Ltd, 1950)

TERTULLIAN

p. 440 *Apologeticus* 11; p. 441 *De Spectaculis* 16, 27, 30 (from T. R. Glover,
Loeb Classical Library, William Heinemann Ltd, 1931)

AUGUSTINE

p. 446 *De Civitate Dei* V, 17 (from R. H. Barrow, *The City of God*, Faber and
Faber, Ltd, 1950)

p. 447 *Confessions* X, 43; p. 449 *ibid.* X, 49 (from F. J. Sheed, *Confessions*,
Sheed and Ward Ltd, 1943. Reproduced by permission of F. J. Sheed)

p. 450 *Confessions* I, 13; p. 451 *ibid.* I, 20; p. 452 *ibid.* IV, 13; p. 454 *ibid.* IV, 28

p. 455 *Confessions* VI, 8 (from Rex Warner, *Confessions of St Augustine*,
Mentor-Omega Books, New American Library, 1963)

A FEW BOOKS ON LATIN LITERATURE

F. E. ADCOCK, *Caesar as Man of Letters*, 1956

R. R. BOLGAR, *The Classical Heritage and its Beneficiaries*, 1954

M. BOWRA, *From Virgil to Milton*, 1945

C. O. BRINK, *Horace on Poetry*, 1963

H. S. COMMAGER, *The Odes of Horace*, 1962

T. A. DOREY & D. R. DUDLEY (editors), *Studies in Latin Literature*, 1964–

G. E. DUCKWORTH, *The Nature of Roman Comedy*, 1952

E. FRAENKEL, *Horace*, 1957

M. GRANT, *Roman Literature*, revised edition 1964

E. A. HAVELOCK, *The Lyric Genius of Catullus*, 1939

G. A. HIGHET, *Juvenal the Satirist*, 1954

G. A. HIGHET, *Poets in a Landscape*, 1957

W. F. JACKSON KNIGHT, *Roman Vergil*, revised edition 1966

C. W. MENDELL, *Latin Poetry: the New Poets and the Augustans*, 1966

B. OTIS, *Virgil: A Study in Civilized Poetry*, 1963

V. PÖSCHL, *The Art of Vergil*, 1962

K. QUINN, *The Catullan Revolution*, 1960

M. R. RIDLEY, *Studies in Three Literatures*, 1962

N. RUDD *The Satires of Horace*, 1966

J. P. SULLIVAN (editor), *Critical Essays on Roman Literature*, 1962

R. SYME, *Sallust*, 1964

R. SYME, *Tacitus*, 1958

E. A. THOMPSON and others, *Roman Historians*, 1966

J. A. K. THOMSON, *Classical Influences on English Poetry*, 1951

J. A. K. THOMSON, *Classical Influences on English Prose*, 1955

P. G. WALSH, Livy: *His Historical Aims and Methods*, 1961

L. P. WILKINSON, *Golden Latin Artistry*, 1963

L. P. WILKINSON, *Ovid Surveyed*, 1962

S. J. WILSON, *The Thought of Cicero*, 1967

INDEX OF AUTHORS AND TRANSLATORS